THE BASQUES, THE

D1642940

Daniele Conversi's book is a comprehensive introduction to Basque and Catalan nationalism. The two movements have much in common but have differed in the strategies adopted to further their cause. Basque nationalism, in the shape of the military wing of ETA, took the path of violence, spawning an efficient terrorist campaign. Catalan nationalism, by contrast, is generally more accommodating and peaceful.

Rooted in cultures that long predate the modern state, and bound by languages and traditions that divide them from their Castilian neighbours, the Basques and Catalans have struggled for centuries to retain their ethnic identities in the face of modernisation and state-enforced assimilation. The latter reached its severest form under Francoism, especially in the early years after the Civil War.

Daniele Conversi examines and compares the history, motives and methods of these movements, considering the influence of such intertwined aspects of nationalist mobilisation as the choice of language, race and descent as core values; the consequences of large-scale immigration; and the causes and effects of political violence.

Daniele Conversi obtained his B.A. at the University of Rome and his Ph.D. at the London School of Economics. He has taught at Cornell and Syracuse Universities.

.006

To my mother

The Basques,
the Catalans and Spain

Alternative Routes to Nationalist Mobilisation

DANIELE CONVERSI

HURST & COMPANY, LONDON

First published in the United Kingdom by
C. Hurst & Co. (Publishers) Ltd.,
38 King Street, London W2CE 8JZ
Copyright © 1997 by Daniele Conversi
2nd impression, 2000
Manufactured in the United States of America

ISBN 1-85065-268-6

PREFACE

The completion of this book would not have been possible without the help and support of a number of people and institutions in several countries. First and foremost, I am deeply grateful to Professor Anthony D. Smith, my supervisor, for his incisive guidance, comments, suggestions and encouragement.

There is a long list of people whose experience and opinions gave me insights into some subtleties which have influenced the content and form of this work. Among them, my most heartfelt thanks are due to my friend Jacqueline Kaye for reading drafts of different chapters and making pertinent comments. Charles Ehrlich and Josep Murgades helped me with very useful comments on Chapter 2, and Chapter 3 benefited from the insights and suggestions of two of the major historians of Basque nationalism, José Luis de la Granja and Ludgwer Mees. I also acknowledge gratefully the comments of William Douglass and Joseba Zulaika on Chapter 4. Xosé M. Nuñez Seixas helped me with many insightful comments, particularly on Chapter 6. Gurutz Jáuregui's comments on Chapters 4, 6 and 9, have proved particularly helpful. Although not all comments of these scholars could be incorporated, I tried to include as much as I could.

For the final draft, I owe my thanks to my colleague Alison Palmer for her suggestions and corrections of Chapter 4, 5 and 6. Mark Perkins, formerly at the inter-library loan service at BLPES, helped to track down hard-to-find publications.

I am also indebted to several organisations and founding bodies. For the research in Chapter 4, thanks are due to the Basque Studies Program, University of Nevada, Reno, which allowed me a unique opportunity to investigate primary sources such as pamphlets, interviews and other documents by Basque leaders. For the research underlying Chapter 5, thanks are due to the Institut d'Història Contemporania de Catalunya, and in particular Professors Josep Benet and Josep Maria Solé i Sabaté. Some of the material included is the fruit of a long interview with Josep Benet.

My research on Catalan nationalism predates my interest in the

Basque case, and in the years immediately before taking my doc-
torate at LSE, I was given very useful help and advice by several
scholars, most notably Professors Salvador Giner and Carlota Solé.
In Italy I also wish to thank Professor Franco Ferrarotti for
encouraging me to undertake both an interdisciplinary and a
sociological route.

In 1991 I founded, together with a colleague, the Association for
the Study of Ethnicity and Nationalism. This enterprise took several
months of work which has proved well worthwhile, since the
association has grown to become a respectable international body
with a worldwide membership. I was also the founding editor of the
ASEN Bulletin, a publication acknowledged by most scholars in the
field.

My 'intellectual' debts are numerous. In my theoretical approach
I owe much to several books by Anthony D. Smith, articles by Jerzy
J. Smolicz and Frederik Barth, and numerous other publications.
For my Catalan case-study there are too many authors to be
mentioned. For the Basque case the reader will find repeated
references to three authors – Javier Corcuera, Gurutz Jáuregui and
Robert Clark – but I have consulted many other excellent studies.
My research diverges in significant aspects from all the quoted
authors, and responsibility for my views is mine alone.

Last but not least, I acknowledge the patient and skilled work on
the text by the publisher Christopher Hurst.

For the names in Basque I tried to use as much as possible the
official (*batua*) spelling except for those few names, such as Navarre,
which have an English form. In the quotations from Basque leaders
and intellectuals writing before the 1980s, i.e. before *batua* was made
official, I use instead *their* original spelling (for example, Arana's use
of Euzkadi and Euskera, rather than the standard Euskadi and
Euskara).

Rome, Italy   D. C.
November 1996

CONTENTS

Contents

MAPS

GLOSSARY

BASQUE TERMS

aberrietsai	enemy of the fatherland
aberrigabe	person with no country
aberrigabetasun	state of being without a country
aberritasun	patriotism
aberriordeko	adopted homeland
aberrikeria	national chauvinism
Aberri Eguna	Day of the Fatherland (coinciding with Easter Sunday)
abertzale	patriot (pl. *abertzaleak*; Sp. *abertzales*)
abertzalekeria	chauvinism
abertzaletasun	patriotism
abertzaletu	to become a patriot
alderdi	political party
aldikatzia, aldikatze	act of alternating, substituting
batzar	meeting, reunion, session
batzoki	meeting place (referred to the PNV centres)
baserri	farmhouse, homestead (pl. *baserriak*)
baserritar	farmer, country dweller, peasant (pl. *baserritarrak*)
batasuna	unity, union, unification
batua	standard unified Basque (from *bat* = one, *batu* = to unify)
bertsolari	troubadour
Donostia	San Sebastián
ekinkide	militant
ekinkideria	militant group
ekintasun	persistence, perseverance
ekintza	action, activity, undertaking; ETA's action, normally a killing
ekintzaile	activist

erdara/erdera	foreign language (normally, Spanish or French)
erdaldun/erdeldun	Spanish-speaker, popularly used as 'foreigner'
Ertzainza	Basque police
Euskadi/Euzkadi	Basque country (as a political entity)
Euskal Herri/ Euskalerria etc.	Basque country (historical name)
euskaldun	Basque-speaker, Basque population (= autochthonous; originally, Basque speaking)
euskaldundu	to become Basque and to learn Basque
euskaldunberri	new Basque speaker (not necessarily an immigrant)
euskaldun-zaharra	old Basque speaker (*zaharra* = old)
euskaltegi	Basque school or language centre
Euskaltzaindia	Basque Language Academy
euskaltzale/euskozale	Bascophile
euskaltzaletasun/ euskozaletasun	love of all things Basque
euskara/euskera	Basque language
Euskaros	members of the Asociación Euskara
Euskalerriacos	members of the Asociación Euskalerria
Eusko Jaurlaritza	Basque-government
etarra	ETA member
foruak/fueros	local charters and laws
Gasteiz	Vitoria (capital of the Autonomous Community of Euskadi)
gudari	warrior, soldier, fighter (part. Basque soldier) (pl. *gudariak*)
Hegoaldea	South; Southern Euskadi (the four Spanish provinces)
herri	country, nation; people, population; town, village
Iparralde	North; Northern Euskadi (the three French provinces)
ikaratzaile	terrorist
ikastola	Basque school
ikur	symbol, sign
ikurrin/ikurriña	Basque flag

itzjostaldiak or *itzjostaketak*	literary competitions
kulturgintza/euskalgintza	promotion of [Basque] culture, cultural activity
lehendakari	president (of the Basque government)
maketo	pejorative for non-Basque immigrant (used by Sabino Arana, no longer used)
mendigoizale	mountaineer , mountain climber, alpinist

CATALAN TERMS

barri	quarter, borough
Jocs Florals	Floral Games (poetry contests)
Modernisme	Modernism, local variant of Art Nouveau, Liberty, etc.
murciano	From Murcia, extended to most immigrants in the 1930s
rauxa	impetuosity, propensity for violence
sardana	Catalan national dance
Els Segadors	Catalan national hymn
seny	common sense
senyera	Catalan flag
tertulies	informal group of friends who regularly meet to discuss
xarnego	pejorative for immigrant (lit., half-bred)

SPANISH TERMS

aldeano	rustic
andereños	Basque teachers, especially in the *ikastolas*
anteiglesia	old Basque administrative division (broadly, parish)
barrio	quarter, borough
bunker	the extreme right (esp. the military during the Transition)
caciquismo	mainly referred to electoral corruption during the Restoration
conciertos económicos	special tax privileges granted to the Basques

desarrollismo	ideology of development as panacea for all social diseases
Diputación	provincial assembly/government
españolista	pejorative for Hispanicist (sometimes used as 'traitor')
fuerismo	foralism, defence of the fueros (esp. in local historiography)
gobernador civil	civil governor, appointed by Madrid
hidalguía colectiva	collective nobility
interior	inside Spain (as opposed to exile)
limpieza de sangre	cleanliness of blood
milagro económico	economic boom
nacionalcatolicismo	official Francoist doctrine merging Spanish nationalism with the defence of Catholicism
obrerista	dedicated to the working-class struggle
peneuvista	member of the PNV
rojoseparatistas	epithet which the Falangists used to address their common enemy, 'reds' and 'separatists' (both terms to be intended in a very broad sense)
tercermundismo	Third-Worldism

MAPS

Note

Map 1 shows the present administrative division of the Spanish state into *Autonomous Communities*. Map 2 specifies which are the three *historical nations* which share with the Castilians the multinational character of the Spanish state. By comparing these two maps, we see that the historical territories claimed by Basque and Catalan nationalists do not fully correspond to those of their autonomous communities. For instance, all Basque nationalists claim Navarre as an integral part of Euskadi, and most of them are also willing to include the French Basque provinces. There is less unanimity concerning possible Pan-Catalanist claims, as mainstream nationalists have refused to get involved in territorial disputes with other Autonomous Communities. As in other nationalist movements, a certain ambiguity over the precise borders of the nation appears unavoidable, even necessary.

Map 3 shows the present diffusion of the *languages* of the three historical nationalities. The map also shows the supplementary indication of three other regional languages which do not have official status (*aranese*, *bable*, and *fabla aragonesa*. See chapter 6).

Regarding Map 4, Catalan nationalists consider Catalonia as only one of the Catalan regions, referring occasionally to it as the *Principat*. This is divided into four provinces (Barcelona, Girona, Lleida and Tarragona). The other regions, as defined by the spread of Catalan, are: the Valencian country (Alacant, Valencia, Castelló), the Balearic islands (Mallorca, Menorca and Ibiza/Eivissa), a small fringe of southern Aragón; outside Spain, we can find Roussillon in France, the Principality of Andorra, and the town of L'Alguer in Sardinia, Italy.[1] These are called Catalan countries (*Països Catalans*), and they have more than 10 million inhabitants, over 7 million of whom are Catalan-speakers.[2]

[1] The Catalan language does not have equal status throughout its territory. In the *Principat* it enjoys a relatively high prestige, in competition with Castilian. In other Catalan-speaking territories, especially Valencia, it is considered a stigmatised variant associated with peasants and left-wing intellectuals. For several reasons, this situation is a mobile one, and Catalan is making decisive inroads into new domains and, to a lesser degree, is also spreading in the other Catalan-speaking regions. In Valencia, the second city in the Catalan countries and a traditional rival of Barcelona, regionalist feelings are strong.

[2] The comparison between the 1986 Censuses for the three main regions

Regarding Map 4, Basque nationalists define *Euskadi* (the Basque country) as composed of seven provinces: in Spain there are Alava (*Araba*), Vizcaya (*Bizkaia*), Guipúzcoa (*Gipuzkoa*), which form the Autonomous Community of Euskadi (established in 1980), and Navarre (*Nafarroa*), which forms a separate autonomous community (*Comunidad Foral de Navarra*); the remaining three provinces are in France: Labourd (*Lapurdi*), Soule (*Zuberoa*) and Basse Navarre (*Baxanabarra* or Low Navarre). Basque nationalists call the former area Euskadi Sur (*Hegoaldea*) and the latter Euskadi Norte (*Iparralde*). Euskadi Sur includes 85% of the Basque land mass, more than half of which lies in Navarre. There is a more 'neutral' term to define the same area, *Euskal-Herria*, which is partly devoid of nationalist connotations.[3]

The focus of this book is limited exclusively to the Spanish side of both ethno-regions. In Euskadi we consider all the four provinces, with particular attention to Vizcaya and Guipúzcoa, while for the Catalan case we concentrate only on Catalonia-Principat, the historic heartland of Catalanism, omitting all other Catalan-speaking areas.

Statistical data

With its 6,077,000 inhabitants (1988 data), corresponding to 15.9% of the Spanish population, Catalonia occupies 31,932 square km., corresponding to 6.3% of the landmass of the Spanish state.[4]

In Euskadi (map 5), 2.3 million people (over 90%) live on the Spanish side, 200,000 on the French side. This makes an aggregate area of 20,600 square km. and over 2.5 million inhabitants. Euskadi Sur (including Navarre), which is the only focus of my book, occupies 17,600 square km., about 3.5% of Spanish territory. Its inhabitants amount to 7% of the Spanish population.

(Catalonia, the Valencian country and the Balearic islands) puts the number of people able to understand Catalan at 8,623,202 (the Balearic islands and Valencian country censuses only included items on 'passive competence', i.e. the ability to understand Catalan). The distribution of Catalan 'understanders' is as follows: 5,287,200 in Catalonia (*Principat*), 2,775,007 in the Valencian region, and 560,995 in the Balearic islands. No reliable data is available concerning the other Catalan-speaking areas. See *Avui*, 21 April 1988, pp. 1–3.

[3] On the use of this term, as opposed to *Euskadi*, see chapter 3, pp. 64–5, particularly note 48.

[4] See *Xifres de Catalunya 1988/89*. Barcelona: Generalitat/CIDC

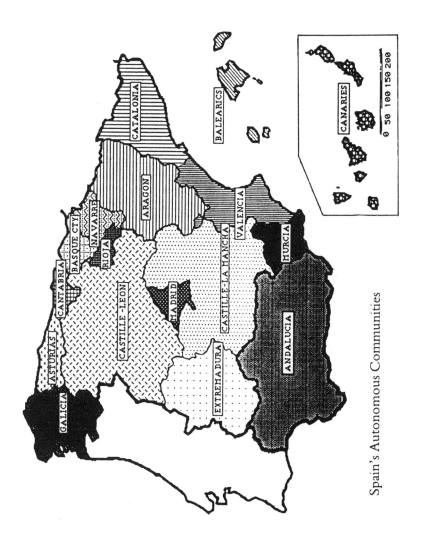

Spain's Autonomous Communities

GALICIA
ASTURIAS
CANTABRIA
BASQUE CTY.
NAVARRE
RIOJA
CASTILLE-LEON
ARAGON
CATALONIA
MADRID
EXTREMADURA
CASTILLE-LA MANCHA
VALENCIA
ANDALUCIA
MURCIA
BALEARICS
CANARIES

0 50 100 150 200

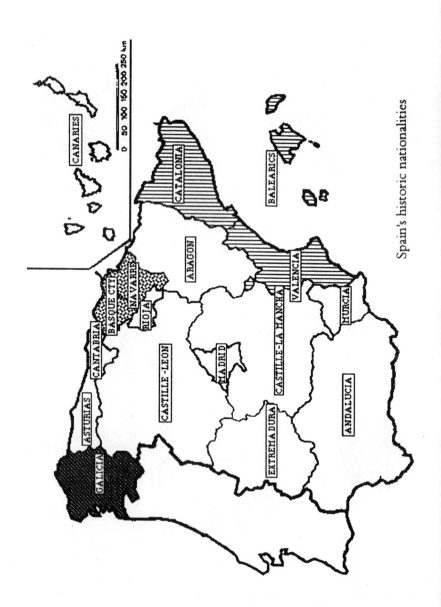

Spain's historic nationalities

CANARIES
CATALONIA
BALEARICS
ARAGON
VALENCIA
BASQUE CTY
NAVARRE
RIOJA
CANTABRIA
MURCIA
CASTILLE-LEON
MADRID
CASTILLE-LA MANCHA
ASTURIAS
EXTREMADURA
ANDALUCIA
GALICIA

0 50 100 150 200 250 km

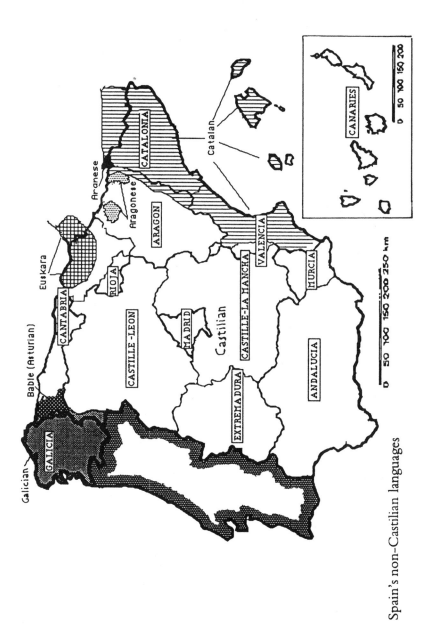

Spain's non-Castilian languages

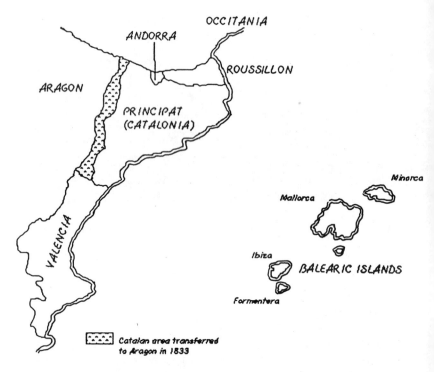

Catalonia and the other Catalan countries

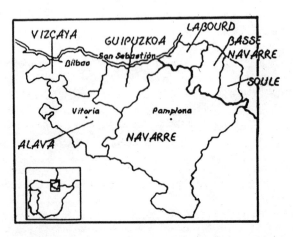

Euskadi (the Basque country) and its seven provinces

1

INTRODUCTION

This book compares Catalan and Basque nationalism and seeks to chart the main differences in their development. It concentrates on specific aspects neglected by previous research: in contrast to most previous studies of Basque and Catalan nationalism, comparative or non-comparative, my research focusses on national culture and symbols, their systematisation and manipulation by nationalist élites, and their relationship to political violence. The aim is to contribute to a sociological paradigm which takes into account the oppositional character of nationalism.

The book is not about economic factors, class cleavages or other variables. These have been adequately covered by many others, but will be referred to in the book. Nor does it seek to define culture; this is a study of the people who define it – the nationalists – and how they have done so.

No country's politics exists independently of its culture. Culture is about *values*, which include attitudes, prescribed behaviour and expectations, as expressed in symbols and as preserved in the nation's material heritage. The concept of value has been widely discussed in sociology. In Parsons (1975, 1991) shared values act as standard-bearers and pillars of the social order.[1] They are internalised through both primary and secondary socialisation.[2] Every society must be supported by shared values, or it risks disintegration. However, both in times of rapid social transformation and ethnic conflict, values are bound to change and are likely to clash with one another. When

---

[1] 'Values held in common constitute the primary reference point for the analysis of a social system as an empirical system. Such a system of societal values may, of course, change over a period of time, but it is the most stable component of the social system' (Parsons 1991: 8).

[2] In stateless nations, socialisation is often carried out by non-state agents, i.e. unofficial media, informal education, self-taught research and voluntary associations. I refer to this occasionally as *nationalist socialisation*.

the values of a stateless nation challenge officialdom, they compete with those of the nation-state. In time- and space-related changes, some values emerge stronger than others, representing focal points for mass mobilisations.

It is also important to remember that most ethnonationalist movements in Europe are based on cultural claims and in particular linguistic ones.[3] The prominent position of language in many ethnic claims has, if anything, increased over the 1970s and 1980s.[4] The exploration of this dimension highlights important differences between Catalan and Basque nationalism: if we accept the assumption that the primary focus and means of legitimation of *most* contemporary European nationalism has been, and is, language, a contradiction between this accepted precondition and the lack of a shared language has necessarily emerged within Basque nationalism. No such contrast has appeared within Catalanism.[5]

Several scholars have acknowledged *en passant* that the distinctive character of the two nationalist movements is related to cultural factors. 'Catalan nationalism has always been more cohesive than that in the Basque Country, in part stemming from the strong cultural and linguistic ties . . .' (Hannum 1990: 267). Some have gone so far as to assert that violence in the Basque country was a consequence of the lack of a vibrant and shared cultural tradition. 'It was [the Catalans'] cultural self-confidence that made terrorism superfluous, a terrorism that perhaps suited the more racist nationalism of the Basques and their emphasis on physical prowess and exuberant youth. In contrast, . . .the democratic opposition achieved in Catalonia a degree of unity and co-operation without

[3] Language features to different degrees in European nationalist claims, with the Scottish and Northern Irish cases having the least linguistic content.

[4] Most independence movements in the former Soviet Union started from linguistic claims (Estonia, Moldova, Belarus etc.), although this was not particularly the case of Yugoslavia and Czechoslovakia before their disintegration. For Brittany, Wales and several other West European stateless nations, language features as a prominent element in nationalist programmes.

[5] My approach considers the language as the carrier of culture, rather than conflating the two terms. This raises the question whether we can conceive a distinctive culture without a distinctive language as its vehicle for expression. Many nationalists will deny that, but there arises the vexed question of how to define a culture. The very effort of defining a culture as opposed to another implies a process of border creation. Hence the choice of language as the crucible of nationhood is related to its availability as an 'ethnic marker'.

parallel in Spain' (Carr and Fusi 1981: 161). However, these authors do not provide a deeper, more systematic analysis for their intuitive assertions. As far as we are aware no study has followed this perspective – to relate cultural variables, or the lack of them, to violence – in either sociology or other social sciences. Even in comparative studies on other areas of the world, such an approach has not been given the attention it deserves.

It will be useful to list here the main research in our field. Interestingly, systematic and large-scale comparisons between the two movements are few, either in Spanish or in other languages. There are studies in English by Payne (1971, 1976), Mansvelt Beck (1992), Medhurst (1987) and in French by Loyer (1990). Miguélez (1984) has attempted a sketchy comparison in Catalan and Euskara. The only large-scale systematic comparison of Basque and Catalan nationalism has been carried out by Díez-Medrano (1995); however, its focus is mainly political and economic.

The mutual relationship between Basque and Catalan nationalism is analysed by several authors, among them Nagel (1987, 1991) on the period before 1923.[6] Hernàndez, Mercadé and Oltra (1983) compare the ideology and platform of several regionalist and nationalist movements in Spain. Comparisons are also occasionally included in more general studies: Linz (1973, 1975) balances survey data with historical insight. Perceptive comparisons are available in Payne (1975), as well as in Elorza (1984), Corcuera (1984) and Olabarri Cortázar (1981). Other authors have contrasted specific aspects of the two economies, electoral turnout, social systems etc., but without focussing on nationalism: Carreras (1985), Izard (1985), González Portilla (1985), and Roiz Célix (1984). Finally, Silver's (1988) interpretive essay does not offer a systematic comparison.

More studies are available comparing each nationalism with similar movements abroad. Scottish nationalism has been compared to its Catalan counterpart by Brand (1985), Ehrlich (1993) and Moreno (1988) and to Basque nationalism by Zirakzadeh (1991) and Watson (1992). Michael Keating (1988) compares the relationship between the state and regional nationalism in Spain, Italy and Britain, as well as nationalist movements in Catalonia, Quebec and Scotland (Keating, 1996). Pierre Birnbaum (1988: 146-55) has attempted a comparison between Scottish, Breton and Catalan

[6] For an up-to-date bibliography, see Conversi (1993).

nationalism. Khatami (1990) has compared Eritrea and Euskadi; Kimmel (1989) Brittany-Euskadi-Quebec, Mayo (1974) Brittany-Euskadi-Wales, and Waldman (1989) Northern Ireland-Euskadi-Quebec. A special issue of the *Journal of Baltic Studies* was devoted to comparisons between the Baltics' and other national movements, among them Basques and Catalans (Johnston 1992, Kasla 1992, Laitin 1992, Shafir 1992).

Few of these studies give a prominent place to culture, but it is impossible to isolate cultural factors from economic or structural ones. A solution is to compare two cases which offer similar economic, structural and social variables, while differing sharply in the cultural variables. This, of course, does not imply a refusal to take into account other dimensions, which will be considered throughout the book.

The violent character of Basque nationalism has inspired much research in the Basque country, both scholarly and otherwise and from several disciplines and viewpoints. By contrast, Catalan social scientists still tend to treat nationalism as a given, as an unaccountable collective feeling, often as something not worthy of analysis. With a few exceptions, the Catalan contribution to the literature on nationalism is entirely limited to historians.[7] Perhaps it is true that 'as scholarship is reactive, the spilling of ink awaits the spilling of blood' (Horowitz 1985: 13).

Moreover, the study of Catalan nationalism has attracted left-wing historians more than nationalists as such. The latter are more prolific in Euskadi. Nuñez (1992: 5, 1993) explains this contrast: 'While in [Euskadi] an extremely clear-cut division exists between nationalists and non-nationalists, and, within the intellectual circles, between [radicals] and moderates, in Catalonia the situation is much more flexible. Catalan culture and language serves as a vehicle for the integration of foreigners and non-nationalists into publishing houses and reviews concerned with propagating Catalan culture.'

General orientations

Given the similarity of economic or structural factors in Catalonia and Euskadi, I attempt to relate the development of the two

[7] Such exceptions are worth mentioning: in sociology Giner (1980, 1984, 1986, 1987), Hernàndez (1983) and Mercadé (1982); in philosophy Bilbeny (1984, 1988); in political science Colomer (1984); in anthropology Pujadas (1983).

ethnic movements to the vitality of shared culture and values. Where the latter flourish, not only do they become a central part of the nationalists' claims, but they also add cohesion to their struggles; i.e. the availability of pre-existing cultural 'markers', which help to differentiate the group from its neighbours, facilitates the organisation of united political action. The common elements chosen as core values can work both as mobilising symbols and as points of reference for a wide political platform and large constituencies. Conversely, the absence of shared cultural distinctiveness is likely to encourage political fragmentation within nationalist movements. In this case, the movement is bound to rely on an 'antagonistic identity'. Such an identity is one constructed essentially through the opposition of the ingroup to one or more outgroups. All identities are in some way based on opposition, but an antagonistic identity focuses more on the need to define one's own group by negative comparison to others, and by exclusion. This border-definition process is carried out by a radical re-evaluation of the positive traits of the ingroup and a parallel devaluation of those of the outgroup. Borders are stressed rather than content, i.e. the group's culture. Culture can also be oppositional, as when it is used in opposition to another culture, generally the dominant one. But when the ethnic culture is weak and ill-defined, the whole group must be opposed to the outgroup, generally the dominant one. Hence, a possible common bond can be provided by violent political mobilisation. Given particular historical conditions (state repression, dictatorship and censorship), violence can become a source of cohesion and the principal means of forging a community and fostering the long-awaited 'rebirth of the nation'.

To understand the source and legitimacy of most nationalist movements, especially cultural ones, one must also take into account the feeling of threat.[8] In the age of the nation-state, minorities do not generally feel protected or safe. Their very cultural survival is at stake under the joint pressures of centralisation and modernisation, and to ensure their survival they try to achieve some political control over their destiny. This is only feasible by exercising some form of

[8] Some authors treat this fear of extinction as a non measurable variable. For instance, Horowitz (1985: 179) speaks of a fabricated 'anxiety-laden perception' which is potentially endless (175–81). However we will show that this perception is rooted in historical events which have direct consequences upon cultural and political practices.

jurisdiction over an established geographical territory. Modern
nationalism cannot be conceived without this spatial dimension.
Territory lies at the heart of all nationalist programmes, hence the
importance of maps and mapping in their strategy. Ultimately, in a
world of nation-states, an ethnic group can only feel fully protected
if it achieves the formation of its own nation-state. However, if a
group has a sufficiently strong identity and feels confident about its
future survival within an existing nation-state, demands for independence or separation may become politically irrelevant.[9]

Definitions, sources and methods

This book speaks of Catalan and Basque nations and nationalism.
It also uses the suffix *ethno-* (ethnonationalism, *ethnies*, ethnic groups,
ethnic borders, ethnic identity, ethnic conflict, ethnicity etc.) to
refer to the broader comparative dimensions.[10] The term
'ethnonationalism' refers exclusively to movements acting on behalf
of stateless nations.[11] The more wide-ranging term 'nationalism'
refers to both state and non-state nationalisms. In most European
languages the distinction between the two concepts is blurred
and uneven: in fact, while 'ethnonationalism' is used to describe
stateless nationalism, there is no specific term to define state
nationalism as a distinctive phenomenon.[12] Indeed, some Catalan

[9] Memories of past oppression are difficult to erase. The collapse of Yugoslavia,
the Soviet Union and Ethiopia reminds us of the all-pervasive strength of such
memories of collective sufferings and their potential for explosion once free
expression has been reinstated. As a consequence, the group may perceive that the
over-arching nation-state can again represent a threat to its future survival. Hence,
apparently quiescent ethnic communities often keep a 'separatist' reservoir that can
be revived in case of a crisis in the group's relation with the centre. The main
variable is again the behaviour of the central government in its relationships with
the periphery.

[10] Far from being used in a genetic sense as coterminous with *race*, the term 'ethnic'
will generally be used to take into account the dimension of putative descent, which
is indeed central to any ethnic identity and distinguishes ethnic groups from other
groups sharing similar cultural elements.

[11] For a discussion of the concepts of ethnonationalism, ethnic nationalism and
related ones, see Yan (1990).

[12] For a discussion of the terms 'nation', '*ethnie*', 'minority' and related concepts
see Riggs (1986). Riggs (1991a, 1991b) concludes that 'ethnicity' is the most
general and scientifically undefined of these concepts.

scholars[13] have pointed out that the only justification for using the term 'ethnonationalism' lies in an ill-starred confusion between state and nation. Walker Connor (1972) claims that this confusion is historically unwarranted, since nations are nothing but 'self-aware ethnic groups': many previous ethnic groups turned into nations and eventually into states. Yet for most West European scholars and lay people the term nationalism is inextricably associated with *state* nationalism, with all the negative traits normally attached to it.

In their reach for some form of self-determination, nationalists use the instrument of the 'nation' as an ideological vehicle. It is exactly the latter's situational, transitory and instrumental value which makes it so difficult to define. The nation cannot be defined because its purpose is to define. It is a conceptual tool and a boundary perception through which an ethnic group wishing to be represented in a state attempts to establish and define its own space of action. Central to this definition is the demarcation of a territory through an ideal reference to a historical past.

My research integrates documentary material (mainly the nationalists' recorded declarations and writings), sociolinguistic surveys and other data (such as language censuses, sociolinguistic analyses and other derivative data on the relation between identity, language, nationalism, voting behaviour etc.). I rely both on primary and secondary sources. Particularly in chapters 4, 5 and 6, primary data, such as political pamphlets, communiqués, biographies, excerpts from newspapers and magazines, and personal interviews, are used.[14]

The book focusses on those individuals – the intellectuals and the intelligentsia – who set the agenda of nationalist mobilization. Many of the founding fathers of the two movements were primarily cultural nationalists who felt that the national culture was being threatened by state centralisation. As the state was needed to protect the culture, the cultural nationalists needed to ally themselves with political nationalists in order to reach the state. Thus they formulated

[13] In particular, Professors Salvador Cardús, Josep Llobera, and Rafalel Ribó, whom I thank for their insightful comments. Salvador Giner (1984) uses the term 'ethnic nationalism'.

[14] As a general bibliography on the national question in Spain from 1939 to 1983, I have consulted Beramendi (1984), as well as the more up-to-date and comprehensive reappraisal of studies of nationalism in Spain by Nuñez (1992, 1993).

their regenerative programmes in political, terms. Finally, in
Catalonia they aimed to form alliances with economically
hegemonic classes in order to gather the necessary financial support;
hence they had to adapt their cultural arguments to the needs of
economic élites and frame their programmes in ways that did not
clash too harshly with the latter's interests.

The role of a sociologist can be compared to that of a photog-
rapher. By changing the perspective and the colour of the light filter,
the same scene may assume a different appearance, revealing new
and unexpected aspects. Eventually the whole picture may change.
The aim is indeed to explain the same phenomenon in a new light,
rather than a new phenomenon in the same light.

Plan

The book is divided into two parts: the first historical and the
second more theoretical, in which the main scholarly theories of
nationalism are tested.

The historical part consists of five chapters. Chapters 1 and 2 deal
with the formation of early Basque and Catalan nationalism, the
establishment of their respective programmes and definitions of
national identity. Chapters 3 and 4 explore the transformations
undergone by the two movements during the Francoist dictatorship
and illustrate how the changed demographic, political and cultural
conditions precipitated a radical re-formulation of the two movements. Chapter 5 focusses on the democratisation process and the
legitimacy crisis of the centralised state inherited from Francoism.
The rapid political changes are charted, taking into account the
influence of peripheral nationalism in the creation of the new state
and vice versa.

The book divides the history of Catalan and Basque nationalism
into two broad periods: from their foundation to the Civil War
(1936-9) and from the latter to the beginning of the democratic
Transition (1975-82). The reason is that the Civil War was a
clear-cut severance and a radical break with the past. In the minds
of those old enough to have survived it, the war is 'a rupture so
complete that it divides time in two; there is "before the war" and
everything that came afterwards' (Di Giacomo 1984: 31).[15] Also

---

[15] As Termes (1986:18) puts it, the enormously negative impact of the Civil War,

nationalism was at the root of the Civil War, which can be seen as a conflict between official Spanish nationalism and centrifugal trends.[16]

The second part deals with three deeply intertwined aspects of nationalist mobilisation: the choice of language as opposed to other core values (Chapter 6), the consequence of large-scale immigration (Chapter 7) and the cause and effects of political violence (Chapter 8). Chapter 6 shows how two different sociolinguistic situations influenced the nationalist leaders' attempts to forge a bounded national identity: language maintenance influenced the moderate and unified course of Catalan nationalism; language shift created a vacuum in the Basque programme, to which the leaders responded by emphasising other elements, but never agreed on which of them to choose. The selection of different core values can result in the development of different nationalist programmes. We delineate two broad patterns of nationalism, *inclusive* and *exclusive*. Stress on language as the achieved epitome of a group's culture creates the preconditions for the development of an inclusive form of nationalism. Stress on race, descent and other ascriptive elements creates the preconditions for an exclusivist form of nationalism.

Chapter 7 analyses the contribution of immigration to the nationalist movement and identifies the different ways in which nationalist proto-élites reacted to the challenge. Immigration both reinforced and modified local core values. Encouraged by the high level of language maintenance, the Catalan pattern emphasised cultural integration through language. By contrast, immigration in Euskadi increased the original fragmentation, inspiring a more radical form of nationalism whose goal was to involve the immigrants in the national struggle. Nationalist mobilisation became increasingly based on action, voluntary participation, subjective involvement and the playing down of primordial symbols. New core values were selected and stressed in the process.

a war which 'disintegrated nearly everybody', has been inadequately studied. In Euskadi the change was also abrupt: 'The tragedy of that war left unforgettable images and experiences in the memory of those who lived it. These were vividly described to us youths during our upbringing. After five decades . . . Still the great divide is "before the war" and "after the war"' (Zulaika 1988:16).

[16] This historical reality is often neglected by many, especially English, historians who prefer to emphasise the ideological or class nature of the conflict. This issue is discussed in the chapters on Francoism.

Chapter 8 attempts to relate the above to violence. Two factors are highlighted to explain the drift towards violent action. First, *internal* cultural, ideological and political fragmentation impinged upon the radicals' resort to *external* confrontation with the state; secondly, state repression was needed for violence not only to begin but also to spread. Having related cultural assimilation to political fragmentation, I argue that the latter two, together with state violence, are ideal preconditions for the rise of violent confrontational politics.

A brief Epilogue sets out the main themes which emerge from this comparison, drawing up some general conclusions and confirming the hypothesis (of cultural nationalism, core values and state repression) expressed in the previous chapters.

2

FROM THE FOUNDING OF CATALAN NATIONALISM TO THE CIVIL WAR

This chapter tackles the issue of when Catalonia began to be defined as a nation in the modern sense, i.e. when Catalan nationalism arose. We see that this development was slow, and many early Catalanists were often at pains to stress their Spanishness. Initially, Catalanness began to configure itself in the form of a distinct vision of the world and a distinct set of customs and laws. This vaguely defined identity began by attributing to a different mentality the existing economic gap between Madrid and Barcelona. Hence, at the beginning, Catalan identity was not a clearly defined notion, and several cultural revivalists wrote in Spanish. Only gradually did some consensus begin to emerge around the centrality of culture and, within it, of language.

Catalonia had had an imperial past – in the time when the Mediterranean possessions of the confederal Crown of Aragon extended as far as Southern Italy and Athens. After a period of decline, its autonomy within the kingdom of Spain was brought to an end by Philip V (1716). A Royal Decree (*Nueva Planta*) banned most Catalan institutions, laws and customs, including the language, and imposed a uniform centralised administration. Although the local institutions were slowly eroded, the country recovered economically. As a consequence, the gap between the region and the rest of the peninsula increased, possibly helping to inspire the forthcoming regionalist movement. The establishment of the steam-powered Bonaplata mill in Barcelona in 1832 is commonly taken to be the beginning of modern Catalan industry.[1] Catalonia became

---

[1] However, its precursors date back to the early eighteenth century (calico-printing was inaugurated in 1728), and in the 1770s and '80s cotton production expanded to unprecedented levels. But this industry eclipsed suddenly and totally in the first decade of the nineteenth century (Thomson 1992).

the one Mediterranean exception to the tendency of early industrialization to be concentrated in Northern Europe (Thomson
1992).[2]

On the pretext of a dynastic dispute, the First Carlist Wars erupted
in 1833. The Carlists were supporters of Don Carlos María Isidro,
the legitimate heir to the throne.[3] However, behind this loomed
more deeply-rooted reasons: Catholic traditionalists, defenders of
local charters and proto-regionalists fought on the Carlist side.
However the Carlists were defeated after a bloody civil war and
Isabella II (1830-1904) was elected Queen of Spain. The defeat of
Carlism (1839) prompted the introduction of social and economic
reforms, the disentailment of ecclesiastical properties, the suppression of guilds (*gremis*) and freedom of commerce. These measures
favoured Catalan textile industries, but the repression of Catalan
institutions continued.[4]

A military *pronunciamiento* (an officers' revolt) overthrew Isabella
II in 1868 and led to the installation of the First Spanish Republic
(1873-4), which assumed an overtly federal arrangement (Hennessy
1962). Nowhere were Republican ideas as welcome as in Catalonia,
where there were sincere expectations that more than a century of
centralism would be reversed. But the enthusiasm for autonomy and
federalism spread too quickly, running out of control. In many
provinces, particularly in the south, several cantons declared independence from Madrid. In 1874, the Republic fell after another
pronunciamiento, preparing the way for the regency (1885-1902) of
Queen María Cristina, wife of Alfonso XII and mother of Alfonso
XIII. Meanwhile, the Carlists attempted another popular rebellion:
a Second Carlist War (1872-6) erupted more than thirty years after
the first one, but was mostly confined to the Basque provinces. As

---

[2] Thomson maintains that state support was essential to the take-off of the cotton
industry.

[3] Ferdinand VII (who ruled till 1833) wanted to be succeeded by his only daughter
Isabella, but succession in the Bourbon family could only pass through the male
line. Don Carlos María Isidro, Ferdinand VII's younger brother, was supported by
the Church and the traditionalists, while his rival and niece Isabella was supported
by the army, the liberals and foreign powers, notably France and Britain.

[4] In 1834 Catalan tribunals were abolished and in 1837 the coinage was suppressed.
In 1845 Madrid decided to abolish the *cadastre*, a financial agreement designed to
compound the last remaining taxes.

we see in the next chapter, its end meant the demise of traditional Basque liberties.

According to some local historians, Catalanism was generated by the confluence of four distinct strains: cultural revival, traditionalist Carlism, Republican federalism and industrial protectionism.[5] The first of these forces, which is of particular concern to the present work, is described in the next section.[6]

The Renaixença (1840s-1870s)

The cultural movement of the *Renaixença* (Renaissance) provided an ideal basis for the subsequent spread of nationalism. Its beginnings as a literary movement during the 1830s and '40s were slow, and at the start it seemed no more than a local expression of regionalist pride. The poem *La Pàtria* (The Fatherland) by Bonaventura-Carles Aribau (1798-1862), published in 1833, is generally identified as the first literary document of the *Renaixença*. However, this is more myth than history.[7] Much more crucial to the Catalan revival was the work of the poet Joaquim Rubió i Ors (1818-99) who, under the pseudonym of '*Lo Gayter de Llobregat*', published several poems in Catalan. The verses were collected in the anthology *Poesies* (1841). In its preface he mentioned for the first time the idea of recovering Catalonia's distinct stature.[8] Since his call had a vast response, it was rightly considered as the manifesto of the *Renaixença*. From that moment onwards, modern Catalan literature began to develop until its outstanding epic, lyric and dramatic poets became the vanguard of Spanish culture at the turn of the century. Before Rubió, men of letters had considered Catalan

---

[5] This is the opinion of both the historian Jesús Pabón (1952) and the nationalist Rovira i Virgili (1930, 1982). However, Vicens Vives (1958) disagrees with this interpretation, reminding us that a sense of grievance and consciousness – which he calls *provincialisme* – already existed before these four factors reached their peak.

[6] On pre-modern Catalan 'national' consciousness, see Simon (1993).

[7] Apparently, Aribau himself was not interested in political Catalanism and was surprised by the success of his composition, which he wrote as a homage for his employer's birthday. Both he and his boss were Catalan expatriates working in a Madrid bank (Miquel i Vergés 1944).

[8] As a starting point for the association between political and cultural nationalism, Rubió announced Catalan literary independence, asserting that Spain is no longer 'our Fatherland'.

no more than a dialect of Occitan, and Aribau himself called it *llemosí.*[9]

The *Renaixença* was not an exclusively bourgeois phenomenon, as some authors imply (i.e. Vilar 1977).[10] Indeed, the Catalan bourgeoisie was enthusiastically pro-Spanish in the 1830s (Fontana 1988: 49–50). Moreover, the *Renaixença* was not simply a version of Romanticism (as with the Provençal *Félibrige*), since it kept on producing new forms of literature once the latter faded away (Balcells 1983: 41-2). The *Jocs Florals* (Floral Games), ancient poetry contests and history pageants from the fourteenth century, were revived in 1859 on the initiative of a group of poets, historians and literati (Joan Cortada, Victor Balaguer, Joaquim Rubió i Ors, Manuel Milà i Fontanals, Antoni de Bofarull) with the aim of re-establishing the prestige of Catalan.[11] They succeeded in obtaining the sponsorship of Barcelona's *Ajuntament* (municipality), in whose building the first *Jocs Florals* were celebrated, providing a unique stimulus for the great poets of the *Renaixença.*[12]

In Catalonia, by contrast with the lethargy of other Spanish regions, a musical, artistic, literary and political wave of creativity swept every sector of society. The *Renaixença* touched all fields of the humanities – poetry, theatre, architecture, painting, sculpture, philosophy – and spread all over the Catalan-speaking regions from

[9] The word was originally designed to describe the *langue d'oc* (Occitan, including Provençal), since the most famous troubadors came from Limoges, north of Toulouse (Sanchis Guarner 1972: 23-4). Provençal literature exerted a strong influence on all nearby Romance literatures, but particularly on the Catalan. Catalan poetry was often written in Provençal. However, Provençal was never used in prose. All kinds of treaties, laws, novels, holy books etc. were already written in Catalan by the thirteenth century. The term *llemosí* was indeed used to differentiate from the latter the poetic works written by Catalan authors using the language of the troubadors (Sanchis Guarner 1972: 23).

[10] Its initial impetus was élitist. The first representatives of the *Renaixença* considered poetry just as an intellectual exercise, and did not feel particularly compelled to reach the wider public (Sanchis Guarner 1972: 177).

[11] The original *Jocs Florals* were a literary competition held in Provençal at Toulouse from 1324 onwards. The Catalan attendance at those functions was so great that the *Consistori de la Gaia Ciència* (Poetry Committee) was transferred to Barcelona in 1393.

[12] These kinds of poetic contest can be found among most European stateless nations, where they often acquire a political meaning, e.g. the Welsh Eisteddfod (see Morgan, in Hobsbawm and Ranger 1983, and Edwards 1990).

the Balearic islands to the French Roussillon, from Valencia to the Sardinian port of Alguer.[13] Theatre blossomed, though at first only in Castilian. In the realm of philosophy Ramon Martí d'Eixalà (1808-57) and Francesc-Xavier Llorens i Barba (1820-72) introduced German idealism and the Scottish Philosophy of Common Sense (Batista i Roca 1959). Relying heavily on Herder, Llorens affirmed that every people has a national spirit (*Volksgeist*), which is reflected in all its cultural manifestations, including philosophy (Llobera 1983).[14] Llorens was an influential thinker also in the rest of Spain: among his disciples were Torras i Bages, Prat de la Riba and Menéndez y Pelayo (Bilbeny 1988: 60), of whom we shall consider the two former later.

The *Renaixença* was initially centred in Barcelona, but slowly spread to other towns and villages. According to Fradera (1990, 1992), the middle to upper echelons of rural society were keen to participate in the revival inasmuch as it suited their own ends. The rural intelligentsia reviled urbanisation, sensing the threat it posed to their traditional lifestyles and customs. Nationalism provided an ideal vehicle with which to voice these apprehensions. As bourgeois nationalism was gaining ground in Barcelona, it tried to forge an alliance with the people living in its agricultural hinterland, the *muntanyesos*. The latter warmly embraced the programme of the *Renaixença* proposed by the urban bourgeoisie, yet they were determined to resist capitalist and urban encroachment. The *muntanya* (hillside, countryside) was seen both as a base from which insurrection against the state could be mounted, as during the Carlist wars, and as the last bastion of rural values which were being crushed by urbanisation. On the one hand, the *Renaixença* offered these rural diehards a means of redemption whereby they could boost their self-esteem; on the other, it embodied for town-dwellers a nostalgic desire to recapture a pre-modern past. Although the two groups came from opposing standpoints, they nevertheless joined together in the creative celebration of the beauty of nationhood. The greatest Catalan poet of the time, the priest Jacint Verdaguer (1845-1902), spent much of his life in the countryside. Lamenting the loss of

---

[13] On the manifestations of the *Renaixença* in Valencia, Roussillon and the Balearic islands, see Jorba *et al.* (1992). On Mallorca, see Melià (1968).

[14] A very cautious scholar, Llorens always spoke in the name of a Spanish nation. Nevertheless, he was puzzled about the wide divergences between Barcelona and Madrid in the realm of philosophy, economy and culture (Fradera 1992).

Catalan traditions and mores, he became 'the person who best condensed these values . . . by accomplishing a complete synthesis between popular and high culture' (Fradera 1990: 63). But the driving force behind the movement remained firmly city-rooted: the Liberal politician, historian and journalist Victor Balaguer (1824–1901) was the first to popularise Catalan historical drama and poetry. He began to write in Spanish, but from 1868 onward shifted to Catalan. An intensely active man, skillful politician and popular writer, he can well be defined as a 'moderniser'. Imbued with Romantic and historicist spirit, Balaguer made full use of the new publishing techniques, such as the popular *feuilleton* (in periodic instalments), taking full advantage of the opening markets of his time (Fradera 1992).[15]

A respectable interpretation identifies the *Renaixença* as a response to the disruption and violence brought about by modernisation. This led to the disillusionment of a previously Liberal intelligentsia who turned to the past 'as an escape route to avoid confronting the problems of modernity' (Fradera 1992). One of the key schemes of the movement was the historicist reconstruction of an idealised past, focused especially on the Middle Ages.[16] Of all the arts, poetry acted as the core of the *Renaixença*, yet poetry was itself historicist and oriented towards the past. The success of the *Renaixença* and the rich output which Catalan literature has produced ever since constituted a solid base upon which political nationalism could draw its stable legitimacy. Once established as a political movement, Catalanism had to rely on a pre-existing definition of Catalan identity. By then, this work had already been completed by the cultural revivalists which preceded the political nationalists.

On a parallel and sometimes independent track, a form of political nationalism emerged. Some scholars consider *Cataluña y los catalanes*,

---

15 This seems to confirm Benedict Anderson's vision of the *print revolution* as a driving force behind nationalism. The novel and the newspaper provided 'the technical means for "representing" the kind of imagined community that is the nation' (1983: 30).

16 This was accompanied by a drive to reach those areas of Catalonia where modernity had not yet claimed its toll. In this research resided the link between historiography and other intellectual endeavours: the past had to be rediscovered in the present. The result was a selective exaltation of those elements of popular culture which more suited the aspirations of the dominant urban classes (Fradera 1992).

written in 1860 by Joan Cortada (1805-68), the main promoter of the Floral Games, as the earliest statement of political nationalism. However, its occasional sentences on the topic were still too ambiguous and did not present an outright political programme.[17] Still others see in *Cataluña en España* (1855) by Joan Illas i Vidal (1819-76) a prelude to political Catalanism, but the book did not envisage any separate political development for Catalonia.[18] The publication in 1887 of *El Regionalismo*, a collection of articles by the influential journalist Joan Mañe i Flaquer (1823-1901), put forward a tenuous plan for regional autonomy. Flaquer's quasi-traditionalist leanings were based on a defence of local customs and laws, linking them with the interests of the Catalan upper classes (Mañe 1900). However, the paternity of political Catalanism must certainly be ascribed to Valentí Almirall, whose work we analyse next.

Almirall and the federalist tradition

The first explicit nationalist programme was formulated by Valentí Almirall (1841-1904) in his *Lo Catalanisme*, published in 1886, which outlined the transition from regionalism to nationalism in a federalist framework. In contrast with the historicist and culturalist generation of the *Renaixença*, Almirall can be defined as a 'moderniser'. One of his aims was to reconcile the traditionalist and progressive strands within Catalanism, adding to them the ingredient of the defence of Catalan economic interests. Since the 1830s Catalan industrialists had pressed unsuccessfully for protective measures to shield their industries against foreign competition. As a failed hegemonic class they represented a precious ally to the regionalist cause, and some of them soon rallied in support

[17] Far from presenting a nationalist programme, the book simply defined Catalonia as a homeland. Cortada recalled Catalonia's historical glories in order to demonstrate that the Catalans 'are different from other Spaniards'. He stressed that Spain's historical, cultural, and economic cleavages made centralist attempts far more difficult than in other European cases. However, he demanded that Catalan interests be accommodated within the Spanish state (Ghanine 1995).

[18] As the Castilian title indicates, there was no concept of 'separating' Catalonia from Spain. In his timid outline of the Catalan question, Illas i Vidal protested the abuse of Catalan interests by the Spanish state, proposing a greater measure of self-government and a change of economic policy on a reformist line. Illas i Vidal was a politician, lawyer and protectionist economist, who actively participated in the Jocs Florals.

of Catalanism, providing conspicuous financial backing for both political and cultural initiatives. Prominent Catalan industrialists often acted as patrons, financing art production, literary festivals, theatres and opera. However, this class remained unconditionally pro-Spanish at heart (Fontana 1988).

Almirall singled out the outstanding aspects of the Catalan character and mentality, and language began to move centre-stage, though as one means of defining national identity among others. As mentioned previously, political regionalism was the fruit of the fusion of four currents: the cultural revivalists, the progressive federalists, the anti-Bourbon traditionalists and the representatives of the industrial bourgeoisie. The first alliance in which Romantic literati, conservative lawyers and protectionist industrialists were prominent was created under the aegis of Almirall. Which factors triggered this successful union? The lack of political power for industrialists, the absence of protective measures for the Spanish economy, and the threats to abolish the Catalan civil code were probably the most immediate catalysts for the formation of this first alliance. But underlying the whole process was the memory of the lost freedom of Catalonia and the desire to strengthen a renewed ethnic identity under the guidance of the cultural revival.

One of Almirall's most important achievements was the drafting of the *Memorial de Greuges* (grievances) presented in 1885 to King Alfonso XII (Nadal *et al.* 1986). This 'Memorial in defence of the moral and material interests of Catalonia' was signed by a committee of businessmen, industrialists, intellectuals, professionals, artists, workers' delegates and literary figures (such as Verdaguer and Guimerà). The Memorial was quickly forgotten after the King's death the same year, yet it was a milestone in the evolution of Catalan consciousness. Its two immediate achievements were the creation of a broad front representing several social sectors and interests, and an unprecedented attempt to enter the 'citadel of power' through a direct dialogue with Madrid (Peers 1937: 130).

We have seen how, at the beginning, Catalanism was made up of a few poets, lawyers, local historians and other intellectuals – also how their alliance with politicians came about. The trend towards the politicisation of cultural Catalanism increased in the years that followed. Greatly concerned with linguistic normalisation, Almirall set up the first daily newspaper in Catalan, *Diari Català* (f. 1879). As the organiser of the First Catalanist Congress (1880), he attempted to coalesce around his federalist principles a group of poets and historians (Figueres 1985). They were members of *La Jove Catalunya* (Young Catalonia), founded in 1870 by a group of literati.[19] But this group of cultural revivalists was not particularly concerned with political activities, despite its name suggesting youth-centred Mazzinian principles. They were active in the organisation of the *Jocs Florals*, but their conservatism barred them from espousing the progressive federalist principles which Almirall inherited from his Republican upbringing. Thus Almirall's first attempt to bring together political and cultural nationalists failed as a result of ideological divisions. Yet two main agreements emerged from the Congress: the drafting of a document in defence of the Catalan law and the foundation of a political organisation, the Centre Català (1882). At a Second Catalanist Congress (1883) convened by the Centre Català, political affiliation within Spanish parties by Catalans was condemned for the first time. Motions in favour of the Catalan law, the co-official status of Catalan (alongside Castilian), economic protectionism, and a central government for Catalonia were also passed. With these initiatives political and cultural Catalanism were finally merged.

Almirall was heir to the Republican tradition of Pi i Margall, who in his *Las Nacionalidades* (The Nationalities, 1877) summed up his vision of a federal Spain based on both pragmatic and historical arguments. He foresaw greater possibilities of carrying out a separate programme for Catalonia in which federalism would be anchored to local traditions, rather than relying on 'abstract' rational and internationalist principles (Llorens i Vila 1993). This led him to break with Pi and the Spanish federalist party and found the Centre Català. In turn, Almirall's idealism soon clashed with the bourgeois interests and political conservatism prevailing in his group. A particular source of friction was his opposition to the Barcelona Universal Exhibition in 1888, which had the backing of almost the entire Catalan establishment. This stance cost Almirall the defection from the Centre Català of its most right-wing members, which formed a separate Lliga de Catalunya in 1887.

[19] As indicated by the name, they were inspired by Giuseppe Mazzini's *Giovane Italia* (Young Italy) and the Romantic awakening of European stateless nations, in particular by Italian, German and Irish nationalisms.

From the Lliga de Catalunya to 1898

Since the restoration of the monarchy (1874), Spain had been dominated by two parties, the Conservatives and the Liberals, who alternated in power through a complex rotation system based on political corruption. Key regional issues were fought in this all-Spanish framework. Only from the early 1890s a new political option started to gain ground in Catalonia – and afterwards in Vizcaya. The decision adopted by the Second Catalanist Congress to condemn political affiliation within Spanish parties was crucial to this development. A new possibility of political allegiance outside the two main Alfonsist parties (and outside Carlism) began to emerge only with Catalan regionalism. In its early stages, the regionalist movement did not aim at separation from Spain. On the contrary, it wished to influence Madrid's political choices by intervening in central Spanish affairs. The Catalan bourgeoisie's efforts to secure a hegemonic position within the Spanish state were thwarted by the latter's incapacity for self-modernisation due to the predominance in its ranks of a centralist landowning oligarchy permeated by Jacobin ideals. The rightist split from the Centre Català, which led to the formation of the Lliga de Catalunya, was once again guided by literary men, although they clearly represented vested interests: the Lliga was founded by the playwright Angel Guimerà (1845-1924) and the lawyer Joan Permanyer (1848-1919). At the beginning, it appeared to be a revival of conservative and 'floralesque' regionalism. Soon they were joined by the young students of the Centre Escolar Catalanista, founded about one year before, among whom was Enric Prat de la Riba (whom we encounter later). Under the leadership of the Modernist architect Lluís Domènech i Montaner (1850-1923), the Lliga become the protagonist of the regional scene. Domènech i Montaner was one of the chief planners and builders of the Barcelona Universal Exposition of 1888, which had been opposed by Almirall. As with other nationalist movements, Catalanism was made up of planners and artists. The planners (intelligentsia) needed an infrastructure (the state) in order to achieve their aims. The artists provided both the emotional inspiration and the framework of ideas for the nationalist goal.

The first salient act engineered by the Lliga was a successful campaign for the defence of the Catalan Civil Code, which Madrid attempted to stamp out in 1889 in order to unify legal procedures.

Meanwhile, Almirall's Centre Català became isolated from mainstream politics and was finally dissolved (*ca.* 1890). The recurrent schisms besetting incipient Catalanism gave rise to a general awareness of the need to create a more broadly encompassing body. Hence, the Unió Catalanista was founded in 1891 as the first coalition to reunite the whole gamut of groups with the aim of propagating regionalist and federalist ideals (Llorens i Vila 1993, Riquer 1977: 48). Their delegates assembled in 1892 at Manresa, a town north of Barcelona, drawing up a seminal document known as the *Bases de Manresa.* Its programme, much more radical than the Memorial de Greuges, included *inter alia* political autonomy, the replacement of the artificially imposed provinces with more 'natural' *comarques* and *municipis* (town councils), the reservation of public appointments for Catalonians (by virtue of either birth or 'naturalisation'), and Catalan as the only official language (Termes and Colomines 1992). The powers attributed to Catalonia should encompass taxation, coinage, legislative and executive authority, civil, penal and mercantile legislation, specific Catalan units for the army, a regional police force, and control of education by the *municipi* or the *comarca.*[20] These proposals, albeit ambitious, represented the first basic agreement on political terms among Catalanist forces and a stable basis on which slow and more uniform progress towards the attainment of regional consensus was later made possible. However, the Bases of Manresa had a limited popular impact and thus achieved their unitary aims only at an élite level.

In 1897 an international dimension was added to the conflict when the Unió Catalanista sent to the Greek king, George I, a message of sympathy for the Cretans in their struggle against Turkish rule. But Madrid could not tolerate any hint of autonomous foreign policy initiatives from Catalonia and its response was brutal: a wave of repression struck the region, with closure of newspapers, proscription of meetings, house searches, closing down of clubs and societies, and the arrest of leaders (Riquer 1979: 22). The occupation of Catalonia was not lifted till 1901, when free elections were allowed and for the first time the Catalanists topped the poll (Riquer 1979: 46). In a typical pattern, repressive measures only reinforced the popularity of the persecuted leaders.

---

[20] *Comarca* (pl. *comarques*) is a traditional unit that stands between the municipality and the province.

Barcelona fin de siècle: a flourishing cultural life

In the 1870s, Catalan literature entered a stage of maturity. Its foremost representatives were the dramatist Àngel Guimerà, the poet Mossen Jacint Verdaguer and the Realist prose writer Narcís Oller (1846-1930), founder of the modern Catalan novel.[21] The period from about 1882 to 1906 is known in Catalonia as *Modernisme*.[22] It began with the lyrics of Joan Maragall (1860-1911) and his articles in the journal *L'Avenç* (Progress),[23] published in 1881-4 and 1889-93 (Grilli 1984). *L'Avenç* contributed to the translation and dissemination of European artists and thinkers, but its role in the development of Catalan nationalism is particularly tied to a campaign for the creation of a unified Catalan orthography, which, as we shall see, only succeeded some decades later, thanks to the work of the linguist Pompeu Fabra. The term *Modernisme* was probably coined in 1884 in an article published in *L'Avenç*, where it was used to signify the will to receive 'cosmopolitan' influences. Modernism was a reaction against the conservative Romanticism of the *Renaixença*, and a scramble for all things new and 'modern'.[24] Modernist intellectuals were 'Almirall's heirs insofar as they attempted to justify Catalanism not in nostalgic or historicist terms..., but as a vehicle of progress and a way to see this progress as a regenerating factor for the Catalan collectivity' (Termes and Colomines 1992: 79).

---

[21] Verdaguer's main success was the great epic poem, *L'Atlantida* (1876), but the spirit of the epoch was more fully reflected in his other poem *Canigó* (1886). Oller's novel *La Papallona* (1882) was translated into French with a preface by Émile Zola.

[22] The movement received different names in different countries. *Art Nouveau, Liberty, Modern Style, Jugendstil, Sezessionstil* etc. Its origins lie in the English *Aesthetic Movement* of the 1870s, generally accepted as a prelude to the Parisian *Art Nouveau*. Catalan architects were already at the forefront of the movement in the 1880s, culminating in the 1900 Paris Expo. As an outstanding symbol of the movement, the café-cabaret *Els Quatre Gats*, a work of Puig i Cadafalch immortalised in a painting by Picasso became a centre for *tertulies* (informal and friendly talks) for artists and intellectuals at the turn of the century(Valenti 1973).

[23] Not to be confused with the present-day historical monthly *L'Avenç*, founded in 1977. On the role of L'Avenç, see Valentí (1973).

[24] As a paradox common to many nationalist movements, Modernism, which aimed at the creation of a national art, brought about a cosmopolitan art which was the polar opposite of its original aims (Castellanos 1986, Valentí 1973).

Through Modernism a new brand of intellectuals entered Catalanist politics. They had previously remained aloof because they did not share the conservative tone of the *Renaixença*. Modernism succeeded in incorporating into Catalanism such variegated groups as Esperantists, naturists, occultists, Theosophists, rural teachers, office clerks, theatregoers, members of charities and parish churches, small traders and shopkeepers (Castellanos 1986:30).[25] Of all the arts, it was in architecture that Modernism excelled.[26] The years between 1880 and 1906 were a period of great urban renewal. A *Modernista* desire for novelty, universality, and openness towards Europe were widespread too among other artists, in particular writers (Cacho Viu 1984: ix). Such xenophile tendencies were not always contradictory to political Catalanism, and were indeed an antidote to Spanishness.

In music, the Republican Antoni Clavé (1824-74) laid the foundations for the cherished traditions of the *Orfeons* choirs, or choral masses, devoted to the diffusion of both classical and Catalan traditional music among the working class.[27] Felip Pedrell (1841-1922) undertook the systematisation of musicological studies, propounding the reform of religious music and the creation of a national opera. The theatre and concert hall *Liceu*, founded in 1837,

---

[25] A measure of Modernism's popularity is given by its survival in a plethora of local domains well after its intellectual demise: small town opinion leaders and local writers assumed the messianic overtones of Modernism and 'thanks to it, they found a new place and a sense of life in the world' (Castellanos 1986: 32 ff.). On modernism's relationship with messianism and myths see McCarthy (1975).

[26] In 1878, Domènech i Montaner published 'In Search of a National Architecture' (*En busca d'una arquitectura nacional*), inaugurating a movement which later produced the great masterpieces of Antoni Gaudí (1852-1926), Josep Puig i Cadafalch (1867-1957) and others. In architecture, the group is also known as the *nova escola catalana* (new Catalan school) (Rohrer 1984). Although ideologically Gaudí was a Catholic integralist, i.e. an anti-Modernist, aesthetically he was the main representative of Modernist architecture (Mackay 1985).

[27] The effort was systematised by Lluís Millet (1867-1941): in 1891 Millet created the *Orfeó Català* mixed choirs, which would provide an ideal milieu for Catalanist assertion throughout the years (Vinyes 1990, Renart 1992). Joan Maragall composed *El cant de la senyera* (Song of the Catalan flag) as the Orfeo's hymn, with music by Lluís Millet. The choir's popularity has persisted till the present (Poblet 1973). In chapter 5 we mention the role of choral and other amateur societies in promoting Catalan resistance under Francoism.

became the paradigmatic cultural institution of the Catalan élites (McDonogh 1986: 188 ff.).[28] Vicens Vives described its creation in the following terms: 'The Catalan bourgeoisie of the industrial revolution needed an institution which could serve as a weapon to propagate its hegemony. Deprived of a court and without rooted social traditions, the bourgeoisie intuitively forged the organ which expressed its arrogance, focussing on the only root of spirituality still existing after the crisis of values of the turn of the century: the love for philharmonic art' (1958: 136).

Yet cultural life flourished at all levels of society, and cultural associations blossomed in every environment. Among the most important were the *ateneus* or academies. The original athenaeum was a 'scientific and literary association dedicated to elevate the intellectual level of its associates through discussions, conferences, courses and lectures' (Alegret 1977: 318).[29] The majority of their members were artisans and day labourers (*jornaleros*), although not all of them had this popular orientation. They were sustained mostly by members' fees, although some of them received substantial contributions from generous patrons and philanthropists. Some were educational, others were devoted to music, especially choirs, still others to tourist excursions (Solà 1978: 39-44). Between 1860 and 1910 the 'people's academies' (*ateneus populars*) aimed at diffusing literacy and modern knowledge among the workers (Pi-Sunyer 1971, Solà 1978: 39-ff.). At the beginning of the century, Anarchist and Marxist groups also organised their own centres under the 'cover' of cultural activities (Solà 1978: 39-44). This widespread *associacionisme* was often strictly linked to Catalanism (Llorens i Vila 1992). The tie between excursions and politics dates back to the nineteenth century. For instance, Jaume Massó Torrents (1863-1943) was at the same time a co-founder of *L'Avenç* in 1881 and a

---

[28] 'After using an expropriated convent for its first performances, the group made plans for a permanent building on the Ramblas. The building was begun in 1844 and finished in 1847. This triennium also witnessed such economic milestones as the foundation of the Bank of Barcelona (1844), the Barcelona Saving and Loan (1844), and the giant textile firm La España Industrial (1845) (McDonogh 1986: 189).

[29] They first appeared in France (*Athenée de Paris*, 1785, *Athenée des Arts*, 1792) and in England (*The Atheneum*, 1824) as part of the Enlightenment's programme to achieve universal dissemination of the fruits of reason and science. In 1820 the *Ateneo Científico y Literario* was founded in Madrid (Solà 1978: 40).

co-founder of the *Centre Excursionista de Catalunya* (Catalan Touring Club) in 1891, which aimed to encourage Catalan national consciousness.[30] Jacint Verdaguer's poetry was inspired by his solitary walks in the Pyrenean wilderness from 1875 to 1878.[31]

Catalan nationalism has been an underlying force beneath much of the contemporary avant-garde movement (Kaplan 1992). During the 1910s, the Cubist period of Pablo Picasso (1881-1973) was influenced by international anarchism as it blended with Catalan nationalism and the symbolist movement in Barcelona. But around this date Modernism was already being replaced by a new artistic and intellectual trend (see below, pages 33-6).

The crisis of 1898 and the rise of conservative nationalism

The loss of Cuba in 1899 symbolised the final demise of the empire and, hence of a powerful and respected Spain. The interests of Catalonia were particularly at stake, since 60 per cent of its exports went to the island. On this occasion the Catalans became the staunchest defenders of the empire.[32] However, 'for most people in Spain the key issues were neither social nor economic, but the patriotic and emotional appeal of sustaining the Spanish flag' (Payne 1973: 2: 510). Nearly a quarter of a million troops were sent to Cuba to face one of the first modern guerrilla campaigns. The Spanish army inflicted enormous suffering on the Cubans, who also had to confront the atrocities of both the guerrillas and the local *españolistas*. An uncompromising line prevailed in Madrid, together with tough support for unbridled repression. But the United States was soon dragged into the conflict, and Spain had to surrender, losing not only Cuba but also Puerto Rico, the Philippines and the lesser Pacific islands. The Spanish empire now consisted only of a few possessions in Africa.

[30] See his *Croquis Pirenencs* (Pyrenean Sketches), Barcelona: L'Avenç, 1896.

[31] This inspiration is manifested in Verdaguer's *Canigó* (from the name of a peak in the Pyrenees), dedicated to the Catalans of France. Recounting a medieval legend set in Roussillon, the novel recalled the historical links that spanned the frontier and called for a unified Catalonia

[32] The Lliga de Catalunya was especially worried about the prospects that autonomy would allow the opening-up of 'their' Cuban market to American products. When Spain surrendered Cuba, there was an explosion of protest in Catalonia.

This defeat represented one of the major traumas in modern Spanish history, the psychological impact of which indelibly marked its intelligentsia. The loss of empire provided the name for a whole generation of intellectuals, the 'Generation of '98', who joined in a wide intellectual and political current named *Regeneracionismo*, calling for the 'regeneration' of Spain. The Catalan response to this generalised Spanish malaise was couched in regionalist terms: Catalanism was part of the Regenerationist movement, but in Catalan eyes the Cuban defeat appeared as the foreseeable outcome of years of faulty centralism by a putrescent corrupt administration.

For a short while it seemed the Catalan aspirations could find a sympathetic echo among a few progressive Spanish politicians. In particular, General Camilo García de Polavieja (1838-1914) proposed the unification of the four Catalan provinces under a single administration, autonomy for the university, the compounding of taxation, municipal reorganisation and respect for the Catalan civil law. Hence many Catalanists joined the Polaviejista party. This led to a split in the Unió Catalanista: in opposition to the Polaviejistas, a group led by Enric Prat de la Riba founded the Centre Nacional Català in 1899. However in 1901 Prat's group allied again with the Polaviejistas, obtaining a sweeping triumph in the general elections. Immediately after this largely unexpected outcome, they declared their permanent union under the name Lliga Regionalista. This was the first fully-fledged Catalanist political party and was destined to dominate Catalanist politics up till the Republic of 1931. The moderate Lliga, hostile to political radicalism in any form, was dominated by industrialist leaders, notably the self-made millionaire Francesc Cambó (1876-1947). In the municipal elections, Cambó was elected and entered Barcelona city politics.

The Church was soon dragged into the movement for the rediscovery of the Catalan personality. After the disappearance of *L'Avenç* (1893) and the eclipse of Modernism, conservative Catalanism re-emerged, finding its foremost representative in Josep Torras i Bages (1846-1916), later Bishop of Vic, who published in 1892 one of the key texts of Catalanism, *La tradició catalana*. This work, inspired by the Catholic apologist and neo-Thomist Jaume Balmes (1810-1848), stressed the Christian origins of Catalonia in the Middle Ages, so that the Catalan 'spirit' and Catholicism were seen as inseparable. However, religion never played a central role in Catalan nationalism. The first stirrings of Catalanism had been expressed in the secular idiom of Almirall. Furthermore, Almirall's progressive attitude was at the root of the right-wing split which brought about the foundation of the Lliga de Catalunya, but despite its conservatism, the latter could not drop altogether its secular ideological baggage. Likewise its successor party, the Lliga Regionalista, 'had no specific religious character or platform, and did not need one' (Lannon 1987: 140); it never presented itself as a Catholic party, nor was the defence of religion an essential aspect of its programme. Although much of the electorate was conservative and religious, religion was considered an established fact that did not need to be stressed (Molas 1972: 1: 163). Catholicism remained in the background, more as the creed of individual Catalanist leaders. In sharp contrast with Basque nationalism, religion could not be used in Catalonia as an oppositional factor *vis-à-vis* Castile. Bages' work represented a belated attempt by the Church to 'Christianise' a movement which was born under the mark of secularism. Previously, the Church had been an ally of Carlism, but as soon as it was evident that ever larger numbers of Carlists were turning to Catalanism, it had to change its tactics. Immersion in a secular environment gave Catalan Catholicism a particular flavour. A characteristic of Catalonia became 'the active presence . . . of an enlightened and tolerant Catholicism. Its Catalanist orientation forced it to compromise itself in a public project of national revival, which is certainly Christian at its root, but without a confessional or exclusivist character' (Cacho Viu, cited by Massot 1986: 182). In chapter 7 it is explained why language, rather than religion, became the hallmark of Catalan nationalism.

Catalan solidarity, anti-Catalan populism and the failure of popular regionalism

The Lliga proved victorious once again in the 1905 municipal elections, and the victory banquet which it organised provided the occasion for a caricature published in the satirical Catalan magazine *Cu-cut!* The anti-militarist tradition of Catalan nationalism was only rivalled by that of the Anarchists. This innocuous illustration was sufficient to exacerbate the easily aroused sensibility of the Army. Hundreds of officers and cadets assaulted and seized both *Cu-cut!* and the Lliga's organ *La Veu de Catalunya*, and the authorities, rather than punishing the authors of the misdeed,

attacked the victims: the editor of the *Veu* was jailed and publication
of *Cu-cut!* suspended. In the wake of this row, the government
was beset by one crisis after another and three ministries fell in
a few days. In 1906 the Prime Minister Segismundo Moret (1838–
1913) introduced in the Cortes a 'Law of Jurisdiction', whereby
offences against the Army and national symbols (such as the flag,
the name or the anthem) were punishable by military tribunals.[33]
With the closing down of the newspapers infringing the law, the
legislative measure provoked an uproar throughout Catalan society.
Progressives and conservatives, Left and Right, immigrants and
natives, regionalists and former centralists united in protest. Nearly
all Catalan parties joined in a coalition named Solidaritat Catalana.[34]
More than 200,000 demonstrators assembled in Barcelona in May,
probably the greatest mass political event seen in the city up till
that time. At a similar meeting in October, protesters defiantly
stood in silence waving thousands of handkerchiefs.

At the 1907 elections Solidaritat's victory was sweeping: it
provided 41 out of the 44 deputies to be returned to the Cortes for
the constituency of Catalonia (in Barcelona it won all of them).
Catalan historiography represents Solidaritat Catalana as a nearly
mythical event. It is often depicted as the culminating moment when
all sectors of Catalan society were united as a single entity of soul
and action and the 'imagined community' became embodied in a
tangible reality. Joan Maragall described the movement as 'the living
affirmation of the existence of Catalonia as a self-conscious
collectivity'.[35] Solidaritat's success was ephemeral and could not
withstand the rapid changes of mood in the anarchic Barcelona of
the first decade of the century. When Solidaritat was defeated in
Barcelona's parliamentary by-elections of 1908, the Republicans
abandoned the coalition. This created a favourable environment for
the affirmation of their pro-centralist rivals, Lerroux's Radicals, who
won the March 1909 municipal elections. The demagogue
Alejandro Lerroux (1864-1949) is one of the most emblematic
figures of modern Catalan history. His blend of anti-clerical

---

[33] This law, which was aimed principally at Catalonia, was upheld until the Second
Republic.

[34] Only the Radical Republicans, headed by Alejandro Lerroux, did not participate in the platform.

[35] In his *Obres Completes* (Maragall 1929-55), also cited by Peers (1937: 150).

Republicanism and 'proletarian' anti-Catalanism, coloured by populist vehemence, quickly won him the support of a large part of the Catalan proletariat (Alvarez Junco 1990, Cullà 1987). Lerroux's rhetoric struck a sensitive chord among immigrants, who found it difficult to identify with the host society at a time when an intolerant bourgeoise scorned any concessions to the working class. The movement, known in Catalan historiography as *Lerrouxisme*, sounded an alarm bell for Catalan élites, making them realise that the bourgeois character of much in Catalanism had produced a fracture within society and made Catalanism incapable of integrating the newcomers. The experience was instrumental in bringing about the subsequent formation of a Catalan Republican left. This, in turn, created increasing political fragmentation. However, more than before, cultural nationalism functioned as a unitary reference for all Catalanists, beyond party allegiance.

Since Catalonia was the first region of Spain to be extensively industrialised, it was also the first to experience the explosion of social conflicts and the advent of working-class politics. As military conscription extended its grip in response to a Moorish revolt in Morocco, the Anarchists and Syndicalists declared a general strike in 1909.[36] Martial law was imposed, but a revolt of huge proportion suddenly broke out, with bombs, widespread murders, barricades, blowing up of bridges, desecration of tombs, random killing of clergy, and the burning of churches and monasteries.[37] This event became historically known as the *Setmana Tràgica* (Tragic Week): five days of shootings, looting and savage destruction which left an indelible mark in the consciousness of many Catalans. It also acted as a perpetual warning of the dangerous threat posed to social stability by radical extremism. Once the Army, the Civil Guard and the police reestablished control over the city, the head of the Spanish Conservative government, Antonio Maura (1853-1925), could not avoid addressing the Catalan question. He drew up a plan which

---

[36] In a country still deeply traumatised by the Cuban debacle, anti-militarism was widespread among all social classes. Hundreds of impaired and disabled war veterans still begging in the streets of Barcelona bore visible witness to past horrors and inspired average people with a visceral hatred for all wars (Josep Benet, personal suggestion).

[37] These attacks on religious centres, peoples and symbols were part of a pattern which was often repeated until the end of the Civil War (Estivill and Barbat 1980, Alvarez Junco 1990).

included the creation of *mancomunidades*, administrative bodies
closer to the historical· reality of each region to be given powers
superior those of the provinces they encompassed.[38] Maura's plan
provided the first practical opportunity to bring about a minimal
degree of self-government after so many years of failed aspirations.
Such an opportunity had to be used to the full, since it was not likely
to be repeated.

Catalanism's maturity, Prat and the Mancomunitat (1914-1917)

A final transposition from regionalism into a fully-fledged
nationalism was the work of Enric Prat de la Riba (1870-1917).
Already in his 'Catechism' of 1894, we find a clear separation
between the two concepts of state and nation: Catalonia is the
fatherland of the Catalans, while Spain is merely a state (Prat
1894). Prat formulated this vision in much deeper terms in a
seminal collection of lectures and articles published in 1906 as
La nacionalitat catalana (Prat 1978). This remains the key text for
the study of Catalan nationalism up to the present day. However,
the moderate strand remained: while Almirall talked about federation rather than independence, Prat likewise avoided any reference
to separatism. Yet he adopted a more radical stance *vis-à-vis* Madrid,
while defending conservative interests at the social level. We discuss
in chapter 7 the details of his organicist political vision.[39] In 1907
he was elected President of Barcelona's *Diputació* (provincial government). Prat's years were marked by intense activity in all realms
of culture, politics and society. In 1906 the Estudis Universitaris
Catalans was founded in order to provide university-level classes
in Catalan history, law, language and literature. The greatest leap
forward was achieved with the creation of the Institut d'Estudis
Catalans (IEC) by the Diputació of Barcelona in 1907. The

[38] It was the first time that a prominent Spanish statesman seemed to meet Catalan
aspirations, although most Catalanists considered his proposals too weak. This
precipitated a split within the Solidaritat alliance between Cambó's Lliga supporting
the plan and the Left opposing it.

[39] Organicism was not just confined to Catalanism. The entire 'Regenerationist'
movement conceived Spain as an organic whole, as a human 'body' gifted with its
own personality and spirit. Jaume Brossa (1875-1919) and Joan Cortada applied
this principle to Catalonia, asserting that Spain hampered a full development of the
Catalan character (cited in Castellanos 1986: 25).

Institute's task was the thorough investigation of all the elements of Catalan culture, and for this purpose it was divided into three main sections: science, philology and archaeology (with history). In its philological section, the linguist Pompeu Fabra (1868-1948) elaborated a wide programme of linguistic reforms culminating in the creation of a unified standard language: the 'Orthographic Norms' (*Normes Ortogràfiques*) were published in 1913, followed by a 'Catalan Grammar' in 1918 and by a 'General Dictionary of the Catalan Language' in 1932, all of them the work of Pompeu Fabra. This work contributed to turning Catalan into the vivid expression of an increasingly rich and articulate modern culture. The lively and affluent character of Catalan civil society allowed for the spread of a Catalan high culture through a plethora of intermediate bodies. The National Library (Biblioteca Nacional de Catalunya), with its network of smaller public libraries, has been a centre of Catalan culture ever since the mid-1910s.[40]

In 1911, the idea of uniting the four provinces of Catalonia under a single administrative umbrella began to take shape, and accordingly Prat presented his proposal to José Canalejas (1854-1912), then Prime Minister of Spain. He agreed to it along with the leaders of most of the other parties, but just before the Bill could be ratified, Canalejas was assassinated in Madrid by an anarchist. The project was placed on file for nearly two years but then a massive demonstration in the streets of Barcelona succeeded in focussing the government's attention.[41] Under pressure from the Catalan MPs, it passed a decree carrying into law the first article of the proposed Bill. It was the most crucial one, empowering the *diputacions* to group together in *mancomunidades* for administrative purposes. The Mancomunitat de Catalunya was officially set up in 1914, in the same building as Barcelona's provincial government. It worked as the administrative liaison and coordinating body of the four *diputacions* of Barcelona, Tarragona, Lleida and Girona (Camps i Arboix 1963). The Mancomunitat soon became intensely active in all fields, since Prat had already paved its way by the time he was elected President of the Diputació in 1907. Many institutions were created or ex-

[40] Even today the seat of the IEC lies in the same building as the Biblioteca, a magnificent fifteenth-century palace whose interior is decorated with Catalan majolicas and ancient furniture.

[41] The demonstration was attended by representatives from 990 municipal councils (out of 1,072 in all Catalonia).

panded under the aegis of the Mancomunitat. Its infrastructure was used effectively 'to improve education, roads and local services and to foster regional culture, giving Catalonia by far the most intense cultural life of any region in Spain' (Payne 1973: 2: 606).[42] Particularly innovative were the changes in education. The Association for the Protection of Catalan Teaching was charged with the supervision of private schools where Catalan was the medium of instruction and was entrusted with the publication of the relevant text books. Prat, this 'eminently creative genius, who lived apart from the noisier exponents of his creed', with 'his serene and imperturbable optimism' (Peers 1937: 164), died suddenly in 1917 at the height of his activities. His successor at the head of the Mancomunitat was the architect and art historian Josep Puig i Cadafalch.

The international upheavals of 1917 and the post-war settlement had their impact on Catalan politics. In 1917 there was a sharp increase in terrorist attacks, strikes, boycotts, lock-outs and various forms of violence. The regime's persistent centralism spurred the nationalists to radicalise their ideology. As soon as it was clear that the monarchy would never accept any change in the *status quo* governing its relations with the periphery, Catalanism turned more and more towards republicanism. At the same time, it became more radical and nationalist in its manifestations: incidents such as assaults on the Spanish flag became commonplace and Catalan began to be used illegally in the University. As a response to Madrid's intransigence, Francesc Macià (1859-1933) founded in 1922 Estat Català, a party advocating straightforward separatism. Macià a former colonel in the Spanish army, lived through a personal evolution from federalist principles to 'independentism' (Jardí 1977). He left the army in 1906 to join Solidaritat Catalana. He was a man of action, not a thinker, and wrote no major book on Catalanism. As we shall see, he became in his later years a living symbol of Catalanist struggle.

In the same year 1922, the less conservative elements of the Lliga abandoned the party and formed Acció Catalana, which attracted the support of the Left.[43] The party won the elections of 1923. One

---

[42] Among other achievements, we can quote the Social Museum, the School of Dramatic Arts, the School of Fine Arts, the Agricultural School, the Industrial University, the Work School, the School of Local Administration, the Professional Orientation School, numerous technical schools, archeological excavations, restoration of ancient buildings and programmes of urban renewal.

of its most ambitious achievements was the creation of a Triple Alliance (1923) with the two other historical nationalities of Spain: the Basques and the Galicians. All these developments were brought to an end by the dictatorship, but before describing its impact and evolution, we analyse the development of a national culture under the Mancomunitat and its link with political action.

Culture and politics: the Noucentista experience

Most artists and intellectuals found in the Mancomunitat an ideal source of support, which was translated in the emergence of the *Noucentista* movement. *Noucentisme* ('Nine-hundred-ism', referring to the new century) was 'an ideological movement which . . . typified the hegemonic aspirations of the most active sectors of the Catalan bourgeoisie . . . Through the creation of its own iconography and a complex corpus of linguistic signs, it formulated . . . patterns of social behaviour which could facilitate reformist action' (Murgades 1986: 105).[44] The entire ideological debate was addressed to a reform of Catalan society, an objective effectively achieved under the Mancomunitat. *Noucentista* intellectuals made extensive use of the administration's powers, aiming to transform society through an efficient apparatus of self-government. They started to operate in 1906, when the Lliga entered the government of Barcelona's province.[45]

More than ever before, the project of cultural Catalanism was the common unifying platform for a galaxy of interests, ideologies, parties, voluntary associations, art schools and professionals. The heart of the project was in fact centred around language and its orthographic unification. The creation of the Institut d'Estudis Catalans (IEC) in 1907 was a turning-point, since many outstanding

[43] Its leaders were the Republican journalist and historian Antoni Rovira i Virgili (1882-1949), the *Noucentista* poet Jaume Bofill i Mates (1878-1933) and the medievalist Lluís Nicolau d'Olwer (1888-1961).

[44] In Catalan, '*nou*' stands for 'new', giving a further flavour of novelty to the movement.

[45] The fact that the Mancomunitat also attracted Modernist exponents, although they rejected Prat's conservatism, is a clear sign of the increased perception of the centrality of politics in the realm of culture. Moderate Republicans, such as the engineer and economist Carles Pi-Sunyer (1888-1971), were drawn into the development projects of the Mancomunitat.

intellectuals were co-opted into the running of the Institute. This was also the Catalan bourgeoisie's answer to the sclerotic state university: the Institute's sections were devised to reflect university faculties. The subsequent step was the creation of the National Library in 1914 to stimulate scientific research, together with a network of public popular libraries (*biblioteques populars*). The 'national' library was to be the centre of cultural production, while the smaller town and *barri* libraries were to be centres for cultural dissemination (Murgades 1986). All these activities stemmed from the desire of the regional bourgeoisie to produce its own cadres and expertise. Professional qualification was an indispensable need for a class aiming at reform and political rule. This ambition required both technical expertise and ideological orientation, the latter an antidote against extempore political radicalism, whether in the shape of national separatism or of working-class agitation. With the Mancomunitat, political power transformed the *Noucentista* ideology into an operational praxis. In its turn, this ideology contributed to the legitimacy of the process of social reforms engendered by the regionalists.

There are some parallels between *Modernisme* and *Noucentisme*: both encapsulated a drive for social reform, both were Catalanist, admired Europe and disliked traditionalism, which should obviously be distinguished from conservatism. But, whereas the Modernist intellectuals moved in a power vacuum and thus relied on militant action, the *Noucentistes* acted within the institutions. This distinction is also reflected in two conceptions of language reform, in which the Modernists tried to engage at the level of informal discussions, in particular from the editorial columns of *L'Avenç*. Reacting against the purist pundits of the *Renaixença* and their archaising proposals, they pursued a language suitable to all cultural and scientific purposes, not just for the glory of *belles lletres* (Castellanos 1986, Murgades 1986). Pompeu Fabra himself, originally a chemist, participated in the Modernists' debates. However, their impact was limited and their decisions were unlikely to be respected, since they lacked the authority to agree on them and the means to spread them. What they needed was some kind of central authority. In the anarchic ambience of Modernism, no single authority was acknowledged.[46]

---

46 The Modernist longing for novelty welcomed everybody who had something

The scenario changed radically with *Noucentisme*. Fabra was called upon by Prat to work in the IEC, an invitation he enthusiastically accepted knowing that through the power which Prat represented it was possible to establish a first base of consensus for the stand-ardisation of Catalan. Indeed, one year after the *Normes* were published under the auspices of the IEC, the Mancomunitat took upon itself their diffusion through its large school and publishing network. Only then did the petty disagreements over 'correct' orthographic forms cease to vitiate the scientific debate. While the Modernists' linguistic disquisitions were bedeviled by ideological radicalism, the *Noucentistes* found a balance between opposing trends under the umbrella of political power. In the name of political realism it was necessary to reach a consensus. Thus everyone was compelled to give up some cherished options.

Among other things, *Noucentisme* glorified city life. The urban space was the locus of rational planning and social reform where people could operate and shape its environment. Under the Man-comunitat the main network of roads was established to link the city with the countryside, together with other infrastructures. The emphasis was always unidirectional: it was the city which lavished all these benefits on the countryside, and the epitome of the city was Barcelona, traditionally identified as the *cap i casal* (head and home) of Catalonia.[47] The triumph of bourgeois ideals conveyed a message of repression of instincts and affections. Passion and *rauxa* (im-petuosity) were to be eliminated in favour of reason and contain-ment. Everything was subordinated to obtaining subsequent gains. This attitude is the opposite to Modernism. In literature the trend was reflected in an effort to eradicate all kinds of irrational effusions and exaggerated sensuousness (Izard 1986, Castellanos 1986). Neo-classicism came again to the fore as a weapon against Romanticism.

---

new to say. Different trends and attitudes coexisted, and there was a constant curiosity for everything new. On the contrary, *Noucentisme* selected only those trends which were consistent with the Catalan bourgeoisie's interest for reform.

[47] The concept of *Catalunya-ciutat* (Catalonia city) was later coined by Gabriel Alomar to express the unity between the intellectuals of the *comarques* and Barcelona. Urban-oriented ideologies still today permeate the attitude of some Catalan intelligentsia. In such a vision the countryside is merely seen as an appendix of the capital city. On the other side, the concept acknowledges the radical historical importance of urban centres for any programme aimed at promoting social and administrative reform.

This reflected a rational faith in culture as a tool for influencing social development. 'Culture was no longer seen as a gratuitous activity – art for art's sake – or as a fruit of desperation – rebellious art. Culture had to become an efficient collaborator of social reform engineered from above' (Murgades 1986: 109).[48]

However, in the end this positivist zeal marked the failure of bourgeois nationalism, and fomented a split between the upper classes, imbued as they were with such a puritan ideology, and the rest of society. Yet nobody can deny its lasting effects in the establishment of a Catalan high culture. But the latter risked remaining a ghetto phenomenon if it failed to become the patrimony of the wider community. Immigration from other regions only increased this risk. The first social chasm was brought to light by the Lerrouxist revolt. Lacking any means of coercion the Catalan bourgeoise proved incapable of tackling increasing social chaos. The lack of a state was at the root of this failure. The regional élites needed a stable power structure to sustain their reform plan. *Noucentisme* ended symbolically in 1925 when Primo de Rivera abolished the Mancomunitat. Hitherto we have seen the thriving vitality of a stateless culture; in the next section we see the state's attempt to crush that culture, and the overall lack of success of that attempt.

The dictatorship of Primo de Rivera (1923-1930)

General Miguel Primo de Rivera (1870-1930) declared the dictatorship on 13 September 1923. At the beginning, most Catalanists hoped that it would bring back some stability in a region plagued by social conflicts, but within only a few days a royal decree banished the Catalan flag and language and had all offences against the unity of the country placed under the jurisdiction of military courts. Catalanist organisations were dissolved, meetings were prohibited or monitored by Madrid's agents, and political leaders were arrested on trivial pretexts. A royal decree also imposed the national syllabus on all Spanish schools, with a ban on teaching any subject not included in it. When Primo de Rivera realised that Catalanist leaders could never accept his policies, he first

---

[48] This confirms that nationalism is a movement aimed at controlling social change, rather than bringing it about (i.e. being favourable to, or against it). Its aim is to control particularly one type of social change, the one which questions the very basis of one's own ethnic identity.

deposed the President of the Mancomunitat and then suppressed it altogether in 1925.

Despite all these prohibitions, Catalan culture persisted in a semi-clandestine environment (Roig Rosich 1992). The Bernat Metge Foundation (founded in 1923) for the study of Greek and Latin classics encouraged scientific research and the translation of the ancient classics, under the sponsorship of Cambó. It also opened a translation school, organising lectures both in Spain and abroad. The Catalan Biblical Foundation (f. 1922) was devoted to editing and publishing biblical texts, again with the sponsorship of Cambó.[49] The Church's Catalanist attitude was reinforced under the dictatorship, whose attempts to suppress the use of Catalan in the liturgy it resented. From his exile in Paris, Francesc Macià organised a military expedition to 'liberate' Catalonia; however, before it could even set foot in Spain, his quixotic army was rounded up in Prats-de-Molló near the border. This semi-glorious defeat, without a single person killed or wounded, created a mythical aura around the figure of Macià and his heroic dedication to the Catalan cause. More than sixty years old, he became the admired Great Old Man, the grandfather (*l'Avi*) of Catalonia (Jardí 1977).

Lacking popular support and increasingly out of touch with the population, the dictatorship slowly burnt itself out, until it came to a sudden end in January 1930. Its late phase demonstrated in embryonic form what would be the result of anti-Catalan policies under Franco. At first, the ban on the Catalan language only disturbed a few intellectuals and politicians when their lectures and speeches were interrupted by police and government agents. However, more wide-ranging actions such as the removal of street name-plates and the ban on displaying or using Catalan sign-boards in shops, and the use of Catalan in public masses and for teaching the catechism, aroused resentment among wide sectors of the population. At the same time, wherever its use was not restricted, the language was used with increasing frequency (Roig Rosich 1992). Thus with the return of democracy, the language was already experiencing a comeback and the new freedom found a fertile ground for its further diffusion. With the dictatorship's demise,

[49] From 1928 to 1948, it published the Catalan version of the Bible in fifteen volumes, directly translated from the original Hebrew and Greek. A new version in a single volume was produced in 1978.

hundreds of *ateneus* blossomed throughout Catalonia, especially in
Barcelona. Many of them were dedicated to the diffusion of educational ideas, but others were devoted to naturism, vegetarianism,
Esperanto, sport, hiking and other forms of recreation, antiqu-
arianism, politics, trade unionism, religion, theatre, cinema, science,
poetry and history.[50]

The Second Republic (1931-1939)

As soon as the injunctions against the use of Catalan were lifted,
a new dynamism was released. The intelligentsias of Madrid and
Barcelona experienced a rare moment of reciprocal entente. The
President of the Spanish Academy, Ramón Menéndez Pidal (1869-
1968), visited Barcelona and commended the benefits of bilingualism. In turn, Catalan intellectuals were grateful to their Madrid
fellows for having raised their voices against their persecution
under the dictatorship. The use of the Catalan flag, anthem and
emblems was restored. At a convention held in San Sebastián
(Euskadi) in 1930 different Republican parties signed the Pact of
San Sebastián a pact to bring down the monarchy. The pact
resulted in the creation of a 'Republican Revolutionary
Committee', which in 1931 was to become the provisional government of the Republic. Three Catalan parties sent their delegates:
Estat Català, Acció Catalana and the newly-formed Acció Catalana
Republicana. They subscribed to full-blown cooperation with their
counterparts from other regions in exchange for recognition of
Catalan distinctiveness. Their final agreement incorporated the
principle of self-determination for Catalonia.

A major outcome was the foundation in March 1931 of Esquerra
Republicana de Catalunya (ERC – Catalan Republican Left), a
coalition of several minor groups centred around the charismatic
figure of Francesc Macià and including the signatories of the pact of
San Sebastián. The coalition swept to victory at the municipal polls

---

50 They were a sign of the times: in those days, before the advent of mass-media,
to hold *tertulies* (conversations, informal and friendly talks) with friends, to 'go to
the café' and discuss social events, was a daily habit and an imperative social need
(Corredor, cited by Solà 1978: 43). Social networks were much more close-knit,
and through them the diffusion of ideas was part of every individual's social life.
The contrast with today's inward-looking individualism is, indeed, stark and
dramatic.

of April 1931, less than a month after its creation. The Lliga, which had collaborated with the dictatorship, was utterly defeated. Cambó's staunch anti-Republicanism was the other main cause of the final demise of his party.

The Statute of Autonomy (*Estatut*) was approved in a plebiscite by 600,000 out of 800,000 voters in that same year (1931). In the ensuing elections for the new Catalan Parliament, the ERC won votes from both the middle and working classes. The Generalitat (the autonomous Catalan government) was re-established in 1932 and Macià was elected as its President and remained so till his death the following year, when he was succeeded by Lluís Companys (1882-1940). Many reforms were inaugurated during the Republic. In several areas Catalonia became a theatre for the most radical innovation. The Catalan school system was transformed into one of the most progressive in Europe.[51] During the first two years (*Bienni Reformista*), the Republican-Socialist government embarked on a policy of moderate reforms. But its 'slow' pace aroused discontent among the impatient under classes. Badly worked lands were handed over to day-labourers, but the speed of reform did not satisfy the peasants and only irritated the landowners. In the cities, labour unrest was aggravated by the economic crisis. The situation prompted the central government to dissolve the Cortes and call for new elections. The Right, grouped under a united cartel, the CEDA (Confederación Española de Derechas Autónomas, Spanish Confederation of Autonomous Rights), achieved a broad victory against the divided parties of the Left, while the Anarcho-syndicalists campaigned for abstention.

The victory of the Right was less sweeping in Catalonia than in the rest of Spain. In the ensuing *Bienni Negre* (black biennium, November 1933–February 1936), the Left continued to rule in the Generalitat and in most Catalan municipalities. But an increasingly

---

[51] Candel (1972: 91-8 and 273-81) recalls his own experience as a child of Southern immigrants: 'It was a European education. Sunny, ventilated classrooms, courtyards with plants and flowers, boys and girls together, no parrotlike memorization. We learned while we played. We sang, we studied, we danced. The students weren't lined up in rows. Instead of desks, we had large tables, as at a get-together, with vases of flowers. The school had all the most modern facilities: a library, first aid station, showers, an anatomy model, a skeleton, an air pump, a microscope, maps, large illustrative sheets . . . In the summer, they took us away for a month to camps' (Candel, cited in Rosenthal 1991: 119, as note 14 of ch. 1).

right-wing Madrid government paralysed most reforms. A bill in favour of small tenant farmers (*rabassaires*) was approved by the Catalan parliament in April 1934, but through their powerful lobbies the landowners stirred up anti-Catalan sentiments in Madrid against a Catalonia dominated by the Left, and Madrid established that the autonomous government had no authority in social agrarian matters, an allegation that minimised Catalan autonomy *de facto*. This and other actions carried out by Madrid provided the main rationale for the revolt of the Generalitat, when Lluís Companys proclaimed the 'Catalan Republic'. The Republic lasted only a few hours and ended in disaster, with the arrest of the 'coup' leaders and of more than 3,400 Catalan politicians. Censorship and a state of emergency ensued for months, and the *Estatut* was suspended. Since Companys was also jailed, the Generalitat was stripped of all authority.

In the February 1936 elections, the Left presented itself in a united Popular Front (Cat. *Front Popular*), resulting in a historical victory. Released from prison, Companys and the other Catalan leaders were returned to the Generalitat. However, the Anarchists soon came to dominate the scene. Under the Popular Front government (February–July 1936) a new set of revolutionary reforms was carried out in a highly radicalised atmosphere. The government of the Generalitat contained Anarchists, Syndicalists and Marxists, but it proved incapable of stemming the tide of popular revolt and the pressure for further revolutionary change.

Many reasons have been given to explain why Anarchism took root with such extraordinary power in Catalonia. Certainly, the Restoration governments (1874–1931) had hindered any normal development of working-class organisations. However, for a student of nationalism, aware of the latter's overarching pervasiveness, the most convincing hypothesis relates to the region's history. Anarchism found an ideal arena for expansion in Catalonia insofar as it advocated 'a drastic decentralization of Spain . . . It is presumably to this fact that Joan Maragall referred when he said "Within every Catalonian there is an Anarchist". . . The Anarchist finds no more support in Catalonia than elsewhere, but having once obtained a foothold he is able, by exploiting the Catalan character or by other means, to strengthen it. . . . Anarchism . . . was greatly helped by the cantonal risings, the vogue of federalist ideas, and the unrest which followed the deposition of Isabel II' (Peers 1937: 156–7). Its nerve-centre moved slowly from southern Spain (particularly Andalusia) to Barcelona, in part following waves of immigration. However, there is another explanation of the widespread political radicalism in Barcelona. A frustrated bourgeoisie, incapable of asserting its control over the state's means of coercion and labour regulation, developed an intransigent attitude towards workers' organisations. The bourgeoisie could always blame social unrest on Madrid's anti-Catalan policies. At the same time, we find in Madrid a state dominated by economic élites whose interests conflicted with those of the Catalan industrialists; the former were uninterested in settling labour disputes in Barcelona up till the moment when matters got seriously out of hand, threatening the very integrity of the state. Only at these moments did the central élites intervene, with much brutality, against both workers' and regionalist associations. Repression was obviously even harsher against those sectors espousing both regionalism and socialism. For them was coined the word *rojoseparatistas,* which became popular under Francoism. The ultimate target was the regionalist movement, and with this aim Madrid élites skillfully exploited labour unrest to stamp their control on Catalonia, letting class disputes rage until the moment when repression was strongly requested by regional élites. In this way, Madrid condemned Catalan industrialists to depend on state intervention rather than give them any direct power. Thus, a lack of state intervention was counter balanced by ruthless state repression. The state became a vicious machine increasingly delegitimised in the periphery, and in the end it could rely only on brute force to impose its will.

On 18 July 1936 the Spanish garrison in Morocco, under the command of General Francisco Franco (1892-1975), revolted against the dual threat of 'socialism' and 'separatism'. The Civil War had begun. The militant workers decreed a general strike, preparing for an armed insurrection. In Catalonia, the initiative passed to the leadership of the Anarchist mainstream CNT-FAI (Confederación Nacional del Trabajo–Federación Anarquica Iberica). The CNT entered the Generalitat, which acted more and more as the government of an autonomous state, and which in October launched a massive campaign of collectivisation. In November Hitler and Mussolini recognised Franco's government. The Civil War brought about extensive destruction, hundreds of thousands were killed or wounded, and there was unprecedented displacement of population. In January 1939, after the 'conquest' of Barcelona, the Generalitat was dissolved and the Catalanist leaders were either executed or escaped into exile. The end of the Civil War in April 1939 ushered in the Francoist era.

We have seen how Catalan nationalism emerged initially as a moderate regionalist movement imbued with progressive Republican ideas at a time of relative economic prosperity. Its first inspiration, the cultural revival known as the *Renaixença*, coincided with the interests of an emerging industrial bourgeoisie, who tried to use political regionalism as a lever in its difficult dialogue with Madrid, especially for its protectionist campaign. Yet cultural Catalanism from its inception was also a popular phenomenon. At the turn of the century, the political movement was dominated by the upper bourgeoisie, but it slowly came to represent middle-class interests, and finally filtered down to the proletarian classes.[52]

The bulk of nationalist thought was conceived between the publication of Almirall's *Lo Catalanisme* (1886) and Prat de la Riba's *La nacionalitat catalana* (1906) (Llobera 1983: 343). Since then there has remained a stable body of doctrine which was kept broadly and unchanged up till recent decades. Catalonia was conceived as a nation by virtue of its linguistic distinctiveness, and hence the relationship between language and nation was always central to all nationalist discourse. When the Catalan language was attacked by the dictatorship, its political importance increased. Thus, cultural nationalism provided the shared horizon for a movement which was politically fragmented. Political pluralism persisted, and even in-

---

[52] Refuting the classic interpretation of Catalanism as evolving from regionalism to nationalism, Termes (1986) identifies an opposite direction, with four distinct phases. At first, there was the doctrinaire nationalism of 'organic intellectuals' such as the Federalist physician and writer Josep Narcís Roca i Farreras (1830-91) and the cultural revivalist Sebastià Farnés (1854-1934) (1986: 17). The latter clearly formulated Catalan identity on the basis of linguistic distinctiveness (Bilbeny 1988: 64). In the aftermath of the 1898 defeat, a bourgeois regionalism emerged. From the end of the First World War till the Second Republic, a new popular nationalism developed in working-class milieux. Finally, after 1931, left-wing nationalism moved towards demands for self-determination. This right was invoked by all Marxist parties without exception, from the Troskyists to the Stalinists, from the 'Bolsheviks' to the 'social-democrats'. All of them favoured the creation of a Catalan state (Termes 1986: 18).

creased, under the hegemony of the Lliga (Brunn 1992). Indeed, the Lliga could exert only limited influence over a host of small and short-lived Republican parties (Casassas 1989). They finally united under Macià's populist leadership (Sallés 1987). However, the splits were purely political, and concerned attempts to dissociate themselves from the bourgeois character of the Lliga and to approach the working class. Hence, the fragmentation was purely political and did not reflect opposite visions of Catalan identity. It did not reflect debates, ambiguity or confusion over Catalan identity, nor did it result from tensions between radical separatists and moderate regionalists, although groups such as Estat Català were born on a separatist platform. The aim was to fill the gap between the upper and lower classes and between natives and immigrants.

3

BASQUE NATIONALISM FROM ITS
BEGINNINGS TO THE CIVIL WAR

The Basques have long been identified as a separate people by foreign travellers, classical writers and local scholars. Prehistoric evidences of what were probably the ancestors of today's Basques are plentiful in several caves and archeological sites found in the region (Collins 1986: 16-30). Roman historians and Greek geographers, such as Strabo, recorded their existence as early as 7CE, with the name of 'Vasconians'.[1] The Romans never succeeded in subduing them or absorbing their culture, nor did the Visigoths, the Muslims, the Franks or the Normans.

Basque-speakers, who called themselves *Euskaldunak*, had long used the term *Euskal Herria* to define their area. Navarre was the last region of the Iberian peninsula to come under direct control from Castile, and did so only when the Duke of Alba conquered Pamplona and Ferdinand of Aragón established the 'union' of the two kingdoms under his crown (1512).[2] The first book written in Basque of which we have knowledge appeared in 1545 by the hand of the poet Bernard Dechepare (Villasante 1979: 49 ff., Sarasola 1982: 35-9).[3] A sense of separate cultural – and political – identity had existed in the area for many centuries. The Jesuit Father Manuel de Larramendi (1690-1766), often quoted as a pioneer of Basque 'irredentism', conceived the Basque provinces as a unit which Castile and France had no right to rule (Ortzi 1975: 57-8). The French Basque chronicler and local historian Augustin Chaho

[1] *Vascones* for later Latin authors (Collins 1986: 31-7).

[2] However, Navarre's constitutional liberties were not suppressed till the end of the First Carlist War (1841).

[3] A New Testament in Basque was published shortly afterwards (1571), followed by other books and translations aimed at converting the Basques to Protestantism (Sarasola 1982: 40-2).

(1811-58) saw all Basque history as a history of national defence against outside encroachment.[4] From his pen comes the first mention of Euskal Herria as an oppressed 'nationality'. Chaho was also among the earliest scholars to interpret the First Carlist War as a national struggle for the freedom of the four provinces (Corcuera 1979: 54, Juaristi 1987: 76-106). Such interpretation became a common refrain in a tradition of local historiography which saw Carlism primarily as a catchword for proto-nationalism. It was also part of a popular primordialist interpretation which sees nationalism as a pre-modern force springing up from the soil and soul of the people. Thus nationalism followed as a natural conclusion from the 'foralist' (see page 45) and Carlist reading of history, readily evoking a widespread resonance (Corcuera 1979: 211).

The structural pre-conditions

To highlight the difference between the Basque and the Catalan cases, one must consider the circumstances in which modernisation occurred. Unlike other Spanish regions – Catalan autonomy was abolished in 1716 – the Basque provinces had long kept their local laws and customary privileges intact. They were among the last regions of Spain to maintain their *fueros* (local statutes and charters), under which each province kept a long (through rarely unchallenged) separate record of administration. Although some of them date back to the seventh century, most of the *fueros* were codified in the seventeenth and eighteenth centuries as agreements between the Spanish crown and Basque regional powers. Jealously guarded, they exempted the local population from both military service and taxation, while allowing the provincial assemblies the right to veto royal edicts, although this rarely occurred. According to the centralists, the *fueros* were a special concession offered by the Spanish crown, which always had the power to rescind them. Although the *fueros* were slowly eroded, before their abolition the *señorio* ('seigniory') of Vizcaya was working as a state within the Spanish state, and was even expanding its powers (Agirreazkuenaga 1987).[5] The foral institutions survived several attempts

---

[4] Among other things, Chaho formulated the myth of Aitor, legendary father of the Basques, although it was first conceived by Navarro Villoslada, a *riojano* (from the region of La Rioja) (Juaristi 1987).

[5] The seigniory (or lordship) was a form of government in which the ruler was a

at centralisation. However, the ideology which sustained their preservation was not nationalism, but foralism. Here we shall use the term 'foralism' (Sp. *fuerismo*) to indicate the ideological and political justification for the *fueros*.[6] Local historians played a key role in defending Basque institutions, since their studies of the antiquity, nobility, utility and democratic character of traditional Basque rights served to legitimise (or counter-legitimise) their continued existence. In the plethora of foralist claims and centralist counter-claims, historical research was crucial since each side had to obtain new pieces of evidence from past history.[7]

The persistence of the *fueros* and the centralist attempts to abolish them explains why the Carlists, who theoretically were a Spanish-wide movement, had their stronghold in the Basque regions. At their height, the Carlist wars were almost exclusively fought on Basque territory. Here a high level of mass mobilisation was drawn into the defence of the *ancien régime*, whereas in the rest of the peninsula Carlism was embraced by more limited sectors of the population, linked to the small nobility (Corcuera 1979: 31). Giner (1984) has observed that Carlism was dominant in the rural hinter-lands of those regions that actually spearheaded the process of modernisation and industrialisation. Overall abolition of the *fueros* in Vizcaya would not have penalised the Carlists so much as the Liberals, who formed the richest stratum in the country (Corcuera 1979: 84). The *fueros* were finally abolished in 1876, after two long and violent civil wars.

While their abolition was reluctantly accepted in Alava and Guipúzcoa, resistance was much more tenacious in Vizcaya. Here, led by the liberal foralist Fidel de Sagarmínaga y Epalza (d. 1894), an intransigent line prevailed of refusal to collaborate in levying Spanish taxes.[8] But the Diputación, the representative assembly of

---

señor or lord. On economic growth and social change in Euskadi between 1100 and 1850, see also Fernández de Pinedo (1974). On trade and the mercantile bourgeoisie in eighteenth-century Bilbao, see Basurto Larrañaga (1983).

6 There is a parallel for this defence of local rights and privileges in Justus Moser's arguments in mid-eighteenth-century Germany (Barnard 1985, Knudsen 1986).

7 Probably the most salient product of this historicist tradition was E.J. de Labayru's *Historia General del Señorío de Vizcaya*, the first volume of which appeared in 1895. The foralist tradition received a new lease of life in the aftermath of the definitive Carlist defeat and, also as a reaction to this, most literature appeared after 1878.

8 As a liberal anti-Jacobin, Sagarmínaga conceived the state 'not as a national unity,

the province, was soon suffocated by the central government which replaced it with a more compromising assembly. However, the latter maintained a foralist stand in order to placate the vociferous 'intransigents'. Indeed, the renewed Diputación wrung many concessions from Madrid, parading the threat of a possible exacerbation of Basque bitterness as a lever against the crown (Corcuera 1979: 91-2). The Diputación soon came under the control of the oligarchic bourgeoisie, who struck numerous deals with Madrid. In 1878 the first *concierto económico* was signed, allowing the Basque *diputaciones* to collect taxes and remit their receipts to Madrid. However, the only beneficiaries of this arrangement were the big industrialists who bore a very low share of the tax burden. The rural areas and small towns were penalised, as local merchants, professional sectors and the peasants suffered most of the hardships brought about by new industries and taxes. As a reaction against the abolition of the *fueros*, Basques lent their support to any movement which opposed centralism. Hence the particular popularity of Carlism in Euskadi.

Following the abolition of the *fueros*, industrialisation rapidly developed in the country. Modernisation abruptly swept in, bringing in its wake the sudden destruction of ancient lifestyles. A relatively isolated and balanced society collided with new untamed forces. Its response to the unstoppable tide of events was a neo-traditionalist retreat, first in the form of continuing Carlist support, then through foralism and, finally, as an isolationist form of nationalism.[9]

The abolition of the *fueros*,[10] which were both symbols and instruments of economic autonomy, marked a watershed in relations between the Basques and Madrid. It was the key condition, though

---

but as [an institution] which integrated the different nationalities in a superior unity' (Zabala 1980: 49).

[9] As in other fields, nationalism took up its isolationist postures from a pre-existing underlying trend. Thus, before nationalism, Sagarmínaga voiced a widely-shared desire of non-interference into Spanish affairs: 'Contrary to the Catalans, the Basques must not at all interfere in the problems of the rest of the state' (Sagarmínaga, cited by Corcuera 1979: 123). Since the Basques were heavily represented in Madrid's economic and political élites, such messages were probably addressed to the *españolista* Basques.

[10] In particular, the removal of the customs posts from the river Ebro to the actual Spanish border.

not the only one, for the subsequent appearance of Basque
nationalism. The brutal shock of industrialisation transformed the
pre-existing ethnocentric awareness of a common identity into a
political ideology (Fusi 1984). From the 1880s onwards, the Vizcayan landscape had become scarred by blast furnaces, large
shipyards, steel mills and opencast mines. Modernisation was not
merely an economic matter; it infiltrated every level of society. It
did not spare even the most tightly knit relationships; families were
broken apart and 'foreign' habits gained ground in most walks of
life. Industrialisation was accompanied by proletarianisation and by
the displacement of Basque youth from the countryside to the city.
And there was more: since the demand for cheap labour required
by the bourgeoisie's intense industrialisation programme exceeded
the local supply, immigrants flooded the country. This added
another dimension to the conflict, since the displaced local youth
had to compete on many levels with new arrivals originating from
extremely different backgrounds. Most immigrants came from Castile, the land of the oppressors, and thus were readily identified as
the oppressor's stooges. Although the newly urbanised Basque youth
quickly forgot Euskara and shared a common language with the
immigrants, their background remained very different. Modernisation, therefore, can be seen as a fatal wound for which Basque
nationalism claimed to be the cure – appearing as a providential
alternative to this chaotic human scenario. As in Catalonia and in
the modern world generally, the age of transition to industrialism
was also bound to be one of nationalism (Gellner 1983: 40). Basque
nationalism was 'born of the intersecting of traditionalism and
modernization, and of the need to adjust to and achieve the latter
while preserving as much as possible of the former' (Payne 1975:
64).

Industrialisation

Early Basque industrialism was dominated by a cohesive and fairly
small upper bourgeoisie, which was able to set for itself considerable
economic benefits from Madrid, in particular protection for its
heavy industry.[11] Hence, this autochthonous 'semi-oligarchy' was

---

[11] The first chamber of commerce in Spain was founded in 1881 in Bilbao. In the
immediate aftermath of its foundation 'it began a vigorous campaign for state
encouragement to Spanish shipbuilding' (Harrison 1977: 373).

absorbed into the mainstream of the Spanish economy and politics and rejected nationalism.

However, as the process of industrialisation deepened, a local upper middle class grew and began looking for a political ideology. Like most of the population, this emerging class was pressing for the re-establishment of the *fueros*, but at the same time it could hardly be attracted by the traditionalist leanings of Carlism, then the most ardent defender of the *fueros* – at least in its rhetoric. Both the Liberals and the Conservatives were associated with centralism, although in Vizcaya both of them often defended the *fueros*.[12] Furthermore, the interests of the two main branches of Basque industry – the steel magnates, who controlled Spain's high finance, and the shipbuilders –came into conflict. The latter soon moved over to the nationalist cause, joining the low and middle bourgeoisie, which were not linked to other centres of capital accumulation outside the Basque provinces and thus tended to be more naturally attracted to nationalism (Perez- Agote 1984). Once the Bourbon monarchy passed the post-1876 reforms permitting foreign investment and the export of natural resources, British capital for mines and furnaces poured into Vizcaya, and British orders for iron ore boomed (Zirakzadeh 1985: 254). The yearly amount of iron ore exported from Vizcaya increased from 55,000 tons in 1866 to 4,272,000 tons in 1890. By 1900 252 mines were operating in the province, which produced 13.2% of the world's iron ore (Ortzi 1978: 112). The *Liga de Productores Vizcaínos* (LPV, Vizcayan League of Producers) was founded in 1894 as a go-getting and aggressive corporate association of protectionist Basque steelmakers.[13] The economic development led by the LPV conditioned for nearly a century an industrialisation based on heavy industries and a monoculture of iron.

Economic expansion attracted a legion of wage labourers into the region. Later, in Chapter 8, we consider the dramatic demographic effect produced by this influx and the pitiful conditions in which the immigrants lived. The situation was an ideal hunting-ground for

---

[12] Basque liberals were not necessarily centralist. Many supported the idea of creating a United Provinces of the Pyrenees on the federal models of the United States of America and the Netherlands (Agirreazkuenaga 1991).

[13] The LPV was a tributary of the steel-making process invented by Henry Bessemer during England's second industrial revolution (Harrison 1977). The Bessemer blast-furnaces allowed inexpensive production of metal derivatives from low phosphorus iron ore, which was plentiful in Vizcaya and scarce in Britain.

socialists, anarchists, nationalists and other kinds of populists. However, the uprootedness of the immigrants proved a more fertile
ground for the spread of socialism and similar class-related doctrines
than for nationalism. The main reason for this lack of appeal by early
nationalists was their open rejection of the immigrants. No attempt
was made to attract or incorporate them – at this early stage of its
development, Basque nationalism was a Basque-only affair.

    In 1890 more than 20,000 steel and railway workers and miners
from the west bank of Bilbao's river Nervión (known as the 'Left
Bank', where most industries were and still are concentrated)
organised a general strike, demanding the reform of working conditions, wage rises and shorter workdays. This was the first general
strike by industrial workers in Spanish history and thus a landmark.
The immigrants were now attracted to the socialist cause and away
from nationalism. In the same year, Socialist candidates were elected
to public office for the first time in Spain, winning seats in Bilbao's
city council.[14] However, the post-1876 atmosphere was ripe for a
nationalist counter-attack and there were also weak signals of a
Basque cultural revival.

Euskaros and Euskalerriacos: an aborted Basque renaissance

Although not comparable in quality and size to the Catalan
Renaixença, a small cultural revival took place in the Basque country
before the emergence of nationalism. The *renacimiento euskerista*
was centred in Navarre and, to a less extent, in Vizcaya. The
Asociación Euskara was founded in Pamplona, the capital of Navarre
in 1878 by Juan Iturralde y Suit (1840–1909), with the aim of
studying and propagating the Basque language, literature, history
and legislation (Elorza 1978a, López Antón 1990). Limiting its
membership to top Navarrese intellectuals, its support never spread
to the wider population (Corcuera 1979: 134). The defence of
the *fueros* was the association's mainstay. People of different creeds
and parties joined the predominantly cultural activities. Most *Euskaros*, as the members of the association were called, were moderate
Liberals, and a few were Carlists (Corcuera 1979: 131, Elorza
1978a, Martínez-Peñuela 1989). As professional classes, they formed

---

[14] There was another general strike in 1903, which again met with fierce
repression, like the one in 1890.

the bulk of the Navarrese intelligentsia. Iturralde was the son of a leading banker, and he had studied art in Paris, where Romantic ideas made a profound impact on him. Back in Pamplona, he mixed artistic with political activity as a municipal councillor.

However, the key figure in the movement was Arturo Campion (1854-1937), son of a French official who had first come to Spain with the Napoleonic armies and returned there as a shopkeeper after the war. As with many early nationalists, the abolition of the *fueros* radicalised Arturo's political position. He became a journalist and writer vocal in defence of Basque culture, while undertaking political activities on Pamplona's municipal council and as a deputy in the Spanish Cortes. The Asociación Euskara became marginally involved in politics, but its main activities consisted in organising poetry contests (such as the Floral Games), prizes for historical research, language and music classes, lectures etc. Ibon Sarasola (1982: 135) dates the Basque literary renaissance back to 1879, the year of the first Floral Games in the Spanish Basque country.[15] The *itz-jostaldiak*, literary contests, were added later, organised by the municipality of San Sebastián. In contrast to the Catalan *Jocs Florals*, the Basque ones were not strictly a literary manifestation but a folkloric event where literary competitions were mixed with popular sports and games, folk singing and oral poetry (Sarasola 1982: 136).[16]

In those years another society emerged in Bilbao, with a more political orientation as a vehicle for the aspirations of Bilbao's emerging middle and upper classes. A radical advocate of foralism, the Euskalerria (founded in 1876) society was more concerned with the success of its business than with local history and religion (Larronde 1977: 261-80). Bilbao's shipping magnate Ramón de la Sota and other representatives of the non-oligarchic 'intransigent'

[15] See Arana (1982: 1987-93 and 2155-61). Basque Foral Games were already celebrated in the Northern (French) side's town of Urruña (Labort) over twenty years before, in 1853.

[16] Sarasola (1982: 136) notes that the prize awarded to the best poetry was of one-fifth the value of the prize awarded for the best cow's milk or to the winners of the *pelota* game. The participants were often from the lower classes (with the exception of a few physicians), most being artisans, peasants and local priests. The poetry of the games derived directly from the tradition of the *bertsolariak* (troubadours) who, with their improvised texts, were key protagonists of popular culture (Aulestia 1994).

bourgeoisie, such as Sagarmínaga, were its main figures (Elorza 1978a). As liberal intelligentsia, this group of modernisers was able to produce a political praxis and later express it in a political organisation. That is why, as we see later, the majority of the society's members joined Arana's nationalist party in 1898–9, bringing to it a key liberal contribution (Zabala 1980). This event is probably the true moment of nationalism's birth as a political option, the moment when 'the messianic "assimilationists" try to realize their former vision by adopting the ethnicity solution of the defensive reforming "revivalists"' (Smith 1971: 255, cited in Payne 1975). According to Zirakzadeh (1991), the entry of the *Euskalerriacos* into Arana's organisation, where they soon assumed key positions, totally changed its course, transforming it from a neo-traditionalist group into a fully fledged albeit more moderate nationalist party. However, their entry made the party much more fragmented internally than it had been at its birth. A clash between moderate and intransigent elements accompanied its history throughout. But why was this liberal intelligentsia attracted to nationalism?

The Sota sector felt itself increasingly displaced from the centres of political power controlled by the upper bourgeoisie related to the mining and steel industries (the LPV). The latter used electoral corruption ('*caciquismo*') to monopolise the control of political representation in local governments. The excluded 'modernisers' then searched for a political space to reflect their orientation and interests. Since they did not feel sufficiently represented by mainstream political parties, they found in nationalism a suitable political vehicle. Arana offered them two irreplaceable advantages: a ready-made ideology and a popular following.

Similarities between Navarre's *Euskaros* and Vizcaya's *Euskalerriacos* were limited to foralist ideology and a few cultural activities. Vizcaya was facing rapid modernisation, while Navarre's social structure remained statically rural. The movement assumed clear political overtones among the *Euskalerriacos*, while it remained confined to the realm of culture among the *Euskaros*. The *Euskalerriacos* became nationalists and even separatists, but the *Euskaros* moved no further than regionalism and were often monarchists (Corcuera 1979: 135–6); they were more traditionalist, intensely Catholic and anti-Liberal, and foralist to the core. This reliance on tradition was reflected in their ideological conformity and scant theoretical output. In contrast, their Vizcayan counterpart had to distill its own balanced vision from the interests of disparate social groups, a search which finally led to nationalism. The culturalist *Euskaros* dissolved as an organisation, while the *Euskalerriacos*, former assimilationist intellectuals, decided to join with the nationalists. However, the works of Campión and his friends still remain an important point of reference for Basque scholars and have left an indelible mark on Navarrese historiography and ethnology.

Arana's legacy

Few nationalisms in the modern world can be said to have been permeated and shaped by a single person, but Basque nationalism is an exception, since it owes most of its symbols and values to one man, Sabino Arana y Goiri (1865-1903). Arana single-handedly formulated its first political programme, coined its name, defined its geographical extent, founded its first political organisation, wrote its anthem and designed its flag. Moreover, the anniversary of Arana's 'nationalist revelation' is celebrated every year as the Basque national holiday (*Aberri Eguna*). Let us now examine each of these 'inventions'.

The first political programme of modern Basque nationalism was contained in Arana's *Bizkaya por su independencia* (1892). In this and other early writings he spoke of *Bizkaya* (Castilian: *Vizcaya*) rather then the whole Basque country, since it was the cradle of Basque industrialisation and the laboratory of all the social change that came with it. It was also the province which resisted the surrender of its *fueros* most strongly.[17] The neologism *Euzkadi*, invented by Arana, was later universally accepted as the national name for the Basque country in its recently standardised (*batua*) version, *Euskadi*. Arana synthesised the geographical extension of Euskadi in the motto *Zazpiak-bat* (seven in one)[18] and in the formula '4 + 3 = 1'. 'Seven

[17] Although Arana always perceived the Basques as a single people, he followed the foralist tradition of non-interference in matters of other provinces, since interference was 'contrary to the spirit of the *fueros*'. Hence, he framed his programme for Vizcaya, convinced that the other provinces would spontaneously follow, and, at the same time, intensified his visits and contacts with them. Arana's programme was based on a great degree of decentralisation which allowed each province to separately follow its path, in accordance with the foralist tradition.

[18] This motto was first used by the Navarrese *Euskaros* (Corcuera 1979: 132) to replace the older *laurak-bat* (four in one), limited to the four provinces on the Spanish side (Elorza 1978a: 23).

PNV

in one' alluded to the four provinces on the Spanish side (*Euskadi Sur*) and the three *départements* on the French side (*Euskadi Nord*).[19] It is the aspiration of all nationalists that the seven areas will one day be united in a free Euskadi. The first nationalist organisation, later named the PNV (*Partido Nacionalista Vasco*, Basque Nationalist Party) was founded by Arana in Bilbao, the capital of Vizcaya. Although informally created in 1895, a political 'bureau' was founded only two years later (San Sebastian 1984: 29, Corcuera 1979: 413, Elorza 1978a).[20] Arana composed the anthem of the PNV, '*Gora ta Gora*', in 1895 while in prison. In 1980, after nearly a century, it was adopted as the official anthem by the Autonomous Community of Euskadi and today it is the Basque national hymn. Arana designed the Basque flag, calling it the '*Ikurriña*'. Its red and green colours were adopted by the PNV in 1933, and it became the official flag of Euskadi in 1936 (Corcuera 1979: 226). Finally, the Basque national holiday, *Aberri Eguna* (Day of the Fatherland), celebrates Arana's political conversion which occurred on Easter Sunday in 1882.[21] Thus the Resurrection has special meanings in Euskadi, and its colourful celebrations assume a unique flavour. The fact that nationalist festivals parallel the Christian calendar seems to give substance to the interpretation of the Basques as a 'chosen people'. The description of Arana as a martyr, or even a suffering Christ, helped in this direction. For all these reasons the personal biography of Arana is an important element in understanding the origin of Basque nationalism – more important than the life history of any of the main Catalan leaders and thinkers.[22] In contrast to Prat de la

[19] The presence of an international border running through the Basque nation has hindered Basque collective identity by creating two very different relationships with their respective central governments. The border dissecting the Basque country was established by the Treaty of the Pyrenees (1660).

[20] In 1895, Arana founded in Bilbao the *Bizkai Buru Batzar* or Regional Council of Vizcaya (Elorza 1978a: 149).

[21] The first *Aberri Eguna* was celebrated in Bilbao fifty years later, in 1932, under the suggestion of Sabino's brother, Luis, at that time President of the 'Euzkadi-Buru-Batzar' (García Venero 1968: 516-8, Granja 1986: 236-8). The itinerant character of the celebration was designed to rekindle pan-Basque ties. Thus in 1933 the festival was celebrated in San Sebastián, in 1934 in Vitoria, in 1935 in Pamplona, and so on (in 1936 it could no longer be publicly celebrated).

[22] Most biographies of Arana tend to be eulogistic, even hagiographic (e.g. Basaldua 1977). Larronde's (1977) in-depth study of Arana's works is more detached

Riba, Arana is to be valued more as an inventor of nationalist symbols than for his intellectual contributions (Ortzi 1975: 134).

Sabino Arana was born in 1865 in Abando, a borough (or parish, *anteiglesia*) swallowed up by greater Bilbao during his lifetime.[23] His father, Santiago Arana, was a small shipbuilder and a man fervently dedicated to the Carlist cause. At the time of the Carlist uprising in 1872, he wholeheartedly joined the insurgents' side and hid a leading Carlist general in his shipyard at Ripa. He travelled to England to purchase arms for the rebels, investing more than 50,000 *duros* from his own resources (Basaldúa 1977: 34-5). But the Carlists were defeated and, at the end of the fighting he had to become a refugee, fleeing to Bayonne across the French border. The triumph of the Liberals represented for the Arana family the defeat of all they and the Carlists stood for. Vizcaya had lost its ancestral institutions, Basque traditional values were sinking under a tidal wave of economic greed, and the Catholic religion was threatened by liberalism (Corcuera 1979: 185). But the defeat also badly damaged the financial well-being of the Aranas: all the money they had given to the Carlist cause was lost. Furthermore, in the shipbuilding industry the wooden hull was rapidly being eclipsed by the iron-clad one with its more modern technology.[24] When Santiago Arana

---

and objective. A great deal of original biographic information is available in Corcuera (1979: 184-241). In English, see Payne (1975: 61-86). Ortzi (1975: 137) suggests the need for a comparative biography of Arana and Prat de la Riba, with their two sharply different personalities and ideologies.

23 Urban expansion, the absorption of the native *anteiglesias* and the destruction of the rural *baserriak* (farmhouses) surrounding Bilbao, were a powerful reminder of the perverse effects of industrialisation all through Arana's life. 'In Bilbao . . . live a handful of bad Vizcayans who govern the town by whim and keep a continuous fight against the peasant, the *baserritar*, the native of the *anteiglesia*...'. (Arana 1982: 1281). 'The harm that Bilbao, dreadful foe of the Fatherland, has caused is incalculable' (Arana 1982: 1285).

24 The economic trajectory of the Arana family responded to a common pattern of industrial élites marginalised by economic development. The industrial boom after 1876 'tended to foster the growth of a financial and manufacturing élite which rapidly accumulated a large share of the region's industrial wealth. As a consequence, a number of the members of the bourgeois sector . . . fell into some degree of decline. Smaller firms were absorbed or driven out of business by the large industrial combines. . . . The decline of this sector of Basque leadership was reflected in the shift of their sons from industry into the professions. . . . They were lawyers and doctors, journalists and teachers, artists, composers, and writers, the providers

returned from his French exile, he was depressed: 'The Carlist collapse dealt him a psychological and emotional blow from which he never recovered' (Payne 1975: 65). Faced with the triumph over him of a cruel world which he could not comprehend, he died in 1883, bequeathing to his offspring a legacy of justice denied.

The young Sabino and his brother Luis were themselves raised as Carlists. Sabino later recognised that he was a Carlist by accident, 'insofar as the triumph of Don Carlos of Bourbon seemed the only way to re-establish the *fueros*' (Corcuera 1979: 89). The best account of Arana's education in the Jesuit college of Orduña is contained in Corcuera (1979: 185-8). His schoolmates came from *acomodadas* (well-off) rural or small town families, and many were born in the overseas colonies of the Spanish empire. However, no name in the list of his schoolfellows was linked to big industry (1979: 186). The school environment and the teaching methods, with their strong emphasis on Catholic missionary vocation, had an important effect on his upbringing. At the close of his student years, the devout religiosity which imbues all his writings had deepened. Arana was also 'obsessed at an early age by the desire to know the history and institutions of his country' (Corcuera 1979: 189).[25]

Sabino 'converted' from Carlism to nationalism after an animated discussion with his brother Luis. According to nationalist mythology, this marked the birth of Basque nationalism. It is said that the nationalist idea first appeared in Luis's mind on a trip to Galicia, shortly after his father's death.[26] It is not certain in what circumstan-

---

of services, such as transportation, communication, design and planning. They were the "second" generation of the industrial boom' (Clark 1979: 38) and thus became the main supporters of the emerging ethnonationalist movement. Sabino Arana, son of an industrialist, studied law in Barcelona, while his brother Luis was trained as an architect.

[25] In *Bizkaya por su independencia*, after a *dedicatoria* (preface) in Euskera, Arana presented his own interpretation of four historical battles which he converted into the emblems of Vizcayan independence: Arrigorriaga, Gordexola, Otxandiano and Mungia. Arana can be defined as a classical *ethno-historian* (Smith 1993).

[26] Payne (1975: 65) refers to Luis' train trip to Galicia. The slogan *Vivan los fueros* ('Long live the *fueros*') was carved on his lapel and a travel companion remarked with indignation: 'How could you ask for a privilege to which other Spaniards have no right?' This statement plunged Luis into a deep reflection and made him realise that the Basques were not Spaniards. We can better understand this episode if we consider that the opposite slogan was normally dubbed on the walls of most other Spanish towns in the aftermath of the Carlist War: '*Abajo los fueros*' (Down

ces and after what readings Luis came to this conclusion. Basaldua
(1977:44) recalls that the conversion occurred roughly at the same
time as many small nationalities were awakening in other parts of
Europe.[27] On his return, Luis had a long and agitated discussion with
his brother, from which Sabino came out thoroughly convinced that
Carlism was now a lost cause, useless to the advancement of Basque
rights. Years later, he recalled that 'understanding that my brother
knew history better than me and that he was unable to deceive me,
I entered in a phase of doubt, and promised myself to study with a
serene spirit the history of Vizcaya while adhering firmly to the truth'
(cited by Basaldua 1977: 46).

In 1882 Arana moved to Barcelona to study law, and remained
there until 1888. This was a time when Catalonia was experiencing
a widespread cultural, economic and political revival. Although
Catalanism had little influence on him, he was directly exposed to
it. In particular, the renaissance of the Catalan language must have
impressed him deeply, since he hoped to launch a similar revival for
Euskara. But this proved a hard it not impossible task during his
short lifetime. The Basque language was half-forgotten and derided
by the natives as anti-modern.

From 1885 he dedicated himself to the study of Basque, publishing in Barcelona the first part of a *Gramática elemental del Euzkera
bizkaíno* (1888). As he came back to Bilbao, he entered a competition
for a chair of Basque language at the Secondary Institute of the
province.[28] Among the other candidates was the philologist and
writer Miguel de Unamuno (1865-1936). However, neither was
awarded the place and the competition was won by a priest,
Resurrección María de Azkue (1864-1951), who later became a
prominent philologist (Basaldua 1977: 54). It is possible to speculate
how this event influenced the lives of two prominent Vizcayans,

---

with the *fueros*, Hormaza cited by Corcuera 1979: 82). The Basque provinces were
the only region of Spain where the *fueros* were still preserved, while the aggressive
campaign to abolish them was increasingly perceived by many Basques as a direct
assault. Corcuera mentions the wave of hatred against the Basque country and the
persecutions against the defenders of the *fueros*.

27 However, in his first pamphlets and articles, Sabino Arana (1980: 10) seems to
ignore all of them and only mentions the former Spanish colonies of the Americas
and the Pacific.

28 On the establishment and closure of this chair (*catedra de vascuence*), see Corcuera
(1979: 150-1). See also Arana (1982ca: 1: 621).

Unamuno and Arana. After they failed as professional philologists, both had to dedicate themselves to other endeavours, and somehow they both moved away from language. However, Unamuno turned to cosmopolitan values, rejecting Basque culture entirely, while Arana turned to defining a new nationalist ideology, in which language rarely became the central element. Arana continued his linguistic studies more as a hobby as he became involved in politics, and never completed his grammar book.[29]

After the publication of his booklet *Bizkaya por su independencia* (1892), Arana attracted limited attention in some professional sectors of Bilbao. A few days later about twenty admirers and friends decided to invite him and his brother for a luncheon in Larazábal, near Bilbao. On this occasion Sabino announced to the incredulous company his political creed for Vizcayan independence. For him Vizcaya was now dying, but it would have been preferable if it were already dead. As it was, the province was humiliated, trampled upon and mocked by that weak and miserable nation, Spain. Complete separation from Spain was the only hope, the escape from such misery. Despite the bystanders' cool and even hostile reception, a few years later most of them passed into the rank and file of Arana's party. Hence the Larazábal luncheon is conceived by some scholars as the informal birth of the subsequent nationalist organisation (Elorza 1978a: 148). The average age of the audience was under thirty-two. Most of them were from Vizcaya and from a relatively high social level, representing those urban and liberal elements which emerged with industrialisation (Corcuera 1979: 208).[30] Among them was Ramón de la Sota, a founding member of Euskalerria. The participation of liberal professions in the embryo of nascent nationalism is easily explained in terms of the politico-economic losses suffered by these sectors since 1876.

In 1893 Arana founded the bi-weekly *Bizkaitarra* (the Vizcayan),

---

[29] Professional failure often plays a prominent role in the careers of nationalist leaders. In situations of 'blocked mobility', the evolutionary vision of ethnic historicism has a special appeal for the proto-national intelligentsia (Hutchinson 1987, Smith 1981: 124-8). Although Basques were overrepresented in the higher echelons of the Spanish administration and industry (Heiberg 1975: 181), more important was 'the belief that one's community [is] being disadvantaged, together with a genuine shortage of opportunities' (Hutchinson 1987: 267).

[30] Corcuera (1979: 208) counts two engineers, three tradesmen, one businessman, and other liberal professions.

where he was almost the only contributor, writing articles on grammar, history, ethics and local politics. Its tenth issue (1894) published a plan for the organisation of an *Euskaldun Batzokis* ('EB' or *Centro Vasco*), a recreative society and informal club for nationalists which was to be the germ of 'Bizkaianism' (Elorza 1978a: 148-9). With 150 founding members, the first *batzoki* named a junta (committee), presided over by Arana.[31] A year later, in 1895, the centre assumed the form of a political 'bureau' as *Bizkai Buru Batzar* in order to contest its first municipal and provincial elections (Basaldua 1977: 91). The bureau was closed down by the Spanish authorities, which also suspended the publication of *Bizkaitarra*, and Arana was sentenced to four and a half months in prison.

As we shall see through his quotation, the theoretical production of Sabino Arana is often of a low quality, yet he can be defined as an intellectual, since his main activity was the production of ideas.[32] Furthermore, as a politician and organiser of the nationalist movement he was also part of the intelligentsia. Much of Arana's symbolic importance lies in his dedicated personality sincerely vowed to extreme self-sacrifice. In Larazábal, he impressed everybody by his oath of being ready to achieve the freedom of Vizcaya 'with all my weak forces, sweeping away all the obstacles in my way and preparing myself, if necessary, for the sacrifice of all that is important to me, from the family to friendship right up to social formalities, economic well-being and my very life' (cited in Ortzi 1975: 141). Arana was a traditional man living in a non-traditional world. He embodied a neo-traditionalist route to nationalism. In many ways, he was a man of the past, and this was a past forever lost in the anomic metropolis. Yet he was also a child of his times, and we can see how this contradiction worked at the ideological level.

Arana the racialist

This section analyses in more depth the attitude of Arana and other nationalists towards the immigrant workers who were then

---

[31] In a few years similar *centros* sprang up throughout Euskadi and even among the Basque diaspora in the Americas and the Philippines (Clark 1979: 43).

[32] His main activity was indeed journalism, as writer and editor of his own journals. 'The fact that he was wealthy enough not to have to worry about employment allowed him to devote his time and energy to the nationalist cause' (da Silva 1975: 243).

settling in Vizcaya. One of the consequences of rapid industrialisation was the arrival in Vizcaya of unprecedented numbers of
immigrants from non-Basque regions of Spain. Many of them
came from Castile, the land of the oppressor. The traumatic impact
of immigration is one of the factors which explains Arana's abandonment of cultural nationalism in many of his political statements.
Rather than trying to revive or encourage the spread of Euskara,
he and his followers chose rather to use it as an ethnic boundary.[33]
His aim became not so much to preserve the language as to
preserve a sense of 'unique' Basque racial purity, dividing the
autochthonous population from the newcomers, whom he called
'*maketos*'.

Traditionally, before the spread of nationalism, there had been a
pride among many Basques in the unintelligibility of their language.
The contention that no foreigner had ever been able to master it
worked as a strong psychological barrier against amalgamation and
'evil infiltrations'. According to an ancient legend, the devil once
visited the Basque country to learn the language and make disciples.
He tried for weeks, but was defeated and returned to hell after having
learned no more of the language than *bai* (yes) and *ez* (no) (Clark
1979: 148, Dickson 1968: 50). Thus not only was Euskara God-
given and crucial to the definition of Basque identity, but popular
ethnicity considered already language to be an 'ethnic barrier' against
foreign infiltrations. Hence Arana's refusal to allow the immigrants
to learn the language was not his own idea but derived from
centuries-old attitudes.

It is not certain how justly Arana can be accused of being a racist,
as he is by many of his opponents. Indeed he never espoused a
biological theory of racial superiority, nor did he believe in a
universal hierarchy of races. Most likely, he used race as a defensive
barrier to prevent the corruption of Basque values and culture from
external encroachment. Thus it is clear that his main aim was to
preserve the local culture and way of life by adopting an extremely
defensive approach (Payne 1975: 74, Corcuera 1979). For instance,
his condemnation of marriage between Basques and outsiders cor-
responded to the firm belief that any such marriage would have
inevitably resulted in a loss for the Basque language and values and

---

[33] Language was seen as a border-guard and a wall protecting the besieged
nationalist citadel. On the *muralla* (wall) conception of language, see Sarasola (1982).

in a further expansion of Spanish influence in the family unit. When he was elected to the Bilbao city council, he proposed that the city's prisons be segregated in order to prevent Basque juvenile delinquents from learning blasphemous saying and immoral habits from their Spanish follow-inmates. Arana required that all members of his nationalist organisation be Catholic, and have at least four Basque surnames, or one grandparent who was a native Basque, to prove their 'Basqueness'.[34] At the root of this isolationist posture lay a pervasive insecurity and pessimism over the possibility of assimilating foreigners. This attitude was inextricably tied to the poor diffusion of the language, the difficulty faced by prospective learners, and the unavailability of other national symbols. In the absence of language, race provided a ready-made criterion that proved much more pervasive.

Why did Arana appear so intolerant? Was racial exclusivity a necessary step in the foundation of Basque nationalism? For all nationalist movements a primary task is to instill in the people whom they wish to mobilise a sense of self-confidence. For this to occur, a subjugated nation must unequivocally rid itself of the sense of inferiority and shame to which it has been subjected over the centuries. The reverse of this negative self-image often takes the form of a radical upgrading of all positive traits of the would-be nation. Hence, an openly declared sense of superiority can develop *vis-à-vis* the outgroup.

Arana the believer

Basque civil society was far less secularised than its Catalan counterpart.[35] This was not only in the countryside, which was a well-known bastion of Carlism and Integrism, but also among the urban middle classes and considerable sections of the native working class.[36] Their conservatism was an obstacle to the diffusion of

34 On the highly selective criteria for admission in the *batzokis*, their rigid internal discipline and ideological intransigence, see Elorza (1978a: 148-9).

35 Luis Mitxelena dates this common endowment back to the Council of Trent (1545), 'the effect of which came lastingly to inform nearly all aspects of local life. . . . Its consequence was the now familiar identification between Basqueness and Catholicism' (Mitxelena 1960: 59).

36 On the contribution of the clergy and religious orders to Basque language and culture, see Villasante (1979: 401-7).

new radical ideologies such as nationalism. Arana, who understood this predicament as well as upholding the same religious values, had to stress some aspects of his doctrine more than others. His religious education gave him the ability to understand and sympathise with the devout Christian sentiments of his compatriots. The religious basis of Arana's programme is subsumed in the motto JEL (*Jaungoikua eta Lagizarra*, God and the Old Law).[37]

Arana derived from Catholicism a whole set of ideas which remain the bastion of the PNV's doctrine up to the present time. First, he advocated non-violent methods to achieve his political goals – a vision discarded by post-1959 radical nationalists as a burden, together with most other Aranist precepts. Secondly, he espoused the core of social Catholicism's concern for the poor and needy. Arana deeply resented the materialistic and rapacious attitude of Bilbao's upper classes: 'All of us know that today the poor are inhumanely exploited and treated like beasts by industrialists and businessmen, mine-owners and the property-owners.'[38] As a solution to these injustices, Arana proposed a utopian classless society which he identified as having been his traditional Catholic homeland before the imposition of liberalism and the invasion of the *maketos*. Accordingly, before the arrival of the latter upset labour relations, employers and employees lived in a state of near-harmony where all classes helped each other. The employers did not despise their workers, nor did the workers disobey or clash with their employers. The nationalist union founded after his death reflected this paternalistic attitude and concern for social justice.

Arana's pious vision is stressed as he compared the Vizcayan programme with the Catalan one: 'Do Catalan nationalists, either moderates or radicals, have in their programmes a solution to social problems, which are so important in their land? We do not think so, because they have not adhered to a religious theme, and there is no solution without Christ. Have the Basque nationalists fastened onto a religious theme? Yes, and this is clearly demonstrated in their motto "For God and the Old Law". Their goal is not political but

[37] This was taken from the Carlist-foralist slogan *Jaungoikua eta Foruak* (God and *fueros*), already 'revived' by the '*Euskaros*' (Corcuera 1979: 35, 48–51 and 133). See also Corcuera (1979: 314–27). According to Clark, this was one of the first 'verbal political symbols Basques had ever used in their native tongue' (1979: 42).

[38] Arana, cited in Larronde (1977: 253) and Zirakzadeh (1991: 127).

social: to Christianise the people, the poor as well as the rich. Politics is only to be the means.'[39] He also wrote: 'My patriotism is rooted . . . in my love for God, and its aim is to connect God to my blood relatives, to my great family, the Basque country.'[40] And 'Ideologically speaking, before the Fatherland there is God; but in practical and temporal life here in Vizcaya, in order to love God it is necessary to be a patriot, and in order to be a patriot it is necessary to love God; this is what the Fatherland is all about.'[41] For him political centralisation also meant a conspiracy to deprive the Church of its hold over society and dilute Catholic values of piety and justice in the name of materialism and avarice. Hence, Spain was dominated by sinister anti-clerical forces epitomised by the Liberals and their corrupt electoral system. His own was a crusade against the irreligion and 'immorality' of Spanish reformers who were leading devout souls astray. Indeed, his whole campaign was to provide a new morality and set of values for the emerging Basque society at the very moment when they were lacking and very much needed. The disentailment of Church lands and free-market economic liberalisaton were seen as part of the same plot aimed at upsetting the values of Christian justice, foral autonomy and Basque culture. He also proposed to establish an extremely decentralised autonomous confederation of Catholic municipalities and provinces under the authority of the Church, with each entity having wide powers and even the right to secede.

The motto of the *Bizkai Buru Batzar* was 'For God and Custom'. A logo with the acronym GETEJ (*Gu Euzkadirentzat ta Euzkadi Jaungoikoarentzat*, 'We for Euskadi and Euskadi for God') also frequently appeared in their own documents and on their signs. 'I proclaim Catholicism for my country because its traditions and its political and civil character are essentially Catholic . . . If my people resist it, I would reject my race. Without God we want nothing' (Arana, quoted in Basaldúa 1977: 69). Soon a large part of the Basque clergy were attracted to Arana's nationalism, mainly in rural areas. The PNV became 'one of the earliest Christian democratic parties in Europe' (Clark 1979: 44).[42] As for other nationalist conceptions,

39 Arana, cited in Larronde (1977: 258) and Zirakzadeh (1991: 127-8).

40 Arana, cited in Larronde (1977: 95) and Zirakzadeh (1991: 125).

41 Arana (1982: 615), cited by Jáuregui (1981: 19) and Zirakzadeh (1991: 125-6).

42 Furthermore, Arana 'portrayed an almost sublime faith in the workings of the

for Arana the nation was an extended 'family', and this family was closely linked to God.[43] The nation, for Arana, was to be rejected if it failed to obey God; only if it continued to obey God was it acceptable. This is typical of a belief in 'ethnic election': the Basques are chosen so long as they love God.[44]

Finally, we have to consider that, according to the pre-nationalist Basque tradition, language itself was associated with the Creator. Theological interpretations of the origins of Euskera defined it as the common language of mankind before the Tower of Babel. At the turn of the nineteenth century, the Abbé Dominique Lahetjuzan considered it the first human tongue, spoken in the Garden of Eden (Gallop 1970: 4, Tovar 1957, 1980). Another Abbé, Diharce de Bidasouet, even claimed Euskara to be the language spoken by God (Gallop 1970: 2).

Arana the philologist

One of Arana's legacies had been to distort and complicate Euskara while attempting to purify it of 'Hispanicisms'. Basque was forced to absorb neologisms since it lacked the vocabulary to convey new inventions and concepts. Thus Arana dedicated many years of his life attempting to cleanse its lexicon of Spanish 'borrowings' and interferences. He pursued this goal with a zealous fervour which led him to 'invent' a purified idiom virtually alien from the language spoken by the common people. However, many terms he invented have been successfully adopted by other nationalists and subsequently, with the spread of nationalism, by most average Basque-speakers.[45] He also established an alphabet

---

democratic process . . . If Basque could only learn their history, their culture and their language, and if they had the freedom to vote for candidates who pledged to protect those things, then Basque nationalism would triumph at the ballot box' (Clark 1979: 46-7).

[43] Arana himself declared that 'the patriarchal family, that is the *patria*, is the union of individuals of an historic race for whom time has formed customs and language and on whose behalf history has created a patrimony of liberties which all generations (of that race) have the perfect right to enjoy' (1982: 1762, also cited in Heiberg 1989: 52).

[44] On myths of ethnic election and their pivotal role in maintaining ethnic identity over the centuries, see Smith (1992, 1993b).

[45] Among his successful creations, a few have even entered into contemporary

with a different order, in which, for instance, the letter 'c' is absent and the letter 'm' comes last.[46]

However, all these efforts have been devalued 'by the secondary character which Sabino conferred on language as a defining element of the nation, always second to race' (Corcuera 1979: 395). A further reason for Arana's choice in favour of race was that Euskara was barely spoken in the urban centres, especially in his home city of Bilbao where he was most politically active and created the first nuclei of Basque nationalism. The same Arana clearly perceived this decline when he declared, disenchanted: 'Euskara is fading away. We must acknowledge this fact as an undeniable reality of which everybody is aware' (quoted by Corcuera 1979: 395). He did not conceive a direct link between language and vision of the world (here including way of thinking, culture and general values). To him, learning the language did not necessarily mean changing a state of mind or acquiring a new value orientation. Hence the language revival was fraught with dangers since any immigrant learning Euskara threatened the Basque natives with moral contamination.

At the same time, Arana could not avoid the traditional importance of language as a signifier of Basqueness. For centuries the Basques had been singled out by both external observers and local intellectuals on account of their unique tongue. Hence, for the local people language worked as a readily available and unmistakable sign of distinctiveness. Its importance can be gauged by considering the self-definition of many Basques who still today name themselves *Euskaldunak* (sing. *Euskaldun*), meaning a person who has (*-dun*) the Basque language (*Euskal-*).[47] Furthermore, the word *Euskal-Herria*

Spanish usage, although with reference to Basque politics. Apart from *Euzkadi* and *ikurriña*, we can count *abertzale* (patriot, derived from *aberri* = fatherland) and *azkatasun* (independence or freedom, normally associated with the acronym ETA). I am using here Arana's spelling, not the current *batua*. See Arana (1982 ca: 2: 975 ff.). He also coined many Christian names, such as *Koldobika* for his brother Luis, included in his *Ixendegi* (list of names/calendar) to be used as a baptismal registry. Individual names are today a central feature of Basque identity and it is not uncommon among immigrant families to baptise their children with Basque names. (Arana 1910).

46 Hence, the title of Father de Ibero's catechism, *Ami vasco,* stands for an 'A to Z' of Basqueness (Ibero 1906). This also explains why the present-day Basque education system is divided into three types of school, identified as A, B and D.

47 This term is often Hispanised as *Euskaldunes.* Its antiquity is attested by the fact that both Strabo and the Latin authors probably coined the name 'Vasconians' as a

(or *Euskalerria*) has been traditionally used by the Basques to define their country.[48] It refers, at least in its original sense, to the whole of the people who speak Euskara and means the 'country of Euskara' (*Euskal*, Basque language; *Herri*, country or people).[49] Both terms – *Euskaldun* and *Euskal Herria* – have been in use for centuries, since long before the advent of nationalism, in order to define the collectivity of the Basques through the most visible element of their differentiation, language. The term *Euskal-Herria* appears with different spellings in early Basque literature, hence, according to Estornés Lasa (1965), it was already in widespread popular use by the sixteenth century.[50] We can identify this as a case of pre-modern linguistic ethnicity. Arana's doctrine was directly connected to this pre-existing ethnic base. The Basques defined themselves as nationalists through language: according to Campión, Euskara-speaking Basques would introduce themselves with the words '*euskalduna naiz*' (I am a Basque-speaker), rather than naming a province or town (cited in Estornes Lasa 1965: 3: 27).

The name invented by Arana, Euzkadi (*Euskadi* in contemporary standard Basque),[51] has gained widespread acceptance with the diffusion of nationalism and is used today by non-Basque-speakers, both in the Basque country and, to some degree, in the rest of Spain. At the same time, *Euskal-Herria* is still preferred by many.[52] However, it is important to stress that the winning term, *Euzkadi*, can be translated as 'the place of the Basque race': attaching the suffix *-di*

---

rough translation from the local word *Euskaldunak* (Collins 1986: 32).

[48] The term *Euskal-Herria* does not have political connotations and is universally accepted by all social, cultural and political sectors of Basque society, as well as in the rest of Spain. The more politically salient term Euskadi is less deep-seated (Jáuregui, personal suggestion).

[49] *Herri* means, at the same time, 'town', 'country', and 'people'.

[50] Its first recorded written usage dates back to 1571, in Leizarraga's preface to the New Testament in Basque. It subsequently appeared in 1643 in Axular's *Gvero* and then in several other works (Estornés Lasa 1965: 3: 25-6). The sheer number of local variants of the term testify to the adaptation of the word in several dialects (Estornés Lasa 1965: 3: 27).

[51] In their effort to dissociate themselves from Arana's racialism, present-day language-planners have changed the spelling of many of his words, replacing, for instance, the -z with an -s.

[52] The political implications of the nationalist name, Euzkadi, led to its ban under Francoism, while the authorities tolerated the use of the ancient Euskal-Herria.

(locality) to the word *Euzko-* ('the Basque race', according to Arana), the new toponym was purposely designed to eliminate the cultural component and emphasise community of race.

In recent years language has gained a prominent position in the definition of who is a Basque. A measure of the increasingly inclusive character of today's Basque identity is given by the emergence of a new term, *Euskaldunberri* (*Euskaldun*, Basque-speaker; *berri*, new). This term began to be used in the mid-1960s, referring to those adults, both native and immigrant, who were voluntarily learning Euskara in order to distinguish them from the native *Euskaldun-zaharra* (*zaharra* = old).[53] Rejecting the old dichotomy between *Euskaldunak* (Basque-speakers) and *erdaldunak* (speakers of any other language),[54] contemporary nationalists have chosen to stress the participation of all 'new Basque-speakers' in the making of *Euskal-Herria*.

With the advent in the nineteenth century of comparative linguistics and the study of Indo-European languages, the radical distinctiveness of the Basques from other European peoples was corroborated by scientific investigation.[55] However, in Europe since the late nineteenth century, race has come to be associated with language rather than being opposed to it; biology was linked to other human sciences, and thus the opposition between nature and culture was downplayed if not nullified altogether. In a time of global change, creeping assimilation and widespread socio-geographical mobility, the desire to re-build ethnic borders was pushed towards the extreme of confusing inherited characteristics with acquirable elements, in a desperate attempt to limit that mobility. The Basque intelligentsia were also affected by this Europe-wide shift of perspective. An additional reason was that many international studies of the time cited the Basques as a distinct race.[56] Not only did nationalism

---

[53] This was also a result of the success of the *ikastolak*, a semi-clandestine network of schools where Euskara was – and still is – the only medium of instruction (see chapter 4).

[54] *Erdera* (*Erdara* in standard Basque) = any language other than Basque.

[55] On the studies on Basque by Wilhelm von Humbold (1767-1835), see Eusko Ikaskuntza (1925) and the translation of Humboldt's work into Spanish (Humboldt 1935). On the linguistic research of Prince Louis-Lucien Bonaparte (1813-91) see González Echegaray (1989) and Rodríguez y Ferrer (1976).

[56] On the important contribution by foreign scholars and *vascofilos* (pro-Basques) to the study of the Basques and their culture in the nineteenth and early twentieth

and modernisation appear on the scene together, but racialism soon joined them.

The first nationalist victories

A first limited electoral victory was achieved by the nationalists in the 1898 provincial elections, when Arana himself was elected to the provincial assembly of Vizcaya. In the 1899 municipal elections, the nationalists won five seats on the city council of Bilbao and three in nearby towns. This success was largely accomplished with the support received by the '*Sotistas*', followers of the shipping magnate Ramón de la Sota, then the only leading industrialist who openly supported nationalism, and whose choice determined the subsequent evolution of the movement. Ideological radicalism periodically erupted from the grassroots, producing minor splits. While the heirs of Arana remained in control of the party's ideology, the pragmatists (Sota and other former *Euskaleriacos*) controlled its political praxis. A characteristic of the PNV was the continuous tension between these two trends, yet this tension offered its advantages to the pragmatists, since separatism was an irreplaceable tool of popular mobilisation.

In Arana's later life the PNV moved pragmatically from separatism to more moderate postures. However, in the 1901 provincial elections the nationalists failed to gain a single seat. Arana was jailed for the second time in 1902, when his telegram to President Theodore Roosevelt congratulating the United States for having freed Cuba from slavery, and praising its federal system, was intercepted. What can be called Arana's second 'conversion' from radical separatism to a more compromising and regionalist line was probably inspired by the triumph of the moderate Lliga Catalana in Catalonia (1901).[57] However, it may not have been a decision springing from conviction, but the result of Arana's desperation at being continuously harassed by the central authorities, although he was not ill-treated in prison. Many present-day radical nationalists hold that Arana's moderate ('*españolista*') evolution was merely a

centuries, see Villasante (1979: 407-16).

[57] According to Granja (1986: 18), Catalanism began to influence Basque nationalism from 1901 onwards. However, Arana did not refer to Catalonia or to Galicia as nations, since he considered them to be part of Spain (Corcuera 1979: 188-9). Only the Basques were allowed the 'privilege' of separate nationhood.

tactical device to gain wider popular support and the backing of the ruling classes in a period of great crisis for the PNV, while Arana never gave up his radical convictions. In his prison cell, he apparently pondered the need for a change, since all political activities of the nationalists were being hampered. His message 'could not spread with the required speed at a time of great travail for the Basque nation' (Basaldúa 1975: 74-5). 'When he emerged from jail, the bureau office had been closed, the party was out of money, and his supporters could not have numbered more than several hundred' (Clark 1979: 43-4). Arana's health, which had always been precarious, soon deteriorated with Addison's disease, to which stress probably made him more vulnerable. He had to resign as president of the PNV (his place being taken by Angel de Zabala). Sabino de Arana died on 25 November 1903 aged thirty-eight. He was long remembered among the Basques as someone of irreproachable rectitude, courage and self-sacrifice, a model to all his followers.

That year, the PNV won two seats in the Vizcayan provincial assembly – it is ironical that the greatest victories for the nationalists came only after Arana's death. It is possible that success was due to the fact that the party had became less intransigent and more pragmatic because of Arana's 'second conversion', and thus could attract a wider range of supporters. Soon it became the second political force in Vizcaya, after the Conservatives.

In 1906 the mayor of Bilbao was a nationalist, but in 1907 the nationalists were relegated to third place. That year the abortive Maura plan for the *mancomunidades* (see chapter 2) failed to reach agreement on the degree of autonomy to be granted to the Basque provinces. In 1910 the bureau adopted a new more Catholic-oriented title, Comunión Nacionalista Vasca (CNV, Basque Nationalist Communion), and a less loosely organized structure. A new nationalist and Catholic union was set up in 1911, the Solidaridad de Obreros Vascos (SOV, Solidarity of Basque Workers). Informally linked to the CNV, it became strong among railway workers and among ethnic Basques generally.[58]

Spain's neutrality during the First World War provided an exceptional stimulus for the expansion of Basque industry, boosting arms manufacture, shipping and mining. The ensuing wave of

---

[58] In 1933, it assumed the present-day name of Solidaridad de Trabajadores Vascos –Eusko Langille Alkartasuna (STV-ELA).

economic prosperity brought the first major electoral triumph for the nationalists in 1917 which lasted till 1918. However, their impact was mostly limited to the province of Vizcaya, where they gained an absolute majority of the seats in the Diputación, but achieved only marginal results in Guipúzcoa and Navarre.[59] The nationalists sent a delegation to Versailles in the hope of receiving aid from the Big Four, but to no avail. Urbanisation and industrialisation continually increased the importance of professionals, tradesmen, bureaucrats, administrators and other sectors which were providing most of the PNV's cadres. However, post-war depression and the example of the Bolshevik revolution also led to an increase in labour strife, nourishing an unprecedented fear of Communism. The national question was relegated to the background, as the local ruling classes relied increasingly on the central government to quell working-class unrest. This situation was reflected in the electoral decline of the nationalists. The CNV returned three delegates to the Cortes in the 1919 parliamentary elections, and in 1920 it only gained one deputy. The crisis fed internal dissent, leading to a split and readjustment of the party. The re-emerging party was now called PNV (*Partido Nacionalista Vasco* – Basque Nationalist Party) and became the major force in Basque politics.

The first Congress of Basque Studies (1918) and the nationalists' internal tensions

In 1918, at the height of industrial growth and social change, a group of Basque scholars, professionals, politicians and businessmen gathered in the town of Oñate (Guipúzcoa) to form a Basque Studies Society, *Eusko Ikaskuntza* or *Sociedad de Estudios Vascos* (Urla 1987: 27-60, 1988: 382). They believed that economic growth and social change could no longer be left to the hazards of improvisation. After the 1914 industrial boom, more poor landless labourers were pouring from the countryside into the industrialised areas. Social problems accumulated on a gigantic scale while the state stayed aloof: urban congestion, homelessness, pollution and illness were affecting industrial cities like Bilbao and Renteria. The participants at the first Congress of Basque Studies denounced

---

[59] This was obviously due to the differential impact of industrialisation on the other Basque provinces. Alava and Navarre remained fundamentally rural. For economic development in Guipúzcoa between 1876 and 1915, see Castells (1987).

the lack of planning and pleaded for a guiding role not only in economic development but also in the management of social change. Science and knowledge they believed, were powerful tools in achieving such aims. In this the founders of Eusko Ikaskuntza were children of the Enlightenment and shared a positivist faith in the possibility of influencing and even directing socio-political change (Urla 1987).

The scientific study of the past was an important step in this direction. History had to be rescued from the fetters of nationalist distortion. Language also needed to be re-founded and salvaged from purist amateurism: 'Authority over language reform had to be wrested away from zealous nationalists and handed over to language experts who would guide it according to the rigors of modern linguistic methods', (Urla 1988: 383).[60] A foremost proponent of this approach was the philologist Julio Urquijo (1871-1950).[61] His attacks were directed against the Aranists' obsession with a purified language, with its 'extravagant etymologies' based on 'the most grotesque hypotheses' (Urquijo, cited by Urla 1988: 383). The founding members and organisers of the Basque Studies Society were acting independently of political nationalism. Many non-nationalist intellectuals were interested in the revitalisation of Basque culture without aspiring to an independent state. The Congress represented a clear instance of cultural mobilisation as a movement autonomous from political nationalism. Yet it was hardly thinkable that such a Congress could have taken place without the previous nationalist victories. Behind the curtains the feelings aroused by political nationalism gave the necessary impetus for many such initiatives to occur.

A Basque Language Academy (*Euskaltzaindia* or *Academia de la Lengua Vasca*) was also created in 1918 in Oñate,[62] aiming to work not only on the *corpus* (structure) of Euskara but also on its status: i.e. the goal was not only to create a proper grammar, syntax and lexicon, but also to enhance its social status in terms of prestige, literacy, publishing and use in academic milieux.[63] 'From this new

---

[60] On the extravagant and amateurish character of the first *euskerálogos*, see Corcuera (1979: 398), Sarasola (1982: 81-3), Villasante (1979: 326).

[61] On Urquijo, see Villasante (1979: 370 ff).

[62] On the Academy, see Euskaltzaindia (1976) and Villasante (1979: 394-8).

[63] We introduce here Heinz Kloss's distinction between *corpus planning* and *status*

perspective, the fate of Basque was seen to depend primarily on the nature of its social distribution – who speaks Basque' (Urla 1988: 383). This was the first departure from Arana's restricted conception of language as an 'ethnic barrier'. Urla observes that the concern for language planning 'arose in conjunction with a host of new social concerns – public health, improving the race [*sic*], better schools, safety in the workplace, social insurance, and urban planning – problems that were emerging in the context of deep social and economic transformation. . . . For this, members of the society availed themselves of the latest advances in social scientific research . . .' (Urla 1988: 383). This emphasis reflects a radical shift in perspective from Arana's defensive nationalism to a newly dynamic conception. Now Basque society 'did not so much have to be *sheltered* from contact as it had to be properly *managed*' (Urla 1988: 384).

Meanwhile, major contrasts plagued the political field. Following Arana's tough line on independence and inspired by the Irish Sinn Fein (Conversi 1993), the radicals separated in 1921 from the CNV in order to re-found the party with the historical label of PNV. Their mouthpiece was the journal *Aberri* (Fatherland), founded by Luis Arana, and its main contributor was Eli Gallastegi (1892-1974), who adopted the nickname of *Gudari* (warrior) (Elorza 1977, Espinosa 1993). In 1921 the Spanish police attacked a workers' meeting, indiscriminately killing several participants. Most of the media applauded the police action, and even mainstream nationalists refused to condemn it. Against them Gallastegi wrote a piece in *Aberri* calling for solidarity with the workers: 'There had fallen idealistic men; some men who had struggled and suffered constantly. They are the Communists, as earlier there had fallen members of SOV. . . . The bullets that have entered their chests seemingly have been lodged in our own hearts. We feel the tragedy as if they were our own, because we too, like them, are young, are idealistic, suffer, and are of modest condition.'[64] This piece exemplified a whole trend of Basque nationalism which opposed the *Euskalerriacos'* bourgeois control over the CNV. Inspired by Arana's original concern for the welfare of the working class, this trend increasingly developed into a more

---

planning (Kloss 1967).

[64] Eli Gallastegi, *Fiesta de sangre*, reprinted in Ortzi (1975: 169). See also Espinosa (1993: 108 ff.) and Zirakzadeh (1991).

articulated anti-capitalist ideology and remained crucial when Basque nationalism finally turned towards Marxism in the 1960s.[65]

This and other splits occurred under the banner of a return to Arana's original principles: Arana left a legacy of contradictions and ambivalences that sowed the seeds of future nationalist fragmentation, and each of the opposing forces within the nationalist field claimed to be the true inheritor of his ideal, whether in its moderate or its radical form, its anti-capitalist overtones or its rapprochement with the industrialists, its emphasis on language or on religion, and so on.

Under Primo de Rivera

The precepts elaborated by Arana dominated the PNV right up to the Civil War. From his death till 1931, there is no relevant ideological evolution within Basque nationalism. According to García Venero (1968: 315), the few ideological rifts which emerged were in response solely to tactical considerations.[66] At the local level, the PNV was generous in its alliances with other parties and independent candidates. Most coalition partners were moderate or right-wing businessmen, theocrats and conservatives. The PNV always remained hostile to the Socialists because of their centralising trends, professed atheism, and control of the immigrants' vote through class politics.

Primo de Rivera's dictatorship (1923-30) forced both the PNV and the CNV into clandestine activity. The nationalist journal *Aberri* (Fatherland) and other independent publications were suppressed. Gallastegi fled to Ireland. Under such conditions, the nationalist torch was carried by a few groups around the PNV, the most important of which were the *mendigoizales* or mountaineering groups, which Gallastegi himself helped to establish, inspired by the organisational structure of Sinn Fein (Ortzi 1975: 176-7). 'High atop some remote mountain, the Basque alpinists could meet safely, far

---

[65] Many of ETA's founders were inspired by the works of Gallastegi, which they discussed in informal meetings.

[66] For instance, the splits between the confessional and the secular, or between the democrats and the liberals inside the party. Even the contrast between the CNV and the refounded PNV was based, not on an alternative to Arana's principles, but on a different emphasis on independence or autonomy.

from Spanish police scrutiny, and discuss politics freely' (Clark 1979: 51).[67]

As with most dictatorships, the stronger the repression the more the nationalist feelings were boosted. With the fall of Primo de Rivera (1930), both Catalan and Basque nationalism emerged with renewed vigour, reinforced by years of secrecy. Furthermore, the condition of clandestinity emphasised the importance of culture, since informal cultural and folkloric groupings were the only outlet available to express national sentiments, all political activities being banned. The non-violent precepts of Sabino Arana held the field, as he had counselled that repression should not be met by open resistance, confidently assuming that democracy would prevail. He himself suggested that in times of trouble the Basques could retreat to the safe haven of their mountainous terrain and to the 'mental sanctuary of their ancient culture' (Clark 1979: 50).[68]

As we have seen, the fall of Primo de Rivera prompted the principal anti-monarchist parties to meet in San Sebastián, where they established the basis for a forthcoming provisional government. Although Basque nationalists did not participate in the pact, the Catalanists did. The latter, together with Basque and Catalan Republicans, wrung a promise of regional autonomy from other Republican groups (Granja 1986: 19-23).

Meanwhile the nationalists healed their wounds, agreeing to reunite their two wings (PNV and CNV) under the PNV's banner (Granja 1986: 30-5). The dictatorship had helped to unite the different souls of Basque nationalism and mobilise even wider sectors (Estornés Zubizarreta 1990). The top echelons of Basque nationalism held an assembly in Vergara (1930), where a new generation of political leaders emerged unsullied by former political rivalries (Granja 1986: 48ff).[69] What united them was a return to

---

[67] In the next chapter we observe how important were these – and kindred – societies as forms of resistance to Francoism, especially in Catalonia. In Euskadi they soon assumed a paramilitary form and in the 1960s they became a fertile ground for ETA recruiting.

[68] 'Basques must not engage in open rebellion, but simply continue the slow, steady pressure of cultural resistance, wearing away the chains of tyranny' (Arana, cited by Clark 1979: 47).

[69] These included José Antonio Aguirre, the party's President and future *lehendakari* (President of the Basque Government in exile), the advocate Manuel Irujo and the notary José María Leizaola.

pure Aranist principles, only separatism being toned down. Under the revived motto JEL, race and religion were firmly confirmed as the bastions of Basque identity. Thus two weeks later a fringe group of disaffected leftists broke away to form the secular Republican Acción Nacionalista Vasca (ANV, or *Euzko Abertzale Ekintza*).[70] The latter's anti-clerical stand condemned it to play a marginal role in local politics, yet its ideological impact would become relevant for later generations (Granja 1986: 601-13).[71]

Basque nationalism under the Republic

In the municipal elections of April 1931 the PNV ran a slate with the Carlists. In the June parliamentary elections, this coalition won 15 of the 24 seats reserved to the four provinces at the *Cortes Constituyentes* (parliamentary assembly) (Granja 1986: 180-229, Payne 1975: 122). However, in reaction to state-sanctioned secularism, the Carlists turned increasingly integralist, which finally led them to ally themselves with the far right. In the 1933 parliamentary elections the PNV, running solo, became the largest party in the region, gaining 12 of the 24 Cortes seats (Granja 1986: 397-437). This was the greatest electoral triumph in the PNV's history (Payne 1975: 134) Even more astonishing, a proposed autonomy statute was supported in a plebiscite by 84% of the voters throughout the three provinces, with a turnout of 87% of eligible voters (Granja 1986: 394-6).[72] The latter was 'the highest for any contest in Spanish history' (Payne 1975: 133-4). However,

[70] According to Granja, ANV was more properly a nationalist party, in opposition to the PNV, which subordinated its nationalism to the religious question (Granja 1986: 606).

[71] For instance, ANV attacked the racist trends prevailing in the PNV's rank and file. For the first time, a nationalist party declared that the immigrants could be accepted as Basques, although it also expressed resentment at their moral habits (Granja 1986: 601-13). ANV rejected Arana's foralist idea of a loose confederation of provinces and opted for a centralised Basque state. However, it drew its support from the same urban liberal middle classes which backed the PNV (Ortzi 1975: 176-7). The creation of ANV was inspired by the federalist thought of Antoni Rovira i Virgili and by the foundation of Acció Catalana, a splinter group from the Lliga (Granja 1986: 18).

[72] Dominated by the Carlists, Navarre defected, rejecting the autonomy draft (Blinkhorn 1974, Granja 1986: 289-95).

as we saw in chapter 2, this advantage was cancelled out by the victory of the right-wing coalition CEDA in Madrid.

Since the anti-nationalist Right came to power, the PNV switched from anti-Republican rhetoric to bolster the Left. This shift proved counter-productive electorally as the party lost votes in 1936, going from 12 seats in the Cortes to 7 (Granja 1986: 554). This again testifies to the all-pervasive strength of religion in Euskadi and suggests that for any 'nod and wink' towards the Left a price would have to be paid. It also testifies to the unitary power of religion for the Spanish state, a legacy later expoited by the right. The PNV articulated Basque hostility towards Republican secularism, as its support was based on the Catholic vote. Yet the PNV was also a Republican party, while its Catholic commitment pitted it firmly against other forces of the Left. The torch of radicalism was carried by Luis de Arana's new journal, *Jagi-Jagi* 'Arise'. Most of its articles were a restatement of Sabino's sayings, mottos and principles. The journal implemented its radical stance, devoting more attention to working-class aspirations. Many young writers argued in its columns that proletarian struggle and national emancipation should go hand in hand. Back from his Irish exile, Gallastegi resumed his contributions (Elorza 1977). *Jagi-Jagi's* constant critique of capitalism was to be intended as an attack on capital's concentration into a few hands; in principle, it was not a struggle against private ownership of the means of production (Zirakzadeh 1991).

In the 1930s, with Jesuit support, the PNV became almost a confessional party at a time when secularism held sway in the rest of the state. This prompted accusations by sectors of the Left that a Concordat between Euskadi and the Vatican was imminent, and Indalecio Prieto, the Socialist leader, denounced the plan to establish a 'Vatican Gibraltar' (Hills 1970: 151). Yet the Basque clergy committed themselves to the Republican cause. This infuriated those around Franco who, before the end of the Civil War, ordered the execution of sixteen priests and monks. Subsequently, indiscriminate repression led many Basque priests and monks to join ETA in the 1960s. It was not a complete accident that the Basque country received a statute of autonomy from the Republic in December 1935, only months before the outbreak of the Civil War. This occurred after three different statutes had been proposed between 1930 and 1936 and all but the last one failed to be approved (Castells

1976). The main reason for this failure was anti-Republican opposition from Alava and Navarre (Aguirre 1991).

As soon as the autonomous government was installed, local administration was fully reorganised, making the region 'the most orderly, least revolutionary part of Republican Spain during the next nine months. Revolutionary excesses and atrocitie . . . were brought under control [and Vizcaya] . . . enjoyed greater political harmony than any other part of the Republican zone. Under the nationalist hegemony, direct conflict was largely averted, and relations with the Communists and other leftist groups were generally amicable' (Cortada 1982: 78).

During the Civil War the Basques supplied the Republicans with some of their most effective troops. In 1937 German planes of the Condor Legion, sent to bolster the Francoist insurgents, bombed the town of Guernica on a market day, razing parts of it to the ground and slaughtering hundreds of people. The event, immortalised by Picasso, shocked international public opinion. It was history's first aerial bombardment of a civilian population. Under pressure from a world-wide outcry, the Francoists denied any responsibility.

Autonomy lasted just nine months, as Bilbao was captured by the Spanish 'nationalist' troops in June 1937. The short-lived statute was immediately abrogated, and all political parties were suppressed.

In this chapter we have seen something of the congenital fragmentation of Basque nationalism, its origin as a response to modernisation, and the importance assumed in Basque society by religion, race and other elements before the Civil War. We have seen too the central role of Sabino de Arana in the birth of nationalism and his ability to create unity. Initially his nationalism was a nostalgic re-assertion of ancient values. In himself he reflected the dramatic tension of his time. Since change was radical, the reaction of many Basques was a desperate rejection of all things modern and a plunge into cherished memories, erecting a barrier between the present and the past. What distinguishes Arana from the main Catalan nationalists is that he carried out his arbitral role singlehanded. He was the inventor of almost all the key symbols of modern Basque nationalism; no Catalan nationalist can be credited with for having similarly invented the main 'aesthetic' symbols of Catalanism.[73] Catalanist ideology evolved slowly and steadily from Almirall to Prat and thereafter. On the contrary, Arana formulated Basque symbolism in a void, drawing uniquely from a pre-existing foralist and Carlist tradition.

We have seen that ethnic nationalism is the result of both modernisation and state-enforced assimilation. Very few scholars of nationalism still defend the assumption that modernisation, with its concomitant processes, can erode ethnic identity. However, we have also seen that full-blown nationalism was related to cultural displacement and assimilation rather than simple modernisation. In this sense nationalism was a radical response to the attack by the state on ethnic values, culture and identity. Although in times of democracy nationalism often rests on the cultural heritage of the nation – and it is especially strong where the ethnic language is maintained (Clark 1981, 1984) – the crucial role is played by hitherto assimilated élites (the intellectuals), and later by disaffected modernisers (the intelligentsia). This phenomenon has been noted in the rise of most nationalist movements. The Basque language was generally lost to these regional élites as they were fully assimilated into the dominant Castilian culture. This is especially true for Arana and his acolytes, and for all those who retained a sense of Basque identity without retaining tangible aspects of Basque culture. In the process, they had almost to recreate it from scratch. In Catalonia the nationalist élites were at least bilingual; although they fully mastered Castilian, most could express themselves properly in Catalan. Hence cultural nationalism could thrive in Catalonia, whereas it could hardly even take off in Euskadi.

One of the contrasts between the two consists of their different assimilative power, and the way this power is perceived in each by intellectuals and the intelligentsia. Arana's racial choice was due especially to a 'pessimistic' (but also traditionalist) disbelief in the capacity to conceive Basque culture in assimilative terms. Many ethnonationalist élites in Western Europe learned the ethnic tongue only after their nationalist 'conversion'. Most were – and are – raised in either dominant monolingual environments or imperfectly bilingual ones. Only later did they engage in the recovery of the ethnic culture.

---

[73] Many such symbols, such as the Catalan flag or anthem, pre-existed nationalism, although it is only with the latter that they received their modern political meaning.

Early nationalists, both Catalan and Basque, often met with apathy in rural areas where the language was still widely spoken. In these areas, which normally supported the Carlists, the defence of the ethnic tongue was not an object of mobilisations. In times of rapid urbanisation, it was seen rather as an annoying obstacle to geographical and social mobility. Like most modern nationalisms, Basque nationalism was born as a typically urban phenomenon. Industrialism, urbanisation, increased state control, the abolition of local rights and laws, and particularly immigration from Castile produced an explosive situation that was later to find its political expression through nationalism. Modernisation was a 'challenge to Basque identity and as such it needed to be tackled, and only nationalism could provide the tool for such a task' (Payne 1975). Paradoxically its full success came nearly a century later in the 1980s. Today both Basque and Catalan nationalism can be counted among the most popular recent examples of nation-making in Western Europe. The next two chapters chart this evolution.

4

EUSKADI: DICTATORSHIP, RESISTANCE
AND RESURRECTION

The focus of this chapter is on the 1950s and 1960s, the period when a new nationalist movement slowly emerged departing sharply from Arana's neo-traditionalism. We shall see how deeply the concept of Basque identity changed, relating this change to the massive socio-economic and demographic upheavals resulting from dictatorship and rapid economic development. The period of greatest interest begins in 1952, when the first radical student grouping was formed, and lasts up to about 1970, when all significant ideological debate ceased. Yet it is after 1970 that the message began to spread among the general population. Before coming to the 1950s, we address the historical and structural factors which brought about this radical change. The chapter's data is drawn from both secondary and primary sources (the writings of the nationalist leaders, newspaper excerpts and magazine quotations).

The darkest years

Beltza (1977) divides the period which followed the imposition of Francoist centralisation into four phases: 1939-45 (exile and clandestine activity), when the nationalist government-in-exile was in a precarious position due to the possibility of an Axis victory and the Nazi occupation of France; 1945-47 (the 'golden years'), when the Basque Republicans tried to channel Allied action against fascism in the aftermath of the second World War; 1948-52 (the fall), with the onset of the Cold War and the tacit rehabilitation of Franco as a potential bulwark against Soviet influence; and 1953-60 (the new nationalism), parallel to the radicalisation of the youth, with the slow fossilisation of the PNV after the opening of Franco's Spain to the West.

From 1939 to 1945, the Basque country was subjected to a regime of state terror with no parallel in its history. Once they had occupied the Basque provinces, Franco's troops initiated a vindictive campaign of repression against any sign of Basque identity. Even innocuous aspects of popular culture, such as dance and music, were subjected to suspicion, inquiry and proscription.[1] A sketchy picture of this repression, which paralleled the Catalan one, is included in a message to UNESCO written in 1952 by José Antonio Aguirre (1904-60), then president of the Basque government-in-exile. He denounced the following: closure of the Basque university; occupation by armed force of social and cultural associations; mass burning of books in Euskera; elimination of all use of Euskera in schools, on radio broadcasts, in public gatherings and in publications; suppression of Basque cultural societies and of all magazines, periodicals and reviews in Euskera; prohibition of the use of Euskera during the celebration of Mass and other religious ceremonies; a decree requiring the translation into Spanish of all Basque names in civil registries and official documents; and an official directive mandating the removal of inscriptions in Euskera from all tombstones and funeral markers (Aguirre in Beltza 1977: 134-6 and Clark 1979: 137).[2]

Such were the ensuing atrocities that the Carlist supporters of Franco could no longer tolerate them and intervened to stem the actions of the vigilante squads (Clark 1979: 82). In the very first years after the Civil War, innumerable people were imprisoned or executed on the pretext of promoting 'separatism'. The number of exiles ranged from 100,000 to 150,000, including more than 20,000 children (Legarreta 1984). A Basque diaspora spread throughout France, Latin America, and other Western countries. At the same time, the oligarchic bourgeoisie sided with Franco, thereby stamping a sinister class mark on state repression (Espinosa 1989, Zirakzadeh 1991).

From 1945 to 1947, in the aftermath of the world war, the Basque Republicans tried to drag the Allies into opposition against the dictatorship. The above message by Aguirre, written when Spain was knocking on UNESCO's door, is an example of the international pressures which the Basque government-in-exile tried to exert. Overall, their impact was limited. In 1945, a Basque Consult-

---

[1] On Basque dance as a symbol of national identity, see Lamarca (1976).

[2] On the repression of Euskara, see Nuñez (1977), Urrutia (1977) and Euskaltzaindia (1977).

ative Council (*Consejo Consultativo Vasco*) was set up in exile as an alliance of the most important Basque parties and labour unions, both leftists and nationalists. The Council was charged with coordinating the action of a Resistance Committee (*Junta de Resistencia*) inside Spanish territory. The Resistance Committee announced a strike on 1 May 1947. As 75 per cent of the workers in Vizcayá answered the call, the government reacted with a state of siege and the successful mobilisation slowly died out. This experience taught the activists that an alliance between the nationalists and the Left was capable of mobilising large sectors of the working class, although it failed to ignite other classes and spread to other regions. Nationalism had demonstrated its ability to unite broad sectors of society, transcending class divisions and withstanding harsh repression. Moreover, during the workers' mobilisation, a younger generation started to assume leadership roles in the movement (Clark 1979: 104-6).

Young nationalists had previously attempted an ephemeral political experience. A Society of Basque Students (*Euzko Ikasle Alkartasuna*, EIA) was set up in the 1940s as an apolitical association with its main seat in Leiden, the Netherlands. In 1947 they started to hold political meetings in the French Basque Country, but soon their activity began to spill over across the Spanish border, where they distributed clandestine leaflets and journals. The organisation was easily uncovered by the Spanish police and in 1951 all its local leaders were either arrested or forced to go into exile, leaving EIA completely dismantled. The rapidity with which the police dealt this fatal blow taught them a bitter lesson as they vowed never again to act except in complete secrecy.[3] In this year also a general strike in Bilbao signalled the end of the Resistance Committee. The strike was successful, but as a consequence 'the repression imposed from Madrid was so intense that the network of clandestine cells within Spain was left in ruins' (Clark 1984: 23). At the same time, the Western powers withdrew their support from the Basque government in exile, dominated by the PNV. Thus the Basque country, and especially the nationalists, faced a desperate isolation and most of them lost all hope.

From 1947 onwards with the onset of the Cold War, the Francoists succeeded in slowly coming in from the cold. Clark

---

[3] Interview with Txillardegi (quoted in Ibarzábal 1978: 362). See also Eugenio Ibarzábal (1978), 'Así nació ETA', *Muga*, no. 1, 1979, pp. 77-89.

(1979: 93-102) offers a good description of the precedents and the subsequent steps which led to the overture of the United States towards Franco's regime, lured by the possibility of opening a military base in the peninsula.[4] Spain became successively a member of the World Health Organisation (1951), UNESCO (1952), and the United Nations itself (1955). In 1953 Spain signed a bilateral treaty with the United States and a concordat with the Vatican. Thus the Basques were among the several illustrious victims of the Cold War. The failure of Western democracies, especially Britain and the United States, to isolate and exert pressures on the regime 'led the Basques to conclude that they could not depend on outside assistance' (Clark 1979: 80).[5] This is one of the crucial features which helps to explain the birth of ETA less than ten years later.

From Ekin to ETA (1952-1959)

The PNV which had played a key role under the Republic, now seemed incapable of responding to the new challenges and became increasingly de-legitimised. Its forced idleness and prudent attitude contrasted with growing nationalist unrest among the youth.[6] In the 1950s the Basque economy was still at a standstill, but towards the end of the decade, a phase of expansion began. As a result many Basques, including traditional PNV supporters, began to prosper and benefit from the regime's policies. Fearful of government repression, most PNV members appeared less interested than ever in Basque nationalism, except in promoting marginal cultural events and folkloric activities. However, one should not exaggerate the PNV's passivity. In 1956 a World Basque Congress was held in Paris to celebrate the twentieth anniversary of the Basque government.[7] Financed by exiled Basque businessmen, 363 people of all

[4] On Basque refugees, especially children, see Legarreta (1984, 1985).

[5] Before this, the United States government refused admission to refugees from the Spanish Civil War (Legarreta 1985: 194-6, Clark 1979: 91). Hence most of them chose to live in Venezuela, Mexico, Uruguay and Argentina.

[6] The exiled *lehendakari* José Antonio Aguirre recognised that at a time of general disillusionment 'one of the most consoling phenomena in the last 16 years . . . has been the enthusiastic adhesion of the Basque youth to the ideals of freedom for their people' (cited by Jáuregui 1981: 75).

[7] Its four sections were: Politics, Culture, Socio-Economic Aspects and the Basque Diaspora.

political persuasions were invited to participate (except the Communists, who were excluded in a further attempt to please the Americans). It has been remarked that 'never before had there been such a gathering of the Basque intellectuals and political élite' (Clark, in Aguirre 1991: 13). But all this activity was carried out abroad, and within the Basque country itself a sense of utter despair prevailed.

This situation inevitably created a generational crisis. Tired of the general impasse but also frustrated by the 'obsolete' PNV's ideology, a group of university students in Bilbao started to hold weekly meetings to study and discuss Basque history and culture. In the beginning, in 1952, there were only six or seven of them, all in their early twenties.[8] This clandestine activity 'uncovered for them an unknown world which [state] terrorism under Franco had relegated to the category of a non-existent reality. Thus, in their readings they discovered Basque nationalism and anti-Francoist resistance. Their formative period was relatively long and intense . . .' (Jáuregui 1986: 571).[9] An irregular bulletin, *Ekin* (To do), was their underground organ and gave its name to the group.[10] At the beginning the PNV was kept in the dark about their existence. For four years they worked secretly with ardent commitment, on their own initiative alone, and confined themselves to purely intellectual tasks.[11] But their activities were eventually 'discovered' by the PNV – this was inevitable since they were all raised in nationalist families. The reception was cool, circumspect and ridden with mutual incomprehensions.[12]

[8] Different sources give different names and estimates of numbers for Ekin's early members. Some authors (themselves early members) mention a handful participants in Ekin's seminars (i.e. *Kemen*, 1964, in *Documentos Y*, vol. 1, p. 434), while others claim there were at least a dozen.

[9] At the beginning, they read exclusively nationalist textbooks such as Arana, Eleizalde and Aranzadi, all of which were outlawed and very difficult to obtain. 'What united them was a lively awareness of national oppression, a great interest for the Basque language – the majority of them ignored it and would learn it – and an ethnic vision of Euskadi' (Ortzi 1977: 279).

[10] At the first meetings only seven copies, plus the original, were duplicated for exclusive internal consumption (*Documentos Y*, vol. 1, p. 434), but in a few years the demand grew rapidly.

[11] Despite the name *Ekin*, their actions did not contemplate much direct intervention in political life. They even reproached the PNV youth sections for being too active and 'inconsiderate' (lbarzábal, Eugenio, 'Así nació ETA', op. cit.).

[12] From this moment onwards the scholar is faced with twin materials and

Another group also maintained a modest amount of political activity. This was EGI (*Euzko Gastedi del Interior,*) the youth cell of the PNV. Ekin members worked hard to keep in touch and join forces with the latter. They succeeded for a while (1956-9), when Ekin and EGI merged under the PNV's patronage. Since the intellectual level of Ekin was far higher than that of EGI, the PNV assigned to the Ekin leaders the task of educating EGI. At the same time, the fusion with EGI presented the previously isolated intellectuals of Ekin with a unique opportunity to spread their political credo to a greater numbers of young activists. EGI membership consisted of local militants, most living in small towns and villages within the Basque cultural heartland. At that time, the EGI activists were just beginning to operate more or less in the open since repressive measures had been partly lifted. As EGI's activities were purely nostalgic, 'folkloric' and had scarcely any intellectual impact, they could be tolerated by the regime.[13] But this mixture of inoffensive 'openness' and 'folklorism' appeared to be a serious problem to Ekin members, who were much more ambitious. Furthermore, the partly open character of the organisation threatened their personal safety and deprived them of freedom of speech.[14]

---

diametrically opposed versions of the events, one by the moderates (PNV), the other by the radicals (Ekin). It is a hard task to draw an objective balance between the two.

[13] See *Documentos Y*, vol. 1, p. 76 (*Notas a los 'Cuadernos de Ekin'*). The older generation subsequently reversed the accusation, blaming the Ekin group for being 'culturalists'. Thus, the PNV leader Jesús Solaun recalled that 'our problem with them [was] to demand that they did something more than the promotion of Euskara and the study of history. . . . By that time, Ekin was nothing more than a group dedicated to intellectual labour; they did not admit anybody, neither agreed to do illegal works, since they did not want to arouse police suspicions'. See J. Solaun (1980), 'Memorias de antifascismo', *Muga*, 3, pp. 35-46. While Ekin accused the PNV of 'folklorism', the PNV accused Ekin of 'intellectualism', not a compliment in the reactionary atmosphere of those years (Morán 1982: 268).

[14] In the 1950s the regime felt secure enough to relax repression and its grip on Basque activities. Nevertheless, concealment was still a must for any committed *abertzale*. Ekin worked in the most secretive conditions and its members were bonded by an oath of total silence over their activities (lbarzábal 1979: 78). Some of their early documents concluded with the following sentence: *irakurri ta gero erre egizu* (read it and then burn it). Euskara was rightly deemed to be an extremely difficult tongue to learn by the 'oppressors'. Its use in ETA's internal communications has prompted the Spanish police to set special courses of Euskara for their

Reciprocal accusations between the PNV an Ekin–EGI of being American agents became increasingly frequent after what was perceived as the great American betrayal.[15] Previously Aguirre had been a firm friend of the United States and an admirer of American society, to the point that he believed his party was liable to receive the same kind of American protection as that enjoyed by other European Christian Democratic parties (Aguirre 1991).[16] During the 1940s the PNV's *Servicios*, an intelligence organisation set up during the war for the benefit of the Allies, still used to pass secret information on the internal situation of Spain to the American services. Since the pro-American stance of the PNV remained unchanged over the years, many nationalists had serious reasons to worry that the information which the *Servicios* was passing to the Americans was in turn given to Franco.

Furthermore, the excessively zealous control exercised by the PNV over the youth soon became a hindrance to Ekin's own evolution. The spontaneous character of Ekin and its enthusiastic attitude made it hard to control, thereby arousing the mistrust of the old guard. When in 1959 Ekin definitively broke off its alliance with the PNV, it took with it most of the EGI youth.

The disappointing encounter with the *peneuvistas* (PNV cadres) contrasted with the idealisation of nationalism during Ekin's formative years. The conservative control of the old generation 'collided head-on with the mentality of the members of Ekin, who had been accustomed . . . to investigate and search for an answer to all questions' (Jáuregui 1986: 572, 1981: 81). Pérez-Agote (1984) describes this as a generation break in the face of the alleged inactivity of their predecessors.[17] The PNV had a bad press in most radical propaganda,

---

forces quartered in the region. The mastering of Euskara also has an initiatory component which allows the neophyte to penetrate the holiest of holies of the organisation. However, learning the language was not mandatory and many members could barely understand it.

[15] When the level of tension rose further, some PNV leaders used to blame the Ekin group of being Communists. Similar accusations and other epithets were part of a demonisation propaganda espoused by the old leaders, at a time when Ekin was still far removed from any Marxist leanings.

[16] On Aguirre's pro-Americanism, see Ortzi (1975: 259–71) and Aguirre himself (1991).

[17] One of ETA's ideologues synthesised the problem as follows: 'They [the old nationalists] had obtained something. We cannot deny that they won an

but kept its support among the *baserritarrak* (farmers). Hence, the accusation that it was a bourgeois party is only partly true. The lack of open channels of communication and the secretive environment of those years were an ideal recipe for misunderstandings.

The PNV was then acting as little more than a neo-traditionalist group, since it saw Basque festivals and cultural events as, in themselves, directly political activities (Bruni 1980). Its ideas of culture and nation had to be articulated in a fairly static, conservative and folkloric way so as not to arouse the suspicions of the regime. By contrast, Ekin members were not only committed revivalists, anxious that Basque culture be saved and preserved, but also eager to promote it as a means of expression for a modern community. This goal could only be achieved by political means, and because during the dictatorship this was not an option, it had to be worked out clandestinely. That is, since political constrictions hampered any possibility of cultural self-expression, the 'culturalists' had both to devise strategies of cultural maintenance and to wage a secret struggle to change the order of things.

The 'emerging' generation were young enough to be impatient with the inertia of their fathers, but old enough to remember the atrocities committed by Madrid after the fall of the Republic. They could neither forgive nor forget these atrocities and the impending menace of destruction of the Basque heritage. At the same time, they could not wait for formal niceties or permit the bureaucratic fetters placed by the PNV on any spontaneous initiatives. They therefore decided to take the serious personal risk of organising active resistance against the regime. Probably, much of the PNV members' aloofness and distrust for the Ekin group stemmed from their concern about the danger of such a choice, since it acted as a magnet for many of their children. With the experience of the Civil War and its endless atrocities still fresh, the old generation were terrified by the prospects that their children and country might undergo a similar fate. The leaders of Ekin reacted to this invitation

---

autonomous government during the Republic. Even if not much, this was something, hence they vigorously defended it to their teeth in front of the new generation which was beginning to call them to account for their inaction. But they did not realise that the Autonomy Statute was part of a body called the Second Spanish Republic and that, with the latter's death, the Statute was buried along with it. Thus, they were wishing to keep alive part of a putrescent body' (Krutwig 1963: 11).

to prudence by radicalising their posture with a juvenile defiance which bordered on a belief in immortality.[18]

The main leader and intellectual figure of the group was Txillardegi (José Luís Alvarez Emparanza), then a twenty-three-year-old engineering student and a member of the Basque Language Academy –he later wrote several prize-winning novels in Euskara and rarely used Castilian. Other founding members were Julen K. Madariaga, José Mari Benito del Valle, José Manuel Aguirre and Jon Nicolas, who were later among ETA's founders and leaders.[19] People like Txillardegi felt that the very existence of the Basques was under threat.

Ekin expanded through personal contacts with friends and trustworthy acquaintances, especially in the rural heartland where the preservation of Basque culture was regarded as a guarantee of loyalty and anti-regime feelings. Since the beginning, the group had considered the possibility of armed actions as the means both to defeat Francoism and to revitalise a nation on the verge of losing its cultural identity. This second idea – of violence as a redeeming and regenerating force – was to take root slowly, steadily and almost imperceptibly. Its most ardent proponent was Madariaga, who defined Basque resistance as a form of anti-colonial struggle. The use of violence had been sporadically advocated as early as the 1940s (Garmendia and Elordi 1982: 174 ff.). However, the leadership of Ekin was more prone to follow Arana's mandate of passive resistance at a time when echoes of Gandhism were still in evidence.[20]

---

[18] Personal observation by William Douglass and Joseba Zulaika.

[19] Eugenio Ibarzábal, 'Asi nació ETA', *Muga*, no. 1, 1979, p. 78, mentions also G. Ansola, M. Barandiaran, A. Irigoyén, R. Albisu, I. Larramendi and I. Gainzarain as first members of Ekin. According to Ibarzábal, Gainzarain exercised the main influence. However, this list is not fully reliable, and we have to compare it with other ones. The most reliable data is probably the testimony of the protagonists included in *Documentos Y*, vol. 1, which gives us the following list: Benito del Valle, Txillardegi, Aguirre, Madariaga, Larramendi, Albisu and others whom it is 'better not to mention' (in *Kemen*, p. 434). García de Cortázar and Montero (1983: 1: 259) mention Aguirre, del Valle, Gainzarain, Madariaga and Txillardegi.

[20] Only a few years later, ETA reversed these assumptions holding that 'non-violent methods do not seem to yield results except under relatively honest regimes. Gandhi achieved [Indian] independence from the British socialists, not from a Franco or a Stalin' (*Zutik – Tercera Series*/n.s., no. 6, 1963, p. 9. Reprinted in *Documentos Y*, vol. 2, p. 283).

The greatest single intellectual influence on the formation of the Ekin group, particularly on Txillardegi, came from French existentialism. [21] The later support of Jean-Paul Sartre for the Basque cause, with his sincere sympathy for ETA's liberation struggle, was highly significant.[22] The first 'philosophical' seminars at the University of Deusto were characterised by an extremely eclectic approach, drawing from an array of sources: first Unamuno (as a Basque), then Maritain, Duverger, Nicolas Berdiaeff, Don Luigi Sturzo, Monsignor Ancel and St Paul.[23] The goal of all these discussions was not to proselytise but to reflect on the present situation of Euskadi and find some solution to its problems.[24] At the World Basque Congress of 1956 in Paris, Aguirre and Del Valle presented a paper on the Basque youth.[25]

The disenchantment with the PNV was the immediate cause of the breakthrough event in modern Basque history, the foundation of ETA (*Euzkadi 'ta Askatasuna*, Basque Land and Freedom) in 1959.[26] With the birth of ETA, the PNV ceased to be the only legitimate representative of Basque nationalism, and a whole new chapter of Basque history opened up. The American 'betrayal' of the Basques is one of the key reasons why the organisation subsequently took a Leftist and even Trotskyist turn, the other two key

[21] See Txillardegi's interviews in *Garaia*, vol. 1, no. 1, 1976, pp. 24-5, in Ibarzábal (1978: 363), and his two novels (*Leturiaren Egunkari Ezkutua* and *Peru Leartzako*). In particular, see the paper by Marc Lagasse on 'Le "séparatisme basque". Est-il un existentialisme?' (Lagasse 1951) and the frequent mentions of Albert Camus in several issues of *Zutik*.

[22] Sartre's ideas and the first ETA shared a lot more in common than has usually been admitted. See the notes of the subsequent paragraph on the Burgos trial.

[23] As mentioned by Jon Nicolas, 'El grupo Ekin y los primeros pasos', *Documentos Y*, vol. 1, pp. 25-8.

[24] Jon Nicolas: *Ibid.*

[25] The paper, signed by 'Ekin', dealt with economic welfare of the youth, focussing on the ideological influence of communism. See 'Grupo Ekin', 'Situación social de la juventud vasca' In *Euskal Batzar Orokorra. Congreso Mundial Vasco. 2° aniversario*, Vitoria: Gobierno Vasco/Eusko Jaurlaritza, 1987, pp. 264-5.

[26] Garmendia (1979) quotes four reasons for the birth and expansion of ETA: (1) the persistence of Basque nationalism; (2) a crisis in Basque traditional values resulting from economic changes in the 1950s; (3) the failure of the PNV's policies, especially its pro-Americanism; and (4) the attraction of other liberation movements (Cuba, Algeria, Israel).

elements being immigration (with its class nature) and ideological diffusion (with the leftist vogue spreading over Europe in the 1960s).

The origins of ETA: its first steps and ideology (1959-1968)

ETA was founded on 31 July 1959 by the same group of Ekin youth who broke away from the PNV after uniting with EGI.[27] In the first months their activity was limited to continuing the labour of study and reflection which they had already done as Ekin. The organisation was divided into six branches,[28] and membership fell into two categories: the militants, who swore an oath of silence, and the sympathisers, who did not.[29] A few graffiti on walls and the hanging of *ikurriñas* (Basque flags) was the sum of their external activity (Garmendia 1979: 21).[30] Originally, ETA was essentially a cultural movement, concerned with the fate of Euskera and local culture.[31] For years it remained a marginal group, appealing to a few hundred young activists and sympathisers disillusioned by the lack of impetus and political activity of the PNV. The industrial development of the 1960s brought about an impoverishment and radicalisation of the small bourgeoisie and the proletarisation of rural people (Garmendia 1979), and many ETA members came from such backgrounds. The conflict was exacerbated by immigration.

Immediately on its formation, ETA chose an intransigent line rekindling old Aranist idiosyncrasies, i.e. the rejection of all things Spanish through the re-appropriation of Arana's myths (Basque primitive independence, egalitarianism, social justice, the idea of the

---

[27] Most of EGI's youth followed the new organisation. In Gipuzkoa three-quarters, in Vizcaya six-ninths and in Navarra and Alava all of the EGI sections joined the successors of Ekin.

[28] The six branches were: Secretariat (which edited internal bulletins and other publications), Groups (which organised study classes), Euskara (dedicated to the study and diffusion of the language), Legal Action (entrusted with the promotion of semi-legal actions), Propaganda (devoted to printing and distributing all publications) and Military.

[29] See *Documentos Y*, vol. 1, p. 22.

[30] On the banning of the *ikurriña* and on those patriots who risked their lives flying it, see Bereciartúa (1977). On Basque nationalist graffiti, see Chaffee (1988, 1993).

[31] According to Pérez-Agote, it is impossible to understand the birth of ETA without considering its initial evaluation of language (1984: 91).

Basques as a noble, democratic and freedom-loving people). However, it also rejected the centrality of race and religion, the two basic tenets of Arana's ideology. The shift from race to language as a preferred vehicle of Basque identity implied a new anxiety to halt the fading of Basque cultural distinctiveness: as declared by ETA, 'once language is lost' race could not sustain Basque identity.[32] Thus the people were 'chosen' by their history, mores and language, not by their religion or descent.

The first acts of political violence occurred in 1961, when a few explosions shattered government buildings in different cities, but responsibility for them was not claimed. On 18 July ETA placed an explosive pack on a railway line in an attempt to derail a number of trains carrying Francoist Civil War veterans. The plot was easily discovered since the explosion was far too weak to derail the train but was still clearly heard.[33] A wave of arrests followed among Basque activists and their sympathisers: 110 ETA members were imprisoned, many of them were tortured, and another 100 or more were forced into exile (Ibarz 1981: 95). These numbers testify to the impressive growth of the organisation. In 1953 Ekin had been made up of five militants in Bilbao, and as many in Donostia. By 1960 more than 300 militants had passed through its *cursillos de formación* (training courses).[34]

Despite this blow, ETA continued its underground activity, inaugurating a long period of reflection. Although deeply imbued with Aranism,[35] ETA's intellectual were quite knowledgeable about European progressive thought, Third World struggles and Marxist analysis. In the early 1960s ETA's leaders started to bring to light

---

[32] From *Cuadernos de ETA*, cited in Garmendia (1979: 22). As observed by Garmendia (1979: 23), ETA seemed occasionally to revert to racial essentialism, especially in its panegyrics for persecuted militants. The noble racial features of an imprisoned or murdered activist were idealised and his/her martyrdom presented as an edifying prototype worthy of imitation. But this aesthetic of 'race' was not associated with racism, which was firmly rejected by ETA as Arana's most pernicious legacy. The aesthetic of masculine beauty and physical strength is still visible in traditional sport competitions.

[33] 'Characteristically for that time, the attempt was made with such precautions that it failed to derail even a single car, and there was not so much as one injury' (Clark 1984: 35). See also Hollyman (1976).

[34] Interview with Txillardegi, reported in *Garaia*, *op. cit.*

[35] Jáuregui (1981) defines ETA's foundation as a revival of Aranism.

the results of years of study and discussion. The first issue of the journal *Zutik* ('Stand up!')[36] and the circular *Cuadernos de ETA* (also called *Cuadernos de Formación*, Training Notes) began to appear respectively in 1961 and 1962.[37]

ETA's First Assembly was held in exile in 1962, and on that occasion the leadership promulgated a 'Declaration of Principles' synthesising the previous activities and outlining the organisation's trends.[38] ETA was defined as a 'revolutionary Basque movement for national liberation' (Garmendia 1979: 19-21), yet it advanced no clear political programme or new theory. However, the organisation was henceforth structured into cells of *liberados*, full-time activists who were to be totally dedicated to its mission and to live in secrecy. A radical change came with the infusion of Marxist ideology and, especially, with the opening up to Third World perspectives. The first full ideological formulation and political programme to be adopted by ETA appeared in the book *Vasconia* (1963) by Federico Krutwig, the son of a German industrialist living in Bilbao, who adopted the pseudonym F. Sarrailh de Ihartza. Krutwig, described as a 'solitary franc-tireur' (Ortzi 1977: 280), was an ex-secretary of the Basque Language Academy and had never been a member of ETA.[39] Despite its numerous distortions and exaggerations, *Vasconia*

[36] The early 1960s were still a period of reflection and debate. *Zutik* warmly solicited its readers to submit any kind of criticism on its contents. It also issued calls for papers, projects, ideas, various information, data etc. (*Documentos Y*, vol. 2, p. 317). All ETA's historical debates were published in *Zutik*. 'Most of ETA's political history is inseparable from the efforts to publish in *Zutik*. . . . It is possible to say that for many years ETA existed in the measure in which *Zutik* was published. And the internal conflicts and schisms focussed around the control of *Zutik*' (*Documentos Y*, vol. 2, p. 380). Thus 'control of the magazine came to be highly prized in the infighting that ensued over the years. When splinter groups split off from the parent organisation, they usually established a counterpart journal to maintain the flow of words and ideas' (Clark 1984: 29).

[37] Every issue of the *Cuadernos de ETA* was dedicated to a single theme. As in Ekin's days, each leading member of the organisation was charged with investigating a specific topic and preparing an ensuing *cuaderno* (notebook). Each issue had an essential bibliography, on the basis of which it is possible to establish the international ideological influences exerted on the militants (Conversi 1993).

[38] As a consequence of repression, only four members of ETA remained in Spain after the First Assembly. This precariousness did not deter ETA from launching a series of frenetic activities, such as the adhesion to workers' struggle, the enrollment of women, the extension of activities in Navarre, printing, producing propaganda, etc. (see *Documentos Y*, vol. 2, p. 5).

remains the key text of contemporary Basque nationalism, and is probably the only work which has been welcomed by ETA as *vox populi*. Txillardegi defined it as 'the most important book on Euskadi published in this century'. Why did this provocative book attain such unparalleled success? The answer probably lies in its straightforward language and the way in which controversial statements are put forward as indisputable truths. Its dry prose admits no doubts, yet the book's many contradictions and ambiguities seem to satisfy most of ETA's currents: the Aranists, the European federalists, the proponents of armed struggle, the believers, the secularists, the Marxists and the 'culturalists' (Jáuregui 1981: 223-4). Interpreting the new spirit of defiance to dictatorship, *Vasconia* offered the new generation both a youthful sense of immortality and a mission.[40] It provided a series of cleverly presented dogmas which served to solidify the otherwise fragmented movement.

A double shift: from religion to secularism, from Americanism to Marxism

Krutwig's programme included an updated recovery of many elements of Aranism, but, as mentioned earlier, the latter was cleansed of its racial and religious overtones. Race was replaced by the concept of *ethnos*, as manifested through language and culture, and the missionary fervour implied in Arana's Christian vision was replaced by the idea of politics as a vocation. *Vasconia* was also a ferocious attack on the Church as an agent of de-nationalisation and an enemy of the people (Krutwig 1963: 75ff.).[41] Ancient

---

[39] At the first World Basque Congress in Paris (1956), Krutwig presented a hasty report on Basque language and territory, which many attendants saw as the rantings of a lunatic, but which nevertheless stimulated a vivid debate. He argued that 'violence' was necessary to create a Basque nation: 'The Americans would have not backed Franco if a group of organised violence was opposing him. . . . If the Basques will keep on acting as a docile people, the world will never take them seriously'. Also language was 'more important than the Rh factor in blood groups'. At first Krutwig stressed a federalist (or cantonalist) union of Basque territories. See Federico Krutwig, 'El echo vasco, el euskera, y el territorio de Euskadi', in *Euskal Batzar Orokorra. Congreso Mundial Vasco. 2º aniversario*, Vitoria: Gobierno Vasco/ Eusko Jaurlaritza, 1987, pp. 130-1.

[40] Personal communication by Joseba Zulaika.

[41] An enormous distrust towards the Church radically opposed Ekin to the old nationalists; it was defined as an 'aconfessional patriotic movement' (Ortzi 1977: 279).

Basque paganism was 'recovered' as an alternative to the current Church's impotence, and the Basques' late conversion to Christianity was put forward as a further proof of their immemorial independence. Although the Christian ethic was still part of ETA's vision, this did not imply the primacy of the Church over the state, the latter ideal having been abandoned even by the post-war PNV. In particular, since the Church was associated with the regime through the doctrine of *nacionalcatolicismo,* only the most universal principles of Catholicism were retained. This did not clash with the subsequent Marxist evolution of ETA, but rather reinforced the militants' commitment in their drive for social justice. Indeed priests, monks, and former seminarians continued to flow into ETA till long after its Marxist–Trotskyist 'conversion'.[42]

A constant feature of Basque life since the end of the Civil War has been astonishment and resentment at the Church siding with Franco and 'betraying' the Basque cause. After the phase of Falangist 'terror', many firm believers tacitly questioned the Church's behaviour, asking repeatedly 'Why this silence by the [Catholic] hierarchy?' (Sierra Bustamante 1941: 204-11). The memory of anti-clerical atrocities was not a sufficient excuse for justifying repression on such a scale.[43] The Church came under fire from most of the clandestine opposition. Basque priests and seminarians were

[42] Many people raised in Catholic seminars entered ETA's ranks between 1967 and 1972. This period has been ironically described by the playwright Father Pierre Larzabal as the 'clerical phase' of ETA (cited in the entry 'ETA', *Enciclopaedia General Ilustrada del Pais Vasco,* San Sebastian: Auñamendi, 1970- [21 vols, last vols still in preparation at time of writing], vol. 12, p. 126). Again, Krutwig compares the guerrilla fighter to a crusader, for 'the spirit which pervades him must spring up over all sides as the faith of the medieval knight. Revolutionary war is thus an ideological combat similar to the medieval one. To a certain extent it is a religious war, and, as in the latter, the revolutionary must promise to redeem the humble' (Krutwig 1963: 330).

[43] Even President Aguirre, leader of the PNV, normally described as a Christian Democratic party (Brezzi 1979), emphatically recalled that the atrocities committed by Franco's troops were far more devastating. 'Both the "Red hordes" and the "White hordes" were guilty of burning, pillaging and murder. But when all the truth is known, the world will be even more horrified by the bloody accomplishment of the White hordes than it was over the tales of the "Red atrocities". I can state categorically that the victims executed by Franco's regime are far more numerous than the victims made to suffer at the hands of certain hangers-on of the Republic' (Aguirre 1991: 307-8).

particularly sensitive to such recurrent accusations (Iztueta 1981). In 1960, three years before the publication of *Vasconia* and less than one year after ETA's creation, the lower clergy came out into the open for the first time: 339 priests of the dioceses of Gasteiz (Vitoria), Donostia (San Sebastián) and Bilbao signed a joint petition to their bishops denouncing the political and cultural oppression of Euskadi. With unprecedented courage, the manifesto defined the official policy as 'reactionary and anti-human to the point of genocide'.[44] The importance of the Basque language as an instrument of evangelisation was particularly stressed. With this action the Basque priests put their personal safety seriously at risk, but the Church in other parts of Spain (and the Vatican) did not display solidarity with the protesters. This stiff attitude on the part of the Church was another factor in encouraging many believers to join ETA or support its activists.

Another mainstay of *Vasconia* is the stress on action. According to Jáuregui (1981: 152), Krutwig's ideas were directly derived from Ernest Renan's (1823-92) voluntaristic view of the nation as a 'daily plebiscite'. As discussed later, the concept of voluntary participation is central to the evolution of all present-day Basque nationalism. However, *Vasconia's* most relevant contribution was strategic with its choice of guerrilla war as the only way to liberate Euskadi. In this choice, Krutwig was directly inspired by the Algerian and Cuban experiences. A further impulse in this direction came from the works of Franz Fanon (1925-61). Fanon rationalised anticolonial violence as a liberating and purifying principle, essential to the psychological well-being of the 'oppressed'. This 'Third-Worldist' approach was opposed to the pre-existing pro-European and federalist trends, and the underlying opposition it implied continued right up to the 1990s (Conversi 1993b).

A further step forward in the definition of ETA's programme came in 1963 with José Luís Zalbide's booklet *Insurrección en Eus-*

---

[44] *Escrito presentado a los excmos. obispos de Vitoria, San Sebastian, Bilbao y Pamplona, con las firmas de 339 sacerdotes de dichas diocesis, el dia 30 de Mayo de 1960,* reprinted in *Documentos Y,* vol. 1, 128-33. Most of the signing priests were PNV members who took a considerable risk in raising their voices after decades of silence. Once the first 339 priests signed the document, many more added their signatures. An overall climate of scepticism and rebellion began to creep amongst the lower clergy pitting it against the upper hierarchy. This is a frequent occurrence in nationalist movements (Smith, personal observation).

kadi,[45] which synthesised those parts of Krutwig's programme dealing with armed struggle. Intended as a guerrilla manual, it can be
seen as the cornerstone of the strategy of ETA's military branch. The
influence of Mao Tse-tung and Ho Chi Minh is evident in many
parts of the pamphlet.[46] The theses of Krutwig and Zalbide were
approved in ETA's Second Assembly (1963), in which Euskadi was
divided into six operative zones (*herrialdes*) with the aim of carrying
out the revolutionary war. Thus local theorists began to conceive
armed struggle as their primary concern, with violence as the only
means of rescuing Euskadi from its secular torpor.[47] In 1963 ETA
participated for the first time in the organisation of working–class
strikes. Although the theorists kept a low profile and a secondary
organisational role, they had to bear the brunt of the repression; the
state could barely allow the airing of economic grievances, but it
could never tolerate ones couched in ethnic terms.

The Third Assembly (1964) wholeheartedly adopted Krutwig's
approach defining ETA as an anti–imperialist and anti–capitalist
organisation working for the liberation of Euskadi and the emancipation of the working class. Zalbide wrote his *Carta a los intellec-
tuales* ('Letter to the intellectuals') which postulated the basic
principles to be adopted by ETA.[48] At the same time, the founding
fathers of Ekin/ETA were expelled from France and compelled to
seek refuge further away in Belgium. Henceforth, the physical
distance considerably hampered the flow of communication between the old and experienced leadership and the 'base', which

---

[45] Published anonymously as a special issue of *Cuadernos de ETA*, no. 20 (1964),
Bayonne: Goitziri. Reproduced in *Documentos Y*, vol. 3, pp. 20–71. The bibliography includes the main works of Che Guevara, Mao Tse-tung, Krutwig and,
especially, *La Guerre Révolutionnaire* by Claude Delmas, entire sections of which are
reproduced. It may also be possible that *Insurrección en Euskadi* was written by
Madariaga, ETA's first proponent of armed struggle.

[46] Especially appreciated in radical milieux was the famous Maoist aphorism of
the guerrilla fighter who moves among his people as a 'fish in the water', a natural
element which he needs in order to survive (Krutwig 1963: 330). One of ETA's
features was indeed its symbiosis with the human environment of the Basque
hinterland.

[47] Still in 1962, there was no agreement on the use of violence within ETA. For
instance, *Zutik* no. 19 reported that 'between Gandhi's non-violence and a civil
war there are intermediate methods of struggle . . . which we want to put into
practice' (*Zutik*, 19 reported in *Documentos Y*, vol. 2, 229).

[48] Reprinted in Garmendia (1979: 287–303).

began to act on its own initiative. ETA then came under the control of young radicals who advocated revolutionary war.

During the Fourth Assembly (1965), the first one which took place *en el interior* (within Spain), the programmatic link between social and national struggle was firmly adopted. Class struggle and national liberation became the two faces of the same coin. Zalbide's *Insurrección en Euskadi* provided the guidelines of this turn of events and was approved by ETA as an article of faith. Its central tenet was Krutwig's theory of the 'cycle of action/repression/action', which held that 'where popular protest against injustices met with oppression, the revolutionary forces should act to punish the oppressor. The occupying forces would then retaliate with indiscriminate violence, since they would not know who the revolutionaries were, causing the population to respond with increased protest and support for the resistance in an upward spiral of resistance to the dictatorship' (Sullivan 1988: 42-43). This theory was to provide the overall framework of ETA's strategy throughout its long evolution since the publication of *Vasconia*. ETA started to assume a paramilitary form. The first direct armed attack was the robbing of a bank courier in 1965.

The main ideological rift of this period was the struggle between Trotskyists and Third-Worldists (*tercermundistas*), of whom the latter followed Krutwig's call for a Third World-style mass insurgency. This tension was at its peak when ETA convened its watershed Fifth Assembly (1966-67), which was spread over a long period of time.[49] Its first half (1966) consecrated a 'holy alliance' between the *tercermundistas* and the 'culturalist' faction (the one immediately descending from Ekin). This alliance occurred at the expense of the Maoists who formed a separate *ETA-Berri* (New ETA). It was the first split within ETA, but more were to follow. In the second and crucial half of the Fifth Assembly (1967), the new concept of *Pueblo Trabajador Vasco* (Basque Working People) was elaborated to rein-

[49] Garmendia (1979) confers a key importance to this period, when, after Zalbide's fall and the exile of many leaders, ETA was left under the control of the Political Bureau (*oficina política*) led by Paco Iturrioz. The theory of 'action/repression/action' was dismissed and a new cleavage arose between patriotic workers and alleged 'bourgeoise' nationalists. ETA began actively supporting the CC. OO. (*Comisiones Obreras*, the clandestine pro-Communist labour union) and to participate in unions' struggles.

force the notion that class struggle and nationalism were in pursuit of common interests.

ETA was divided into four fronts: cultural, economic, political and military. In the years to come, the great debate would be confined to the latter two, of which the Military Front eventually emerged victorious. The 'culturalists' and other original Ekin members formed a separate group, called *Branka* (1967), based on the name of their journal.[50] Each of these splits was preceded by intense ideological debate, mostly in a violent atmosphere of confrontation further polarised by secrecy and the fear of police intrusions. The political environment of those years could not allow the luxury of pluralism. Furthermore, ETA's logic demanded that one simple and unchallenged ideological choice be made in order to attract more conscripts from all classes. What occurred instead was a process of political fragmentation from which new leaders emerged or splinter groups were formed in an unceasing process of self-definition. Since the times of Ekin, discussions were marked by 'a permanent oscillation between humble claims of the mere right to doubt to the fanatical rejection of those who dared to question what just happened to become an unquestionable truth' (*Documentos Y*: 1: 10). It is important to consider that most people in Euskadi were unaware of these internal conflicts and saw ETA as a homogenous body. Holding a belief in ETA's ideological continuity, its external supporters and sympathisers understood these conflicts as nothing but detail.

The beginning of armed struggle

In the mean time the spiral of violence slowly escalated with the first armed bank robberies. Following one of these, on 7 June 1968, a car transporting two *etarras* (ETA members) was stopped at a roadblock. A gunfight erupted and a member of the *Guardia Civil* (Civil Guard) was killed, the first victim of ETA, but the car managed to escape.[51] However, at a second roadblock one

---

[50] This tradition of naming a group after the journal or bulletin which was their mouthpiece (*Ekin, Branka, Saioak* etc.), testifies to the spontaneity of the process and the lack of formalities in their creation and, generally, in the overall Basque political evolution during these years.

[51] '7 de junio de 1968. ETA aprieta el gatillo por primera vez', *La Vanguardia*, 5 June 1988, pp. 6-7 (report published on the occasion of the 20th anniversary of the beginning of armed struggle).

of the two *etarras*, Txabi Etxebarrieta, was hauled from the car and shot in cold blood. This was the *'casus belli'* for which the theorists of armed struggle were waiting. Popular indignation at the killing of Etxebarrieta broke out in mass demonstrations in every major city, town and village of Euskadi, and for weeks priests held masses in his memory. Etxebarrieta was now a hero and 'ETA's ranks swelled with new arrivals' (Clark 1984: 49).

Although the use of violence had been theorised at least since the late 1950s, the first premeditated political murder was carried out only in 1968. When the police commissioner, Melitón Manzanas, a notorious torturer, was about to enter his house on the afternoon of 2 August, he was shot dead with several bullets by a single assailant in front of his wife.[52] The government response was swift and ruthless. During a 'state of emergency', scores of suspected ETA sympathisers were rounded up, illegally detained, beaten and intimidated. Meanwhile, people filled the street in mass demonstrations. The first phase of the 'cycle of action/repression/action' had begun, but its heavy toll on the organisation forced its leaders to rethink its applicability. In 1968 Zalbide wrote from jail a new booklet, *Iraultza* or *Hacia una estrategia revolucionaria vasca* (Towards a Basque Revolutionary Strategy), which replaced his anti-colonialist thesis with a broader anti-imperialist perspective (Jáuregui 1981: 417).[53]

In 1969 the structure of ETA was severely disrupted by a further wave of arrests. Most of the leaders were forced into exile, where they rejoined the other main factions. The Sixth Assembly held in 1970 represented ETA's last serious theoretical debate, but ideological confusion reached its peak and a host of groups emerged from it more separate than ever. The Red Cells (*Céllulas Rojas*), focussing on the magazine *Saioak* ('Essays') and led by José Ezkubi, championed the extension of the struggle to the rest of Spain through contacts with working-class organisations. The *Milis*, originating

[52] Manzanas was one of the most hated figures in Euskadi. An article signed by Madariaga claimed that persons like Manzanas 'will pay dearly for their crimes' (*Zutik*, 1962, reprinted in *Documentos Y*, vol. 3, p. 301). These accusations were reiterated in other ETA publications (such as *Zutik*, no. 2, December 1961, in *Documentos Y*, vol. 1, p. 406).

[53] After being criticised by Krutwig and Beltza, Zalbide reformulated his thesis in *Fines y medios en la lucha de liberación nacional* (1970), which was subsequently adopted by the new post-1971 ETA.

from the Military Front and led by Jon Etxabe, refused any contacts with Spanish organisations 'pursuing an anti-Marxist line' and maintained a radical intransigence in their quest for national sovereignty. Other factions followed their paths.[54] However, all of them remained somewhat aloof from the heat of the debate in their French or Belgian exile. With nearly all the experienced leadership either detained or in exile, ETA's Executive Committee was now in the hands of an inexperienced youth who tried to patch up the pieces by attempting to placate each of the exiled factions. However, the participants of the Sixth Assembly were not representative of this ideological variety: the assembly became at first dominated by the Red Cells to the exclusion of the other factions. They expelled the *Milis*, but were in turn expelled by the Executive Committee, while other members resigned in bitterness. Finally, the *Milis* and the old leaders (Krutwig, Beltza, Madariaga, Txillardegi *et al.*) ruled from exile that all the participants to the Sixth Assembly be expelled from ETA. That meant that they re-founded the organisation and that for a while there were two ETAs.

In 1970, sixteen *etarras* charged with the murder of Manzanas were brought before a military tribunal in Burgos. The famous Burgos trial was an historic watershed for the whole Basque movement as well as for the Spanish opposition (Halimi 1971, Sullivan 1988: 92–112). For weeks the international media focussed on the Basques' struggle. All over Europe mass demonstrations and solidarity committees sprang up in support of the condemned. Renowned leftist intellectuals joined the chorus.[55] European ambassadors were

---

[54] The *tercermundistas* tried to strike the balance between the goal of independence and a residual commitment to Marxism-Leninism. The culturalists of *Branka* tried insistently to form a broad coalition, which was referred to as 'national front'. Other leaders of the *Ekin* days and early ETA, such as Madariaga and Beltza, maintained good relations with Branka.

[55] See Jean-Paul Sartre's introduction to Halimi (1971). Sartre saw Euskadi as a colony exploited by a fascist state allied with American imperialism. In general, he showed considerable understanding for the problems of European national minorities, and accused the European Left of uncritically assuming the French bourgeoisie's cultural Jacobinism (Ortzi 1977: 380–1). 'I wish to oppose the abstract universality of bourgeois humanism to the singular universality of the Basques. . . . A heroic people, led by a revolutionary party, has shown us another [face of] socialism, tangible and decentralising: this is the universality of the Basques, which ETA justly opposes to the abstract centralism of the oppressors' (Sartre 1972: xxix-xxx, in Halimi 1971). Obviously Sartre was referring to the ETA of the Burgos

recalled for consultation and the Vatican pleaded for clemency. Popular demonstrations were held in many parts of Spain, while in Euskadi priests celebrated masses, general strikes paralysed most activities, and universities were closed. In Madrid, dissident lawyers occupied the Palace of Justice, and massive demonstrations were held in other cities. Its legitimacy crumbling under the pressure of a powerful public opinion, the Spanish regime was now agonising.[56] As a consequence, ETA rose as a symbol 'above public censure. Open criticism of ETA was judged as open support for the regime' (Heiberg 1989: 107).

The trial came at a time of maximum internal strife for ETA, with factions at odds with each other and many disillusioned militants leaving the organisation. The day before the trial started, the *Milis* kidnapped the West German consul in San Sebastián. Apparently, their double agenda was to put pressure on the regime and regain control over ETA. In the limelight of the Burgos trial, the *Milis* were provided with direct access to the international media through their spokesman Telesforo Monzón (1904-87).[57] The kidnappers asked for a more lenient treatment for the Burgos sixteen and for the commutation of death sentences. Following secret negotiations, the consul was released unharmed and subsequently Franco commuted all the death sentences. In this way the *Milis* had gained unprecedented authority.

However, ETA's internecine conflicts continued in the following months (early 1971) as the old guard renamed itself ETA-V, from the Fifth-Assembly, while the followers of the Sixth Assembly came to be known as ETA-VI. The latter had almost dropped their nationalist emphasis, embracing Trotskyism and class struggle.[58]

---

trial, which emerged as an international champion of resistance against oppression.

[56] The regime was now being abandoned even by the Church as, since 1969, the Opus Dei technocrats left the government coalition (Hermet 1986: 455 ff.).

[57] Monzón, an independent-minded old man attracted by the enthusiasm and good-will of the new generation, resigned from the PNV in 1977 in order to join the Left *abertzale* movement. See Idoia Estornés Zubizarreta, entry 'Monzón', in the EGIPV, vol. 29, pp. 254-8.

[58] The only earlier abandonment of nationalism dates back to the already mentioned founding of *ETA-Berri* in 1966 by the followers of the Maoist leader Paco Iturrioz. In 1970, ETA-Berri changed its name into *Movimiento Comunista de España* (MCE, Communist Movement of Spain) in order not to be identified with ETA and avoid police persecution.

Euskadi was then still conceived as an internal colony, but especially as an urban developed society in which the working-class movement was to play a decisive role in the building of Basque socialism. Yet, at least in Bilbao, the workers were largely immigrants, therefore the emphasis had to be on class conflict rather than ethnic conflict. Clearly, the presence of immigrant workers played a key role in repeatedly shifting ETA's ideology to the far left. The need to mobilise immigrants resulted in an increasing radicalisation of the process. Indeed ETA's radicals quickly found out at the expense of the moderates that the immigrants were more likely to be involved whenever actions prevailed over theory and over 'abstract' debates on Basque identity.

In order to understand this mechanism, we have first to presuppose that newcomers are willing to integrate into the host society. Even when they chose not to do so or to give up their efforts at integration, they normally encourage their children to become full members of the host society and share its culture. However, this step is particularly difficult to accomplish in a society which is unable to offer shared and accessible core values. Until recently, race and religion worked as conscious obstacles to integration, while the language was not widely available and extremely difficult to master.[59] At the same time, in a polarised society mass mobilisations began to attract the immigrants' offspring. Their participation in these public events encouraged them to share the natives' common myths and symbols. They certainly were not concerned with 'purity of blood': what was at stake was their social peace and very existence, since any mobilisation carried with it the risk of being killed by the 'occupation forces'. Simultaneously, Left-wing nationalism carried a progressive message to the immigrants, while ETA's daring violence exercised an irresistible charm in many juvenile sectors. The more ETA's *ekintzak* (armed actions) involved a direct confrontation with the state, the more ETA's star would rise among

---

[59] Although immigrants and natives nominally share the same religion, the reality is more complex. Religious practice per Sunday varied from 80% in Euskadi to 15% in Andalusia and Extremadura (Duocastella 1965, quoted by Martin 1978: 254-5). Castile, where most of the immigrants came from, occupied a middle ground. Martin observes that Catholic weekly practice is at its optimum where it is the expression of a repressed nationalism (1978: 152): in Eire, Poland, Euskadi and Brittany. On the regional distribution of religious practice in Spain see Duocastella (1965).

non-native proletarians. Thus violence became a vehicle of integration into the nationalist struggle.

The move away from ethnicity to class produced continuous splits within the *abertzale* movement.[60] The young members who drifted towards workers' mobilisation and finally dropped the nationalist cause became unavoidably alienated from the ethnic Basque base, which still formed the backbone and leading force of the movement. The class orientation of the now Trotskyist ETA-VI, its inactivity, and its miscalculation of the possibility of mobilising Basque workers on class lines, together with the arrest and imprisonment of its leaders, spelled its decline and subsequent end. ETA-V, a wider interclass alliance of various nationalist forces, took the lead of the movement. ETA-VI then vanished into the cauldron of extra-parliamentary Spanish left-wing organisations,[61] while some members joined mainstream left parties and still others were drawn back to their radical nationalist roots. As Clark puts it, 'ETA served as the point of departure for a number of splinter groups that would occupy positions of radical intransigence throughout the Spanish and Basque political spectrum' (1984: 44).

But other forces were also at work, trying to smooth over nationalist discord. In 1971 there was much talk of a proposed *frente nacional* ('national front') reuniting all Basque forces from both Left and Right. The main promoters of this idea were the 'culturalists' of the Branka group. Again, cultural nationalists played a key role in reinvigorating political nationalism by attempting to build up an inter-class alliance of all nationalist forces. The project would eventually fail, because of the predominance of Marxists inside ETA who refused to make common cause with 'bourgeois' nationalists.

The early 1970s saw an unprecedented outburst of cultural activities. The spearhead of the cultural revival was the movement

[60] As a protest against the Marxist-Leninist turn of ETA in the mid-1960s the old leadership (Txillardegi, del Valle, Imaz) left the organisation: 'ETA is no longer a means to achieve our goals and it has been converted into a Marxist-Leninist party. . . . Since we do not accept any of the basic tenets of this political philosophy and praxis, we have decided to abandon ETA' (*Por que dejamos E.T.A.*, by J.L. Alvarez Emparanza, J.M. Benito del Valle, X. Imaz, 14 April 1967, pamphlet reprinted in Caracas [1967?] by Eusko Gastegi).

[61] In 1973, ETA-VI was definitively absorbed into the Trotskyist LCR (*Liga Comunista Revolucionaria*), the Spanish section of one of the rival Fourth Internationals.

of the *ikastolak* or schools in Euskera. Established during the Second Republic, the *ikastolak* were forced underground and nearly ceased their activity under Francoism (Arpal *et al.* 1982, Tejerina 1992: 129-37). The first timid re-openings by the regime in the 1960s were quickly seized upon by the movement, which started anew, first in private homes, then in kindergartens, and in the following decade spread to every city and village of the *Euskaldun* area.[62] The *ikastolak* were entirely financed by parents' contributions and had all sorts of legal hindrances placed in their way by the Francoist authorities. The fundraising was carried out village by village and represented a high point of collective mobilisation. The revival was supported by many non-nationalists as well, in particular the Left, since at that time the struggle on behalf of Basque culture was considered parallel with the one for democracy. In 1960, the first three *ikastolak* were opened in Gipuzkoa (Lasa 1968). Their number increased at a spectacular rate, going from 520 pupils in 1966-5 (Nuñez 1977) to 40,000, distributed in 185 schools, in 1977 (Euskaltzaindia 1977, 1979). A literary revival also started in this period, culminating with the mythical novel *Obabakoak* by Bernardo Atxaga.[63]

From Marxism back to nationalism

ETA's Workers Front, known as *obreristas* ('workerists'), was soon accused of *españolismo* (Hispanicism, pro-centralist attitudes) since it promoted collaboration with Spanish parties on the ground that the proletariats of Euskadi and other regions shared a common struggle against bourgeois capitalism. The accusation of being *españolista* was particularly onerous for people who had to live in

[62] Benito del Valle's declaration that the first *ikastolak* were created by Ekin (*Punto y Hora*, no. 134, pp. 44-5, 1979) is firmly rebutted by Ibarzábal (*Muga*, no. 2, 1979, p. 4. See also *Muga*, no. 3, 1980, pp. 10-13). However, Txillardegi also mentions Ekin's failed attempt to promote *ikastolak* from 1954 to 1959 (*Garaia*, vol. 1, no. 1, 2-9 September 1976, p. 25.). The *cursillos de formación* organised by Ekin gave primary importance to the teaching of Euskara, which was one of the main subjects and often also a medium of instruction. After the 'joint venture' with EGI, these initiatives spread to many villages and attracted more and more pupils.

[63] For an anthology of recent Basque fiction, see Lasagabaster (1990). See also Coco (1992). However, only Atxaga's novel stands out as a great literary achievement and has been translated into English (Atxaga 1992). For a review of the novel and its implication, see Cameron (1992).

absolute secrecy and for whom the slightest leak of information could have dramatic consequences, including arrest and torture.

Once its rival ETA-VI disappeared, ETA-V joined an important fraction of the PNV's youth branch (EGI) and merged – for the second time – under the single initials of ETA (as formally agreed in 1972). The infusion of 500 youths from EGI reinvigorated ETA and renewed its informal contacts with conservative nationalists. They wholeheartedly adopted the ideological principles of the Fifth Assembly (second half), thereby fusing class and national struggle. This new turn was translated into a stepping up of violent actions. In 1972, armed assaults reached an unprecedented peak. The turning point was the kidnapping of the industrialist Lorenzo Zabala as part of a labour dispute in early 1972. This was the first action directed against an ethnic Basque who, furthermore, spoke Euskara. As the workers of his factory had gone out on strike for a raise in wages, the company responded by firing all the striking workers. This action provided a unique opportunity to assure the working class that they could count on ETA for the defence of their interests, drawing them into the struggle for the liberation of Euskadi. The fact that Zabala was an *euskaldun* (Basque-speaking) only added strength to ETA's claim of acting on behalf of the workers and beyond strictly ethnic interests. The four conditions set out by the kidnappers were all met with minor modifications by the employers: increased wages, the rehiring of the sacked workers, the payment of wages lost on days while on the strike, and recognition of the workers' committee charged with negotiating a wage settlement. Zabala was released unharmed after only one week of being held incommunicado (Ibarra Guell 1987, Bruni 1980, Ibarz 1981).

The success of the operation proved to the regime that ETA was still alive and had regained considerable strength after the dark days of the Burgos trial. This action initiated an unprecedented wave of guerrilla attacks, unleashing renewed repression upon the whole Basque country. A new generation of leaders emerged, among them 'Txomin' and 'Argala'. Four ETA members were killed on separate occasions. The new brand of Marxism and nationalism (this time, without rejecting the latter) attracted the important moral support of the Burgos prisoners, whose statements appeared in *Zutik* (Ortzi 1975: 390-1).[64] As a consequence, ETA reached a period of une-

[64] See *Zutik*, no. 63, 1972, reprinted in *Documentos Y*, vol. 12, pp. 347 ff.

qualled expansion. The fusion between Marxism and nationalism
proved highly attractive in a country which, as we shall see, has
traditionally stressed egalitarian values and a thirst for social justice.

The most notorious act by ETA was the killing of Admiral
Carrero Blanco, the expected successor of Franco, in December
1973. This act created a spate of international concern and admira-
tion of ETA, as well as a diplomatic focus on the Basque question,
a general sympathy for the Basques and even a few art works, such
as the book and movie *Operation Ogro*.[65] But ETA's fronts started to
argue among themselves, acting autonomouly and competing in
their actions, as did different sub-factions within them.[66]

In 1974, a bloody terrorist attack at the Café Rolando in Madrid
killed nine people and left scores injured. ETA accused the security
forces of being responsible for deliberately not evacuating the place
after its bomb alert. However, the repercussions of the attack
brought about an acrid confrontation and a new split between
ETA-m (ETA-Militar) and ETA-pm (ETA-Político-Militar). The
latter convened its own 'second half of the Sixth Assembly' in 1975
and decided to expand armed struggle. After the imposition of a state
of emergency in Vizcaya and Gipuzkoa, two *etarras*, Txiki and
Otaegi, were executed. This gave the signal for a new series of mass
protests, which in turn prompted further states of emergency. But
the Francoist regime could no longer stem the tide of popular
discontent. Hence its *raison d'être*, the drive to keep the country

---

[65] The book was written by Eva Forest (1974) under the pseudonym of Julen
Aguirre. See also the critique of the movie by the Italian writer Alberto Moravia,
'La Memoria e i suoi figli' in *L 'Espresso*, 21 Oct. 1979. Its director Gillo Pontecorvo
became famous in the 1960s for his *La battaglia di Algeri* (battle of Algiers) on the
Algerian revolution. *Operation Ogro* was much less well received than its predecessor, not just in the Basque country. This was possibly due to the director's rejection
of armed struggle, an allegedly 'moralistic' choice influenced by the impact of
contemporary dramatic events in Italy, namely the array of murders, kidnappings
and other terrorist attacks carried out by the Red Brigades. This overlap and
confusion was one of the reasons why Basque nationalists were so disappointed by
the movie's overt message that ETA should drop armed struggle, although the
movie recognised its legitimacy as a tool against Francoism. In some way, the
'outrageous' confusion of ETA's struggle with an international terrorist band with
the sole common denominator of Marxism contributed to distance some sectors
of ETA from Marxism. Paradoxically, Pontecorvo's mistake was to have
misunderstood the 'Fanonian' connection between Euskadi and Algeria.

[66] In 1974, both the Workers' and the Cultural fronts split off to form autonomous
parties.

tightly united, risked becoming its greatest failure (Preston 1993). In late 1975, Franco was on his death-bed and the whole region was in turmoil. Crucial changes were unavoidable.

In the late 1950s, under the full impact of Francoism, the Basque country began to undergo a rapid process of radical socio-economic change.[67] Clashing with the dictatorship's stalemate, the new socio-economic changes inspired a rethinking among underground opposition circles and set the bases for impressive future political upheavals.

ETA's main ideological text was written by a non-member, Federico Krutwig, who never participated in organised politics. This gives him a different historical role from that of Sabino de Arana; nevertheless, he and Arana were both marginal intellectuals. Arana was castigated by his contemporary intellectual colleagues as a quaint reactionary,[68] and Krutwig was considered mad. Both were viscerally anti-bourgeois and saw urban capitalist society as a major cause of Basque decadence. Both were Castilian-speakers and learned Euskara at a later age, as a central part of their nationalist socialisation. In their choices, both Arana and Krutwig were inspired by, and synthesised, pre-existing trends. Arana drew upon the Carlist tradition which he inherited from his family's background. To a certain extent he was also influenced by liberal foralism (Sagarminaga, Iturralde *et al.*) and by the strong bonds persisting between city and countryside. Krutwig drew instead on the intellectual debate initiated by Ekin, which was later put into practice by ETA. However, they sharply differed in their choice of core values for Basque national identity. Krutwig was vehemently anti-clerical since he saw the Church as an instrument of oppression against the Basque people. He also proclaimed himself to be anti-racist and did not believe in the purity of blood and other dogmas. Therefore, he castigated his predecessor Arana as being 'more racist than Hitler'.[69]

[67] The Basque economy had been heavily penalised during early Francoism. It began to recover from about 1959 and in the 1960s reached boom proportions. As Madrid created bureaucratic difficulties for the local economy, some businessmen suspected that Madrid was trying to undermine it. Nationalism has thus been interpreted as a means of greater control over the regional economy (Zirakzadeh 1985, 1991).

[68] See the statements by Unamuno and Maetzu in chapter 9.

[69] From an interview in *Cambio 16*, 23 Jan. 1984 (quoted in Gilmour 1985).

He was so anti–clerical that he defined the Catholic Church as an 'army used to enslave the Basque spirit, the army of the most odious of the oppressors' (1963: 67). Yet there is a common thread between Arana and Krutwig: paradoxically, it is a desperate search for cultural regeneration in a world that has only contempt for tradition. In this search they both turned to language. Yet at a certain stage they both laid language aside and replaced it with something else, more attuned to the times and circumstances. Arana chose race and religion. Krutwig redefined Basque identity in terms of language, but in practice placed it second after voluntary participation and activism, as epitomised in 'revolutionary violence'. Race and religion were no longer feasible instruments of mobilisation.

A key feature in Basque politics and within ETA has been the continuous clash between cultural and political nationalism. Furthermore, after ETA had definitely chosen the path of armed struggle, a more dramatic conflict emerged between these two kinds of nationalism and a purely military one. With the increase of killings by the police and the Guardia Civil, and with the indiscriminate repression of the Basque people and culture, ETA fighters were raised to the status of martyrs and heroes. In this connection it is important to remember that all the founders of Ekin and ETA were primarily cultural nationalists: one of their central concerns was in the fate of Euskara. In the late 1960s ETA-V and then ETA-VI drifted towards a purely political brand of nationalism, focussing on class struggle. That occurred after their leaders opted for mobilising the immigrant working class.

This chapter has also illustrated the fissiparous trends within ETA and how these were overcome through the use of violence, generating a vicious circle of internal fragmentation and external confrontation. The trigger for the cycle of armed struggle has been the violent, often indiscriminate, oppression under the dictatorship. We have also seen that ideological tensions were related to cultural fragmentation, in the form of immigration, rural/urban divide, class cleavages, Castilianisation etc. The dynamics of fragmentation and state repression is analysed in the final chapter. In the next chapter we examine how the interaction of different internal variables with state repression generated a different pattern of national mobilisation in Catalonia.

5

CATALONIA UNDER FRANCO

Francoism adopted the most radical politics of assimilation against non-Castilian cultures in modern Spanish history.[1] The dictatorship's early stage (1939-*ca*. 1945) was known as the Falangist period due to the predominance in the government's ranks of members of the Falange Española. Most authors divide Francoism into two broad periods: from the Civil War to the advent of the 'technocratic era' (1939-59), and from the latter to the dictator's death (1959-75). Thus 1959 is a watershed year, although other authors have pointed to different periods and focusses.[2] In this chapter an historical overview of the Francoist oppression and resurgence of Catalanism underlines its strong cultural character and the reasons why it developed as a broad non-violent, inter-class and inter-party alliance. In contrast to the Basque case, we see that the all-encompassing cultural nature of Catalanism worked as a stimulus for bridging ancient ideological rivalries, creating the basis for a non-violent democratic movement which swelled local politics with the collapse of the dictatorship. It is interesting that the period of most acute repression (1939-42) has attracted the attention of nationalist historians, some of whose data have been incorporated in the present work. More detached analyses are still hard to find.

The drive to cultural homogeneity (1939-1942)

Before his assassination, the Finance Minister José Calvo Sotelo (1893-1936) loudly proclaimed: 'I'd prefer a Red Spain to a broken

---

[1] Before 1939 the Spanish state failed to articulate any serious process of nation-building (Arbos and Puigsec 1980, Giner 1986: 447).

[2] As an example, Vilar (1967) focuses on 1956 as a watershed. 1956 is also the year in which Spanish Television started broadcasting from Madrid, but its programmes could be picked up in Catalonia only in February 1959 (Culla 1989: 349).

Spain' (cited in García Venero 1968: 561). This sentence synthesised
the driving force of the Falangist and Francoist campaigns, namely
an obsession with 'national unity'. Thus political hatred was directed
against the 'separatists' even more than against the Left. Eventually
the two categories were bundled up into a unique concept and
propaganda tool as *rojoseparatistas* ('red-separatists').

The propagandists of the Falange attacked the 'separatists' for
'ignoring the unitarian reality of Spain'. Yet in practice such unity,
far from being 'natural', was based on the imposition of a single
language, Castilian (Spanish), backed up by police repression and a
centralised education system. The Jacobin idea of a common language, culture, race, history and territory as necessary prerequisites
for state-building was deeply entrenched in the Falangist ideology
which accompanied early Francoism. The Fascist and Nazi models
of a strong unitary self-sufficient state were also imported and
adapted to the Spanish reality.[3] Hence everybody had the duty of
'fluently speaking the tongue of Spanish unity, the ecumenical
language of our *hispanidad*'.[4] Spanish was the language of the empire
(*idioma del imperio*) and, for this reason, 'it must be spoken all over
the state territory'.[5]

Many of these ideas were inspired by the philosopher José Ortega
y Gasset (1883-1955).[6] Although Ortega was at pains to stress that
he was not a nationalist, he repeatedly emphasised that Spanish unity
could only be preserved at the cost of accepting the dominance of
the Spanish state and imposing its cultural symbols – first of all the
Castilian language. Hence his anti-regionalism offered a providential
tool of legitimation for the far right's ideology.[7] He cried out for a
policy of *nacionalización* aimed at forging a 'vertebrate, upright Spain'

[3] For a comparison of the Fascist, Nazi, Francoist and Vichyite models of cultural
assimilation, see Ille (1990).

[4] Quoted in Eduardo Alvarez Puga, *Diccionario de la Falange*. Barcelona: Dopesa,
1937, pp. 12-3.

[5] Ibid., p. 36 (emphasis added). The quoted text also refers to the new directive
of placing noticeboards in different Catalan public places intimating '*Habla el idioma
del imperio*' (Speak the language of the Empire, i.e. Spanish).

[6] Ortega's *España invertebrada*, a sort of Bible for many Spanish fascists, is openly
quoted in the *Diccionario de la Falange*, op. cit., p. 52.

[7] In this one can trace a parallel with the German philosopher Martin Heidegger.
On the affinities and friendship between the two, see Regalado García (1990).

(cited in Dobson 1989: 87).[8] Ortega therefore 'found himself painted into a corner, defending precisely the type of Spanish nationalism he always hoped to avoid. . . . Only the shell of the idea – the Nation was left, and others were to make unscrupulous use of it' (Dobson 1989: 94). That was what eventually happened, and Ortega's ideology was quickly picked up and upheld by the Spanish ultra-rightists of the Falange.[9]

Backed by the intellectual authority of opinion-makers like Ortega, the Falangists proceeded in their campaign of annihilation of all vestiges of ethnopolitical identity. This far-reaching persecution assumed Orwellian overtones and 'jail sentences were imposed for even casual conversations carried on in the [regional] language on public streets' (Clark 1979: 81). Oriol Pi-Sunyer states that 'a totalitarian system attempted to control the totality of civil culture; it was not simply the Statute of Autonomy that was abrogated but any entity that might seem to pose a challenge to the state, whether a boy scout troop or a choral society' (1980: 108-9). However, the intellectual influence of the Falangists was minimal: in Catalonia, a land with a highly developed associative and intellectual tradition, the Falange had a very low prestige. Not even the bourgeoisie, who called for its help against the 'reds', wished to deal with it.[10]

As soon as Barcelona fell to the Francoist troops, Catalonia was submitted to a special regime of occupation for six months (Benet 1973: 221-77). In a frenzied 'hunt for the separatist' all Catalan-language references were erased from public access (Jones 1981), and hundreds of thousands of books in Catalan were consigned to the pulping plants or burned in public.[11] Patriotic statues and

8 Ortega also confused his adversaries by waving the standard of 'decentralisation', which he claimed to regard as a generator of widespread public responsibility and thus of commitment to the 'nation'. In rhetorical contradiction with these statements, he also claimed that 'internal demands for autonomy had to be seen in the same light as the loss of Spain's colonies – as a symptom of the collapse of the nation' (cited in Dobson 1989: 94). He was therefore a sworn enemy of all regionalist and 'separatist' movements and for this reason his quotations became an ideal tool to be manipulated by the far right.

9 On the ideology of the Francoist regime, see Arbos and Puigsec (1980).

10 Josep Benet, personal suggestion.

11 The 'Library of Catalonia' became the 'Central Library', and 'Catalonia Square' (*Plaça de Catalunya*) was renamed for a few weeks 'Spanish Army Square' (*Plaza del Ejército Español*) (Fabres *et al.* 1978: 76, Riquer 1989: 101).

monuments were smashed (Benet 1973: 369-71). All posters, placards, notices, signposts and labels in Catalan were removed, and people who opposed these measures were heavily fined or jailed (Benet 1973: 269-73, 295-309, 371-5 and 380-2). In the workplace Catalan was banned even as a spoken language: a civil servant caught in the act of speaking Catalan risked immediate dismissal (Benet 1973: 309-14). Municipal and state teachers suspected of Catalanist sympathies were forcibly removed from their jobs, or transferred to other regions, while others more loyal to the regime were 'imported' from the rest of Spain (Benet 1973: 328-9).[12] In the University of Barcelona, all subjects dealing with Catalan culture were abolished, and the purge of the University staff reached levels unparalleled in other Spanish regions (Benet 1973: 355-6).[13] The Institut d'Estudis Catalans was closed down and replaced with an Instituto Español de Estudios Mediterráneos which existed in name only (Benet 1973: 360-7).[14] All symbols of Catalan identity such as the flag and anthem were outlawed (Benet 1973: 387). Contemplating this labour of destruction, the Francoist journalist Manuel Aznar could triumphantly boast: 'The theory of small nationalities is dead. The German, Italian and Spanish empires are the vital forces of the new Europe' (Benet 1973: 403-4).[15]

There were attempts to proscribe the *sardana* (the national dance) and Catalan songs.[16] 'Gothic' liturgical vestments were defined as

[12] Between April and August 1939, 700 teachers from Castile and Extremadura were despatched to Catalonia to replace the deported Catalan ones. Given their total ignorance of the local language, culture and history, they were supposed to work as an instrument of assimilation. All the pedagogical advances registered by the pre-war Catalan school system were erased.

[13] More than half of the teaching staff (135 professors) were expelled from Barcelona's University.

[14] According to Manent (1976), these figures were high if compared with the total figure of the exile from Spain, 450,000.

[15] This penchant against small minorities was typical of Francoism, and was inherited from the ideological armour of the Fascists and the Nazis. Note its similarity with Frederick Engels' attack on 'peoples without history' and its influence on Marxist ideology.

[16] In one edict, the *sardana* was accursed as a 'differentiating agent' (Benet 1973: 386). However, according to Brandes (1990: 34-5), the dance was prohibited only in some locales in and around Barcelona, not in the countryside. 'No doubt because the dictatorship considered the *sardana* to be relatively innocuous, the dance was allowed to flourish as a form of what we might call 'peaceful protest' against the

'separatist' and priests were advised to utter even their Latin homilies with a 'Spanish' pronunciation (Benet 1973: 435-6). The regime tried to build up far-fetched analogies between anti-semitism and anti-catalanism in order to earn Hitler's favour.[17] Censorship led to the destruction of private correspondence written in regional 'dialects' (Benet 1973: 314).[18] Punishment for the offenders ranged from simple fines to dismissal from the workplace, exile and prison. In the first years of the dictatorship, many people were accused of 'separatism' merely for 'daring' to speak in Catalan.[19] Denunciation and spying became common (Riquer 1989: 82).

The scope of all these measures was not simply to suffocate Catalanism but to eradicate Catalan culture and any sign of a separate Catalan identity at its very roots. Their result was devastating: 'Barcelona, the city of revolutionary anarchists and experimental artists, of thronging boulevards and excited discourse, had become another grey provincial Spanish town. Its political and cultural leaders were gone – some dead, some in exile. A defeated silence fell over the entire nation, a silence that for years would remain virtually unbroken. When it was broken – furtively and sporadically – it would be by the sound of bitter weepings' (Rosenthal 1991: 45).

More than 500,000 people fled into exile in 1939, 200,000 of whom came from Catalan-speaking areas (Pi-Sunyer 1980: 109,

---

regime's more effective and oppressive campaign to eliminate the public use of the Catalan language' (Brandes 1990: 35).

[17] The Falangist identification of the Catalans as Jews resulted in the coining of the neologism *Judeo-catalanes* (Benet 1973: 128-37). Both the Nazi and Fascist governments agreed with a policy dedicated to the destruction of regional 'particularisms', avoiding at all costs the 'creation of a Catalan state' (Benet 1973: 218). On the deportation of Catalan Republican refugees in France to Nazi concentration camps, see Roig (1992). Of the 6,000 Republicans who died in Mauthausen, about one-third were Catalans or Valencians. However, Franco slowly tried to dissociate himself from the Axis, especially after Japan entered the war. Thus anti-Nazi refugees and several thousand Sephardic Jews from the occupied Balkans were given sanctuary in Spain or transit visas. Many were granted full Spanish citizenship (Avni 1982).

[18] Until 1941 private correspondence was scrutinised by the censors, but mail censorship lasted up to 1948 (Riquer 1989: 102, Gallofré i Virgili 1991, Gubern 1981).

[19] On the regime's equation between Catalan language and separatism, see Benet (1973: 89-1).

Sauret 1979). The latter were thus deprived of part of their intelligentsia. In only six days, 1-6 May, 1939, 266 people were executed after sentencing by summary war councils (Benet 1973: 241-2, Solé i Sabaté 1986).[20] The president of the Generalitat, Lluís Companys, was shot by a firing squad in October 1940 after being seized in France by the Nazis who handed him over to the Falangists (Benet 1990). Between 1946 and 1953 most literary output was produced in exile.[21] The *Jocs Florals* were alternatively celebrated in America or Europe (Benet 1973: 386-7). The Catalan intelligentsia who remained in the country was thus forced underground and had to meet in small family-based circles of friends.[22] As in Euskadi, the family emerged as the extreme bulwark and redoubt against Castilianisation, as an inviolable space where discussions on Catalonia's destiny could be carried out in Catalan.[23]

The Franco regime tolerated regional culture only in the form of 'folkloric' remnants. While the attempts to crush Euskara were openly aimed at its eradication, the anti-Catalan polity included a supplementary strategy of 'dialectisation': that is, the authorities tried to promote the view that Catalan was a mere dialect, a sub-variety of Spanish. They also tried to break up its linguistic unity by supporting non-standard varieties.[24]

After the war Catalonia was a broken society and apathy penetrated all walks of life, preventing any possibility of political

[20] Solé i Sabaté (1986) gives an estimated number of 3,350 executions. As often happens (it has been common practice in Guatemala, Iraq and other totalitarian countries in the early 1990s), repression reached its most gruesome levels in the countryside, away from public opinion and the media's attention.

[21] According to Manent (1976), 450 books and 180 periodicals in Catalan were published in exile between 1939 and 1976, the majority of them in Mexico and France.

[22] Hence, a characteristic of postwar Catalonia was the absence of intellectual cadres in the country. The few who remained, such as Ignasi Augustí and the group *Destino*, were forced to abandon the use of Catalan (Josep Benet personal suggestion).

[23] On the role of the family as the main instrument of nationalist socialisation, see Barrera (1985), Johnston (1991) and Rossinyol (1974: 409).

[24] The term 'dialectisation', introduced in sociolinguistics by Heinz Kloss (1986), refers to deliberate policies aimed at undermining the unity of a language, by promoting its internal fragmentation and refusing to recognise it as a single language. On Catalan see Benet (1973: 72-3); for a comparison with Occitan, see Lafont (1977).

mobilisation (Riquer 1990). The poet Salvador Espriu (1913-85) reflected this tragedy in his writing. Speaking for many of his generation, he expressed a 'tactical withdrawal from a fraudulent public life into a few trusted realities. . . . In the background, of course, is the civil war itself, at once a collective and deeply personal tragedy: 1,200,000 dead and 500,000 exiled. The sense of drifting in a sea of spectres – the ghosts of dead friends, enemies, acquaintances and relatives, all speaking a language itself mortally threatened' (Rosenthal 1991: 46-9).

A slow recovery (1942-1959)

After the Allied victory against Fascism, Catalan expectations were raised (Rossinyol 1974: 405). Indeed, the outcome of the war contributed to Madrid's decision to grant some symbolic cultural concessions to the opposition: a few printed classic works, theatrical performances in Catalan, and concerts of the *Orfeón Catalán* choirs were finally permitted.[25] The regime needed to break its international isolation through a façade of feeble liberalization, the minimum necessary to present the world with the appearance of ongoing change. Hence, from 1946 Catalan culture began, in semi-clandestinity, to reawaken (Galien 1987).

As soon as the yoke of repression was slightly eased, Catalanism gave signs of renewed vitality. Every niche of freedom was exploited by the cultural activists. Despite endless difficulties, the language began to have a modest revival. Since 1942, clandestine classes in Catalan history, language and literature had been set up at the Estudis Universitaris Catalans, and attended by small numbers of people. From 1944 the Institut d'Estudis Catalans resumed its activities, albeit only in a token way, lacking resources and continuously harassed by the regime. New literary prizes were established. Before 1939 the organisation and financing of such events would have been the responsibility of the Generalitat, but now every initiative had to stem from private enterprise (Samsó 1990).[26] Exiled intellectuals, such as the poets Carles Riba (1893-1959) and Pere Quart (1899-1986), returned home and began to contact the new generations.

[25] On the modern Catalan tradition of choirs and their political content, see Artís i Benach (1980).

[26] For the academic and literary prizes under the Generalitat, see Benet (1973: 54-7).

The Selecta publishing house was founded in 1946, through the efforts and dynamism of the entrepreneur Josep Maria Cruzet (Riquer 1989: 240). The first non-religious book, the complete works of Jacint Verdaguer, was allowed in 1946, but – in keeping with the regime's policy of 'dialectisation' – not in standard Catalan. The printing of books in Catalan slowly but steadily increased: output increased from twelve books in 1946, to sixty in 1948 and ninety-six in 1954. In 1960 there were more than 200. Catalan was first used in public at the 'Seventh International Conference of Romance Linguistics', celebrated in 1953 at the University of Barcelona. Because of the strictly philological character – and the international appeal – of the conference, it was able to pass the scrutiny of the regime's censors.

Unofficial historiography thrived under the stimulating leadership of Jaume Vicens Vives (1910-60).[27] Throughout modern Catalan history, local historians played the role of reawakeners of the national spirit. Many works by Vives' predecessors were largely apologetic eulogies, where rhetoric and mythical constructs took precedence over detailed scientific analysis. This myth-making function is crucial to any nationalist movement and characterizes Catalan historiography from its inception to the present day. Vives broke radically with this tradition, nevertheless many of his works were permeated by a Catalanist spirit. In his classical *Notícia de Catalunya*, published in 1954, Vives asserted: '[We must] make an effort to improve the knowledge of ourselves before we begin precise plans. . . . We have to define ourselves. If we want to construct an acceptable edifice, we must know who we were and who we are' (Vives 1984: 9).[28] The book provided some answers to

---

[27] Jaume Vicens Vives was the man who first sought to explain Catalan historical identity in concrete economic, demographic, social and psychological terms. Often referred to as Spain's first modern historian, he championed the methodological input of the French *Annales* school (Braudel, Le Goff, Leroy Ladurie *et al.*). Yet he envisaged the historian as social activist and catalyst for the recovery of Catalonia, striving to rebuild her culture, her institutions and her national spirit, However, this aim was to be achieved through impartial and factual analysis, rather than via old-fashioned panegyrics and eulogistic writings.

[28] Therefore, he developed the discipline of economic history, adopting statistical and demographic analysis. He also created a network of international scholarly exchange, providing instruments like a bibliographical index and an historical journal (Enders 1984).

these questions: the new Catalan identity was to be open, malleable, seaborne, reflective.

In 1955, Selecta published Josep Ferrater i Mora's (1912-90) *Les formes de vida catalana*,[29] another key text which defined the essence of a renewed Catalan identity and influenced political Catalanism in the years to come. It was not a typical nationalist text, and indeed its tone was overtly anti-separatist (Ferrater i Mora 1980: 149). Yet as an eloquent interpretation of a pre-existing Catalan character, Ferrater also formulated a new collective self-perception: the Catalans were 'reinvented' for the benefit of a more pluralistic vision of Catalanness.

The various cultural initiatives analysed in this section contributed to the emergence of a slight optimism among some intellectuals, who perceived Catalan culture as being no longer on the verge of extinction as it was a few years before. However, being prevented from spreading their message to the masses, they had almost no social impact. In the 1950s, there was a moment of real danger that Catalan would become a family language, extinct in the public sphere. Up till 1945-6, many people believed that a great change would take place at the end of the World War, and a clandestine press thrived in the expectation of major upheavals. When it was clear that the Western world was not interested in a prompt re-establishment of democracy in Spain, the hopes of the Catalan intelligentsia waned: in 1946 the clandestine press ceased its activity because of disillusionment, and the Communists were forced out of the opposition as a consequence of the Cold War.[30] At this point the danger of a violent turn for Catalan nationalism was vividly present. But the most impatient activists and the youth found a means of expressing their anxieties in cultural nationalism. We shall analyse this briefly.

---

[29] The book was first published in 1944 in Santiago de Chile in a limited edition. It was then known by only a few people, among them Vicens Vives, who openly quoted it as one of his main sources of inspiration in *Notícia de Catalunya* (1984: 190 ff.). To have a clear idea of the new Catalan identity, the two books should be read in tandem.

[30] Josep Benet (personal suggestion) stresses the Castilianisation of the youth (since 1955-6) who did not live through the Civil War, since only Castilian was allowed at all levels of instruction.

Economic 'miracle', immigration and language revival

In 1959 Franco reshuffled his cabinet at the expense of both
Falangists and Carlists, allowing the Catholic technocrats of the
Opus Dei to enter key positions. The latter's Stabilisation Plan
favoured a market economy 'where prices would control the
allocation of resources, and the integration of that market into
the capitalist economy of the West. . . . [The Plan] would cure
the economy of its inherited impurities . . . [and] rapid growth
would take care of all problems' (Carr 1980: 156-7). This implied
that Spain had to open up to the world, allowing a gleam of
hope for democratic reforms.

These expectations were disappointed because its economic
performance became the only subject on which the regime could
tolerate criticism. Indeed, the development plan became the traditional target of Left-wing criticism, since 'the technocrats' faith in
private enterprise . . . reinforced the hold of a narrow financial
oligarchy ensconded in the "big seven" private banks [as] only the
private banks could finance industrial growth' (Carr 1980: 157).

From 1963, the *milagro económico* (economic miracle) had begun,
and the Spanish growth-rate 'outpaced all capitalist economies other
than the Japanese' (Carr 1980: 157). Foreign loans, especially from
the United States, poured into the country, feeding a burgeoning
economy. Mass tourism to what was then one of the cheapest places
in Europe led to the irreparable destruction and over-building of
large stretches of the Mediterranean coast.[31] Finally, the remittances
from migrants in the richest European countries helped to alleviate
the economy of the poorest areas of Spain. The stress on aggregate
growth led to the concentration of industries in a few regions,
especially Euskadi and Catalonia, although the regime tried whenever it could to favour Madrid as a financial and industrial centre.
This did not help redress the imbalance between the rich and poor
provinces. As a consequence, the three regions began to experience
the largest influx of immigrants in their modern history; this
phenomenon, as we see later, caused severe social strains and was a

---

[31] The number of tourists attracted to 'the playground of Europe' rose from 6
million in 1960 to 40 million in 1980. Most of the Mediterranean coast from
Catalonia's Costa Brava to Malaga's Costa del Sol was spoiled to the point of
resembling Romania's 'systematisation' projects under Ceausescu, reaching its nadir
in Alicante's Costa Blanca.

crucial factor in the process of re-defining Catalan and Basque identity which finally led to the creation of new forms of nationalist opposition.

The region's upper classes were generally satisfied with the regime's performance, at least on the surface. However, dissatisfaction boiled deep within some sectors and the comparison with other European countries was inevitable.[32] Much of the blame was directed at the Spanish state because of its decisionist role in the economy. According to a member of the emerging regionalist bourgeoisie, Raimon Trias Fargas (1972, 1974), the surplus extracted by the state removed the surplus necessary for profit and reinvestment in Catalonia. Only 52% of that taken by the state was returned to the region, while the percentage of all state funds granted to Catalonia had decreased to 11% in 1970. Furthermore, through government control of banking, 45% of savings were regulated by Madrid for development programmes of the INI (National Institute of Industry), and were not available for reinvestment in Catalonia (Trias Fargas 1972: 82-3). 'The increasingly close integration of Catalonia into a market economy of continental dimensions . . . worked to alter the economic balance: from a developed zone within the Spanish economy, Catalonia [was] being transformed into an appendage of a much more powerful system' (Pi-Sunyer 1979: 60). The alternative solution proposed by the regionalist bourgeoisie and rejected by Madrid was that these savings must be retained in Catalonia to promote development by increasing investment and improving local productivity (Trias Fargas 1974). Encouraged by the economic boom, these upper classes followed the Christian Democratic orientation of their European counterparts. Most of them advocated, both at a rational and emotional level, the revival of Catalan culture in all its aspects, centering particularly on language, and as we see later, a few regionalist industrialists and small entrepreneurs were a crucial source of funding for several cultural enterprises.

In 1959 Luís de Galinsoga, the pro-Francoist director of the most popular Barcelona newspaper *La Vanguardia*, launched a tirade against the use of Catalan while he was attending a mass in Barcelona, and in his fury shouted his famous 'aphorism' '*Todos los catalanes son*

---

[32] The Catalan bourgeoisie perceived itself to be in a state of 'relative deprivation' in relation to its European partners.

una mierda' ('All the Catalans are shit'). Taking advantage of the fuss
created by such a desecration, several grassroots groups organised a
boycott of the newspaper, which resulted in a sharp drop in
subscriptions and advertisers.[33]On direct orders from Franco, Galinsoga was sacked. This was a triumph for the opposition and
demonstrated that 'Catalonia [was] alive, conscious, reasserting
herself, and once more will be thriving.'[34]

On the occasion of Franco's visit to Barcelona, some slight liberal
reforms were approved such as the compilation of Catalan civil law.
However, repression reared up again on some trivial pretexts. At a
concert in Barcelona's Palau de la Música the audience struck up
Maragall's *Cant de la Senyera* ('Song to the Catalan Flag') in the
presence of some Francoist ministers. Twenty people were arrested,
and the nationalist leader Jordi Pujol, whom the police identified as
the main organiser, was sentenced to seven years in prison.[35]

From 1959 *Serra d'Or*, the first large-circulation magazine written
entirely in Catalan, prospered under the auspices of the Montserrat
Abbey. With 12,000 subscriptions in 1964, it represented a significant achievement given the times and the religious character of
the publication.[36] Children's books and magazines, such as *Cavall
Fort* (founded in 1961), became important elements in the Catalan
educational panorama (Rossinyol 1974: 446, Tremoleda 1967).
Finally, with a circulation of 100,000 copies, *Tele-Estel* (founded in
1966) became one of the four best-selling magazines in Spain.

A key event was the foundation in 1961 of *Òmnium Cultural*, a
patronage society dedicated to promote Catalan culture in all walks

[33] Most of these organisations were Catholic-based. The main organiser of the
boycott was Jordi Pujol's CC, which also underwent the harshest measures of
repression in the aftermath of the event.

[34] Statement from the main promoters of the campaign, chiefly the Catholic-based
Acadèmia de la Llengua, quoted by Culla (1989: 302).

[35] On this episode and its consequences, see Crexell (1982). Despite police
beatings, Pujol denied having taken part in the events at the Palau, although he
'confessed' to being the person mainly responsible for the *Vanguardia* boycott.
Nevertheless, the CC group led by him was the chief organiser of the Palau's act
of civil disobedience. Pujol spent two and a half years in prison. After his release
he showed less inclination to engage in direct political confrontations, turning
instead to economic and cultural revival.

[36] In the words of the literary critics Josep Maria Castellet and Joaquím Molas,
Serra d'Or soon became 'the most free and best informed magazine in the entire
peninsula' (quoted by Culla 1989: 311).

of life (Rossinyol 1974: 449-51). With the help of funding from a few industrialists and entrepreneurs, it subsidised in particular Catalan language classes. Closed down by the regime in 1963, it was allowed to resume its activities only in 1967, and subsequently established scholarships and prizes, such as the *Premi de les Lletres Catalanes* (Prize for Catalan Literature) awarded yearly from 1969.[37]

The media world was shaken by the impact of the *Nova Cançó* (New Song) movement (García Solar 1976). In 1961, a group of singers and songwriters known as *Els Setze Jutges* (literally, 'the Sixteen Judges') burst on to the scene, while the record company EDIGSA was established to promote Catalan songs. Songwriters performed freely in universities, parishes, Boy Scout camps and artistic centres of cities and countryside (Culla 1989: 306-7). The song movement was one of the most effective vehicles for the propagation of national consciousness among the masses. The success of singers such as Raimon from Valencia and María del Mar Bonet from the Balearic islands rekindled national consciousness in all Catalan-speaking areas (Fuster 1988). Raimon's version of Salvador Espriu's poetry *Assaig de càntic en el temple* ('Trial Hymn in the Temple') became virtually an opposition anthem.[38] Espriu's poem was 'an attack on the postwar prostration of Catalonia, in which there was almost no immediate resistance to the Franco regime' (Rosenthal 1991: 51). Catalonia was conceived as a dormant nation waiting for its bards to be re-awakened:

> *Oh, how tired I am of my*
> *craven old brutish land,*
> *and how I'd like to get away from it*
> *to the north,*
> *where they say people are clean*
> *and noble, learned, rich, free,*
> *wide-awake and happy.*
> *Then, in the congregation, the brothers would say*
> *disapprovingly: 'Like a bird who leaves his nest*
> *is that man who forsakes his place',*
> *while I, now far away, would laugh*
> *at the law and ancient wisdom*

[37] In 1976, Omnium Cultural numbered 22,000 members. On the crucial activity of this association, see *Omnium Cultural. 1961-1986.* Barcelona: Omnium Cultural, 1986.

[38] On Raimon's political role and artistic achievement, see Fuster (1988) and Racionero (1985).

> *of this, my arid village.*
> *But I must never follow my dream*
> *and I'll stay here till I die.*
> *For I'm craven and brutish too.*
> *And what's more I love, with a*
> *desperate grief, this my poor,*
> *dirty, sad, unlucky homeland.*[39]

Of the phrase 'Like the bird . . . thus the man' Rosenthal writes that it 'echoes both style and the imagery of parts of the Old Testament. It is also the poem's first patriotic expression, and suggests a parallel between Catalans and Jews, two peoples often persecuted for being more industrious and progressive than their neighbours. Another parallel is a common sense of deep and sometimes fatal attachment to national identity' (Rosenthal 191: 51).[40] In Espriu's most famous book, *La pell de brau*, Spain is referred to by its Hebrew name 'Sepharad', and other Hebrew words punctuate the text. As the name 'Sepharad' suggests, Spain could be emulated and desired only in its pre-1492 form.

On 11 September 1964, the first public *Diada* (Catalan national holiday) was celebrated by 3,000 citizens.[41] This was the first postwar Catalanist street demonstration. Seven people were arrested and heavy fines were imposed on participants. On the institutional side things were also moving fast. The struggle for the language could not be carried on without re-founding the education system, and a petition for the introduction of Catalan at all levels of education and the media gathered momentum in 1963. The educational centre Rosa Sensat, created in 1965, established the first summer schools to train teachers of Catalan. Classical and contemporary works were translated from foreign languages into Catalan, helping to open up the regional culture to universal currents.[42] A press law (*ley de prensa*)

[39] Translated by David H. Rosenthal, (1991: 50). Also quoted in Hooper (1986: 234).

[40] In the Basque case parallels with Judaism were less usual. On the contrary, Arana took as a matter of pride the weak Muslim and Jewish influence in the Basque Provinces.

[41] The meeting took place where the statue of Rafael Casanova (1660-1743) once stood. Casanova was a hero of the Barcelona siege (1714) and the last *conseller en cap*. As a symbol of the defence of Catalan constitutions, the monument receives homage annually on the *Diada*, the Catalan national holiday (11 September).

[42] When censorship began to soften its grip in 1958, translations of foreign works into Catalan were the first items to benefit (Gubern 1981).

suppressed preventive censorship in 1966, but this served only to restrict public debate and critical analyses of political reality still further. Indeed, penalties were increased for those publications that 'threatened' Spanish unity, instigating a new style of self-censorship. Important publications were not spared this onslaught: the magazine *Destino* was closed down for two months, its director was sacked and it was subjected to heavy fines for its anti-conformism. Such 'exemplary' punishments, together with another state of emergency in 1969, were designed to intimidate journalists and media professionals.

Yet the half-muted revival continued unabated. An ambitious campaign to celebrate Pompeu Fabra's birth centenary was articulated in 1968 through hundreds of public events under the title *La llengua d'un poble* ('A people's language'). All the political forces of the opposition were involved in the celebration. The first of fifteen volumes of the *Great Catalan Encyclopedia* appeared in 1969. The basis and action programme for a future government of Catalonia were now in place. It was evident that only political autonomy could allow an effective cultural normalisation and democratisation. Thanks to the strength of their culture, Catalanist militants acquired a new confidence in their fate as a nation. Although most political expression was outlawed, the Catalans could always find comfort in the study and contemplation of their heritage in the certainty that it would survive and thrive again. This was in sharp contrast to the Basque country where no such hopes could be cultivated by a disillusioned nationalist intelligentsia, who had been historically betrayed by their Castilianised élites.

How can this cultural revival be explained? Catalan culture was already firmly established before the Civil War. Repression from above and immigration from below threatened its vitality, but could hardly erase the awareness of a strong cultural potential. Postwar Catalonia was like a fertile field which had been covered with concrete, flattening all forms of life on the surface; grass soon started to grow up again through every available crack until nature reconquered what had once been its own.

Moreover, the Catalan language assumed an unequivocal political meaning. This was a telescoped repetition of what happened had under Primo de Rivera. In a spiral process, the state wanted to erase Catalan culture because it attributed a political meaning to it but culture itself increased its political meaning as a consequence of state repression: the flame of cultural nationalism still burned under the ashes of the Civil War. This contrasts to the experience of Euskadi, where cultural nationalism was weak from the start and its place was taken by military nationalism. Thus with the Basques the move from cultural to political nationalism (Hroch 1985, Hutchinson 1987) was replaced by a move from political to military nationalism, since military action provided the cohesive force which a declining Basque culture could not provide.

Also, thanks to the cohesive force of the cultural claim, Catalan opposition became united in a loose front encompassing not only nationalists but also Communists, Socialists, Catholics and even some Anarchists. In the same period, Basque nationalism remained ideologically fragmented due to the lack of a common platform, such as it had from its inception. All Catalan political parties, voluntary associations and labour unions joined in their demands for linguistic rights. 'It was in the obstinate adherence to language that the Catalans manifested the most decisive proof of their vitality and will' (Rossinyol 1974: 409).[43] Political autonomy – rather than independence – was the limited goal needed for such linguistic rights to become a meaningful reality. This assertive stance was derived from the inner conviction that Catalonia possessed a distinctive high culture with a unique literary and artistic heritage.[44] By contrast, Basque culture was derided by people like Maetzu and Unamuno (see chapter 9), an attitude with few parallels among Catalan intellectuals. Euskara was scarcely spoken and was country-rooted, but at the same time it represented a unique expression of ethnic distinctiveness. All Basque nationalists at some stage conceived Euskara as the quintessence of Basque identity. But its promotion was denigrated by mainstream intellectuals as a throwback to a culture that was degraded and oriented towards the past. Further-

---

[43] One of CC's founders, Miquel Coll i Alentorn described the importance of the cultural revival in the following terms: 'Cultural questions were our concern since the beginning, as we saw that the people were condemned to ignore their own culture' (interview by Colomer and Mascarell 1977: 51).

[44] Already in 1965, Pierre Vilar asserted that 'the stage of deep decadence is left behind and Catalonia lives now an indisputable moment of ascension' (Vilar, quoted in Rossinyol 1974: 414). This optimistic *Zeitgeist* was reflected in a positivist will to 'reinforce and improve Catalonia in all domains, to prepare her better to face the new stages of her existence by placing her in the context of Western society and the Europe of natural communities' (Rossinyol 1974: 414-5).

more, the fact that Euskara was scarcely spoken, especially in the cities, meant that it could not properly work as a tool of mass mobilisation, as with the Catalans. For many nationalists, especially the 'cultural' ones, dream and reality clashed. Arana dreamed that through his efforts alone, and with the help of a few trusted friends, Euskara could be revitalised, but he had to abandon this ideal as soon as he realised that Basque nationalism could not be based on language alone. He therefore chose race and religion, sowing the seeds of fragmentation and ambiguity in the nationalist message. Along with this fragmented character went an intransigent and radical emphasis on separation from Spain.

Before passing to the specific developments of the national struggle in Catalonia, we should reiterate the main argument of this chapter, relating it to the overall thesis. The strong cultural emphasis in Catalonia created the condition for a peaceful nationalist revival in which most opposition forces were accepted, independently of their ideology. This evolution has been made possible by a lively pre-existing regional culture, especially in terms of language and literature. The contrast to the Basque case has shown the importance of a lively cultural basis which is capable of resisting the impact of the state's assimilation policies. The lack of shared elements of cultural distinctiveness has been an important factor in determining the adoption of a strategy of violent action by the Basque nationalist leaders.

Paradoxes of a secular society: the Church as refuge of the nation

After the horrors of the Civil War, when hundreds of priests, monks and nuns were massacred by the Republican forces, it is no wonder that most churchmen and women received the Francoist troops as liberators.[45] Indeed we have mentioned that anti-clerical pogroms were a feature of Catalan 'progressive' politics from at least the turn of the century. Through the doctrine of *nacional-catolicismo*, the regime presented itself as saviour of the faith – and the country – and this was one of the pillars of its legitimacy. As the Vatican accepted the new Church hierarchy proposed by the

---

[45] Riquer (1989: 22) calculates between 8,500 and 9,000 victims of Republican repression. Nearly a quarter of them, 2,500 men and women, were clergy-people. For a collection of testimonies of the massacres, see Massot (1987).

regime, the Church became an instrument of assimilation.[46] For eight years, its higher echelons attempted unsuccessfully to de-Catalanise the regional clergy and all religious practices. Anti-Catalanist bishops were appointed in Tarragona, Lleida, Barcelona and Tortosa. As we have seen, Francoism attempted to influence celebrations of the mass to the extent of changing liturgical parapher-nalia and ceremonies. For many years, mass in Spanish became the rule. The Church hierarchy, particularly these anti-Catalanist bishops, were 'conscious instruments of Castilianisation, acting, more than as pastors, as servile functionaries of a regime which they identified with ideologically' (Culla 1989: 309-10).[47] However, the local clergy soon started to resent these attempts, offering the first possibilities of public gatherings where Catalan could be used.[48] Eventually, the regional priesthood became the main actors in the national revival of the early 1960s.

This leading role of the Church needs explanation. As we have seen, Catalan society is strongly secular. In 1963 only 15% of the population of Barcelona considered themselves to be Catholics, against 82% who claimed to be indifferent.[49] Paralleling the decrease in religious practice, the Church strove to recapture its role as a spiritual guiding light of social values. Young parish priests of urban origin who had not lived through the Civil War were beginning to enter the parishes (Gil-Delgado 1975, Hermet 1986). They were alert, active and intellectually aware. Ten years before the Second Vatican Council ('Vatican II') some of them were already attracted by the example of the French worker-priests, who 'merged a Christian concern for the poor with progressive issues and leftist politics' (Johnston 1991: 71).

The Benedectine abbey of Montserrat became the centre and symbol of this resistance, and people travelled there from all over Catalonia to hear a mass in Catalan. The catalyst event was provided by a celebration for the enthronement of the Virgin of Montserrat

---

[46] On the shifting Vatican policies towards Catalonia and its clergy, see Carreras de Nadal and Manent (1971).

[47] The only exceptions were the Bishop of Vic and, from 1963, the Bishop of Girona.

[48] On the role of the Church during the Civil War and its immediate aftermath, see Massot (1978).

[49] Diocesan sources, quoted by Culla (1989: 308-9).

on 27 April 1947. Three years before, the abbey had launched an appeal to raise money for the construction of a throne for the icon of the Virgin. As popular contributions reached an extraordinary level with kilos of gold and silver being donated, a few people organised a feast for the event by a series of parish meetings. Some of them, such as the historian Josep Benet, were not monks, but Left-wing secular nationalists. The success was beyond all expectations: about 100,000 people converged on Montserrat by every available means, on foot, by mule or in cars, from every corner of Catalonia. For some the pilgrimage lasted two or three days. 'That night, very few people slept because there were not enough cells for the pilgrims' (Fabres *et al.* 1978: 126-9).

In this first mass event of Catalanist affirmation, Catalan words were spoken publicly for the first time. A huge *senyera* (Catalan flag) was flown from the peak of a mountain, and the Civil Guard were unable to remove it for many hours. Aware that all this fervour was likely to be used by the Catalanist opposition, the *governador civil* (civil governor) nevertheless had to concede that 'it would have been a political mistake to refuse permission to speak Catalan at Montserrat' (cited by Fabres *et al.* 1978: 129). This unique event proved two things: the persisting strength of Catalanist sentiment among the faithful (and beyond), and the ideal position of the Church to act as ark and sanctuary for Catalan culture. But the regime unleashed a strong repression on both organisers and participants so that nothing remotely similar could be enacted again for many years. Henceforth, religious opposition to the regime's appropriation and misuse of *nationalcatolicismo* remained muted. But, given the regime's bias in favour of Catholicism, Churches and monasteries all over Catalonia were turned into safe havens for Catalanist militancy. They were the only environment where Catalanists felt protected from police irruptions and censorship.

Things started to change again in the 1960s. The example of the 339 Basque priests who in 1960 denounced the Church's support for the regime and thus risked Franco's wrath (see previous chapter) had a strong impact on the Catalan clergy. But the great stimulus for the clergy came after the election of Pope John XXIII in 1958, when he unexpectedly convened Vatican II (1962-5). His encyclical *Pacem in terris* (1963), the 'encyclical of freedom', condemned cultural and political repression against national minorities, which stirred up enthusiasm among the open-minded clergy. Non-believers too followed the developments of the Council with unusual attention.[50] As an unseen religious awareness permeated the country in the early 1960s (Culla 1989: 309), Church and civil society became re-united in a singular way: Catholic-inspired political activities sprang up all over the country and secular families sent their children to Catholic-run schools and leisure centres. The revival covered several fields: the *Publicacions Abadia de Montserrat* engaged in the publication of books and magazines that no private publishing house would dare to print. In the field of social work, there were about twenty associations of the lay apostolate which catered to local needs throughout Catalonia (Pi Sunyer 1971: 132).[51]

Under the aegis of the abbot Aureli Escarré (1908-68), the abbey of Montserrat became the core of Catalanism.[52] In 1963 Escarré released a famous interview for the French newspaper *Le Monde* in which he spelled out the toughest condemnation of the regime ever uttered from the *interior*. His declarations caused an international uproar and achieved unprecedented publicity for the Catalan cause. The accusation against the Spanish regime was that it had abjured fundamental Christian principles behind its façade of defending Christianity.[53] This was a burning indictment of the regime, since its legitimacy rested on Catholic backing. However, any direct attack on the rebellious clergy would have spelled disaster. Repres-

---

[50] The encyclical was directed to 'all men of good will', independently of their religion or belief. 'Universal peace', the Pope said 'is a good which interests all mankind without exceptions.' See John XXIII, *Enciclica Pacem in Terris*, presented and annotated by Joaquín Ruiz-Giménez, Madrid: Espasa, 1963. According to Ruiz-Giménez, the unprecedented relativist and tolerant character of the encyclical is evident: it does not present 'the minimal condemnation against any system as erroneous, nor the minimal concession to polemics. The only attitude which is openly condemned is racial prejudice.'

[51] The great popularity of the Church in the 1960s, which included a boom in religious books, made many people conjecture about 'irreversible Catholic hegemony' (Lorés 1980: 23).

[52] At least till 1947, Escarré was not an opposition sympathiser. His turnabout resulted probably from the impact of the Montserrat gathering in 1947, which he himself helped to organise (Minobis 1988).

[53] He claimed with words of fire: 'The real subversion existing in Spain is that of the government. . . What we have behind us is not twenty-five years of peace, but only twenty-five years of victories. The conquerors, including the Church, which was obliged to fight on their side, have done nothing to close the gap between victors and vanquished. . .' (cited in Read 1978: 203).

sion was a harder task after Vatican II when 'the opposition could quote Vatican guidelines in support of its actions' (Pi-Sunyer 1971: 132). Yet two years later Escarré was forced into exile, where he remained till his death, and the Vatican removed his title of abbot. Escarré's combative stance made him a hero for most Catalans, and a massive crowd attended his funeral in 1968 (Minobis 1988).

In 1966 the local Church joined the student movement and 130 priests demonstrated in front of Barcelona's police headquarters (*Jefatura*) against the ill-treatment of a student. When the procession was attacked, astonished bystanders could see the priests in gowns being chased in the streets and beaten with batons by police (Crexell 1992). The Christian Catalanist youth had its spearhead in the CC (Crist-Catalunya, later Comunitat Catalana) under the leadership of Jordi Pujol, the future president of the re-established Generalitat (Marcet 1987). CC was founded in 1954 as a highly informal group of friends imbued by social Catholic doctrine, mostly expressed in a paper called *Ponència* by their main ideologue Raimon Galí (b. 1917). This paper was a compendium of contemporary philosophy from a neo-traditionalist standpoint and was adopted as CC's ideological stand for five years (Lorés 1980: 10-21, Marcet 1987: 3-7, Muñoz 1979, 1990: 94-108).

The shift from religion to secularism was compounded by a new interest in Marxism among former seminarians and lay intellectuals. The rapprochement was mutual and paralleled by the abandonment of traditional anti-clericalism by the Communists. Religious organisations then ceased to be the vectors of the movement, as the torch passed on to the Left, notably the underground Communist Party.[54]

---

[54] According to Lorés, the change was sudden and irreversible: in a secular society like Catalonia, 'the coherence of Catholicism was maintained thanks to those 'values of rationing' typical of a postwar economy, [which proved] unable to withstand the impact of the 'values of consumerism' that displaced them in the 1960s . . . [This] was paralleled by a generational crisis of Marxist dogmas, of the unidimensional meaning of militancy . . . and by the appearance of all sorts of cultural 'heterodoxies', accompanied by an expansion of knowledge which invalidated many of the acritical Catholic and Marxist approaches' (Lorés 1980: 30). On the eclipse of CC, see also Fabre and Huertas (1981).

Paradoxes of internationalism: the Communists as makers of the nation

After Pujol's imprisonment, a small number of his followers started to focus on class struggle, developing their own brand of revolutionary socialism and finally abjuring Catholic confessionalism (Culla 1989: 304, Muñoz 1990: 166 ff). This evolution paralleled ETA's massive shift at the same time towards Marxism, although revolutionary socialism remained an epiphenomenon in more moderate Catalonia. From 1964 the Communist Party (PSUC, *Partit Socialista Unificat de Catalunya*) achieved primacy in the Catalan opposition. Nearly all active political opposition situated itself to the Left, while the Catholic nationalists led by Pujol limited their activity to cultural and economic enterprises devoid of political content. From the mid-1960s a grassroots movement for the propagation of national awareness and culture appeared under the motto '*Fer poble, Fer Catalunya*' (To make a people, to make Catalonia). This represented a break with pre-war Republican Catalanism, which Pujol and other nationalists held jointly responsible for the escalation which led to Civil War (Culla 1989: 300). The movement's Catholic inspiration was reflected in a concern for people's welfare, although it remained aloof from working-class organisations and interests. Its initial character was non-partisan. Convinced that the regime was destined to remain in power, Pujol preferred to devote his efforts to '*Fer País*' (Make/Build the country), i.e. to build up a private cultural and economic infrastructure as a bulwark against 'de-nationalisation'. In this way, it was possible to stimulate national socialisation with the spread of Catalanist values and symbols (Culla 1989: 304). That meant partly renouncing clandestine action and taking the maximum possible advantage of the occasional snippets of freedom bestowed by the regime. The politics of *Fer País* was conceived by Pujol as the 'central ground' (*terreny*) for action, and his group only timidly supported overt political activities (Culla 1989: 368, Lorés 1980: 21-8, Marcet 1987: 7-10).

By contrast, the PSUC was highly organised into political fronts which covered a huge variety of fields and emerging struggles, such as the neighbourhood associations and the feminist movement. Its magazine *Nous Horitzons*, written entirely in Catalan, became an arena for political debate in which leading nationalist intellectuals took part. The PSUC exercised a prominent influence on the unofficial labour union Workers' Commissions (*Comisiones Obreras*) and the student movement. Most important, the PSUC was able to make its activities appear legal, while assuming an open attitude to the other opposition forces (Culla 1989: 368). The PSUC itself obviously remained illegal – till 1977. The evolution of the Communists towards nationalism was slow but steady. During the first PSUC Congress, held in Paris in 1956, leading militants focussed much of their attention on the 'national question' (Ribó 1977). Meanwhile, atheism was slowly dropped from official Communist ideology. Why this slow opening to Christian ideals and even theology? The new theology emerging from Vatican II, with its semi-official dialogue between Catholicism and Marxism, reinforced the commitment of those 'progressive' elements within the Church who were more concerned with social issues. People of leftist leanings, such as the historian Josep Benet, played an important role in building bridges between the two fields (Lorés 1980: 23, Samsó 1991). It is interesting to note that Benet was a cultural as well as a political nationalist, and that many of his works dealt with the repression of Catalan culture.[55]

On 11 September 1967, the now Communist-led Comisiones Obreras for the first time officially participated in the *Diada* – an important step towards the inclusion of the Left and the labour unions in the broader Catalanist movement. For the first time, many immigrants attended. A new alliance between working-class organisations, the local Church and the nationalist intelligentsia was being forged. Two main issues brought together the Church and the Communists: the social question (particularly the integration of immigrants) and the national question (particularly language rights). The 'bridge' across the ideological gap was provided by the defence of Catalan culture, identity and interests.

The students between nationalism and radical fragmentation

From the 1950s Catholic students gave increasing attention to social problems, especially those concerning the immigrants. The universities were another sector where the regime decided not to intervene too heavily. One main reason was that most students came from the upper and upper-middle class families which sup-

---

[55] On clandestine postwar Catalan culture, see Samsó (1992) and Galien (1987).

ported the regime. Students were granted limited freedom to have their university organisations, but they increasingly resisted compulsory membership in the government-sponsored syndicates.[56] At the same time, universities reeled under the heady impact of foreign ideas and became an obvious forum for political opposition. This situation of contact with the outside world also gave them some leverage and the opportunity to publicise the regime's excesses. The University became a place of relative freedom, a laboratory of ideas, and a centre of recruitment for the opposition, while the regime considered university life to be a barometer of public order (Culla 1989: 371).

In March 1966, 500 student delegates, professors and intellectuals met to set up a new syndicate, the *Sindicat Democràtic d'Estudiants de la Universitat de Barcelona* (SDEUB, Democratic Student Union of the University of Barcelona). This event became known as the *Caputxinada*, after the name of the Capuchin convent in Sarrià, a suburb of Barcelona, where it took place (Crexell 1987). Again the Church worked as an active supporter of the opposition, and the assembly's location was an important factor in making the police initially desist from a frontal attack. Nevertheless, the police burst into the friary after a two-day siege. The news spread rapidly in the region, engendering a solidarity movement which had dramatically positive consequences for the consolidation of the opposition. It led to the creation of a coordinating body, the *Taula Rodona* (Round Table), under the initiative of the PSUC. For the first time in the postwar period, a vast array of opposition groups joined forces in a loose front: Communists, Socialists, Nationalists, Christian-Democrats and various independent figures.

The SDEUB acquired nearly unanimous support from students, 20% of whom were actively involved in its events. During the academic year 1966/7, it developed intense political and cultural activity in the shadow of Catalanism, the high point of which was a massive recital by Raimon. The regime responded by expelling over 100 students and professors, and suspending for one year the registration of all the students of the University of Barcelona.

Repression stifled much of the student movement, but in May 1968 the echoes of the European student revolts brought to the universities a previously unknown *gauchisme* ('leftism') resulting in

---

[56] On the student movement, see Colomer (1978).

the proliferation of several far left groups. These groupuscules tried to 'compensate for their lack of support with extremism and violence' (Culla 1989: 372), which provided the regime with an excuse for escalating its repression. In turn, the subsequent state of emergency drove the groups further towards ideological radicalism, and they proliferated in numerous violently militant teams. Before the spectre of endless fragmentation the struggle for Catalan identity offered a solid standpoint to many disaffected leftists, who in turn radicalised their posture, e.g. in claims for self-determination.

The vitality of Catalanist social networks: the Scout movement, hiking groups, football supporters, neighbourhood associations

We have mentioned the importance of the family in rearing and consolidating feelings of Catalanism and national identity. A major consequence of censorship was that every expression of national identity had to be acted out in limited circles of trusted friends and relatives. The result was the enlargement and reinforcement of solidarity and interaction within small groups. This led to the emergence of a Catalan middle-class network consisting of individuals from all ideologies and political tendencies who knew each other well. They formed a 'relatively homogeneous élite [who] inhabited a circumscribed physical and social space. Under such a situation, a village-like situation [arose] . . . that mitigated against anonymity and made it possible for almost everyone to know everyone else' (Pi–Sunyer 1971: 129). This seems to confirm visions of the nation as an extended family. As in Euskadi, fear of repression led to the gradual formation of 'loosely structured, often *ad hoc*, networks and cliques' (Pi–Sunyer 1971: 129). At this stage it was impossible for the authorities to regulate and check the activity of a myriad of *penyas* (get-together meetings held weekly at restaurants, bars and other public venues).[57]

The range and scope of quasi-formal associations which could by-pass the regime's control increased. Under the guise of shared professional or leisure interests, clusters of families socialised their children into the same groups. Associations of *sardanistes* (*sardana* dancers), folk-singers, hikers and excursionists, as well as choirs,

---

[57] The *penya*, with its 'fairly flexible membership . . . provides an excellent forum of discussion. Since everyone knows everyone else . . . the atmosphere is relaxed and talk is spirited' (Pi–Sunyer 1971: 130).

alumni associations, hobby groups, private clubs, football supporters, and Scout and Guide gatherings all served to encourage Catalanist socialisation.[58]

The Scout movement (*escoltisme*) became one of the most fertile grounds for the cultivation of Catalan culture and nationalism (Balcells and Samper 1993, Johnston 1985, Serra i García 1968). Many future politicians and school teachers had been through its ranks. The Scouts enjoyed special protection from the clergy, particularly those of the abbey of Montserrat. The movement expanded and in 1970 it numbered over 10,000 affiliated members. Parish centres organised all sort of social activities.

Excursion groups linked to a late eighteenth-century tradition of 'rediscovering' the countryside also flourished (Torres 1979, Johnston 1985). The intimate bond between the territory and its inhabitants is a crucial component of all nationalisms. Since nationalism is *per se* a territorial ideology, the cult of the territory assumed a central role in the ideology of groups like the *Centre Excursionista Català* (Nogué i Font 1991). Excursions were conceived as a means to communicate with nature – scientific excursions, and to identify with the national community – revival of folklore.

Voluntary associations have been a constant undercurrent in postwar Catalonia. In periods of harsh repression, they have provided a safety–valve for culture expressions which could not be voiced otherwise. Under Primo de Rivera, excursion groups and all other kinds of grass-roots associations served the crucial purpose of cultural resistance in both Catalonia and Euskadi (Roig Rosich 1992).

During late Francoism several groups began to spread in the cities, involving immigrants. In both Euskadi and Catalonia, the most important ones were probably the neighbourhood associations (*associacions de veïns*), which addressed the lack of welfare provision and urban planning typical of Francoist development schemes. Hence urban social movements in Barcelona were a response to the dearth of state intervention, as the inefficiency of the Spanish state gave rise to urban dissatisfaction (García 1990). Their success when moving from an underground basis to a programme of open participation

---

[58] According to Johnston (1983: 130), social networks play an important role in the growth of a movement 'prior to mass mobilization'.

was due to their mutual contacts within the framework of Catalan nationalism.

Since the nationalists did not have a state at their disposal, Catalan civil society had to rely on the spontaneous initiative of thousands of citizens. Grassroots Catalanist organisations had to work in extremely adverse conditions, as their formal recognition was made impossible by the dictatorship. But Catalan civil society blossomed at every level, with a creative strength not seen elsewhere, which was drawn from a pre-existing individualistic tradition of organisational autonomy (Giner 1980, Estivil and Giner 1985). Hundreds of informal cultural bodies and recreational entities, many of them clandestine, arose in every corner of the country in order to reorganise national cultural life. They did not represent a wholly new phenomenon, as we have seen in the preceeding chapter about Barcelona's rich and intense cultural life at the turn of the century. In the 1940s and up to the 1960s they assumed an informal and underground character. Most of their activities were directed towards maintaining Catalan culture (Johnston 1991).

Many of these organizations acted as a strong integrative force for the immigrants, spreading among them the gospel of nationalism. This socio-cultural participation, heightened by the thrill of fighting against a waning dictatorship, was an important factor in forging an elusive 'alliance' involving both immigrants and natives. The targets of Francoist repression continued to be both Catalan nationalists and working-class organisations. However, it was the former who displayed the most effective symbols of political mobilisation and inter-ideological alliances. Irrespective of their class, regional origin or political belief, most sectors of Catalan society united with the common goal of struggling against Francoism.

Thus the slow recovery of the Catalan culture determined the quality of the opposition's struggle. We have seen a deeply changed picture from the gloomy prospects of cultural genocide following the Civil War to the unexpected revival of the Catalan culture in all fields with the first gleams of freedom. This brought about a diffused sense of optimism, showing the unique value of cultural resistance – and cultural nationalism – in shaping a country's identity without needing to resort to violent strategies. In the conclusion of this chapter, we link this to the general argument of the book: the importance of core values and how they relate to the violent or non-violent choices of the nationalist intelligentsia.

The unitary front and the regime's agony (1970-1975)

In July 1970 Prince Juan Carlos was officially designated as Franco's successor, strengthening the impression of the regime's imperturbable continuity. But the echoes of the Burgos trial in December 1971 reverberated in Catalonia, engendering waves of protest and casting a dark shadow on the regime's authority.

The mobilisation for language rights continued with the campaign *Català a l'escola* ('For a school in Catalan') in 1970. November 1971 saw one of the key events of modern Catalan history, the creation of an unprecedentedly broad coalition of opposition forces which was named *Assemblea de Catalunya* (Assembly of Catalonia). The initiative and the main organisational tasks stemmed from the Communists, but the Assembly included socialists, social democrats, Catholics, nationalists, left nationalists, liberals *et al.* Under the banner *Llibertat, Amnistia, Estatut d'Autonomia*, three main points were highlighted: amnesty for political prisoners, a guarantee of liberty of expression and association, and the re-establishment of the 1932 Statute of Autonomy (Colomer 1976, Batista and Playà Maset 1991).

In a backlash, neo-fascist groups stepped up their activities in the early 1970s with a series of bomb attacks against bookshops, publishers, journals, cinemas and other centres of Catalan culture. Bibliophobic violence worked as a 'complement to legal repression' (Balcells 1980: 362). At the same time as the killing of Admiral Carrero Blanco by ETA clarified the crisis faced by the regime, Catalanist opposition turned increasingly to politics. From 1974 moderate members of the regime such as Fraga Iribarne sought to introduce reforms. In that year Radio Barcelona broadcast its first programme in Catalan, and a concert by the songwriter Lluís Llach in the Palau de la Música attracted an enthusiastic audience. Cultural nationalists then began openly to turn to political nationalism. In January 1975 Jordi Pujol called on the middle classes to take political action as the next phase, following the linguistic and cultural revival.

We have seen that the 'new' postwar Catalanism developed out of a series of historical events: the defeat in the Civil War (1939), strong cultural and political repression (1939-42), underground cultural resistance followed by a slow linguistic revival (1942-59), the economic boom (1959-72), unprecedentedly heavy immigration (1959-72), and a slow de-legitimation of the regime (1971-5). The main forces promoting Catalanism, especially in its cultural forms, were the Church and the Left (first of all, the Communists). Most social classes, with the notable exception of the upper bourgeoisie, joined in. Furthermore, the very economic success of Catalonia helped to reinforce group identity (Pi-Sunyer 1985: 262). Contrary to theories of economic deprivation, internal colonialism and the like, it was not a clear sense of economic grievance from a poorer region which engendered nationalism. True, economic complaints were often voiced, but they were summed up in demands for less state control and more freedom of enterprise. What, then, was the rationale of the opposition? Summarising, it can be said that nationalist mobilisation was deemed necessary in order to redress other kinds of injustice: cultural repression, lack of political freedom, and economic 'exploitation' (the middle classes and chunks of the bourgeoisie resented Madrid's centralised development plan).

We have also seen that the Catalanism emerging from the ashes of the dictatorship was partly new. Franco's ruthless repression and sweeping social change together instigated a re-definition of Catalan identity. As the traditional elements of nationhood came under heavy attack, the intelligentsia attempted a counter-mobilisation, first by addressing the contentious issue of whether 'Catalonia' still existed. This process of introspection began in the 1940s, and culminated in the publication of a few books on the 'Catalan character' (Ferrater i Mora 1980, Vicens Vives 1984).[59] The fierceness with which the dictatorship tried to suppress Catalan culture is seen by many observers to be the main cause of the re-emergence of Catalan nationalism.[60] The latter thus developed essentially as a reaction to the attacks against Catalan culture. Whether or not this interpretation is correct, it must be recognised that since at least the 1940s Catalanism was centred, perhaps more than ever before, on the issue of language and its recovery. The new Catalanism of the 1970s therefore had its roots in this dramatic violation of human and

[59] The phenomenon was echoed by the intelligentsia of two other Catalan-speaking areas, Valencia (Fuster 1977) and the Balearic islands (Melià 1967).

[60] For example, Salvador Giner argues: 'The intent to suppress the key features of a national community can produce a reaction opposed to the desired one. It is external oppression and not a pretended national essence which legitimizes nationalism' (Giner 1986: 447).

linguistic rights, around the defence of which all democratic forces converged. This concern for language stemmed from a long-standing tradition, analysed in chapter 7.

There was a vast section of people – especially religious people – who accepted the dictatorship as the lesser of two evils, the other being left-wing repression. Franco presented himself as the saviour of the country's stability against revolutionary anarchy and separatism (Preston 1993), but once this aim had been achieved and no sign of overt opposition had been seen for years, some sectors became increasingly impatient with Franco. Among the first to change their attitude were the local clergy, as they slowly welded alliances with the Catalanist opposition and, at a later stage, even with the Left.

The first nucleus of this covert opposition was formed in Montserrat, and the symbol of this turnabout was Escarré's shift to the democratic opposition. Previously a staunch supporter of Franco, the abbot became slowly convinced that the regime had gone beyond its legitimate aims and lost its *raison d'être*. The need to defend Catalan culture and to allow democratic reform played a key role in this re-awakening. However, after bitter years of unbridled repression, the dictatorship had to come to terms with the fact that Catalan culture could not be erased by decree. Defying formidable odds, the regional culture showed unexpected signs of strength, and began to revive as soon as the bans were slowly slackened. Most sections of Catalan society coalesced in the defence of the threatened culture, but the simple realisation that it was still healthy gave the whole movement a non-confrontational and optimistic character. Freedom was to be gained by everyday struggle rather than by eschatological solutions. All chinks in the armour of the regime had to be exploited. Dialogue and moderation became Catalanist keywords. The nationalist poet Salvador Espriu sang in his *La Pell de Brau* (The Bull's Hide):

> *Always remember this, Sepharad,*
> *keep the bridges of dialogue safe*
> *and seek to understand and love*
> *your children's diverse motives and tongues . . .*
> *That Sepharad may live forever*
> *in order and in peace, in work*
> *in difficult and deserved liberty.*[61]

---

[61] Translated by David Rosenthal (1991). As previously, mentioned, Sepharad was the name Espriu gave to this ideal Spain where all cultures and religions could

Espriu echoed a committed sense of empathy and solidarity not only with the other forces of the democratic opposition but also with other oppressed peoples, and *La pell de brau* 'did play an important role in opening new "bridges of dialogue" among the nations of Spain, with their 'diverse motives and tongues"' (Rosenthal 1991: 54).

In the late stage of Francoism, far-reaching social changes, such as immigration and a booming economy, shifted the focus onto new issues. In response, new political movements (Marxism, 'independentism' etc.) addressed these new challenges by trying to adapt to, and re-define, national reality. This process of re-definition was important in the intellectual arena, with the emergence of a new historiographal tradition and its related methodologies. This reflects a contrast between the two stages of defeat and renewal: early forms of opposition were virtually eradicated after the fall of Barcelona and barely survived till 1952 in the form of intermittent and weak guerrilla actions.[62] But a new moderate opposition grew out of the social upheavals released by the *milagro económico*.[63]

In contrast to the Basque case, accounts of repression and resistance to the regime are often pervaded by a sense of irony.[64] This can only be afforded in an atmosphere of ultimate self-confidence when the bases of collective 'integrity' are not under radical threat. The philosopher Ferrater i Mora (1980: 89 ff.) conceived *ironía* (irony) to be one of the four defining elements of the Catalan personality, along with *continuitat* (continuity),[65] *mesura* (measure), and *seny* (wisdom, good sense, judgement).[66] In the Basque case, it

---

live harmoniously side by side. The reference is to Spain before 1492, to the Inquisition and to Liberal Jacobinism.

[62] On Spanish guerrilla bands until 1960, see Pons Prades (1977).

[63] On Spanish opposition to the dictatorship, see the collection of articles in Tusell *et al.* (1990).

[64] See, for instance, Fabres *et al.* (1978).

[65] *Continuitat* refers not simply to tradition and history, but to everyday persistence. The value of *treball* (work) inspires every Catalan 'to finish always what s/he has begun and to give the final touch to all enterprises' (Ferrater i Mora 1980: 42-3).

[66] As the English journalist John Hooper has stressed, 'There is no exact translation of *seny*. Perhaps the nearest equivalent is the English term "nous" -good old common sense. Respect for *seny* makes the Catalans realistic, earnest, tolerant and at times a bit censorious. Yet it sits uneasily with their frequently tumultuous history' (Hooper 1986: 234).

is unusual to find the same sense of irony, living evidence of a strong underlying cultural identity. The Francoist attempts to eradicate Catalan culture had a grotesque character which was not lost on the opposition. Although its impact on Catalan culture was disastrous, the democratic forces recognised a sense of inner moral superiority in the face of centralism. Thus many accounts of repression given by Catalanist intellectuals, historians and social scientists, are pervaded by a subtle irony tempered by the bitterness of experience.

The Catalanist programme was carried out in the name of 'prudence and clarity'. This is the opposite of the programme that emerged from Ekin's days of reflections, which ended in radicalism and confusion, with no hegemonic project on which all sectors of the Basque movement could agree. This resulted in dividing the radical youth from the moderate *peneuvistas*.

From the 1960s onwards, the regime's previous 'policy of frontal assault was softened to one of slow suffocation' (Rosenthal 1991: 7). The main restrictions remained in force, while a steady flow of immigrants began to enter the region. This massive influx radically altered Catalonia's demographic balance (as it did in the Basque country), producing drastic cultural and social changes. At this point, the new nationalism hitherto confined to intellectual élites started to spill over into the general population, a process which the increasingly de-legitimised dictatorship could not hold back. The main concern for progressive intellectuals was the re-establishment of democracy and autonomy. But at a popular level the upsurge of nationalism also betrayed an apprehension towards large-scale immigration with its concomitant identity problems. This apprehension did not turn into a clash thanks to the previous formulations of the local intelligentsia.

Catalanism first re-emerged in purely cultural manifestations, and then slowly took a political form once the prohibition was relaxed. That was, step by step, the same process used at the time of Primo de Rivera and, before that, during the *Renaixença*, reflecting a general pattern of evolution of stateless nationalism (Hroch 1985, Hutchinson 1987). The fact that this itinerary could not be thoroughly followed in Euskadi because of the weakness of the local culture, and hence of cultural nationalism, has been mentioned in the previous chapter and is fully analysed in the final chapter.

6

THE TRANSITION TO DEMOCRACY

FROM CLANDESTINE ACTION TO THE
EUROPEAN COMMUNITY (1975-1986)

Franco's death and the beginning of the 'Transition'

On 20 November 1975 Francisco Franco died. Two days later Juan Carlos de Borbón was named King of Spain. The process of democratisation which immediately followed came to be known as the 'Transition' (*Transición*). On 25 November, only three days after his accession, the King proclaimed a first general amnesty, and about 15,000 political prisoners and exiles were freed.[1] The issue of a total amnesty was the crucial factor in the relations between the Basques and Madrid throughout the 'Transition' period.

The inability of the Franco regime to stay abreast of the radical changes brought about by large-scale industrialisation spelled its decline. At its end, not only was Francoism doomed but the very idea of the Spanish state was no longer legitimate in Euskadi.[2] This remained the case at least until the late 1980s, well after the Transition had run its course.[3] Nationalist unrest spread all over Euskadi, with demands for a general amnesty and popular demonstrations, while ETA's violence reached its peak. 'The Basque region during these days was like a pressure cooker about to explode. Sentiments for change had been so sharply suppressed during the

---

[1] The *abertzale* magazine *Hitz* published a list of 749 Basque nationalist prisoners soon after Franco's death. ('749 Gudari gizon eta ematze espetxeetan', *Hitz*, no. 5, January 1976, pp. 6-13). The pardon had affected fewer than 10 per cent of them (Preston 1986: 82). However, the demands for an amnesty concerned a much larger number of exiles.

[2] On the problems of the state's legitimacy in Euskadi, see Pérez Agote (1982).

[3] 'Arzallus dice que el Estado español no está legitimado en el País Vasco', *El Periódico*, 12 October 1987.

dictatorship of Franco that there had been little opportunity for the expression of dissent. With the dictator gone, Basques now sought to release the pressures built up over the preceding forty years' (Clark 1984: 90).

The period spanning the first general elections of 1977 to the approval of the Constitution in 1978 was one of crucial decision-making. As with passing of most dictatorial regimes, the success of minority nationalism in Spain was tightly bound up with the democratisation process. The prospects of democracy meant the first real possibility in decades for submerged nationalist feelings to find their voice freely (Gunther, Sani and Shabad 1986).

In 1976, the King appointed the first cabinet under the leadership of Adolfo Suárez. The unitary character and superior organisation of the democratic opposition on the periphery, particularly in Catalonia, compelled the Spanish political forces to confront the Catalan and Basque question (Balcells 1992: 203). The initiative passed from the Assembly of Catalonia to the political parties, most of which were legalised under Suárez's government. After being passed by the parliament, the democratic transition was formally accepted by popular referendum. The Law of Political Reform was approved by 69% of the Catalan electorate. As a consequence, the main Catalan political parties decided to abandon their vision of 'democratic break' or 'rupture strategy' (*estrategia de ruptura*) and endorsed a smoother process, omitting the question of the legitimacy of the monarchy and dropping any demand to 'purge' the state apparatus of former Francoist cadres (Balcells 1992: 204). In contrast, all Basque nationalist parties maintained a more intransigent line.

The initial procrastination of Madrid over fully accepting democratic reform was cut short by huge mass mobilisations in most Spanish cities. Catalonia was by far the most mobilised region of Spain in terms of popular demonstrations and civic initiatives. On the *Diada* of 11 September 1977, more than a million people attended the great demonstration in Barcelona called by all the opposition to demand 'freedom, amnesty and statute of autonomy'. Hailed as the biggest demonstration in postwar Europe, it gave an unmistakable signal to Madrid that the time for dismantling the centralist state had come. All the democratic forces contributed to its organisation, but the Left, rather than the nationalists *per se*, were its main instigators. The impact was immediate: on 29 September a decree established a provisional Generalitat and in October Josep Tarradellas, the president of the Catalan government in exile, was recalled home and became its first President.

In Euskadi popular mobilisations were continuously disrupted by violence. In March 1976 nearly 80% of the work force in Vitoria demonstrated to demand pay increases. After several days of barricades and police charges, in which popular marches swelled with new participants, five people were reported to have died. (Clark 1979: 269-71, Preston 1986: 82-3). Strikes, protests and street violence erupted in most Spanish cities in support of the Basque workers. As with most of the mobilisations following the Burgos trial, such manifestations of solidarity proved that the Spanish opposition as a whole was more interested in achieving full democracy than in the Right's abstract claim that the unity of the Fatherland was in jeopardy.

In Euskadi the first general elections in 1977 saw the PNV establish itself as the main Basque party, but it came a close second after the PSOE, Spanish Socialists (Llera Ramo 1985). In Catalonia, a huge victory was won by the Left, with the regional Socialists (PSC-PSOE) and the Communists (PSUC) heading respectively for first and second place.

Spain's path to devolution: from the Constitution to the Comunidades Autónomas

The new Constitution was approved in 1978. Various articles concerned the so-called 'autonomous communities'. Conferring official legitimacy on the regionalisation process, article 3 runs *verbatim*:

> Castilian is the official language of the State. All Spaniards have the duty to know it and the right to use it. The other Spanish languages will also be official in their respective Autonomous Communities according to their own Statutes. The richness of the distinct linguistic modalities of Spain represents a patrimony which will be the object of special respect and protection.

But any possible 'over-interpretation' of these rights was corrected by article no 2: 'The Constitution is based on the indivisible unity of the Spanish Nation, common and indivisible fatherland [*patria*] of all the Spaniards. It acknowledges and guarantees the right to autonomy of the nationalities and regions which form it and the solidarity among them.'[4] An important corrective to the latter sentence may be provided by article 145:[1] 'No federation between Autonomous Communities will be permitted under any circumstances'.[5] The patent aim of this article was to curb possible unifying trends among the regions. Pan-Catalanism spoke in the name of Valencia and the Balearic islands, while in Euskadi the question of an '*irredenta*' Navarre began to fuel nationalist fire.[6]

However, the most important point of the 1978 Constitution was its acknowledgment of the existence of other 'nationalities' (*nacionalidades*) within the one and indivisible Spanish 'nation' (*nación*). The three historical nationalities, which were not explicitly mentioned in the Constitution, are Catalonia, Euzkadi and Galicia (Gispert and Prats 1978). But the obvious trick was to extend decentralisation to most other regions, thereby 'relativising' the potential impact of Basque and Catalan autonomy. There are now seventeen 'Autonomous Communities' (*Comunidades Autónomas*, or *CC.AA.*) on the official map, some entirely invented.[7]

[4] '*La Constitución se fundamenta en la indisoluble unidad de la Nación española, patria común e indivisible de todos los españoles y reconoce y garantiza el derecho a la autonomía de las nacionalidades y regiones que la integran y la solidaridad entre ellas*' (art. 2 del Título Preliminar de la Constitución Española).

[5] *Constitución española/Regulamento del Senado* (1982). Madrid: Publicaciones del Senado.

[6] On the definition of Navarre as a 'Basque Ulster', see Blinkhorn (1974). However, in contrast to Ulster, religious cleavages are absent and the main conflict is between pro-Madrid 'regionalists', who want a limited degree of autonomy within Spain, and the nationalists, who defend Navarre's autonomy within a unified Euskadi. Navarre itself is divided between an *Euskaldun* north which is sympathetic to radical Basque nationalism, and a Castilianized south which supports autonomy within Spain. The capital Pamplona (Iruñea) is broadly situated at the intersection between these two areas.

[7] For instance, autonomy statutes were granted to Cantabria, an area whose ancient name was La Montaña, and La Rioja, both regions culturally and historically part of Castile. Madrid has been detached from its historical hinterland, Castile, and established as a separate *Comunidad Autónoma*, a sort of 'federal district' on the pattern of Canberra, Washington or Mexico City. Recently, local historians have been mobilised in order to confer on these administrative units a new regional dignity.

Not everybody is satisfied with the present status, and some regions claim a separate autonomy based on alleged historical roots. Thus some organisations in León wish their region to 'secede' from the Autonomous Community of Castile.

The Constitution can hardly be understood without taking into account the decisive role played by Catalan and Basque nationalism in the debates preceding its approval. Once approved by the parliament, the Constitution was submitted to popular referendum and was accepted all over Spain, by Euskadi. Most Basque nationalist forces opposed it, while the PNV abstained in the parliamentary vote.[8] The reasons for boycotting the Constitution were numerous and all related to the ambiguities of its provisions about Basque rights. In the ensuing referendum, the abstention rate reached 56% in Gipuzkoa and Bizkaia. Such a figure shows the small extent of the Spanish state's legitimacy in Euskadi, a situation which provided fertile ground for the continuation and spread of violence.

The next important step was to transform the Constitution's regionalist ideal into practice by creating the instruments of regional self-government. With its robust tradition, Catalonia was the obvious candidate to be granted this honour first. The Statute of Autonomy of Catalonia (*Estatut*) was approved in 1979 after a popular referendum: 61% of the eligible voters cast ballots and 88% of those supported the *Estatut*. Catalonia achieved an autonomous government (the Generalitat) and its own parliament. The Statue's charter declared Catalan the 'proper language' (*llengua propria*) of Catalonia, although it had to share the status of 'official language' (*llengua official*) with Castilian (Moll 1983).

The Basque Autonomy Statue was approved in the same period as the Catalan one and both were inspired by the experience of the Generalitat under the Republic.[9] Again a popular referendum ratified its approval in 1979, with 61% voting and 89% supporting the statute. Jesús María de Leizaola (1896-1980), the successor of Aguirre as president of the Basque parliament in exile, returned from France and so ended the forty-three-year-old 'government-in-exile'. In April 1980 Carlos Garaikoetxea, at that time leader of the PNV, became the first post-war *lehendakari* (head of the Basque government).

[8] On the Basque nationalists' attitude towards the Constitution and the Statute, see Hills (1980) and Tamayo (1988).

[9] During the Republic, according to Clark (1979: 349), 'the Catalan example proved to be the only one of negotiation over the transfer of powers. Since the Catalan regime was the first to be developed, its powers were subject to more bargaining. Subsequent regional entities, such as the Basque General Council, would have to follow the pattern established by the Catalan Generalitat.'

The ghost of Spanish nationalism

However, for some the process of devolution went too far. Provoked by the rapid spread of democratisation and regional autonomy, as well by ETA's assassinations, the most reactionary elements in the military were anxious to put a halt to the process. On 23 February 1981 a plenary session of the Spanish parliament was interrupted by a group of Civil Guards led by Colonel Antonio Tejero, who seized the assembly and held the MPs prisoner for more than one day. A providential intervention by the King apparently prevented the attempted coup, nicknamed the *Tejerazo*, from becoming an open military revolt.[10]

The shock of this adventure had long-lasting and damaging implications for the young democracy and halted further democratic progress, especially in matters of regional devolution. In a move conceived to pacify the 'bunker'[11] and banish rumours of a more serious coup, Madrid tried to pass a basic law (LOAPA, *Ley Orgánica de Armonización del Proceso Autonómico*). The law was officially designed to 'harmonise' the devolution process, but its surreptitious aim was to curtail the powers of the two main autonomous communities, Catalonia and Euskadi, by standardising the political power and representation of each region. Its attempted introduction in 1982 stirred vigorous popular protest from most of the opposition.[12] The impending threat of another *golpe* (*coup d'état*) had been

[10] The King has played a key role in transforming the regime while preventing a *coup d'etat* by the army. His firm behaviour in the face of the abortive coup by Tejero in 1981 caused the military revolt to subside, and the Transition to continue its course. The former leader of the Spanish Communist Party, Santiago Carrillo, has often remarked that without the King Spain would be embroiled in civil war (cited in Alba 1983). He has probably been the most popular political figure in Spain during the whole transition period. A survey carried out by DATA in 1977 indicated that 59% of the Spaniards chose monarchy, 19% were indifferent, while no more than 18% preferred the republic (cited by Linz 1979). The reason for this preference does not relate simply to the King's personality but is also historical. Since Spain's two previous republican experiences were fraught with conflicts and civil wars, republicanism does not have a positive profile in Spanish politics. The monarchy is seen as a supranational symbol of unity and stability.

[11] The term 'bunker' was often used in Spain 'to cover the extreme right committed to fighting democracy from the rubble of Francoism' (Preston 1986: 232).

[12] 'El PNV se sentirá desligado del estatuto si se 'nivelan' las autonomías, afirma Sudupe', *'El País*, 1 November 1984. Apart from all Basque and the Catalan

one of the main 'justifications' for promoting the LOAPA, but in August 1983 it was held by the Constitutional Court to be *ultra vires* and dropped after its enormous unpopularity became clear.[13]

Another event put the Transition process in Catalonia under considerable strain. Barely a month after the *Tejerazo*, a manifesto signed by a few sociologists (the complete list of names was never revealed) claimed that Castilian-speakers were subject to discrimination, and made an implicit call to oppose Catalanisation by political means. The reaction was immediate, but contrary to the one sought by its authors. Within five days, a counter-call 'in defence of the Catalan language, culture and nation' (*Crida a la solidaritat en defensa de la llengua, la cultura i la nació catalanes*) was published with the support of over 1,300 institutions and voluntary associations. Its organisers set in motion a vast mobilisation campaign, culminating on 24 June 1981 in a festival *cum* demonstration which filled up the *Camp Nou*, the largest football stadium in Europe. On 14 March 1982, the *Crida* with other groups organised a huge anti-LOAPA demonstration.

In a pattern recurring throughout Catalan history, what started as a reaction against an attack on Catalan culture turned into an increasingly political movement, but because this attack occurred within the framework of autonomy agreed by the nationalists with Madrid, the declared objective now became separation from the rest of Spain. The Crida's leaders capitalised on the threat to the core values of the nation, claiming that only with independence would Catalonia be liberated from the *españolista* threat. In order to counteract the radical independentist movement, which was popular among the youth, Madrid had to move rapidly and grant concessions to Catalonia. In the end, only the success of the Generalitat's politics of linguistic normalisation could curtail those who proclaimed that only independence would grant cultural freedom to Catalonia.[14]

In the 1982 general elections, the PSOE won an absolute majority

---

nationalists, the anti-LOAPA front also included the Communists (PCE) and the Andalusian regionalists (PSA). The law had been agreed on by the PSOE and UCD.

[13] For a legislative assessment of the LOAPA and the entire decentralisation process in comparative perspective, see Hannum (1990: 263-79).

[14] For a comprehensive, albeit partisan, history of the Crida, see Monné and Selga (1991). For a more critical viewpoint, see Candel (1985: 197-248, especially p. 239) and Laitin (1989).

in the Madrid's *Cortes*. For the first time Spain was ruled by a Socialist government, which remained in office till the spring of 1996.

The end of the PNV's monopoly over Basque nationalism

Since 1970 all relevant ideological activity within ETA has ceased. Yet, with the decline of Francoism, the ideological debate which originated in the 1960s spread among the wider population. From the first elections held in 1977, the nationalist parties grew continuously until they achieved an absolute majority of the vote (over 70%).[15] The spread of nationalism has enveloped all areas of society. It is difficult to relate this expansion to political violence. Certainly, many nationalists from all over the political spectrum believed that ETA still played a useful function to put pressure on Madrid. Moreover, active logistical support for ETA has been discovered in many respectable sectors, such as law firms, unemployed welfare societies, religious orders and so.[16] The PNV was the first party to benefit from democratisation, as it emerged reinvigorated from the political process which promoted autonomy. However, democracy and autonomy triggered the people's will to express their grudges and claims through other forces. In a pluralist system the PNV could no longer claim to be the only representative of Basque nationalism.

The situation was complicated by the persistence of political violence, which put pressure on the whole nationalist movement. A large sector of nationalist opinion still operated underground and looked to the 'heroic' gestures of the ETA activists rather than the moderate *peneuvistas*. Hence the challenge to both democracy and nationalism became – and remains to this day – the question of how to integrate this widespread support for the radical cause into the democratic game. As we see in the following paragraphs this process had resulted in the formation of three new nationalist parties.

Once Euskadi was granted an autonomy statute, ETA-pm, then the main branch of ETA, decided to drop the armed struggle altogether, while ETA-m continued its attacks. Many ex-militants of ETA-pm, together with a relevant sector of the local Communist

[15] Iñigo Gurrutxaga 'Avance costante de los partidos nacionalistas', *El País*, 2 December 1986, p. 16. See also Clark (1987).

[16] 'La policía cita a HB, comités de parados y a los abogados de San Sebastián dentro del "complejo ETA"', *El País*, 13 September 1987.

Party, formed in 1976 the electoral alliance Euskadiko Ezkerra (EE-Basque Left).[17] When it was founded, EE adopted a Marxist and pro-independence line, but eventually it moved on to an overall acceptance of the regional autonomy framework. The renunciation of violence was a slow process and had to pass through a period in which armed actions were used to supplement legal action whenever the results of the latter were insufficient. As Preston (1986: 125) points out, 'the abandonment of violence was to cause internal division, schisms and a nostalgic longing for armed action'. This testifies to the thesis that violence served a functional unifying imperative and, whenever it was abandoned, fissiparous trends emerged within the 'pacified' organisation.

At the same time, the continued use of violence was advocated by important sectors of Basque public opinion, which uncompromisingly vowed to achieve independence. Since the Spanish state was still perceived as the main enemy, the whole democratisation process was seen merely as a façade disguising the perennial Spanish attempt to eliminate Basque identity. This was the 'sectarian view that the elections were a stunt "to legitimise fascism" [and that] Spanish tyranny was now masked by the trapping of a fraudulent democracy' (Preston 1986: 126). Notwithstanding the autonomy concessions, the radical leftists declared that the Basques were 'persecuted more than before'.[18] Indeed, the 'occupation forces' were still massively present in the region as a reminder of Madrid's past attempts to crush Basque aspirations. Hence important sectors saw the severing of all ties with Spain as the only viable solution. To achieve this goal, ETA's actions were considered not only justified but necessary.

Herri Batasuna: the universe of anti-state protest

Eventually, those important sectors which supported radical separatism and gave moral endorsement to the use of violence had to be democratically represented. In November 1977 the veteran *abertzale* leader Telesforo Monzón (1904-87) called a meet-

---

17 On Euskadiko Ezkerra, see Ross (1993).

18 In 1983 the exiled leader F. Letamendia (Ortzi) declared that the Basques in general, not only the nationalist Left, were more persecuted than years before. 'Lo vasco, en general, y no sólo la izquierda abertzale, está ahora más perseguido que hace algunos años', *Egin*, 16 July 1983.

ing of these forces in Alsasua, Navarre, in which they agreed to form an electoral coalition named Mesa de Alsasua. In April 1978 it adopted a new name Herri Batasuna (HB–Popular Unity). The plethora of groups forming the HB coalition had a vested interest in the continuation of ETA,[19] on which some of them had been accused of being directly dependent.[20]

Like ETA, HB never had a proper leader or central figurehead,[21] and it has been characterised by an unparalleled flexibility in the renewal of its cadres.[22] An interesting feature has always been its ideological heterogeneity. Marxists, environmentalists, gay activists, neo-traditionalists, anti-nuclearists, cultural revivalists, punks, pacifists, feminists, unemployed, priests, small-town businessmen, students, peasants and every other imaginable sector from both urban and rural milieux are all well represented in what is probably one of the most unorthodox, unconventional and *sui generis* parties in Europe. What united all these groups was the rejection of both the Spanish Constitution and the Autonomy Statute, and the aspiration to independence. What kept their disparate interests in a single front was the confrontational character of the struggle, the blanket division of the world into oppressor(s) and oppressed. Violence and counter-violence turned into the *leitmotivs* and the glue of this multitude of social actors. Since independence was the key goal, all ideological differences were momentarily put aside. Thus the main inspirer of the Mesa de Alsasua, Telesforo Monzón, was a traditionalist *jelkide* (follower of God and the Old Laws) from the conservative wing of the PNV, but he declared himself willing to make alliances with anybody who was prepared to fight for national sovereignty.

HB and its predecessors seemed to have the capacity to absorb and make their own any conflict that emerged in Basque society. Thus all contemporary cleavages and social movements have been

[19] Probably, if one of these parties decided to go it alone it would fail to gain any relevant support. At most it could achieve the control of some minor municipality.

[20] 'Javier Solana dice que los partidos integrados en HB dependen de ETA', *El País*, 24 December 1987, p. 15.

[21] Rather, its leadership was beset by endemic discontinuity and power shifts. See Clark (1984: 204–18) on the internal organisation and hierarchical structure of ETA in 1981. However, such kinds of hierarchy were continuously changing.

[22] 'Herri Batasuna renovará a primeros de año a todos los componentes de su mesa nacional', *El País*, 24 December 1987, p. 15.

skilfully appropriated by radical nationalism finding a 'natural' means of expression in its milieux. A good example is the anti-nuclear struggle before the formation of HB.[23] In July 1977 an estimated 150,000 to 200,000 people demonstrated in Bilbao against the nuclear power plant of Lemoniz. Most of the mobilising efforts were carried out by the *abertzale* Left. The event, 'hailed as the biggest anti-nuclear demonstration ever' (Rüdig 1990: 138), triggered other political activities which culminated in ETA's attempt to blow up part of the installations. Also in this case, we can acknowledge the radical nationalists' ability to capitalise on key social issues, and their awareness of both popular feelings and burning contemporary problems. Although Lemoniz was 'primarily used as a political resource to further the appeal of Basque nationalism, . . . it is one of the few European nuclear stations which have been abandoned at a well-advanced stage of construction' (Rüdig 1990: 138-9).

By the 1980s HB became the first party in Gipuzkoa, the third in Bizkaia and the fourth in Alava and Navarre. HB was voted for by the youth of other regions as well, including Madrid,[24] where it has attracted the anti-state feelings of a few relevant sectors, especially students, fringe intellectuals and the unemployed. In these cases, the vote for HB was not so much in favour of Basque separatism as against 'the system'. In Catalonia HB became in 1987 the most popular of the lists not represented in the parliament (and the seventh among all parties, with over 40,000 votes), providing a vehicle for expressing the separatist feelings of the Catalan radical youth.[25] Herri Batasuna was finally legalised in June 1986'.[26] although many Socialist leaders opposed the move on the ground that it could stimulate its electoral growth to the prejudice of the PSOE.[27]

23 On the anti-nuclear struggles in Euskadi, see the pamphlet by Altabizkar (1974). A good synthesis is available in the international manual by Rüdig (1990: 137-9 and 212-13).

24 See *Anuario de Euskal-Herria*, 1987. Bilbao: Editorial de Amigos del Libro Vasco, pp. 163-4.

25 'La presencia de Herri Batasuna en Barcelona ha sido mayor que la del resto de grupos minoritarios', *El País*, 10 June 1987; 'HB es la séptima lista más votada en Cataluña para el Parlamento Europeo', *El País*, 13 June 1987.

26 'El Supremo ordena la legalización de Herri Batasuna', *El País*, 3 June 1986, pp. 1, 12, 15 and 16.

27 'Benegas relaciona el ascenso de HB con su "legitimación" por los tribunales', *El País*, 25 June 1986.

The challenge posed by the increasing popularity of the *abertzale* movement created strong tensions within the moderate nationalist field. In October 1986 a new party, Eusko Alkartasuna (EA–Basque Solidarity), arose as a splinter group from the PNV. The split precipitated early elections for the Basque parliament, since the PNV lost its ruling majority. In the ensuing election (30 November 1986), EA won 14 seats in the 81-member Basque parliament, exactly the same number as the PNV, a remarkable achievement for a completely new party.[28] The success was partly due to the charismatic personality of its leader, Carlos Garaikoetxea, the former *lehendakari*.[29] A major reason for EA's breakaway move was the PNV's governing alliance with the PSOE, which was considered not to be nationalist enough, threatening to erode the centrist position in favour of HB and the radical Left. Another reason which strained Garaikoetxea's relations with the PNV was the issue of centralisation.[30] Garaikoetxea aimed at concentrating powers in Vitoria (Gasteiz, the capital of the Autonomous Community) in order to avoid further administrative fragmentation,[31] but his modernising approach was opposed by the PNV's old guard, who advocated an articulation of provincial interests, especially in Alava.[32] The PNV's position was a tribute to the Aranist idea of a 'confederacy of free territories' honoured by a centuries-old tradition of provincial autonomies. As a non-violent party occupying the middle ground between the PNV and EE, Euzko Alkartasuna soon gained the support of hundreds of mayors and local councillors.

[28] In those same elections, the PSOE became the first party with 19 seats, HB increased its representation to 14 seats, and EE received 11 seats. Overall, parties advocating more autonomy or straightaway independence gathered more than 70% of the vote.

[29] Garaikoetxea had been the *lehendakari* from 1980 to 1984, when he was forced to resign.

[30] 'El PNV lleva ante los tribunales del partido a Carlos Garaikoetxea', *El País*, 21 July 1986, pp. 1 and 14.

[31] Patxo Unzueta, 'Identidad nacional y territorios históricos', *El País*, 25 November 1986, p. 17.

[32] The Ekin generation consistently criticised the PNV's old guard for the loosely decentralised structure of the party. They accused it of being *cantonalista* and tied to parochial interests, thereby hampering any possibility of a coordinated policy across provincial interests (see *Documentos Y*, vol. 1, 13, 19, etc.).

Basque and Catalan social networks

Young people have been the main protagonists of Basque radical nationalism.[33] Their nationalist socialisation was accompanied by the creation of a counter-culture different from that of the forefathers, yet assertively Basque. A main vehicle for the explosion of nationalist slogans was the rock concert. The new cultural universe thereby shared many elements of contemporary international mass culture. Yet it retained a strong militant flavour, expressed in the singing of lyrics in Euskara.[34] City and countryside met on such occasions. Although youth nationalist culture was made up of this unique blend of local, urban and cosmopolitan elements, the core of radical nationalism was firmly entrenched in the countryside.[35] The rural population formed the bulk of the support for the *abertzale* parties.[36] Another channel for the diffusion of nationalism has been sport, both traditional and modern.

The anti-nuclear struggle was carried out mainly by neighborhood organisations, fishing collectivities etc. The professional middle classes – doctors, architects, academics and those involved in cultural and leisure organisations – also took up the issue (Rüdig 1990: 138).

In the Basque country the crucial problem around which the whole Transition process revolved was the call for a total amnesty (*Amnistiak Osuna*), and all nationalist parties have included this demand in their programmes.[37] Amnesty demonstrations sprang up in every corner of Spain, but in Euskadi they assumed a special overtone; 'Frequent demonstrations were backed by labour dis-

[33] Rafael Castellano, 'La extrema juventud radical' *El País*, 1 December 1986, p. 19. Alfonso Péez-Agote, 'Euskadi, la nueva generación', *El País*, 2 December 1986, p. 11.

[34] 'Al trepidante ritmo de Euskadi, Folkis, punkis, jivi', *Punto y Hora*, no. 442, special issue, August 1986. 'Rock vasco deseo de cambio', *El País Domingo-Historia del Rock*, p. 563. See also Blasco (1987) and Lahusen (1993). On the movement of the *nueva canción vasca*, parallel to the Catalan *nova canço*, see also *Muga*, 8, 59, 1986, pp. 4-23.

[35] The town councils have been the principal political scene of HB's political activity, especially in the small villages of Gipuzkoa.

[36] 'El voto más radical se asienta en zonas rurales', *El País*, 12 February 1984. See also Clark (1981, 1984: 185-203, 1987).

[37] 'Carlos Garaikoetxea propone una amnistía sin restriciones en el País Vasco', *El País*, 23 September 1987.

putes, sit-ins hunger strikes and mass resignations by municipal officials' (Preston 1986: 82). From 1976 the spearhead of this kind of mobilisation was the *Gestoras Pro-Amnistía* (Pro-Amnesty Committees).[38] These were classical awareness-raising groups, as well as associations for the moral and material support of prisoners and their families. Each of the four provinces had its own committee, while their representatives toured Western European capitals to publicise the Basque prisoners' plight. Their stalls selling badges, stick-on labels, T-shirts and publications could be seen at any major Basque *fiesta* or street market. They participated in rallies and demonstrations, held press conferences, and raised money for the prisoners' families. They also provided medical aid for those lucky ones who were released from jail. Finally, they had contacts with international human rights groups, such as Amnesty International, which monitored any possible human-right abuse by police forces during the Transition. The fruit of years of popular mobilisations in favour of amnesty was Herri Batasuna. The coalition derived much of its strength from the periodic, cyclical and quasi-ritual character of such mobilisations: as ETA would continue its armed attacks, 'there would always be, no matter how many amnesties were granted, a fresh supply of ETA prisoners as a focus to rally the HB rank and file through amnesty mobilisations' (Preston 1986: 152).

Catalan social networks functioned in a different way, since there was not the catalyst of political violence. With the establishment of democracy, many formerly private and semi-clandestine initiatives passed into public hands. The nationalist movement was itself formalised and articulated in different political parties.[39] But, as political struggle became institutionalised, the civil society, which was previously its only support, began to lose its former central role. The neighbourhood associations which were the backbone of the urban social movement in the mid-1970s were on the wane and

---

[38] On the Pro-Amnesty Associations and the struggle for unconditional amnesty during the first years of democracy, see Clark (1979; 277-300) and Ortzi (1991: vol. 4: ch. 1: paragraphs 1-9; ch. 2: paragraph 84: vol. 2: ch. 6: paragraph 77).

[39] Since 1909, state-wide parties have not stood a chance of success in Catalonia if they have not been 'Catalanised' through either semantic arrangements or the establishment of regional sections. Left parties are among the strongest advocates of Catalanism: many members of the Communist Party endorse Catalonia's right to self-determination and even independence, while the Catalan Socialists propound a broad federalism for the existing Autonomous Communities.

nearly disappeared (García 1991). After achieving a massive peak during the mobilisations of 1977 and 1978, labour union member-ship drastically declined (Balfour 1989). Furthermore, Catalonia was not able to produce a nationalist union, perhaps an indication of the gulf existing between immigrants and native Catalans. In contrast, the Basque nationalist union STV-ELA became the biggest in Euskadi.[40]

Both in Euskadi and Catalonia, popular *fiestas* (*festes* in Catalan) represent a culminating moment for the expression of national identity. Local events, celebrations, folkloric, religious and even pre-Christian festivals acted as a catalyst of nationalist expression[41] –their integrative role is also mentioned in the chapter on immigra-tion. The basic unit of any mobilisation, and indeed of all social life in Euskadi, is the *cuadrilla*, the informal group of friends who meet regularly.[42]

Nationalist mobilisation was conducted against the backdrop of a general secularisation of society. In Catalonia we have seen the sudden decline of religion as a mobilising factor in the late 1960s. A survey in the mid-1980s has shown that about 75% of the Basques are believers, although only one-third are practising Catholics.[43] The present-day *abertzale* movement is basically secular, yet, as we said, it has attracted membership from committed priests and former seminarians.

---

[40] In the elections for workers' delegates held in enterprises in 1986, the ELA/STV took first place in the Basque Autonomous community, with 34.9% of the delegates, entitling it to 'most representative' status at regional level (see *Trade Unions of the World, 1989-1990*, Harlow: Longman, 2nd edn, 1991, p. 349).

[41] For an excellent study of the relationship between these *festes* and Catalan identity, see Barrera (1985). One of the most important is the *Patum*, celebrated every Corpus Dominii in the town of Berga. For the renewed importance and shifting meaning of the *Patum*, see Barrera (1985: 99-102 and 245-51), Farras i Farras (1986) and Noyes (1992).

[42] On the *cuadrilla* and other kinds of social networks, see Della Porta and Mattina (1985). Another Basque tradition is the *txikiteo*, which consists in a *cuadrilla* ritually going on a fixed itinerary from one bar to another drinking and eating small quantities of food (Ramírez Goicoechea 1991: 289-97).

[43] 'El 75% dels bascos són creients, però només un de cada tres habitants d'Euskadi és praticant', *Diari de Barcelona*, 19 February 1988. Se also Pérez-Agote (1990).

New developments in language planning

As an outcome of the new process of devolution, striking progress has been made in the field of linguistic rights: use of the three main non-state languages, Galician, Basque and Catalan,[44] is now constitutionally recognised. There are increasing pressures to add two other languages: Asturian (spoken in the region of Asturias) and Aragonese (*fabla aragonesa* spoken in a small mountain area of North-East Aragón). Furthermore, in the Pyrenean valley of Aran within Catalonia, the Catalan government has granted official recognition to Aranese, a Gascon variety of Occitan (see map 2).[45]

As expected, Catalonia played the leading role in the linguistic 'reformation' of the Spanish state. Privileged with a prolific tradition of sociolinguistic studies, Catalans had both the theories and the data to set in motion a policy of language planning.[46] In chapter 8 we mention some of the data which was indispensable to this task. The birth of an autochthonous sociolinguistic school dating back to the late 1960s was a response to the unparalleled Catalan situation – of a 'stateless' language which was not a minority language. Given such uniqueness, which demanded original case-studies, it was difficult to find international examples to emulate.[47] Once the Generalitat was established, the basis was there for a rapid change in linguistic policies. In all realms of culture, the powers of the 1979 *Estatut* far exceeded the ones provided by the 1932 statute (Balcells 1992).[48]

---

[44] Catalan also included its 'Valencian' regional variety. See Ninyoles (1969, 1977) and Sanchis Guarner (1972).

[45] For data on the present status and diffusion of Aranese, see Climent (1986).

[46] For a synthesis of Catalan sociolinguistics, see Vallverdú (1980). For its theoretical contributions, see also Conversi (1985, 1988b, 1992).

[47] Both Catlan sociolinguists and nationalists see the experience of Quebec as the most worthy of emulation, and academic contacts between the two counties are now firmly established. See, for instance, Manuel Parés and Gaëtan Tremblay (eds), *Catalunya, Quebec. Dues nacions, dos models culturals*. Ponències del Primer Simposi, Barcelona, May 1985. Barcelona: Generalitat de Catalunya, 1988; *ibid.* (eds) *Catalunya, Quebec. Autonomia i mundialització*, Ponències del Segon Simposi, Montreal, March 1987. Barcelona: Generalitat de Catalunya, 1990.

[48] In all respects related to culture and language, the powers given to the Generalitat in 1979 considerably exceeded those enjoyed under the Republic. In particular, the Catalans were given an unprecedented freedom in the control of mass media and education (Balcells 1992).

The Generalitat is composed of several Departments. Within the Department of Culture, a key role is played by the *Direcció General de Política Lingüística* (DGPL), an institution explicitly charged with coordinating language planning. In 1982-3, this agency set in motion a campaign aimed at increasing public awareness of language issues. The campaign was carried on with the help of various tools: gadgets, billboards, advertisement spots, strip cartoons, radio and television skits, adhesive badges and stick-on labels, balloons, music, free classes for adults, short movies, sponsored lectures, public debates and so on. One of its objectives was to encourage speakers to use their own languages while able at the same time to understand the language of their interlocutor(s) without expecting the latter to be reciprocate (Boix 1993). Borrowing from the Catalan sociolinguistic school, the DGPL described this 'ideal' practice as *passive bilingualism*, where a speaker would use his/her language expecting an interlocutor to do likewise rather than switching language (Vallverdú 1980). Bilingualism was thus meant to be encouraged as daily practice.

The campaign was a prelude to a new law passed in 1983 by the Catalan parliament with the unanimous approval of all political forces. The *Llei de Normalització Lingüística* (Law of Linguistic Normalisation) set the juridical basis for language use in all public domains (Generalitat 1983). In particular, it established Catalan as the language of instruction.[49] So, step by step, the official use of Catalan was extended, it recovered the space and the status it formerly enjoyed under the pre-war Republican government, and in many cases even improved upon it. Similar Laws of Linguistic Normalisation were approved in Galicia, Euskadi and Navarre. The Basque and, to a certain extent, the Navarrese governments have attempted to make good use of the Catalan experiment, although from a much more difficult point of departure. A promotional campaign was put into action, and a Law of Linguistic Normalisation for Euskera was approved by the Basque parliament in 1984 (Villa 1986).

In short, by the 1980s the use of regional languages in Spain was finally secured through the Constitution, national decrees, statutes of autonomy and laws of linguistic normalisation.[50]

---

[49] For a brief discussion on this law, see Mar-Molinero (1989: 314).

[50] For a chronology of educational legislation in Catalonia, see Petherbridge-Hernández (1990: table 1)

The overall aim in this chapter is to show the portentous expansion of nationalist mobilisation as soon as democracy was installed. In Euskadi, the diffusion of nationalism was characterised by increasing fragmentation, not only among parties but also within them. In Catalonia, the nationalist message also spread and became more diversified, while maintaining a broad consensus around a few central themes.

As we have repeatedly stressed, our main aim is to show the importance of cultural models and symbols, especially language, in the delineation of patterns of nationalist mobilisation. Notwithstanding the extensive changes which the two nationalisms have gone through, the key characteristics of both have been maintained throughout dictatorship and democracy. Catalan nationalism remained moderate and broadly united around a cultural platform. Basque nationalism kept its radical separatist posture and its internal fragmentation. If anything, Basque nationalism increased its radicalism, thanks to state repression.

This chapter also confirms the second main thread of the book, i.e. the relationship of cultural and political fragmentation to political violence. In Euskadi the scattered nationalist scenario was continuously compounded by mass mobilisations resulting from the alleged 'crimes of the occupation army'. Funeral processions of murdered *etarras* or other Basque militants turned into epic events of national self-assertion (Aretxaga 1988). The massive and threatening presence of the police and other mechanisms of state control exacerbated the conflict and ignited popular discontent. The intrinsic confrontational character of Basque mobilisations, a partial fulfillment of the 'action/repression/action theory' envisaged by ETA's first theorists, has in some way handicapped any peaceful solution of the conflict. Since repression was needed to hold such an eclectic movement together, ETA was also needed as a continuous trigger of both 'state violence' and 'nationalist counter-violence' – and as a bonding agent for the nationalist movement.

A key feature of ETA was its all-pervasiveness. The military organisation responsible for terrorist attacks was just the tip of the iceberg of what has been named the 'ETA complex'.[51] A whole

---

[51] 'La policía cita a HB, comités de parados y a los abogados de San Sebastián dentro del complejo ETA', *El País*, 13 September 1987.

oppositional ideology with its own language and separate institutions emerged from the conflict. Lawyers were particularly prominent in the struggle, but other professions were well represented.[52] Slogans, graffiti, posters, *murales*, placards, banners and all kind of visual propaganda inundated the Basque public space (Chaffee 1988, 1993). With democracy this heterogeneous yet tightly bound world burst into the open as a major actor in local politics, finding its electoral expression in HB. This organisation is notoriously accused of being ETA's political wing, but its huge strength in votes and popular support reveals much about the illegitimacy of the Spanish state in Euskadi.

In the twilight of dictatorship, the struggle for democratic rights went hand in hand with the fight for cultural freedoms and political autonomy. These were all viewed in the framework of a single inseparable concern to attain the political goal of civil liberties. Soon after Franco's death, the unitary movement reached its maximum momentum in 1977. Massive street demonstrations, particularly the million-strong *Diada* in Barcelona and the continuous clashes with the police, as in Vitoria in 1976, put an inescapable pressure on the central government's resistance to change. Nevertheless, the unity of democratic opposition started to break down in 1978.

According to a survey in 1982, 38% of the Basque population considered ETA activists to be idealists and patriots, and only 31% believed that they were criminals or insane. However, the same survey showed that only 8% of the Basques claimed to support ETA, while 77% said that they were opposed to its activities (Linz 1985: 614; Olabarri 1985). This blend of justifications and accusations may derive either from a persisting fear of expressing one own's view, or from the fact that some people really believed in the genuine commitment of ETA's activists. However, successive surveys indicate a slow decline in ETA's popularity, especially after 1987 (a period not covered in this book).[53]

Another opinion survey undertaken in 1982 indicates that only 13% of the population in Euskadi felt primarily Spanish, 24% felt a dual Basque-Spanish identity and 60% considered themselves only

---

[52] On the recent 'discovery' of young lawyers as a major secret force behind ETA, see 'Tape traps Eta Lawyers,' *The Independent*, 6 February 1993. On the social class and occupation of ETA's members, see Clark (1984: 144-7).

[53] ETA's popularity certainly declined after 1987 as a result of indiscriminate killings and purely terrorist acts which departed sharply from its original tactics.

Basques. By contrast, 30% of the Catalans felt primarily Spanish, 40% assumed a dual Catalan-Spanish identity, and only 26% considered themselves Catalans (Linz 1985: 527-673, supra note 782).[54] Thus Basque identity seemed to be more accentuated than the Catalan one. Considering that immigration figures were roughly the same in Euskadi and Catalonia, such percentages seem to contradict our basic argument that Catalan culture and nationalism are more integrative than the Basque. But we are considering here the much more elusive issue of identity and feelings of belonging. It is undeniable that under Francoism and in its aftermath the Basques have developed a more inclusive and open identity.[55] However, this new identity has been formulated at the cost of a more moderate brand of nationalism. It was the overall confrontation with the Spanish state and its 'occupation armies' that moulded an overarching identity in which blood-type and surnames no longer mattered. Moreover nationalist leaders saw the Basque nation as verging on extinction, and it was the continuous emergency character of the situation which created an all-pervasive aura of solidarity between all sections of the population. In the end, especially during the Transition when the illegitimacy of the state reached its zenith, all kinds of social issues from class struggle to women's liberation and the environment, were subsumed under the umbrella of radical nationalism. Disguised by a circumstantial unity, Basque culture remained spontaneous and fragmented, while the cultural revival begun in the 1960s only started to be transformed into a unitary 'high culture' in the mid-1980s.[56]

A key feature in recent Basque politics has been the formation of new nationalist parties challenging the PNV's supremacy. Such a development has contributed to the articulation of the nationalist message along different political lines and competing ideologies. In the Basque Country ETA has been the backdrop of such changes.

---

[54] The difference is even sharper as regards working class perceptions: only 14% of the 'Catalan' working class considered itself Catalan, compared with 40% of working-class Basques.

[55] See Jáuregui (1981), Gurrutxaga (1990), Pérez-Agote (1986), Tejerina (1992).

[56] A unified standard *batua* was only proposed in 1964, accepted by the Basque Language Academy in 1968 (Sarasola 1976: 23) and adopted as Euskadi's co-official language after 1980 (Villa 1986). Ever since, this unifying norm has spread through the media, the schools and other means, contributing to create a new shared identity based on language, rather than on any of the previous shifting and divisive values.

Given its popularity and its symbolic value, ETA became an inescapable point of reference for a galaxy of groups, interests, unions and individuals who were seeking representation in the new democratic political arena, but at the same time rejecting the dominant value system.

Nationalist pressures have resulted in momentous institutional changes. Spain was transformed from the most centralised West European state to one of the most decentralized. Though often hampered, the Basque and Catalan Autonomous governments succeeded in being granted considerable powers in many sectors. Now Catalonia has its own parliament, school system, television channels, social welfare etc. Likewise, the government of Euskadi, with its seat in Vitoria/Gasteiz (in the province of Alava/Araba), enjoys similar prerogatives, albeit separately from Navarre; since the early 1980s, the Basque Autonomous Community has its own police force, the *Ertzaintza,* as the Catalans have their *Mossos d'Esquadra.*[57] Gasteiz's government has even moved swiftly into areas previously not covered by governmental action. For instance, it has offered the best official support in Spain for the development of new technologies.[58] Its efficiency, like those of its Catalan counterparts, has been widely acclaimed in the Spanish press.[59]

---

[57] 'La Ertzaintza quiere ocupar su sitio', *El País,* 24 November 1986.

[58] 'El paraíso de las subvenciones públicas', *El País*, 27 November 1986, p. 19.

[59] 'Eficacia autonómica', *El País*, 18 December 1989.

7

LANGUAGE AND OTHER VALUES

This chapter has a twofold aim: first to underline the persisting importance of language in Catalan nationalism, contrasting it with the discontinuous attention which it has received in the Basque context; and secondly, to explore how the stress on a particular core value has influenced the development of two very different nationalist ideologies. The choice of a special symbol of national identity, such as language or race, can have direct political consequences, as reflected in each movement's ideological formulations. This choice is based on the availability of pre-existing cultural 'material' and human resources. In broader terms, historical and anthropological conditions have the power to influence, indirectly but consistently, patterns of political mobilisation.

Three related assumptions can be demonstrated: first that where an ethnic language was scarcely spoken, its absence made the choice of another element of national identification difficult; secondly, that language was a core value for the Catalans, while it was not so for the Basques, at least till very recently – a difference related to the dissimilar diffusion of the two languages; and thirdly, that for the Basques, the absence of a clearly identifiable core element created ambiguity and conflict in the nationalists' political programmes. We speculate on how this difference affected the development of the two nationalisms, relating this difference to their inclusive or exclusive nature. The contrast shows how minority linguistic nationalism, which is the major expression of cultural nationalism, can be *inclusive* and other kinds of nationalism (e.g., racially or religiously oriented) *exclusive*.

Among many elements that a nationalist movement can choose, the Catalan movement was greatly facilitated by the availability of a lively, rich and widespread language. Even today the contrast between the two regions remains stark: whereas over 90% of the population in Catalonia proper (the *Principat*) understand Catalan and more than 60% can either speak or read it (CIDC 1987), in the Basque Autonomous Community only around 20% of the population knows Euskara, with a maximum of 35-40% in Gipuzkoa and a minimum of 4-5% in Araba (Letamendia 1987: 23).[1] Seven main dialects correspond broadly to the seven Basque provinces. A standard form of Euskara (*batua*) is only recently attempting to bridge this segmented plurality. By contrast, the Catalan language was fully standardised at the beginning of the twentieth century by Pompeu Fabra, and is now universally accepted by all Catalans.[2] Catalan represents a paradox in the contemporary European scene, since it may be the only 'minority' language[3] which is rapidly expanding the number of its speakers – this increase is backed by abundant and reliable data.[4]

To understand this phenomenon we must take into account a peculiarity which sets Catalonia sharply apart from other 'minorities', especially from the Basques. In its syntax, lexicon, phonetics and even orthography, Catalan is very similar to Castilian. In contrast, Euskara is completely unrelated to any other known language,[5] being the only remnant of a pre-Indo-European aboriginal stratum. Catalan is a neo-Latin (Romance) language, thereby belonging to the same family as Spanish, Italian and French.[6]

[1] In the three provinces of the Autonomous Community in Euskadi, the number of Basque speakers has recently increased from 21.5% in 1981 to 24.5% in 1986 (Tejerina 1992: 165).

[2] The exception being some 'regionalist' groups in Valencia and centralist forces, which have attempted half-heartedly to foster regional varieties of Catalan.

[3] The term 'minority' is unsuitable to describe the situation of Catalan fully, because it is not a minority language in its own territory but only in respect to the overall Spanish state. Neither are the Catalans conceivable as a minority in a 'social' sense, i.e. as a disadvantaged sector of the population.

[4] In Galicia, Spain's third historical nationality, Galician is spoken by over 80% of the population. However, the nationalist movement has been traditionally weak. Comparing the three regions, it seems that, contrary to most assumptions, the popularity of nationalism is inversely proportional to the diffusion of the local language. Euskera is by far the least diffused of the three languages, both in gross numbers and in proportion to the territory claimed by the nationalists.

[5] The most known, yet unproven, hypothesis claims that Euskara is related to Georgian. Other philologists and linguists have speculated on a relationship with Peul, Berber etc.

[6] A superficial observer may think that it derives from an intermingling of Spanish and French (and even Italian). Its detractors emphasise its *patois*-like character and

This structural similarity and proximity to Castilian explains why immigrants can learn it without excessive effort or investment of time. This also explains why it was easier for nationalist élites to formulate an 'inclusive' nationalist programme, given their faith in the possibility of cultural integration.

Core values and key symbols

A recurring phenomenon among successful nationalist movements is their use of mobilising symbols which are deemed to be central to the self-definition of their community, and which convey widely shared popular values. Since the nineteenth century, European nationalist movements have been particularly concerned with language. Among present-day ethnonationalists, language continues to be the basic criterion of self-definition and nationhood. Few works have attempted to explain the reasons for this emphasis. Gellner's (1983) focus on industrialisation and its need for social mobility seems to refer exclusively to the rise of the nation-state and may be less relevant to more recent ethnonationalist movements, which he explains in term of uneven development. One might argue that, since the model cherished by many ethno-nationalists is the state itself (i.e. they wish to achieve their own separate statehood), they also try to emulate the state's stress on an unified culture, by contrasting their languages to the dominant one. Hence there is a correlation between state intervention in the cultural-linguistic domain (compulsory literacy, homogenisation) and the counter- tendency among ethnonationalist movements to emphasise their language. West European stateless languages have dramatically receded in the last two centuries, and one of the causes of this shift, though by no means the only one, has been official monolingualism enforced by the state (Fishman 1968, 1972, 1980, 1982, 1985, Haugen 1966). Therefore language has acquired a previously unknown political dimension, and its centrality has increased in most nationalist claims. Language shift and language politicisation have developed in tandem. However, imitation *per se* – imitation of state policies – cannot account for the stress on language. Theories of ideological diffusionism (Kedourie 1993)

---

its 'hybrid' features from the border area

thus offer a limited explanation for the spread of the special bond between language and nationalism.

Endogenous psychological and economic factors also play a role. According to different viewpoint, 'an emphasis on language is usually an emphasis on something else – on dignity and economic power. Socioeconomic fights can be carried out under a linguistic guise; language as culture lends the necessary symbolism' (Khleif 1979: 61). However, to assert that language is merely a disguise for civil rights or welfare claims would be missing the point. Language is indeed both a means and an end; it has both an instrumental and a symbolic value, and, as Khleif himself recognises, it is one of the many available boundary mechanisms. Just as symbols are central to national mobilisation and in all processes of border-making, language plays an indispensable role since it is the most elaborated symbolic system available to man. The more so if the symbol in question has the power to subsume in itself the entire identity of the group.

Every ethnic group confers particular importance on a specific element of its own culture. This stress, as well as the element in itself, is subjected to change especially in contexts of inter-cultural contacts and inter-group communication. According to Jerzy J. Smolicz (1981, 1988), there are elements which more than any other appear apt to epitomise the intimate essence of a culture: they therefore become its *core values*. Smolicz defines them as 'pivots around which the whole social and identificational system of the group is organised', insofar as they form 'the heartland of a group's culture and act as identifying values that are symbolic of the group and its membership . . . Removal of such pivots, through enforced 'modernisation' or dominant assimilation, would result in the entire edifice crumbling to pieces' (Smolicz 1988: 394). Different words can be used by others in order to define the same concept. Susan di Giacomo (1989) has applied to Catalonia Ortner's definition of *key symbols* as those 'key elements which, in an ill-defined way, are crucial to [the group's] distinctive organization' (Ortner 1973: 132). At the same time, 'all nationalist movements select from the range of symbols available to them one, or perhaps two, that represents them and their goals' (Di Giacomo 1984: 21-2).

In his comparative studies on immigrant ethnic groups in Australia, Smolicz has observed how each group tends to emphasise a peculiar aspect of its own cultural tradition which is held to be of paramount importance. Such an element can vary from one community to another: in some it is the *religion* which is manifested as a differentiating factor (Smolicz cites the Irish, Arab, Malay and Polish examples),[7] in other groups this role is assumed by the *family* (Italians and secular Jews), in yet others it is the *race* (Chinese).[8] In view of its importance, *territory* could also be considered a core value among the Aborigines and other Native groups. Yet a territorial dimension is present in all kinds of nationalism. The most universal core value in the contemporary world, however, is *language*. It is of basic importance among all literate groups, where it is occasionally superseded by other elements according to a particular historical or political situation and to their relation with dominant or other groups. The significance of language is also heightened among those groups whose sacred texts are written in their tongue, but in these cases religion often has priority exactly because it is a religion written and codified in sacred texts.[9]

This perspective also underlines the situational and historically-determined character of each core value. Periods of oppression or foreign domination are often those in which these values are consolidated. If a particular aspect of one's own culture, especially when it is already perceived as important, is proscribed or forcibly marginalised, then the affections and attentions of the community coagulate with particular energy around it.[10] As an example of this shifting stress on different cultural elements, the core value for Poland was language essentially up till the Second World War. It then became religion, for the very reason that it was this aspect of Polish identity which had been particularly restricted (Smolicz 1981). Likewise, a thorough study of legislative measures against Catalan shows that they have often strengthened the linguistic consciousness among regional élites, even though some of them adopted Castilian (Ferrer i Girones 1985). The next section il-

---

[7] Hutchinson also illuminates the Irish case, arguing that a 'plausible reason for the decline of the [Irish] language is that, as a symbol of nationality, most Irish men and women regarded it as definitely secondary to religion' (1987: 308).

[8] On the centrality of race in Chinese nationalist discourse, see Dikötter (1993).

[9] See the parallel importance of religion and language in such groups as, for instance, the Arabs, the Georgians or the Armenians.

[10] On the oppositional character of national identities, see Scott (1990).

lustrates that Catalan is a classical core value, and that its political importance has been strengthened as a consequence of repression.

The cultural roots of nationalism

In chapters 2 and 3 we saw that both nationalist movements, particularly the Catalan, were preceded by cultural revivals. These revivals were often apolitical and their protagonists conceived regional regeneration in the framework of a Spanish nation. The result was a partly unintentional regional nationalism. A similar process was repeated during the two dictatorships (Primo de Rivera and Franco) when, due to the banning of political parties, people turned to culture as a safe haven for nationhood. But in this case the focus on culture was not unintentional and culture quickly became politicised as the highest expression of nationality. As soon as the regime weakened its grip, cultural resistance gave way to political resistance. This is a known phenomenon: 'The struggle for nationhood in the modern world has been *preceded* everywhere by emerging cultural nationalist movements. . . These movements have formed *recurrently* in post-eighteenth century societies as historic cultural revivals, in order to propound the idea of the nation as a moral community, and have inspired rising social groups to collective political action' (Hutchinson 1987: 2). Indeed, once the political movements were established, they had to rely on a pre-existing definition of what the essence of the nation should be. By that time, this work had normally been completed by the cultural revivalists who, as in most ethnonationalist movements, preceded the political nationalists.[11] However, our stress here is on the type and impact of the cultural revival, since the evolution of political nationalism also depended, in turn, on which aspects of the national culture had been selected as central values.

In Catalonia the *Renaixença* provided an essential basis for the subsequent spread of nationalism. Its success and the rich output of Catalan literature ever since (Terry 1977) constitute a solid base upon which political nationalism could build its legitimacy. In the Basque case we have seen the much more modest precedent of the

---

[11] Whereas this has been the case for Catalanism, it has only been partially so for Basque nationalism. As we have seen, its founder, Sabino Arana, also had the task of being a myth-maker and a creator of values for his nation.

Asociación Euskara (1877- 83), founded in Pamplona by Navarrese intellectuals to preserve the language.[12] The association's estimated membership of 300-400, with a minimal popular influence, seems insignificant in comparison to the great manifestations of the Catalan *Renaixença*. However, the Asociación Euskara assembled people of high standing: researchers, professors, liberals, priests. These were the same categories of people who later became prominent in the Basque nationalist movement (Letamendia 1987: 58). However, the revivalists were not successful in spreading their message of cultural regeneration to the masses. (The other group, *Euskalerria* (1876-99), was not precisely a cultural movement.)

The relatively small success of the Basque revival, in comparison to the Catalan *Renaixença*, can be ascribed to many factors, but certainly the most important is the sparse diffusion of Euskara, coupled with a low language loyalty among the upper classes, and with diffuse diglossic habits among the overall population.[13] Sarasola (1976: 179-83) considers that the overall number of books published in Basque during the sixteenth, seventeenth, eighteenth and nineteenth centuries is slightly over 600. In comparison, the number of publications in Catalan for the same period rises to several thousand.

The concept of *diglossia* is helpful when comparing the Basque and the Catalan case. In a classic article Ferguson (1959) describes it as the uneven coexistence of two languages, or varieties of language, within a single community. The high variety is used in public and formal domains; it has a written and standardised form, and is normally associated with a high status. The low variety is spoken in informal situations, for instance, within the family, among friends *et al.*, and it normally has little prestige. Basque is a standard case of diglossia.[14] By contrast, Catalan has been associated with a high position at least since the nineteenth century, because of the lan-

[12] See Chapter 3, section '*Euskaros* and *Euskalerriacos*: an aborted Basque renaissance'. On the *Euskaros*, see Elorza (1978a: 11 ff.). On the *Euskalerriacos*, see Larronde (1977: 261 ff.).

[13] The concept of 'language loyalty' was coined by Uriel Weinreich (1953) and, since then, it has been extensively used in sociolinguistics (Fishman 1966).

[14] With the Autonomy Statute (1979) and with its final codification in a standardised variety (*batua*), the Basque language has moved – slowly – to a higher (H) position. Yet, it still faces great difficulty to spread among most of society.

guage loyalty of most of Barcelona's middle and upper classes.[15] It therefore has to share its 'relative prestige' with Castilian.[16] *Diglossia* in its simple form has never really prevailed in Catalonia, although daily interactions respond instead to 'diglossic patterns',[17] partly because of the past proscriptions by the central governments. Catalan sociolinguists use the term *linguistic conflict*, rather than diglossia (Aracil 1982, Vallverdú 1972, 1980). A linguistic conflict is conceived as an unstable situation in which two languages compete for hegemony and its final result is either the disappearance of the weaker language (and the triumph of the stronger one) or its full normalisation (Conversi 1985, Kremnitz 1993). *Linguistic normalisation* is therefore defined as the effort to extend the use of a language to all the formal and informal domains which had hitherto belonged exclusively to the dominant language (Vailverde 1980, Kremnitz 1993).

Catalonia: language as a unitary bond

As we have seen, Catalan nationalists consistently focussed on the issue of linguistic rights. For them, as well as for lay people, language was both a symbol and an essential instrument for the diffusion and the expressiveness of their own culture. This can be clearly seen from a rapid glance through the key texts of the principal Catalanist intellectuals and politicians, who persistently saw language as the vessel of national identity (Marí 1987). Such emphasis appeared less pronounced at the end of the nineteenth century than it does today, as reflected by the following statement of Almirall: 'In reality, language is not the most important element of the personality of a people, because what doubtlessly has more importance is the community of moral and material interests. . . However, while not being the most important, it is the most visible. . . A distinct language supposes a distinct character. The

---

[15] Language loyalty was not a constant and universal feature amongst Barcelona's upper classes. See McDonogh (1986: 108-22) for the adoption of Castilian among the upper bourgeoisie, particularly in periods of centralisation.

[16] On the concept of 'relative prestige' applied to the Catalan case, see Woolard (1982).

[17] A lengthy and critical presentation of the concept of diglossia is available in Vallverdú (1973, 1980), who prefers the term 'diglossic patterns' for the Catalan case.

form of expressing ideas corresponds to the way of conceiving them' (Almirall 1979: 77). For Almirall language was merely the main visible manifestation of a people's personality; what seemed to matter to him more was the mentality and 'spirit' of Catalonia. Yet language is deeply associated with his idea of a Catalan character,[18] and he subsequently adds in Romantic overtones: 'The use of our language is the *more eloquent* manifestation of our personality. Until the Catalan language will exist, every attempt at [cultural] unification will be a true act of tyranny, whichever the domain in which it will be exercised' (1979: 78, emphasis added).

The Bishop of Vic, Josep Torras i Bages (see Chapter 2), tried to promote religion as an alternative value. Nevertheless, he also recognised that 'Language is the people . . . the thought of a nation, it is what characterises and portrays it . . . Among all the social bonds, apart from religion, language is the most deeply unifying' (Torras i Bages 1981: 42). Torras i Bages continually stressed the Christian origin of Catalonia in the Middle Ages, so that the Catalan 'spirit' and Catholicism were seen as inseparable dimensions of a single world-vision. He is often quoted as saying 'Catalonia will be Christian, or will not be' (Benet 1968). However, his attempt has remained relatively unsuccessful in an increasingly secular society. In Catalonia, unlike the Basque country, religion did not play a central role. On the other side, the secular Enric Prat de la Riba asserted: 'Language is the most perfect manifestation of the national spirit and the most powerful tool for nationalisation and, therefore, for the survival of a nationality' (Prat 1978: 84).

Prat's vision tended to identify Spain's nationalities with the distribution of its linguistic territories. Therefore he proposed rebuilding the Spanish state on the 'natural base' of four federated regions: Galicia, Euskadi, Catalonia and Castile (this last including Andalusia and all other Castilian-speaking regions).[19] This also implied the reunion of all Catalan-speaking territories under the project of a Greater Catalonia, which would have included the *Principat*, the Valencian region and the Balearic islands. Prat (1978) expressed this project in his theory, but in practice he was a moderate

---

[18] In referring to the national character, Almirall never used the concept of *Volksgeist*, which was later introduced from German philosophy and elaborated by Prat de la Riba.

[19] See Map 2.

politician, inclined to compromise and bilateral negotiations with the central government. Beyond his wider ambitions, he was able to stand firm on a few points: decentralisation and, above all, a full development of the Catalan language and culture. During his presidency of the Mancomunitat, the efforts for the recovery of the language were increased and systematised. (Among the new institutions, we have mentioned the Institut d'Estudis Catalans and the work of Pompeu Fabra.) From Prat onwards, language assumed an ever more central importance, as expressed over and over again by other nationalist leaders:

'Our language, the expression of our people, which can never be given up, . . . is the spiritual foundation of our existence.[20] ... The Catalan problem has as its only foundation the existence of a sense of Catalan distinctiveness [*fet differencial*], of an irrefutable and indestructible Catalan personality. Within this distinctiveness, the least questionable [element] is language and the adhesion of Catalan people to their mother tongue (Cambó 1930: 26-6).

... Of all the elements which constitute a nationality, language is the deepest, the strongest and the most decisive. That value, at once corporeal and spiritual, which Joan Maragall found in the word, turns language into the symbol and the lively expression of the personality of a people (Rovira i Virgili 1982: 208).

... Language is the strongest marker of a nationality. The linguistic map of Europe is, . . . with a few exceptions, the map of its nationalities. Linguistic unity is the synthesis of all other unities: it presupposes in the peoples a long cohabitation, a shared culture, a common history, and a centuries-old brotherhood. Thus it becomes an indestructible spiritual bond (Rovira i Virgili 1982: 97).

... The Catalan personality can only be fully expressed through the intermediary of its language. When the latter recedes, the former fades, weakens and becomes corrupted, . . . the Catalan ceases to be a Catalan . . . [and], in ceasing to be a Catalan . . . he/she ceases simply to be (Ferrater i Mora 1980: 140).

---

[20] Catalonian Cultural Committee, *Appeals on Behalf of Catalonia*, Geneva: Catalonian Cultural Committee, 1924, p. 13, cited by Fishman (1972: 46).

According to the writer and historian Joan Fuster, language is 'not only the result of a previous unity [of all the Catalan people], but also the main thrust for the future and the basis of new bonds of solidarity' (Fuster 1977: 134). Economists, such as Carles Pi-Sunyer (1888-1971), also expressed the idea that language was deeply inter-linked with identity and economic prosperity.[21] This tie between language and identity has been continually stressed up till the present, and in recent years, it has been increasingly emphasised. To mention a recent case, on March 1989, Jordi Pujol met Felipe Gonzalez, the socialist head of the Spanish government. Pujol's speech included the following:

> 'The language issue will indicate whether the relations with the central government are progressing or not. . . *If some issue is absolutely crucial to Catalonia, it is its language and culture,* because they are the core elements of our identity as a people. Catalonia will not deem its historical grievance resolved until the cultural issue is settled. . . *Catalonia did not want autonomy for political or administrative reasons, but for reasons of identity*'.[22]

Pujol re-stated the crucial importance of language when, on a visit to the Emperor of Japan (23 May 1990), he praised King Juan Carlos for being the 'first head of state who has spoken Catalan for many centuries'.[23]

The central importance of language in present-day Catalonia means also that cultural and political nationalism often coincide. In Catalonia social actors concerned with language and politics do not necessarily play different parts, because language is an overriding concern which sometimes supersedes even economic interests.[24]

---

21 Carles Pi-Sunyer (1929) saw the nation as a linguistic and cultural entity. As a nationalist, he claimed that nations aspire to have their own state, but more recently expressed his deep rejection of aggressive expansionist nationalism, such as in pre-war Germany. He contrasted the latter with the liberal and open character of Catalanism (Pi-Sunyer 1975).

22 Declaration of Jordi Pujol, in *El País*, 2 March 1989, p. 14.

23 *El País*, 24 May 1990.

24 To confirm this, it is enough to consider the yearly expenditure which the Catalan government specifically allocates to language planning and to the improvement of the knowledge of Catalan in the school curricula. The initial monetary input directed towards the creation of an autonomous TV channel was also very high.

Whether or not they play different roles, the drama is certainly played by the same actors. Yet many non-nationalist intelllectuals and politicians, while deeply committed to the use of Catalan, are also uncomfortable about the use of language by nationalist.

Euskadi: out of assimilation, fragmentation

Chapter 3 examined Arana's struggle to define the key elements of Basqueness and its ambivalent attitude towards language. In his early formulations, language was not a core value and was replaced by race and religion. The Basques therefore found themselves in a much more difficult position in their attempts to select an element which would carry the symbolic weight of national identify.

There was a further obstacle in the use of language as a unifying national symbol. It was in fact used by Arana and his followers as an *ethnic border*,[25] i.e. its function was to divide the autochthonous population from the newcomers. This is in sharp contrast with the Catalan case, where language has been conceived as a tool of integration. So Arana simply saw language as a means of keeping the Basque people away from mixing with the 'foreigners':

The Vizcayans [Basques] are as much bound to speak their national language, as not to speak it to the *maketos* or Spaniards. It is not to speak this or the other language, but rather the difference between languages which is the great means of preserving ourselves from the contagion of Spaniards and avoiding the mixing of the two races. *If our invaders were to learn Euskera, we would have to abandon it*, carefully archiving its grammar and dictionary, and dedicate ourselves to speaking Russian, Norwegian or any other language, as long as we are subject to their domination. For the Catalans it would be a great glory if the Spanish government appointed Catalan as the official language of all Spain; on the contrary, if it were to do the same with Euskera, it would be for us the final blow of unavoidable death dealt from the most refined diplomacy (Arana 1982: 404).

---

[25] The concept of language as an 'ethnic boundary' has been applied to Welsh by Khleif (1979), though with a more general meaning.

Yet this attitude of Arana is paradoxical in so far as we know that one of his main concerns was the recovery of his country's ancestral tongue. Arana's strategy was also to utilise the language (at least in part) as an instrument of political mobilisation, albeit only among the *Euskaldun* population. However, this strategy could not be pursued in the cities, especially in Bilbao where Arana operated and his PNV was founded, had its first meetings and achieved its first electoral successes in 1907.[26] Here Euskara was hardly spoken.

This seems to be a basic contradiction: Basque nationalism emerged among those sectors of the population who did not speak Euskara[27] – following a pattern common among nationalist movements worldwide. Arana did not know Euskara and his parents did not speak it at home (García Venero 1968: 239, Ortzi 1975: 124). However, he learned the language through sheer determination – a measure of his commitment.[28] The nationalist periodicals and magazines of the turn of the century (even the official organ of the PNV), were written 80% in Spanish, 'an essential condition, if this kind of press were to attract readers' (Letamendia 1987: 25). Probab-

---

26 However, it is also true that for the last ten years the centre of gravity of Basque nationalism has shifted eastward from Bizkaia to Gipuzkoa and today the highest proportions of nationalist voting can be found in the countryside and small towns (Clark 1987: 437). Other anthropological studies deny the rural character of Basque nationalism. In the French Basque country, the youth's renewed interest in nationalism was not shared by most elders (Ott 1981: 28) and nationalism is much weaker than in the Spanish side. Among some plausible reasons, one is at once economic and tied to state-building: 'The people realize that they owe much of their recent economic prosperity to the French social security system and the various government subsidies, which now provide them with more than half their annual cash income' (Ott 1981: 28). Thus, in the case of France, it could be said that the all-pervasiveness of the welfare state had a de-mobilising effect. State intrusion does not necessarily result in a nationalist reaction.

27 For a different thesis, albeit one which refers to the late 1970s and early 1980s, see Clark (1979: ch. 6, 1980: 81-83, 1981, 1987: 439). According to Shabad and Gunther, today it is in Euskadi 'that the use of the regional language is more strongly associated with attachment to the ethnic group', confirming a shifting trend in Basque identity and in the identification of core values (1982: 450 ff.).

28 Arana himself learned Euskara from scratch during a long convalescence, using as his only source a French-Basque dictionary written by Willem Jan van Eys (1825-1914). He learned it well enough to use it in his political writings (all of them collected in the 3-volume Arana 1982 ca.). Many of his first works were etymologies and it was his intention to write a Basque grammar (Basaldúa 1977: 47, 53). On van Eys's work, see Villasante (1979: 279-80).

ly the nationalist ideology had more appeal to those urban groups which felt a greater sense of dispossession and loss of their culture: this was a grievance to be redressed through political action, although they themselves were incapable of maintaining, let alone extending their own use of Euskera.

These ambivalent attitudes of most early Basque nationalists can therefore be blamed on the scanty diffusion of Euskara: political activists revered it as a national symbol, but they overlooked it as a modern means for communication. In this they were simply perpetuating the *diglossia* which they inherited from centuries of assimilation.

In his consideration of language as an element of national awakening, how far was Arana influenced by his five-year stay in Barcelona? He lived there at a time when nationalism and language revival were both on the rise. Arana's biographers have pondered over the influence of his stay in Barcelona on his formulations, but they could hardly prove that Arana was inspired by Catalanism. On the contrary, 'If there were some influences, they were only negative' (Larronde 1977). His writings on the 'Catalanist errors' are full of pejorative comparisons between 'Vizcaya' and Catalonia. For instance, Catalonia is considered a Spanish region which aspires to mere autonomy, while Euskadi never considered itself part of Spain and strove for independence: 'Catalonia suffers from the ingratitude of her own mother Spain, Vizcaya has been taken over by an alien nation, which is the common Fatherland of Catalans, Balearics, Galicians, Valencians, etc. We can already see how unreasonable is an alliance between the Catalans and the Vizcayans...' (Arana 1982: 406). Arana was explicit about the difference between his programme and the successful Catalan one:

> Catalan politics, for instance, consists in attracting other Spaniards to it, whereas the Vizcayan programme rejects all Spaniards as foreigners. In Catalonia every element coming from the rest of Spain is Catalanised, and it pleases them that urban immigrants from Aragón and Castile speak Catalan in Barcelona. Here we suffer greatly when we see the name 'Pérez' at the bottom of a poem in Euskera, when we hear our language spoken by a *riojano* teamster or a Santander salesman, or by a Gypsy, or when we find a *maketo* [Spanish immigrant] name among a list of seamen shipwrecked in Vizcaya. The Catalans want all Spaniards [immigrants] living in their region to speak Catalan,

but for us it would be ruin if the *maketos* resident in our territory spoke Euskera. Why? Because the purity of race is, like language, one of the bases of the Vizcayan banner [*lema*]. *So long as there is a good grammar and a good dictionary, language can be restored even though no one speaks it. Race, once lost, cannot be resuscitated* (Arana 1982: 404).

We see later the reasons for this preference for race over language. Here language is considered merely as a symbol, it makes little difference if nobody speaks it. The word 'immigrants' is inserted in parentheses because Arana seldom used it, perhaps because he did not want to emphasise their migratory nature, as much as their foreignness and Spanishness; the purpose might well have been to underline their extraneousness and as an alien body which Basque society could not absorb.

Arana's strategy was to adopt a double and contradictory attitude towards the autochthonous and immigrant population. The following shows the ambiguity of his project *vis-à-vis* the language:

'To an *euskeriano*' [native speaker of Euskara]

In the streets of the towns of Vizcaya I have seen many children speaking *erdera*.[29] Are there any Vizcayan fathers in these towns? Yes: But it is not enough to be a son of Vizcaya. It is necessary to be a patriot.[...]

You tell me that you don't love *Euskera*, because it does not have any utility. I perfectly understand this; it is better than loving it [just] because it is beautiful. But is not Euskera the language of your race and of your blood? It is not the language of your fatherland?

If a people loses its tongue, it is because it has become the slave of another people. Do you want to be the child of an enslaved people?

Don't you have a fatherland? If you have it, why don't you love your language?

If you don't love the language of your fatherland, you can't love your fatherland either. If you do not love your fatherland, you cannot love your forbears. Do you want your children and progeny to despise you? (Arana 1982: 1306-7)

---

29 *Erdera* = foreign language (specifically, Spanish). *Erdaldun* = speakers of foreign languages (specifically, Spanish-speakers).

'To an *euskeráfilo*' [non-native speaker of learner of Euskera]

To know Euskera means nothing if one is not a patriot. Patriotism is everything, even if one does not know Euskera.

Euskera cannot save the Fatherland; only patriotism can save it.

Propagate patriotism and, along with it, the language will also be propagated. If you propagate Euskera as a language without Fatherland, the enemies of the Fatherland could be understood and could understand with it.

Many are the Euskerianos who do not know Euskera. This is bad. Many are the maketos who know it. This is even worse.

Great damage can be done to the Fatherland by one hundred *maketos* who do not know Euskera. Even worse is the damage that can be done by only one *maketo* who knows it.

If Euskera dies, it is because there are no patriots.[...]

In the heart of the Fatherland, every *Euskeriano* who does not know Euskera is a thorn; every *Euskeriano* who knows it and is not a patriot is two thorns; every Spaniard who speaks Euskera is three thorns.[30]

This passage is clear evidence of a double strategy of using Euskera as a purely patriotic symbol (one thorn) subordinated to wider nationalist goals (two thorns), while refusing to spread it as a modern communicative means or to assimilate the immigrants (three thorns).

As expressed by another influential figure of Basque nationalism, Father Evangelista de Ibero, nationalist leaders had at their disposal different elements around which a national sense of awareness could be formed: Basque origin, character, language customs, laws, 'glories' (historical past), 'tendencies, aspirations and destinies'. But language was given a secondary role: 'Of all these properties, which one constitutes essentially a nationality? *In the first place, the blood, race or origin; in the second place, the language*. The other qualities are nothing but the consequences of the first two, most specifically of the first' (Ibero 1957: 17).[31] Like other early nationalists, de Ibero stressed race and religion as the key element of national identity.[32]

---

[30] 'La Patria. A un euskeráfilo', *Baserritarra*, no. 8, 20 June 1897, reprinted in Arana (1980 ca.: 1307-8).

[31] Also quoted by Krutwig (1963: 547) and Linz (1973: 37).

[32] On Father de Ibero's Catechism, with its characteristic technique of question and answer, see Martínez-Peñuela (1989: 38-48). Religion came even before nationality: 'Between seeing Euzkadi in full exercise of its rights, but separated from

However, writing three years after Arana's death, he also declared that 'physical difference will never be as important, as intimate, as scientific, as that of language and moral character' (Ibero 1957: 18, cited by Payne 1975: 88).[33]

Race and the concept of collective nobility

The stress was thus firmly placed on race as a substantial characteristic of the *'ser vasco'* (being Basque). The motives of this stress can be found in the peculiar anthropological situation of the region, to which the nationalists tried to adapt. In the Basque country, Euskara had become a minority language, spoken by a minority within the minority. Its destiny of extinction was sensed by many early nationalists and pre-nationalists.[34] The appeal was therefore directed to race. This was a more obscure and less tangible element, although in the Basque case it was charged with mobilising effects. But why race and not any other element or value? Was there no more accessible symbol of identity available? A possible answer lies in the semantic transformation of the ancient concept of 'collective nobility' (*hidalguía colectiva*). This was the 'moral core of the Basque sense of ethnic uniqueness', a fact that 'seems to have few parallels elsewhere in Europe', in so far as 'any Basque able to prove birth of Basque parents . . . was automatically recognized as noble by virtue of purity of blood' (Greenwood 1977: 86).

The historical origins of *hidalguía colectiva* can be traced back to at least 1053, when for the first time, the inhabitants of a local valley were granted permission to bear arms and raise their own popular militia.[35] But the great bulk of these concessions date from the late fourteenth century, coinciding with the first major thrusts towards

---

Christ, and seeing her as in 1901 [i.e. as an integral part of Spain], but faithful to Christ, the PNV would opt for the second' (de Ibero cited by García Venero 1968: 325 and Clark 1979: 44).

[33] For de Ibero, race was then defined by language (quoted by Clark 1979: 45-6). Since race was defined by language, language was in turn conceived as an impenetrable barrier of protection around Basque culture and values.

[34] For instance, Arturo Campión wrote that 'Euskara is *retiring to the mountains in order to die closer to Heaven*' ('El Baskuenze', 1901, cited by Heiberg 1989: 48, emphasis added).

[35] See also Baroja (1971-2: 73) and Aranzadi (1981: 395-431).

Spanish centralisation, and conferred in order to protect the northern borders which the new centralisation trends had made vulnerable to French incursions.[36] 'Unable to afford massive border defences, the Catholic kings and their successors were able to use grants of collective nobility to insure themselves a degree of border control. The Basque sense of ethnic uniqueness and their acceptance of the idea that they were Spanish were at that time easily compatible' (Greenwood 1977: 92).

'Reverse' theories of modernisation (Connor 1973, 1994) claim that ethnic conflicts and wars are a by-product of modernisation (see ch. 1).[37] When economic development irreversibly alters traditional lifestyles, nationalism attempts to reconcile the new state of things with the ancient system of social relations. That is why nationalism ummistakably arises in the cities, since cities epitomise modern disruption. It can eventually spread from the cities to the countryside, but not usually the other way around.

In Euskadi resentment against increased state control, urbanisation, industrialism, immigration and the abolition of the *fueros* produced an explosive situation, which was to find political expression through nationalism only many decades later. Many historians stress the abolition of the *fueros* as a main cause of the subsequent rise of Basque nationalism (Payne 1975, Corcuera 1977). Their abolition was the first blow to traditional Basque identity, and may also explain the difference in core values from Catalonia. While the Basques retained their traditional privileges till the nineteenth century, Catalonia had to relinquish them more than a century before. Yet a distinctive Catalan sense of identity was affirmed from time to time, following a pattern of continuity. Early Basque nationalists found in the persisting notion of a collective nobility a basis on which to build a cohesive sense of distinctiveness. Here we can identify the origin of Arana's deep concern for racial integrity and purity of blood. It was Arana who transformed the ancient concept of 'collective nobility' into the more modern one of 'race'.

A few supposedly objective factors also came to the rescue of

[36] 'In return for the grants, the people swore to personally defend their area without recompense. By doing so, they served as the border garrisons of the Spanish state. When attacks were particularly severe, their resistance gave the time needed to bring the state's army into position' (Greenwood 1977: 91-2).

[37] See Corcuera (1986), Clark (1979) and most sociological studies on Basque nationalism.

racial boundaries. Scientific investigations proved the existence among the Basque population of a high percentage of blood group O and of a rarer presence of blood groups B and AB (Goti Iturriago 1962). There are less well founded claims of district cranial formation and hair and eye colour.[38] Thus the concept of collective nobility emerges from an interrelation of historical, anthropological and biological factors.

Another feature of this concept lies in the egalitarian ethos in which it is entrenched. Because all Basques were nobles, 'a butcher, shoemaker, charcoal burner, scribe or soldier – rich or poor – was a noble' (Greenwood 1977: 87). This myth of Basque egalitarianism is central to the understanding of the strong recent impact of leftist parties and ideologies despite the religious and tradition-bound orientation of most Basque rural society. Modern Basque egalitarianism has its roots in the feature of shared nobility which advocates no in-group differences of status.[39] Otazu (1973) contends that Basque egalitarianism was little more than a myth. However, Sandra Ott's anthropological research on Basque shepherds in the French province of Soule has shown how egalitarian values are deeply rooted in traditional ideals of co-operation and reciprocity. They are the essential basis of the three main local institutions: the household, the 'first neighbours' and the pastoral institution of the *olha*, or *cayolar* (Ott 1981: viii).[40]

It may be argued that the Spanish concept of 'cleanliness of blood' (*limpieza de sangre*) filled a similar place to Basque 'collective

---

[38] Collins dismisses these claims as neither objective nor scientific (1986: 5) and holds that 'they are dictated by the predetermined requirements of a nationalist ideology, rather than by a process of rational deduction' (Collins 1986: 7). According to the same author, language is 'the sole satisfactory tool with which it is possible to approach the question of Basque identity and origins' (1986: 8). For a more recent re-appraisal of genetic factors, see Cavalli-Sforza (1995).

[39] Greenwood (1977: 87) uses the argument of a shared nobility to explain why its vestiges 'presently manifest themselves in the egalitarian and democratic tone of Basque society'. A good account of this egalitarian ethos can be found in Heiberg (1985: 288 ff., and 1989: 32-3).

[40] The *olha* is 'pastoral syndicate which consists of a group of shepherds, their communal herding hut, corral, and the mountain pastures on which their flocks graze during the months of summer transhumance' (Ott 1981: 4). Egalitarianism is furthermore emphasised by the importance accorded to two ordering principles: *aldikatzia*, lit. 'serial replacement, taking turns, or alternation' (Ott 1981:214) and *üngürü*, lit. rotation.

nobility'.[41] However, a comparison reveals two different world views. First, *limpieza de sangre* 'had to be demonstrated by a meticulous process of genealogical investigation' (Greenwood 1977: 87, Amiel 1983), while Basque collective nobility was conferred by the mere fact of being of Basque ancestry. And secondly, Spanish *limpieza de sangre* was also very difficult to prove, because Spain as a socio-cultural entity had been created through the Reconquest. That historical process had been carried out, not only by mass expulsion of the Moors and Jews but also by a fanatical campaign of forced conversion and assimilation. Therefore Spaniards cannot trace back their ancestry to a purely Christian past, untouched by exposure to Islam or by Berber, Jewish or Arab blood. In contrast, the Moors never entered the Basque country which, along with Asturias, remained the last outpost of Christian Spain.

The stress on race therefore had a specific meaning for the Basques, probably with no parallels in other parts of the industrialised world. This very stress has proved untenable in present-day Euskadi after massive immigration at the end of the nineteenth century and, in much greater proportions, since the late 1950s. It was not a coincidence that ETA was created then. By the end of the immigration period, in the late 1970s, ETA reached the peak of its violent campaign.[42] The sheer numbers of immigrants caused great distress among the native population and ETA was to capitalise on these tensions. Immigration as an indirect variable in the popularity of ETA is stressed in ETA's *Libro Blanco*: 'Massive immigration is creating new lifestyles, customs [which are] incompatible with our way of being and which will end up by submerging the Basque people if we do not react.[...] The threat of extinction is so great that we Basques only have one path: to unite, forgetting all differences among us.'[43] Such a concern for immigration occurred despite the fact that most of ETA's founders and intellectuals (Txillardegi, Benito del Valle, Krutwig *et al.*) were themselves from immigrant

---

[41] While preferring the concept of *pureza de la raza* (purity of race), Arana occasionally also used *limpieza de sangre* and other 'Spanish' terminology, such as *hidalguía originaria, nobleza originaria* (Arana 1982: 545 ff.).

[42] The largest number of political killings in ETA's history was carried out between 1978 and 1980 (Clark 1980: 125).

[43] *El Libro Blanco*, reprinted in *Documentos Y*, Donostia: Hordago, 1981.

families (Jáuregui 1981: 135). This also explain why, in contrast with Aranism, the immigration issue was not tinged by racist overtones.

However, ETA has continuously tried to escape the legacy of Aranist ideology. Struggling to define itself in progressive terms, its ideologues have repeatedly accused Arana and his PNV's followers of being racists.[44] This often led to the brink of alienating its rural *Euskaldun* base, which had hitherto accepted the Aranist tenets of Basque exclusiveness. The racially-oriented theses of Sabino Arana are today rejected by all Basque nationalist parties. However, because they embody the first formulations of Basque nationalism, Arana's writings have indirectly conditioned the subsequent choices of the nationalist movement.

The Basque tongue is conceived as an unfathomably primordial element and a still-living proof of the survival of Europe's most ancient people. As Euskara's origins remain an enigma, the origins of the Basque people are also still shrouded in mystery. It was especially because of its value as prehistoric testimony that many early Basque nationalists attached importance to language (King 1994). Thus the situation was made more complicated by the mythic value attributed to Euskara, 'which is the complete identification most Basques make between Euskera and their own cultural identity. Many Basques equate its potential loss with the total demise of Basque identity. . . In connection with their linguistic insularity, Basque identity is founded on an acute awareness of their enigmatic past. Their being a "mystery people" is also what seems to be of most interest about Basques to outsiders. No founding myth or political revolution is a substitute for such an archaic definition of their group origin. Identity runs in an unbroken line from the ancestors. . .' (Zulaika 1988: 7).

The re-emergence of language

Language has discontinuously emerged as a central issue for Basque leaders, especially among the radicals. For instance, Txillardegi considered Euskera as 'the key to the survival of the Basques as a distinct people and he felt astonished that people could consider

---

[44] For instance, Krutwig has declared that 'Arana was more racist than Hitler' (interview in *Cambio 16*, 23 Jan. 1984, quoted in Gilmour 1985). While Krutwig accepted most of Arana's ideas, he could not subscribe to his view on religion and race.

themselves nationalists while failing to speak, study and propagate it'.[45] Txillardegi confesses that his *abertzale* sentiment was 'intimately bound up with the discovery of Euskera' at the end of the 1940s.[46] His autobiographical sketch on the foundation of *Ekin* explains to what extent the development of a new Basque nationalism was related to the will to preserve Basque culture, especially the language:

> We started to reunite in Bilbao. We learned Euskera, we read the existentialists . . . and we began to study the foral legislation, each one choosing the branch of his or her major interest. . . We were young, we loved reading and felt the need to rationalize the Basque problem. We rejected that excess of sentimentalism, affective motivations and good will which, from our viewpoint, was the 'official' nationalism and which was translated into an attitude so incomprehensible for us as the one denouncing the oppression of Euskera, without doing anything to learn it.(cited by Ibarzábal 1978: 364)

> Thus the new nationalism was conceived in ethnic and cultural terms, while the old version was seen as merely political. We were the *ethnic patriots* and the others [the PNV] were the *political patriots*. I believe this definition fully hits the mark and propounds something that in the future will become evident' (*ibid.*, 369).

It has been repeatedly mentioned above that in its origins ETA was mainly a cultural nationalist movement and that Txillardegi's cultural activism was at the root of one of its main splits, which gave life to *Branka*. ETA's two 'organic intellectuals', Beltza and Krutwig, argued that 'as forms of thought depended on language use, Basque socialism must be led by people who spoke Euskera, while nationalists must strive to restore it as the language of the whole of Euskadi'.[47] In another essay they held that only those who spoke Euskera were fully Basque and that other Basques had a special duty

[45] See Txillardegi's interview in Ibarzábal (1978). Also quoted by Sullivan (1988: 29).

[46] See his interview in Ibarzábal (1978: 361). For a critique of Txillardegi's position, see Ereño (1979).

[47] 'Estrategia y Táctica', in *Documentos Y*, vol. 12, p. 298, quoted in Sullivan (1988: 130).

to learn it.[48] *Vasconia* stressed language as the Basque country's basic value: 'Euskera is the quintessence of Euzkadi. While Euskera lives, Euzkadi will live' (quoted by Gurrutxaga 1985: 244). In his definition of a nationality, Krutwig considered five basic and 'objective' factors, in order of importance: language, mentality and culture, religion, race and finally the economic, factors. He held language to be the most important of all, and, as for the second ones (mentality and culture), they were 'both sustained by language: as soon as language disappears, the other two factors also fade away' (Krutwig 1963: 29).

In the writings of most Catalan intellectuals we find a persistent and strong concern for the fate of language. This continual effort gave Catalan nationalism its peculiar strength and stability. It acted as a firm standpoint for its negotiations with Madrid, which in its turn, during the democratic phases of Spanish history, has seen it as a stable point of reference for improvements in its relations with the periphery. By contrast, Basque nationalism, lacking a similar stable basis (and consequently, similarly persistent politics), has, at least in the past, been outwardly more discontinuous in its demands and its negotiating position with the central government and inwardly more ambiguous in its self-definition over identifying the most important values to be maintained and promoted. As we have seen, this does not mean that language was unimportant for Basque nationalism. Indeed, it has been a central concern for all its main theorists and intellectual figures. Yet the sparse diffusion of Euskara and its dialectical fragmentation led most Basque politicians (especially within the main nationalist party, the PNV), to play it down in favour of other factors more related to tradition, such as religion and race.[49] This indeterminacy, ambivalence and indefiniteness helped to shape the development of Basque nationalism.

In Catalonia the emphasis on language provided an instrument both for the consolidation of a coherent nationalist ideology and for

---

48 'Principios de nacionalismo revolucionario', in *Documentos Y*, vol. 12, pp. 20–1, quoted by Sullivan (1988: 130).

49 Basque is divided into at least seven dialects, corresponding more or less to the seven Basque provinces and each having its own spelling.

a slow integration of the immigrants. In this different emphasis lies the characterisation of the *exclusive* identity promoted by early Basque nationalism, versus the *inclusive* identity adopted by Catalanism from its beginning.[50] We shall tackle this dichotomy in greater depth in the chapter on immigration. Catalanism resembles what Hans Kohn (1968) defines as 'open nationalism', directed to absorb and welcome new elements, exogenous stimuli and contributions to its culture. These are endogenously translated and merged into a unique, but articulated, national culture, conceived as in perpetual evolution.[51] Conversely, Arana's programme reflects Kohn's model of a 'closed nationalism',[52] tending to avoid any overlap between the two groups. It is always possible to learn a new language, but it is not possible to change one's forefathers.

Notwithstanding their initial differences, today both movements stress the centrality of language for the definition of their national identity. This viewpoint is shared in Catalonia by all political parties (except by much of the extreme right) and in Euskadi by most of them. However, it is still hard to maintain that language has became

[50] On the shifting patterns of Catalan identity, see Di Giacomo (1984), Woolard (1986) and Llobera (1991).

[51] According to Salvador Giner, *open societies* 'hinge upon the overt recognition of individual responsibility, privacy and citizenship as collective values for the conduct of human affairs. No known collectivity embodies perfectly the virtues of such a society . . . [but] Catalonia must surely be counted among those countries which have managed with relative success to approximate to the distant ideal' (Giner 1980: 14).

[52] If we wish to avoid Kohn's dichotomy, we can question the self-description of Arana's movement as 'nationalist' and, rather, view it as a neo-traditionalist reaction by a threatened ethnocentrism. For instance, Arana takes much from pre-nationalist thought without greatly modifying it: his praise for the excellence of the Basque race and culture was typical of sixteenth-century Basque apologists (Corcuera 1979: 16). His confessional emphasis on 'God and the Old Laws' (the PNV's official motto) is also a neo-traditionalist feature, rather than a nationalist one. Nationalism can be described also as a traditional society's response to the intrusion of modernity. Yet its response is normally syncretic, rather than 'homeostatic', i.e. it must adapt and re-create endogenously the new elements brought by modernisation. This is hardly the case of Arana: Arana's mixture of confessionalism, racism and legal traditionalism greatly limited the spread of his message, at least if we compare it with the popularity enjoyed by Catalanism. Sharing with Catalonia a similar economic structure and patterns of social disruption (urbanisation, immigration, class tensions etc.), Arana's simplistic and oppositional ideology could not be accepted by the local upper classes, while its racist overtones alienated it from the immigrant working class.

a core value for Basque society, although now even ordinary people are starting to see it as important.[53] However, emotional and affective attachment to Euskara often cannot be translated into its active use, due to the intrinsic difficulties of mastering the language, in contrast to the relative ease with which a Castilian-speaker can learn Catalan.

In this chapter we have seen how language played a central role in the formation and programmes of the two nationalist movements. The absence or presence of a powerful element of distinctiveness such as language can affect the relative growth of two otherwise very similar social movements. We have also seen why language has been replaced by race in Euskadi, and finally why this substitution became impracticable with the mass arrival of immigrants. Chapter 8 shows that the latter is not a new phenomenon, since it inspired much of Arana's most visceral tirades. The Aranist concept of 'race' developed with, and against, massive immigration.

A comparative analysis of Basque and Catalan nationalism has shown that regional culture, especially language maintenance, directly affects the development of nationalist movements. The method was a comparison of the ideas of the leading nationalist leaders and intellectuals of Basque and Catalan nationalism shows that the direction taken by these movements is related to existing cultural conditions in the two regions. Two patterns have emerged, which are applicable to other nationalist movements: the Catalan model, based on language, and with a thriving cultural nationalism; and the Basque model, not based on a single value and more confused over its definition of the nation's identity. These two patterns resulted in two opposite reactions towards massive immigration: Catalan nationalism developed an inclusive framework in which immigrants could be considered Catalans after having acquired the culture of the host society; in contrast, Basque nationalism remained more exclusivist from its inception until the early postwar era. The relationship between cultural ambiguity and political violence among the Basques is the subject of the last chapter.

---

[53] For a thesis which stresses the centrality of language in present-day Basque nationalist programmes, see Urla (1987, 1988). See also Tejerina (1992).

8

NATIONALISM AND IMMIGRATION IN CATALONIA AND THE BASQUE COUNTRY

Our aim in this chapter is first to describe the quantity and significance of the immigration phenomenon in Catalonia and Euskadi, and secondly to analyse its impact on both nationalisms. Since the sheer number of immigrants was enormous, there were bound to be inescapable consequences for both Catalan and Basque identity. Nationalist leaders were correspondingly compelled to re-elaborate regional identities and relate them to the new trend. Both the Basque country and Catalonia have been the targets of massive immigration, and both have recently been granted Autonomy Statutes which recognise Catalan and Euskara (Basque) as regional languages co-official with Castilian. But since well before these radical changes, immigrants arriving in the two regions faced very different patterns and possibilities of integration. This is also tied to the relative ease of learning Catalan, as compared with the difficulty of learning Euskara, for an average immigrant arriving from elsewhere in Spain. Catalan historical records, moreover, have demonstrated long-term and durable integration trends. On the other hand, integration in the Basque country has been strewn with difficulties. However, this chapter does not focus on the sociolinguistic problems of learning the two languages, but rather on the effect of large-scale immigration on nationalism and the different responses which it inspired in the local leadership.

As we said in the book's introduction, the wide range of academic literature existing on Basque nationalism, even in English, has not been matched by similar studies of Catalan nationalism, apart from historical ones. In contrast, Catalonia has produced a considerable literature on immigrants, whereas the output of such works in Euskadi is poor. This difference is revealing: in itself, it may be a further proof that in contemporary Catalan social science the main trend has been an optimistic assessment of the issue of newcomers, whereas in Basque scholarship – as in politics – the main issue has been Euskadi's confrontation with the Spanish state. Immigration is no more than a sub-category of that issue. We encounter the same difference in political action. If the main concern in Catalonia has been its self-definition and socio-cultural composition, in Euskadi the problem was 'Spain'. Whereas Arana and the first *peneuvistas* were aiming to separate Euskadi from the rest of Spain, early Catalanist leaders were instead aiming to exert some kind of control over the Spanish state, presenting themselves as an alternative model to Castilian hegemony. Finally, we have also to consider the stunted development of social sciences in Spain under the dictatorship. Once democracy emerged, the two regions had different sets of priorities which resulted in distinct theoretical schools and specialisations.

There now follows a brief historical and quantitative sketch of immigration and of the conflict it generated in the two regions.

Catalonia: historical background

Catalonia terra de pas. Catalonia's special position along the Mediterranean coast and between Castile and France has meant that traditionally it has absorbed multiple cultural influences and movements of people. The population in the coastal area, open to commerce through the port of Barcelona, increased much faster than most of the interior, since the birth-rate and immigration were higher on the coast. Massive immigration also occurred in Valencia (Vilar 1977: 2: 42-94; 1977: 3: map 56). In Catalonia most immigrants came from neighbouring and culturally similar regions, often from southern France (Occitania), and hence had no particular difficulties in assimilating.[1] This helps to explain why the assimilative traditions of Catalonia are often treated as 'primordial'. The past success in integrating Southern French elements created optimism for the future.

After a sharp decline in the fifteenth century, the population of Catalonia increased spectacularly between 1550 and 1620. This was partly due to mass immigration from France. By the end of the

[1] Here Occitan (Provençal) was spoken, the nearest language to Catalan in vocabulary grammar, syntax, morphology and phonetics. Relationships between Catalans and Provençals were mutual and intense. As for cultural matters, many Catalans travelled to Provence to attend the original Floral Games.

sixteenth century, some 20% of the male population were French (Occitan) immigrants (Elliot 1963: 26). Till the nineteenth century, most immigrants came from the North, especially from this region. Important migratory movements occurred during the eighteenth century, when Barcelona recovered part of its economic power (see Nadal and Giralt 1960).

The population of Catalonia-Principat today approaches 6 million; before 1700 it was 0.5 million. Hence, it has increased more than tenfold in 200 years. Only in the eighteenth century do we find a sharp demographic increase: the population doubled from 407,000 in 1718 to 814,000 in 1787. This was a time of economic development, following the setting up of textile manufacturing, the expansion of commerce and a good period for agricultural output. In the nineteenth century the population continued to expand. Steady industrial growth allowed the formation of manufacturing cities and the enlargement of Barcelona. In 1887 the population of the *Principat* reached 1,843,000. The demographic distribution also changed: most of the population moved to the coast or not far from it, gradually leaving the agricultural hinterland depopulated. By 1900, the birth-rate began to decrease and this decline has lasted to the present day. The difference in birth-rates between Catalonia and the rest of Spain drastically increased, but the population continued to grow due to immigration. The overall demographic balance with the rest of the peninsula correspondingly shifted: Catalans, who represented 10.6% of the Spanish population in 1900, had become 15.77% in 1975 (Termes 1984: 132).

Several authors (Ferrater i Mora, Maluquer, Carles Pi-Sunyer, Vives and others have described Catalonia's capacity for assimilation over the centuries: its position along the Mediterranean coast between two large countries, France and Spain (both champions of an intolerant and chauvinist vision of ethnic relations), the constant flux of different peoples, the cosmopolitan nature of Barcelona, its port and its commercial activities, and the character of Catalonia as a *terra de pas* (lit. country of passage).[2] The historian Vicens Vives uses the concept of *passadís* (passageway, corridor, passage):

> The peoples who inhabit these passageways are subjected to considerable human pressures, some peaceful, other bellicose

---

[2] This concept has been elaborated, among others, by the philosopher Ferrater i Mora (1980).

and warlike. The play of both trends continually aroused by the ebb and flow of historic events, engenders a permanent vital tension and develops particular qualities. . . . A passageway people finds itself always in dangerous historical situations, so that powerful currents of resistance rise up in the people, creating and recreating it over the centuries (1984: 20).

This vision may be related to other social theories which ascribe an integrative and accommodating capacity to seaborne societies. In particular, Lenski's (1984) definition of a *maritime society* seems to fit the Catalan case.[3] One of the characteristics of maritime societies is that they are more open than other societies, such as agrarian ones. Their reliance on the free movement of goods and labour endows them with an exceptional ability to integrate with outgroups.

In 1887 immigrants represented only 1.25% of the Catalan population, but this proportion slowly increased to 3.33% in 1897, 4.22% in 1900 and 5.44% in 1910. In 1920 it had reached 14.03% (Termes 1984: 129) as a consequence of the industrial boom caused by Spain's neutrality in the first World War I. This rhythm was kept constant till 1930. Rural immigrants from Barcelona's hinterland were now competing with immigrants from outside Catalonia. However, individuals from Catalan-speaking areas still represented the majority: they came first from Valencia, then from Menorca and Majorca and some from Southern Aragón.[4] Only in 1930, when the non-natives had become 19.61% of the population, did the number of Castilian-speaking immigrants (318, 956) approach that of Catalan-speaking ones (329, 708), at least in the province of Barcelona (Termes 1984: 131).

---

[3] According to Lenski, *maritime societies* are distinguished from agrarian societies by the following key features: their chief source of economic surplus derived from commerce, rather than agriculture; merchants were much more favourably situated; their governments were typically republican and plutocratic, rather than monarchical; militarily, they relied on naval force, more than other forces. Lenski's classical examples are the Phoenicians, the Carthaginians, the Venetians and the mid-fifteenth century Dutch. However, he also consider cases of *hybrid societies* part maritime and part agrarian, mentioning the Athenians from the sixth century BC. until the Roman conquest and England from the sixteenth to the early nineteenth century (Lenski 1984: 191-2). Perhaps, Catalan society may also be included in this latter group, since its government was officially monarchical and its economy was based on agriculture.

[4] These contacts did not result in major linguistic changes, since 'the slight dialect differences did not weigh on the process and were soon erased' (Badia 1964: 107).

During Primo de Rivera's dictatorship, many immigrants were attracted by the salt potassium mines and the preparatory work for the 1929 Universal Exposition. This first generation of newcomers were collectively known as *murcianos* – people from Murcia, even though they came from other regions as well. The economic stalemate of the 1930s produced a decrease in the immigration rate. Finally, the Civil War and its aftermath caused an influx of several thousands fleeing from hunger in Andalusia as well as a huge political exodus from Catalonia. Immigration then halted for a while, and only in the 1950s was the trend reversed. Between 1951 and 1970, 1.16 million immigrants arrived in Catalonia from other parts of Spain, mainly from Andalusia (Rebagliato 1978: 256). In 1970, 37.69% of the Catalan population had been born outside the region (Termes 1984: 132), and finally in 1975 the immigrants reached 39% of Barcelona's population (Rebagliato 1978: 260). Not even in the United States and Argentina at the peak of their receptiveness did immigrants exceeded 30% (Marsal, cited by Termes 1984: 132). However, the phenomenon was unevenly spread as most immigrant families clustered in the newly built *barris* of Barcelona's outskirts. Their highest concentration was to be found in the suburban townships of Cornellà (78.4%) and Santa Coloma (78.7%) (Strubell 1981: 76). Also crucial was the immigrants' higher birth-rate compared to the natives'. By 1965 immigration accounted for 65% of the total growth of Catalonia, while natural growth represented only 35% (Sàez 1980: 26). Thus, if taken together, the immigrants and their children far outnumbered the natives.

All nationalisms attach enormous importance to population figures. The more numerous the population, the more strength the nation has, and a declining population is a bad omen for every sincere nationalist.[5] Demography is therefore a power game. That is why most cases of demographic decline in human groups are bound to generate a counter-trend in the search for a political solution through either self-determination or a campaign to expel immigrants (and sometimes outright racism). Most nationalist movements in history exploded at times of massive population upheavals, huge

[5] In considering several nationalist movements world-wide, it is difficult to find a single one which encourages birth control. This does not mean that this pattern cannot change in the future; China's 'one child' policy may well be dictated by the imperative of economic development and fast growth, which often go together with programmes of national aggrandisement.

transmigrations or, simply, changes in the demographic balances. For instance, the rise of Serbian nationalism, which led in the 1990s to war in the Balkans, was notoriously brought about by a dramatic shift in the demographic balance of the Kosovo province: this region, considered by Serbs as the cradle of their nation, has seen an unprecedented increase in its Albanian component, so that at the time of writing Albanians make up over 90% of its population and the remaining Serbs behave like a 'besieged' minority (Magas 1993).

A decrease in birthrate has also fostered radical visions of Quebecois nationalism.[6] Both Quebecois and Catalan demographers have traditionally lamented population decline, but the hope of integrating the immigrants could cajole separatist elements to moderate their stance. Accordingly, the unity of the Canadian and Spanish states can only be saved by policies which ensure the integration of the non-native population into the regional cultures. Finally, there is a pro-immigrant argument in that the only remarkable population increase in this century in Catalonia came about through immigration. Since immigration stopped in the 1970s, bringing about a zero growth-rate, it is possible that nationalist leaders will be prone to encourage further immigration, once the instruments of Catalanisation are fully available and the immigrants' will to integrate is no longer a matter of controversy.

The failure of racism in Catalonia. Given Catalonia's traditional capacity to absorb immigrants, Catalan leaders were never particularly interested in raising insurmountable barriers between natives and newcomers. Immigrants were not resented as a major

---

[6] Suffering from net emigration, Quebec's share of Canada's population has declined from 29% in 1966 to about 25.5% in 1989. However, the biggest problem in the policy of immigrants' attraction is to give them the incentive to stay longer, since many of them prefer to leave for other Canadian provinces after a while. Quebec's immigration officials award more points for good French proficiency (15) than for English (3). Therefore, Quebec has become the main focus of immigration from some French-speaking countries, notably Haiti (even though Haitian Creole is sharply different from standard French) and Lebanon. Robert Bourassa's government wanted to 'raise the province's annual intake of immigrants from 17% to 25% of an expanding Canadian total', more or less 50,000 to 60,000 per year (*The Economist*, June 10, 1989). However, the fact that many immigrants insist on learning English, rather than French makes many Quebeckers believe that only total independence will make the separate identity of their nation clear to potential newcomers.

threat to Catalan identity; the main threat was obviously from Madrid, which presented a far greater danger to the survival of the Catalan nation. Its policies were a major source of de-Catalanisation. Moreover, due to the strength of linguistic identity, racialist definitions of the nation never gained currency: there have been attempts in this direction, but they have been notably successful. We shall now examine some of these racialist definitions, contrasting them with the more integrative ones which won the day.

At the turn of the century, the positivist writer Pompeu Gener (1848-1920) tried to define Catalan identity on the basis of race and descent. The Northern, Gothic character of Catalonia was opposed to the Arab and Berber nature of Castile. Relying on Nietzsche's vitalism, Gener called for the creation of *super- nationalism*. Since 'science' provided an irrefutable instrument of legitimation, it is not surprising that most European nationalist movements at the end of the nineteenth century developed overt racist rationalisations. Race was considered the most reliable and incontestable way of supporting group differentiation, and 'science' provided a kind of esoteric doctrine through which a self-appointed secular clergy tried to impose their vision grounded on immovable dogmas. The steadfastness of these dogmas was based precisely on the difficulty of demonstrating them. The previous chapter argued that the choice of race was directly related to the absence of other elements of ethnic differentiation. The more difficult it is to identify the differences between groups, the more race comes to the fore as the ultimate identity marker. In Catalonia linguistic consciousness provided an impediment to race-centred ideas, and in the end the racist ideas of Gener and other marginal pundits never acquired legitimacy.

For a while *L'Avenç*, the eclectic Modernist mouthpiece, provided a platform for Gener's ideas with the aim of differentiating Catalonia from the rest of Spain.[7] For the Modernists this was simply a by-product of their scramble for all things modern, scientific and European. Their use and abuse of 'scientific' terminology was a means of distancing themselves from the Romantics and the *Renaixença*. The stress on race was intended to provide a provisional foundation for an allegedly more 'modern' form of nationalism, against previous nostalgic attitudes. But these attempts by Gener and

---

[7] Gener played a more influential role in the radical magazine *Juventut* (Youth, 1900-6) of the Unió Catalanista.

others were quickly forgotten and when, several decades later, a massive influx of immigrants created the conditions for an ethnic backlash, few remembered his name.

A new stream of racial thought appeared in the 1930s.[8] In his pessimistic portrait of Catalonia's 'decadence', the demographer Josep Vandellós (1899-1950) backed up his anti-Malthusian defence of human fertility with a wealth of statistical data.[9] Catalonia was threatened with extinction by the falling birth-rate. As a remedy for what he described as racial decadence and 'generational egotism' he proposed the spread of nationalism. In this Vandellós was influenced by Italian Fascism and German pessimism.[10] Although more influential than Gener, his preoccupation with Catalan 'decadence' as a result of immigration and miscegenation was not seriously taken up by nationalist politicians.

Another author who expressed concern over immigration was Manuel Rossell i Vilar, who linked culture with race. He was preoccupied with immigrant 'ghettos' and the paucity of mixed marriages, but also with possible threats to 'mental purity' resulting from massive inputs of 'foreign blood'. Thus, although inbreeding (*mestissatge*) was desirable in one sense, it would have brought with it long-term 'mental perturbation' (Hall 1983: 77). His writings were even less popular than those of Gener and Vandellós.

Much more important was what can be called the *integrationist* trend, exemplified by several authors and scattered in most nationalist literature.[11] However, its importance only emerged fully in the 1960s as a consequence of massive immigration and the competing danger of an anti-immigrant backlash. At this stage, it was absolutely imperative to rediscover, and appeal to, supposedly 'primordial' integrative trends innate in Catalan society, and the works of Vicens Vives, Ferrater i Mora and others which have

8 Among the forerunners Termes (1984: 138 ff.) mentions several anti-Malthusian hygienists preoccupied with the falling birth-rate at the turn of the century. Later the physician Puig i Sais spoke of the fatal dangers of de-Catalanization and the need to increase the number of Catalans of pure stock.

9 Avoiding the concept of 'race', Vandellós spoke instead of 'racial qualities' (Hall 1983: 77).

10 Vandellós studied with the Fascist statistician Corrado Gini and was also influenced by the German philosopher Oswald Spengler (Bilbeny 1988: 156).

11 Some authors stressed the economic advantages derived from immigration (Muntaner and Nadal, cited by Culla 1989: 339).

already been mentioned served this purpose. But active integration was more easily attainable in the wake of a common opposition to the dictatorship. As in Euskadi, the oppositional character of the nationalist movement helped to mobilise immigrants and natives against a common enemy. In this task, the whole opposition remained united. Memories of the Tragic Week and the potential for communal strife in Catalan society haunted both left and nationalist politicians. The two main representatives of this integrative current are the journalist Francis Candel (b. 1925) and the nationalist leader Jordi Pujol (b. 1930).

Candel (1964), himself an immigrant, published a book defending the immigrants' contribution to Catalan society which became a regional best-seller; significantly, it was titled *Els altres Catalans* (The other Catalans). However, he did not present an overall solution to the problem of cultural integration, especially where language was concerned. His main merit was to have brought to life the immigrants' love for the host land and its people. Candel was criticised by Cruells (1965), who called his own book *Els no Catalans i nosaltres* (The non-Catalans and ourselves): according to Cruells, the majority of the immigrants were not ready to accept Catalan culture (1965: 17) and even connived at the regime's suspicious 'linguistic universalism' (1965: 24). At this stage, the idea of a single Catalan community was destined to remain simply 'a fiction ... if it does not bring what is essential to Catalanity, which is its language' (1965: 12).[12]

The most relevant thinker in this period was Jordi Pujol, whose ideas we have already examined in other chapters. His programme consisted of addressing the immigrants' issue through linguistic incorporation, seeing acquisition of Catalan as a step 'naturally' ensuing from acceptance in the host country: 'Our central problem is immigration and, hence, integration. The basic objective is to build up a community valid for all Catalans. And I would add that by Catalan I mean everybody who lives and works in Catalonia, and who makes Catalonia his/her own home and country, with which he/she incorporates and identifies' (Pujol 1966). Hence, the stress was put on residence in an attempt to build a non-ethnic sense of citizenship (Woolard 1986, 1989). However, within what looks like an unmistakably civic concept of the nation, language (especially its

---

[12] Cruells (1965) attacked Candel's work emphasising the distance between what, he claimed, were two opposite communities: Catalans and non-Catalans.

use in the family) remained the real crucible and badge of successful
incorporation: 'Language is the decisive factor in integration. It is
the most definitive. A man who speaks Catalan and who speaks
Catalan to his children, is already a Catalan at heart [*de soca i arrel*]'
(Pujol 1966: 82-3). Pujol first expressed his vision in the late 1950s
in some clandestine pamphlets. Obviously, such literature could not
have a large circulation, but it was very influential among important
circles of intellectuals who can be defined as 'Catalonia's militant
minorities' (Termes 1984: 154).[13]

Basque country: historical background

Immigration, centralism and modernity. In contrast with Catalonia,
the Basque country did not posses a vibrant tradition of acceptance
of newcomers. The concept of universal or collective nobility
(*hidalguía colectiva*) discussed in the previous chapter served a clear
isolationist purpose. 'All those who wished to be considered as
inhabitants [*vecinos*] were compelled, if they were not from the
country, to prove their nobility. This required a long and costly
legal procedure. The applicant had to finance the journey of two
persons – a bailiff and an inhabitant of the place – to his birthplace,
where he had to prove...his nobility and purity of blood with
witnesses or a baptism certificate' (Fernández de Pinedo 1974:
51). Already in the fifteenth century, people who came from
outside Bizkaia and Gipuzkoa had limited civic rights and duties.
With Bizkaia's *Fuero Nuevo*, the permission of the *anteiglesias*,[14]
villages and towns was needed in order to acquire stable residence.
This implied an investigation into the moral conduct to be carried
out in the applicant's last place of residence.[15] In 1585 the *Junta
Provincial* of Gipuzkoa forbade residence to all who could not
prove their collective nobility (Vazquez de Prada 1978: III: 170-2).
    The abolition of the *fueros* found the local population unprepared

---

[13] Also influential was the Left nationalist activist Antoni Pérez, inspired by social
Catholicism (Muñoz 1990: 166 ff.).

[14] The *anteiglesias* (literally, before the Church) were administrative units roughly
corresponding to municipal districts based on the parishes.

[15] This attitude had been kept in the seventeenth century, when Bilbao's class
structure started to change and expand. The members of the city's Junta periodically
affirmed that its inhabitants were of noble lineage and thus could admit foreigners only
after research into their genealogies (Dominguez Ortiz 1976: 171).

for the vast upheavals to come, and unable to counteract them. The rapid industrialisation of the Bilbao area after 1876 meant that many people from both the surrounding countryside and other regions of Spain flocked into the city, while the locals could not have a say in these developments. Bilbao more than doubled its population from 35,505 inhabitants in 1877 to 83,306 in 1900. By 1900 about 80% of the city's population were immigrants, and only 23.4% had been born there (this figure includes children of immigrants). Nearly half of the immigrants were non-Basques (Corcuera 1979: 73-5).

The amount of social disruption brought about by these dramatic changes in the human, cultural, social and ecological spheres was an essential catalyst for the birth of Basque nationalism. The massive arrival of dispossessed people who appeared incapable of integration was at the root of widespread resentment against Spain which is fully reflected in Arana's words:

> If a foral and *Euskalduna* [Basque-speaking] Vizcaya were morally possible, though of *maketo* race, its realisation would be the most hateful event in the world, the most creeping and abject [*rastrera*] aberration for a people, the most iniquitous and wicked political development and the most amazing falsity in history (Arana u.d.: 1: 197)

> *Maketismo* or *españolismo* [creeps] into every sphere of Vizcayan society: within the cultural and religious authorities, in the press, in recreational and political groups, in professional and religious organisations. . . (189)

> Our race has became despicably dominated by that of its most hard-fought enemy (326).[16]

Indignation and bitterness at the destruction of Basque traditional society were the main touchstones of Arana's thought. The self-righteous outrage over the decline of Basque civilisation, laws, language and values which lay at its base was reflected in Arana's Manichean typologies of the incompatible characteristics of Basques and Spaniards. Spaniards epitomised negative attitudes and behaviour – all that Basques abhorred: they were regarded as lazy,

---

[16] Arana also referred to the preferential allocation of administrative posts to the Spanish immigrants as *maketismo* (326).

violent and prone to drunkenness. By contrast, Basques excelled in the fields where the Spaniards failed.

However, if by racism we mean a hierarchical evaluation of human groups on a universal scale, Arana was only partly a racist, because it was exclusively the Spaniards who were the target of his contempt.[17] His 'racism' was a situational one, driven by hatred of the Spanish mentality and political oppression.[18] In Arana's time, at the turn of the nineteenth century, the concept of race was fashionable: this concept served to legitimise Basque aspirations towards a status equal to that of other modern nations. In this sense race was an even stronger mark and guarantee of distinction than language. Racial exclusiveness pre-existed Arana and was a common sentiment among Bilbao's residents in the third quarter of the century. The Castilianised and pro-centralist upper echelons were no less racist, if not more so, than the Basque-speaking proletariat and petty bourgeoisie. Later both nationalists and anti-nationalists resented the *maketos* as invaders. However, only among the nationalists did they become openly identified with the state, since most of them came from Castile, the land of the oppressors.

We have no reliable proof that Arana had direct knowledge of the works on racial superiority which were popular in Europe at the end of the century, especially in France, which he visited for brief periods. In his self-taught and disordered syncretism Arana rarely, if ever, mentioned his sources. Certainly, he had a lively intellectual curiosity about everything that could reinforce his nationalist creed. Allied with the *fin de siècle* mood of Spanish decadence, European racial theories may have had a strong impact among some Regenerationist intellectuals. Physical anthropologists, both foreign and local, were asserting their theories of Basque racial uniqueness.[19]

---

[17] Indeed, Arana was also able to express some solidarity for other peoples fighting against Spain or similar Western foes, like the American Indians (1980: 189-90) or the Berbers of Morocco (189-90 and 193-4), who were at that time waging their struggle against the Spanish army. Of the latter, Arana ironically asked: 'What kind of culture can the Spaniards bring to the Riff?' (189), implying that Berber civilisation was superior to the Spanish.

[18] On the different meanings which the concept of race assumes relative to prevailing historical conditions and discourses, see Goldberg (1992).

[19] For instance, Telesforo de Aranzadi published at the turn of the century his anthropometric works on cephalic indexes, eye colour and other physionomic peculiarities. The former topic was also studied by the phrenologist Federico

Aranism helped indirectly to popularise these concepts, which became better known after Arana's death. The consciousness of racial superiority 'persisted at the ideological level long after openly racist aspects disappeared from the nationalist programmes' (Corcuera 1979: 386). As we saw, this legacy created internal conflicts and bitter fragmentation during the 1960s, when most nationalists began to consider how to involve the immigrants in their struggle.

In the previous chapter, we suggested that all nationalist movements search for common and shared values through which to mobilise the masses. This search is directed at re-creating the 'essence' of national culture through an effort of syncretism. Core values are no more than symbolic emblems of ethnic cohesion and syntheses of a rapidly changing culture. Arana chose race because other differentiating elements were lacking. He found that race had a stronger mobilising potential precisely because it defined the 'communitarian essence' of the nation as no other element could do.

Our contrast between Catalan openness and Basque exclusiveness refers to the initial period of the two nationalist movements. The original formulations remained substantially untouched till the Civil War; alternative visions could not emerge in the prevailing conditions. After the war, Basque attitudes changed dramatically: the reaction to the second massive wave of immigration in the 1960s was to look for, and create, alternative values so as to include the immigrants in the nationalist struggle rather than reject them. But we will first examine the conditions of the first great immigration and the reaction to it.

The end of traditional society: forerunners of a violent upheaval. At the start, industrialisation was limited to Vizcaya and concentrated in the mining area around Bilbao. Given the impact of subsequent urbanisation and immigration, it was also here that nationalism was born and slowly spread.[20] We have to remember that at first,

---

Oloriz. When race was associated with superiority, we easily find the features of a 'chosen people'. Thus Engracio de Aranzadi in 1904: 'We Basques constitute the aristocracy of the world, the noblesse of the earth' (cited in Corcuera 1979: 386). In this sense, race was not necessarily racist, but resembled more a spirit of caste. Furthermore, these declarations did not form a cohesive doctrine of racial superiority.

[20] Till the late 1950s, Gipuzkoa had relatively little non-Basque immigration. Its

Arana spoke only of a 'Vizcayan nation' and only later extended his nationalist programme to the other Basque provinces, inventing the term Euskadi. This happened as soon as the effects of industrialisation sprawled into neighbouring Gipuzkoa.

Immigrants in the Bilbao area were then living in pitiful conditions. A vivid picture of the appalling conditions in the mining industry was sketched by the Communist leader Dolores Ibarruri, 'La Pasionaria' (1895-1991):

The miners worked from dawn to dusk with no set hours. They left home before it was light and did not return till well after nightfall. The bunkhouses that the mining companies offered as shelter to those who came from other regions resembled the lairs of wild beasts rather than human dwellings.

At night . . . the interior of the [miner's] bunkhouses looked like a scene from Dante. The air was filled with the smoke of harsh tobacco . . . and illuminated by a flickering light. The blurred figures of half-naked men could be seen moving among the cots or seated in their bedrolls in a foul atmosphere compounded of sweat, fermented food and the odours of the latrine, which was located in a small compartment. . . . The men slept on sacks stuffed with hay placed on top of narrow wooden benches.[...]

If one of the men contracted smallpox or typhus . . . he was removed from his cot and taken to a hut where the sick were housed. If he died, his bunk was sprinkled with lime water, and his cot was immediately occupied by someone else. The temporary labourers, most of whom were of peasant origin, were . . . carriers of fatal illnesses and epidemics which spread without control from Vizcaya to Castile and from Castile to Vizcaya (Ibarruri 1976: 17-8).

---

industrialisation was a subsidiary spill-over from Vizcaya, following an eastward trend from the towns at the border between the two provinces towards the French frontier, where it halted. Industrialisation in Gipuzkoa consisted mostly of small industrial enterprises. In this environment, cooperativism flourished, as exemplified by Mondragón. The process was slow and, until the 1950s, it was not as traumatic as in 1880s Vizcaya. The other two Spanish Basque provinces, Alava and Navarre, remained largely agricultural and untouched by industrialisation for a much longer time. The agricultural character of these provinces has retarded the growth of nationalism.

A first natural reaction to the arrival of the immigrants was self-induced isolation. The natives reacted in the typical way of threatened minorities, reinforcing traditional barriers. Efforts in this direction normally fail if the minority in question does not have the (economic) means to implement its wish of seclusion. In the Basque case, isolationist tendencies were encouraged by the natives' economic well-being compared to the immigrants towards whom they could afford to display some kind of 'superiority', as they could hardly do where the central government was concerned.

Again, the population nearly doubled between 1900 and 1930 (Fusi 1984: 15). During the 1930s, religion increasingly became more important than race. The clergy had become involved massively in the nationalist movement, possibly as a response to the secular threat emanating from the Second Republic. In the Basque country religion became an indispensable tool of social cohesion at a time of social instability in the rest of Spain. At the popular level this new religious awareness was expressed in visionary events, religious apparitions and miracles (Christian 1987, 1996), but the cataclysm of the Civil War irreparably destroyed this traditional balance. The Catholic field then became split along ideological and geographical lines, with Navarre and part of Alava siding with the Francoists against Basque nationalism. In the dark night of oblivion which followed, an underground movement slowly emerged that challenged what had hitherto been a static nationalist ideology. This movement focussed on language and on voluntary action. These two elements were to be sources of unity and cohesion.

In the 1960s the Basque economy expanded massively. Immigration had been constant since the 1890s, but the record figures of the 1960s led to inevitable strains on Basque culture and society. The fracture between immigrants and natives was partly healed through efforts to create a new sense of Basque identity carried out by some educators and nationalists. This attempt to achieve 'national' unity is epitomised by the role of the *andereños* (Basque teachers) as agents of the Basque cultural revival. They insisted on creating common schools where immigrant children could learn Basque alongside natives. But their first attempts failed on several occasions, not because of opposition from the immigrants, but, on the contrary, because many villagers were firmly opposed to their children being sent into mixed classes. Only a nationalist explanation – namely the sincere desire and right of the immigrants to become Basques –

succeeded in convincing the reluctant parents of the viability of such schools, chasing away centuries-old prejudices. The root of the problem was the different view the teachers and the rest of the inhabitants had of Basque culture. The *andereños* had a highly positive view of it, which traditionally the villagers did not. In the true Aranist spirit, their main concern was to be kept safe from 'negative foreign' influences – more than to maintain Basque culture. In the early phase of the cultural revival, positive national self-appraisal was still skin-deep.

The perception of their culture as a badge of inferiority is common to many minorities. In particular, social mobility in industrialised societies demands the mastery of a standard language as a vehicle of a homogeneous high culture (Gellner 1983). Hence the retention of unstandardised varieties is seen as a hindrance to social mobility, as well as sign of cultural backwardness. This did not necessarily mean that the Basques themselves despised their culture. On the contrary, they often loved it, but having continually to confront the impact of the dominant culture they did not have the means (political power) nor the knowledge (political skills) to promote Basque culture at a higher level. Centuries of diglossic inertia prevented them from even considering the possibility of transforming Euskara into a vehicle of high culture.

Eventually the old ideology of racial superiority, which *de facto* downgraded Basque culture, waned with the spread of a neo-nationalist ideology which, in contrast, tried to promote Basque cultural manifestations. In 1971 a special issue of *Alderdi*, the underground newsletter of the PNV, was entitled '43 Words for You, Immigrant in Euskadi'.[21] Its editorial called on those who 'came from other lands . . . to assume fully the duties which the impending crucial situation demands from us all'. The call opened with a 'welcome to our land...this is your land, you are Basque. [...] We [the natives] are not better or worse than any others.' A vigorous rebuke to the centralising dictatorship concealed a plea for the respect of all non-Spanish cultures. The immigrants were asked first to respect Basque culture and then to join the struggle for freedom. Immigrants were finally given the possibility of becoming Basques. The only condition was to accept the Basques and their desire for independence and democracy. Hence the stress was mainly on

21 *Alderdi*, no. 270, December 1971.

participation in the struggle for freedom and collective rights. *Faute de mieux*, it was a call to respect at least Basque culture and the Basques' efforts to preserve it. Hence we now analyse the emergence of this voluntary conception of the nation.

Basque country: contemporary period

Voluntary action and political struggle as avenues of national integration.
We have mentioned that religion assumed a primary oppositional character under the Second Republic. There was a further change in the 1960s: through the contribution of Ekin and then of Krutwig's *Vasconia*, language became the new crucible of conceiving Basqueness. The main novelty was precisely that the previous ascriptive requirements for membership of the Basque nation were replaced by a kind of voluntary association centred on personal involvement in the political struggle. Although it remained in the background as a symbol of Basque identity, language was continuously overshadowed by political action. An increasing number of immigrants were enrolled in the armed struggle, and Clark (1984: 147-9 1986a, 1986b) gives interesting figures for non-native membership of ETA.[22] Many activists were sons of immigrants or of one immigrant parent and even immigrants themselves, as were many of ETA's martyrs. Such was Juan Paredes Manot, celebrated for exclaiming 'Long live free Euskadi!' seconds before being executed by the firing squad. Even the most traditionalist Aranists were deeply impressed by this act of ultimate generosity, and their beliefs in Basque purity were deeply shattered. *Action* became far more important than race and generally it was also more important than language as a marker of Basqueness. One of the main reasons for this choice was precisely that immigrants, as well as assimilated Basques, could not be mobilised through race, religion or language revivalism.

This new way of conceiving Basque membership through active participation draws from a pre-existing autochthonous value, *ekintza*

---

[22] According to the surnames of ETA members, 40.1% of them came from mixed ancestry, that is, either the mother or the father had a non-Basque surname. Furthermore, 16.6% came from purely non-Basque ancestry, that is, both surnames were Spanish. In the whole, 56.7% of the *etarras* were not of purely Basque origin (Clark 1984: 147). The Basques follow the Iberian tradition of using both maternal and paternal surnames.

(action).[23] Its inner meaning is a 'commitment as far as possible to implement in secular life what religious belief dictates to be true' (Zulaika 1988: 39). In other words, the Basque defines her/himself as a person by 'doing' (Valle 1989: 127). The nationalists felt that a Basque is one who, 'loving his nation, fights for its liberation'; hence 'a true Basque can only be a Basque nationalist' (Heiberg 1979: 187). This conception was also present in Arana's stress on patriotism as a moral obligation. Also a true Basque is one who actively (and politically) defends the symbols of Basque cohesion and differentiation (Heiberg 1979: 195). Activism is especially a duty for the young and every young person has a particular responsibility to be an *ekintzaile* (activist). The concept contains within it a sense of mission and a striving to 'convert' other people to act likewise (Zulaika 1989: 39). The new post-1960s Basque nationalism extended this sense of mission to the immigrants, where it achieved a new class-oriented meaning. The choice of Marxism as a central tenet was directly linked to this drive for immigrant mobilisation. The root of the concept of *ekintza* is contained in the name of the organisation and journal *Ekin*, the predecessor of ETA. *Ekin* means 'to do' and its young founders conceived of it as opposed to the static, outdated and passive attitude of the old *peneuvista* generation.

The relationship between this concept of self-fulfilling action and violence is clear. *Ekintza* is enhanced whenever the activity involves some kind of risk. Thus, 'the requirement of underground secrecy for the more political type of *ekintza* was a proof of its importance. The high risk involved in following the dictates of one's conscience exposed the intrinsically evil nature of the existing political establishment and gave a moral, almost sacred imperative to the *ekintza*' (Zulaika 1988: 44). Participants in the struggle were not simply Basque citizens, but also Basque nationalists and part of the corresponding 'moral community' identified with it, irrespective of where they were born. The 'targets' of these mobilisation tactics were both Spanish-speaking Basques and the immigrant population. Hence the peculiar conditions of secrecy under the dictatorship transformed each *ekintza* into a daring act and favoured the metamorphosis from simple action and militancy into violence. The

---

23 Zulaika (1988: 36-56) links the revival of this concept to the influence in Euskadi of the pro-regime ecclesiastical movement, *Acción Católica* (Catholic Action). According to the group's representatives, the notion of *militancy* had to be a central Christian vocation (*ibid*: 40).

choice of a voluntarist definition of the nation led to the subsequent mounting spiral of violent actions and reactions.

Conflicting parameters of Basque identity: some data. There are different means of measuring political integration and participation. If we take account of electoral patterns, the high percentage of voting for the pro-independence coalition Herri Batasuna in areas where immigrants are a majority testifies to the immigrants' involvement in nationalist politics.[24] In Rentería, an industrial town of Gipuzkoa, only 19% of the population were natives of the area in 1979, yet the overall nationalist vote was 48.65% in that year (Llera Ramo 1985: 405, SIADECO 1981) and in the 1987 municipal elections (*Anuario El País* 1988, Silver 1988: 124) it rose to 62.7%.[25] The greatest gain was recorded by radical parties: HB (from 19.97% in 1979 to 28.11% in 1987) and EE (from 12.62% to 13.1%).[26] Before the Civil War, when immigrants were a small minority in Rentería, the overall nationalist vote was no more than 36.1%. Moreover, this was exclusively directed at the conservative PNV. In 1979, the PNV's percentage declined to 16.9%, while the radical parties achieved top positions. The conclusion advanced by Silver (1988) is that when immigrants vote for nationalist parties, they tend to vote for radical nationalists.

Such changes occurred on the background of a dramatic demographic shift. The population of Rentería rose from 3,062 inhabitants in 1877 to 45,789 in 1981 – more than a fourteenfold increase in little more than 100 years (Goicoechea 1991: 20). Immigration also caused a change in the age structure and there is a higher percentage of youth than in other cities (*ibid.*: 21). This is a

[24] 'Euskadi, "otro" país. Los partidos nacionalistas entran en la disputa del voto inmigrante', *El País*, 19 June 1986.

[25] The total vote for the nationalist parties (62.77%) was distributed as follows: HB 28.13%, EA 15.92%, EE 13.05% and PNV 5.67%. The PSOE remained the first party with 31.93%. The positive result for the Left parties indicates that the choice of class-related politics by Basque radical nationalism started to yield results and vindicate their initial choices.

[26] See *Anuario Estadístico Vasco 1985*. Bilbao: Gobierno Vasco/Eusko Jaurlaritza, 1986; and *Anuario Estadístico Vasco 1988*. Bilbao: Gobierno Vasco/Eusko Jaurlaritza, 1989. For the data up to 1980, see SIADECO (1981), *Análisis Descriptivo de la Comarca Rentería Pasages*, Donostia: Caja Laboral Popular, pp. 132-51. For a detailed analysis of the 1977 and 1977 elections in the four Basque provinces, see Llera Ramo (1985).

further variable that may be taken into account to explain the strength of radical nationalism. Indeed, the peculiar appeal which nationalism exerts over youth has been highlighted by research in many other nationalist movements.[27]

Most immigrants were non-Basque: in 1975, 40.1% of the inhabitants of Rentería were born outside Euskadi (Goicoechea 1991: 21-2). Of course, this percentage did not include their Basque-born offspring, who were considered as natives, so that, if taken together, the immigrants and their children formed the overwhelming majority of the population. The average of immigrants in the *comarca* (36.3%) was much greater than in Gipuzkoa as a whole (27.77%) or Euskadi as a whole (30%, including Navarre).

As in most other Basque towns, the support for HB in Rentería has increased at every election. After a brief decrease to 16.59% (1982, general election), HB support increased to 24.65% (1983, municipal election), 25.71% (1986, legislative election), 25.44% (1986, regional election) and 28.13% (1988, municipal election). HB has to compete with the PSOE (Socialists), the only relevant Spanish-based party, for the immigrants' vote.[28] Since Rentería has been a special target for repression by the Guardia Civil, the city is a good testing-ground for the correlation between state violence, nationalism, immigration and lack of common culture.

This propensity towards immigrant radicalisation is confirmed by other more general data. Everybody living in the Basque county can identify as either Basque or Spaniard. Thus, many immigrants identify themselves as Basques. In Linz's (1986: 40) sample, 8.4% of immigrants identify themselves as 'more Basque than Spaniard'. Among them 36% want independence for Euskadi, compared with 24% among those natives (i.e. with two Basque parents) who identify themselves as 'more Basque than Spaniard' (not all natives identified themselves as such).[29] Assuming that desire for inde-

27 See, for instance, Alter (1989: 72). Referring to the period of the rise of nationalist movements, Benedict Anderson states that 'both in Europe and the colonies "young" and "youth" signified dynamism, progress, self-sacrificing idealism and revolutionary will' (1983: 109).

28 Given its steady but slow growth, HB also appeared to be the most stable party in the region (Goicoechea 1988: 407).

29 Obviously, these percentages are subject to widely divergent interpretations, since they touch a politically sensitive area (the desire for Basque independence)The percentages of those desiring independence vary greatly according to the source:

pendence is a reliable indicator of nationalism, we can see that nationalism is stronger among those immigrants who claim Basque identity even than among Basques in general (whether they feel they are Basques or Spaniards). When immigrants 'feel' Basque, they are less likely to compromise over independence and other issues. The oppositional mechanism of nationalist mobilisation has resulted in the direct incorporation of many immigrants into the 'moral community'. The crucible for nationalist militancy is thus a shared Basque identity, rather than origin, race or even culture. Furthermore, paradoxically, the percentage of people opposed to independence is higher among self-indentified 'pure Basques' than among all the other groups of immigrant or mixed origin.[30] Linz concluded that 'when immigrants are forced to choose between a primordial and a territorial definition, they naturally incline towards the latter', which is why 'the most extreme nationalism in the Basque country seems to be associated with a *territorial*, rather than a *primordial*, conception of the nation' (Linz 1985: 206).[31] On the other hand, Clark finds a positive correlation between language maintenance and nationalist voting, but he refers mainly to the native population, rather than specifically to the immigrants (Clark 1984, 1987).

Also, among those who favour a centralised Spanish state, the definition of who is Basque tends to focus on birth and descent: this

for instance, a survey promoted in 1983 by the PNV's magazine, *Euzkadi*, claimed that 74% of the interviewed Basques were in favour of independence, 'if this was achieved peacefully'. Only 21% opted against it. As to their perception of identity, 54% assumed that the Basques are a people apart, whilst 32% claimed that the Basques do not differ from other Spaniards. Thus, the percentage of respondents aspiring to independence was much higher than that of those perceiving the Basques (and thus themselves) as a different people. The paradoxical conclusion is that nationalism – the drive to achieve a form of separate statehood – was more widespread than a sense of separate identity – a belief in sharing a different culture and origins. This bears a relation to the lack of core values as discussed in the previous chapter(s). See *Euzkadi*, no. 94 (15 July 1983), pp. 10-15. However, the reliability of this survey from a sample of only 89 interviews is questionable.

[30] Rejection is obviously strongest of all among those who feel themselves to be purely Spaniard: 75% of these firmly reject independence, a far higher percentage than any of the other groups.

[31] Among the 'primordial' traits, Linz includes language, which can obviously be acquired. This is perhaps on the ground that the sociolinguistic nature of Euskera (its scarce diffusion, low prestige and difficult learning) makes it more 'primordial' than Catalan.

stress on putative origin or race is adopted by 80.3% of the pro-centralists. Thus the *españolistas* are unable to conceive an integrative dimension in Basqueness. In parallel, people who define Basqueness by race or descent are 'only' 45.5% of those favouring independence (1985: 215). Thus a racially exclusive conception of the nation is more widespread among the centralists than among the nationalists.

Catalonia: contemporary period

Mass migration and the limits of cultural integration. The regime's propaganda deliberately falsified the causes of migratory movements: they were explained away by the 'attraction exerted on the simple peasant mentality by the city, with its theatres, avenues and elegant women' (Hall 1983: 74-5). Minimising the seriousness of the social problems caused by its policies, the regime's cop-out was to say that 'these are problems common to all developed countries' (cited by Hall 1983: 75). As we have seen, the most crucial period of massive immigration occurred at a time when the use of Catalan was still rigorously forbidden in all public spheres and 'offenders' were liable to prosecution. The immigrants did not stand a chance of learning it formally. At the same time, Catalan remained *de facto* the habitual language among native Catalans. Thus Francoist prohibition made impossible the immigrants' cultural integration at the very moment when a massive effort in that direction was most needed. On the other hand, many scholars were optimistic about the immigrants' gradual assimilation into Catalan culture. For instance, Maluquer (1963: 62 ff.) found that in the Pyrenean industrial town of Campdevànol all the children of immigrants spoke Catalan and behaved like their Catalans peers. He explained this success as resulting from their parents' desire for social mobility and the prestige they associated with the natives as a reference group: 'Their situation of socio-professional inferiority explains the efforts of the immigrants to be similar to the autochthons.' While the natives labelled the immigrants pejoratively as *xarnegos* (lit. half-breed or hybrid), the most relevant finding was that 'this form of verbal discrimination was employed against the newcomers, not only by the Catalans but also by older immigrants, who thus tried to elevate themselves by stressing a social distance' (63). This, Maluquer concluded, was clear proof of successful integration into Catalan culture and society, extrapolating optimistic conclusions for the Catalanisation of future generations: 'Despite the fact that the teaching was carried out only in Spanish, the school children spoke Catalan among themselves and called *xarnegos* those who did not.[...] This [attitude] encourages assimilation' (63). By defining anyone who did not speak Catalan as *xarnego* and thus as a member of an outgroup, the children also testified to the central importance of language in the definition of their identity. These attitudes highlighted prevailing integrative trends, since the immigrants were no longer considered *xarnegos* as soon as their language proficiency was clearly established.

We have seen that these assimilatory trends have old roots and go back to Catalonia's centenary concept of *terra de pas*. In the recent past, this process has led to optimistic attitudes on the Catalan side. Thus in 1965 the linguist Antoni M. Badia i Margarit claimed: 'The possibility that the immigrants would escape assimilation is simply nil' (cited by Vallverdú 1980).[32] Again, still in 1978, the anthropologist Claudi Esteva i Fabregat assumed that the autochthonous culture was still dominant and that a new 'ethnic group' was emerging in the form of 'hybridisation' (*mestissatge*): 'In Barcelona the Castilian-speaking population [i.e. the monolingual one] is losing about 17% of its components by the second generation' (Esteva 1978).

Catalan culture started to show signs of renewed vitality once the trauma of dictatorship was overcome. However, things did not go as well as many expected. Pi–Sunyer (1971: 119) warned that 'the argument that this minority within a minority can, given the right conditions, be assimilated with few problems smacks of wishful thinking and is not borne out by similar historical cases'. According to Hall (1983: 74), since hardly any reliable data on immigration were available even in the 1970s, the gravity of the situation was hidden from many Catalans. An article published in 1979 in the journal *Els Marges* (Argente *et al.* 1979) expressed a strong preoccupation that, without drastic measures on its behalf, the language was condemned to extinction in the space of a few generations.[33] The article achieved a certain resonance also beyond academia. It

[32] He also asserted that 'by the mere act of living in Catalonia, the immigrants have placed themselves on the road which sooner or later will lead to their Catalanisation' (Badia i Margarit 1964: 109).

[33] Similarly, Woolard argues that 'politically motivated claims that there is only one community in Catalonia do not reflect current reality, and the divisive potential of ethnic identity . . . has not yet been overcome' (1986a: 57).

indicated that the main threat to the language was the unprecedentedly large number of immigrants who barely had any occasion to interact in Catalan. The number of monolingual Castilian-speakers was the highest ever recorded in Catalan history, and in these circumstances actual daily use of Catalan was unlikely, even for people who did master the language.

However, assimilation was not the issue. Rather, the issue was the diffusion of bilingualism, which does not imply the loss of the immigrants' culture.[34] Indeed, the very term 'Castilian-speakers' normally refers to the monolingual population (i.e. those unable to speak Catalan), while Catalan-speakers are always bilingual (and normally use Catalan).[35] This concept of two groups, Catalan- and Castilian-speakers, avoids too sharp a delineation of the two communities, since there are both Catalanised immigrants (or immigrants who are undergoing a process of Catalanisation) and Castilianised natives (even though they are a minority and mainly among higher echelons). Linguistic competences form a continuum shading from pure monolingualism to 'perfect' bilingualism, or the preferred use of Catalan as daily language.

To a lesser extent, the same notion of a continuum applies in the Basque case, where most of the literature emphasises a chasm between autochthonous inhabitants and immigrants. In Euskadi we also find a continuum of identities and behavioural patterns rather than a sharp opposition between two groups, although cultural integration is less likely. Several studies tend to present the immigrants as a tightly bound and easily identifiable community, over-emphasising the fracture between them and the host society (this occurs in both nationalist and more balanced analysis).[36]

---

[34] We can find a plethora of nationalist literature on bilingualism, its limits and dangers. The argument against bilingualism (and in favour of Catalan monolingualism) is backed by sociolinguistic arguments (see, for instance, Aracil 1982, Sabater 1984: 37-8).

[35] Catalans tend to use their code daily in most in-group interactions. Language erosion only occurs among very limited sectors of the native population. In fact, most children with two Catalan parents have daily occasion to use Catalan within the family (Strubell 1981: 151 ff.). However, the natives' competence and fluency in Catalan is often superior to their competence in Castilian.

[36] Some studies of Basque society (Escudero 1978, Heiberg 1989) speak plainly of 'two communities'. For the case of Catalonia, see, for example, Pi–Sunyer (1983) and Di Giacomo (1985).

Moreover, since the big wave of immigration ended in the late 1970s, the very term *immigrant* can no longer imply territorial displacement from one region to another.[37] The largest part of those who migrated in the last twenty years are well-established and intend to remain in the host region; this is especially true of the second generations who have virtually no desire to return to their parents' land (Solé 1981: 18-24 and 344-53). Certainly, many immigrants mythologise their land of origin and surround it with an aura of nostalgia. But the myth falls apart as soon as they have a chance to return to their *pueblos*. Here, often unrecognised as members of their own kin by the local population, they are called, ironically, *los Catalanes* (Solé 1986, 1987), After such disappointing experiences, they frequently feel that it is impossible for them ever to be re-integrated into their former homeland. The ensuing identity conflict sometimes results in a desire to acquire a stronger Catalan identity. As older immigrants find making this step difficult, they are nonetheless anxious that their offspring and future generations should be fully integrated into Catalan society and culture, and to have full access to Catalan. This desire is shown by several surveys mentioned in the next section.

The spread of Catalan. We saw in the previous chapter that the percentage of those able to understand Catalan has grown spectacularly from 79.8% in 1981 to 90.3% in 1986; i.e. in only five years it has increased by over 10% (data from the municipal census of April 1986). In the Basque country the increase has been only 3% in the same period, nevertheless it is an increase.[38] Different hypotheses are available to account for the diffusion of Catalan among immigrants. For instance, 'relative deprivation theory' suggests that since the autochthonous group is economically better placed, it acts as a 'reference group' for many immigrants, representing a pattern of behaviour which many migrants aspire to emulate. The reference group's language is part of what people wishing to become members of the group may try to adopt. In

[37] Pascual and Cardelús (1987: 332) note that the fact of being born outside Catalonia does not justify the definition of person as an 'immigrant', since he or she could have been residing in Catalonia for at least twenty years.

[38] However, actual linguistic uses are much more resilient to change. Furthermore, they are difficult to assess statistically: census forms only contained items on language proficiency, not language use.

sociolinguistics the phenomenon is known as *linguistic prestige* (Weinreich 1956) or *status* (Wooland 1989); thus language 'is generally inseparable from the prestige of those who speak it' (Woolard 1989: 93). Many authors tend to see class and ethnicity in Catalonia as overlapping, in that Catalans are concentrated in the middle or upper classes, while immigrants allegedly represent the working class (Woolard 1989, Di Giacomo 1986).[39] Indeed, at first most immigrants fell into semiskilled and unskilled labour pools (Pinilla de las Heras 1973: 105). However, this is only a rough generalisation and we cannot speak of class as coterminous with ethnicity, particularly in more recent years. In fact, some Catalans are likely to be found at the bottom of the social ladder too. On the other side, there are immigrants who have succeeded in reaching the highest ranks of class stratification, thanks to a relatively diffuse social mobility.[40]

The immigrants' highly positive attitudes towards Catalan language and culture has been confirmed by numerous sociolinguistic studies.[41] A large part of the data refers to the respondents' opinions about the introduction of Catalan in the school curricula. The proliferation of such surveys in itself signals the concern of the Catalanists over the possible impact on immigrants' attitudes of the forthcoming linguistic normalisation. The investigations preceded or followed swiftly the recent changes in the local education system. A survey by Badia i Margarit (1969) was the first to unveil a heartfelt desire to learn Catalan among the general population. The first serious quantitative work, by FOESSA (1970), came to more reliable conclusions: in a sample of 'housewives', 97% of the interviewees favoured the introduction of Catalan into the school system (33% were immigrants themselves, while 50% had at least one parent born outside Catalonia). Other surveys were specifically concerned with the attitudes of the overall immigrant population. In the generally rural *comarca* of Osona, 94% of respondents, all born outside Catalonia and in Castilian-speaking areas, wanted their children to

---

[39] Di Giacomo argues that 'the confluence of social class and ethnicity is painfully obvious' (1986: 73).

[40] On social mobility among the immigrants in the 1960s and the first 1970s, see the classical sociological investigation by Pinilla de las Heras (1973). See also Miguélez (1987), Miguélez and Solé (1987) and Pascual and Cardelús (1990).

[41] For an exhaustive review of these studies, see Torres (1980, 1988).

learn Catalan (Reixach 1975). In the satellite city of Cornellà de Llobregat, which had – and has – the highest percentage of monolingual Castilian speakers in all Catalonia (CIDC 1987), 97% of the parents favoured increasing the teaching of Catalan (cited by Torres 1980). According to another study, 90% of an interviewed sample of both native Catalans and immigrants preferred the teaching of Catalan to be extended to the overall territory, while about 80% wanted Catalan introduced as a compulsory subject in all school curricula (Bibiloni and Junyent, cited by Torres 1980). Paradoxically, the zone which showed the strongest support for the teaching of (and in) Catalan were the suburbs of Barcelona, i.e. the place of maximum immigration and of minimum knowledge of the language (Torres 1980: 53). This evidence has been backed by more recent data on the pressing request by immigrant fathers on behalf of their children for 'immersion schools' in the metropolitan periphery (Conversi 1987).[42] The fact that almost all the immigrants expressed a desire to learn Catalan is a measure of its perceived utility. In fact, this desire seems stronger in areas where there is less knowledge of Catalan and, therefore, have a greater need to acquire basic rudiments of the language. However, this pragmatic demand does not guarantee an increasing use of Catalan, or necessarily reflect a positive attitude towards the language.

Some authors indicate a further factor of integration in the solidarity between the immigrant workers and the Catalans generally experienced during the time of Franco in the wake of their common experience of oppression by the centralist state.[43] With its double crusade against 'separatists' and 'reds' alike, Falangist rhetoric reinforced such an alliance. After years of unceasing propaganda against the *rojoseparatistas*, even ordinary people came to perceive some sort of identity among the two dimensions. The experience of the Spanish Republic, when the Catalan nationalists and the Left were allied against the centralist right, was still fresh in popular memory. However, probably the most important factor of integration was that the working–class leaders were themselves raised in Catalanist

[42] For an overview of changes in the Catalan education system in the early 1980s, see Conversi (1987). For the implementation of 'immersion' classes adapted to Catalonia on the Canadian model, see Arenas (1986).

[43] This may seem part of nationalist or leftist mythology, but similar examples are given by numerous authors. On immigrant-Catalan solidarity during later Francoism, see Candel (1964, 1985).

milieux, or directly involved in Catalanist politics. At times
nationalist, communist or socialist leaders were members of the same
families. Due to the common struggle for democracy and against a
common enemy, a bond of solidarity was created among leftist and
nationalist leaders. This brings to the fore once more the role of the
political intelligentsia as the moulder of a new social identity and of
the cultural struggle as a cohesive factor.

Catalan identity: a dynamic process. The concept of identity is among
the most elusive and difficult to define both in general terms and
in terms of any specific identity associated with a given ethnic
group. Frederik Barth (1969) noticed that the intensity with which
group members stress their ethnicity increases when there is intense
spatial-geographical contact between groups. The most isolated
ethnic groups are probably the least self-defined in ethnic terms.
Thus it is more likely that the Catalans and the Basques who
were subjected to massive immigration and overall acculturation,
would become more consciously 'national' than their Galician
counterparts, since the Galicians did not experience anything like
the same amount of cultural interference. Here immigration is
particularly important, because, thanks to the massive influx of
people belonging to a different culture, the average person becomes
conscious of cultural differences every day. As the immigrants'
all-pervasive presence can not be ignored, cultural conflict becomes
part of the life of every individual life. In particular, wherever
immigration occurs on a large scale, it is inevitably perceived as
a form of aggression. Traditional ethnic borders are attacked daily
and plunged into deep crisis. These borders may either be utterly
reinforced by this crisis, as in the early Basque case, or be more
pliable, adapting to new trends, as in the Catalan case. The natives
adopt different strategies to defend their identity. In both cases,
national identity is a concentric process, but the hierarchy of
values is clearer in Catalonia.

The Catalan leaders' attempt to define a specific sense of Catalan
identity have tended to underline territoriality and residentiality. ('A
Catalan is whoever lives and works in Catalonia').[44] On a second

44 For instance, the historical works of the fathers of Catalanism: Antoni Rovira
i Virgili, Francesc Pi i Margall, Enric Prat de la Riba, Valentí Almirall *et al.* Among
the works which are specifically dedicated to immigration, those of the now
president of the Generalitat, Jordi Pujol (1966), lay the foundation for a non

and more inward level, there is the linguistic aspect ('A Catalan is whoever speaks Catalan'), which is not automatic but can be acquired. With the stress on either residentiality or language, ascriptive and hereditary criteria of national memberships ('A Catalan person is a child or descendant of Catalans') have been cast aside. Hence present-day definitions of who is a Catalan include individuals coming from other regions, provided they remain resident in Catalonia. Furthermore, this is also part of the immigrants' self-conception, insofar as 'second-generation immigrants' (i.e. immigrants' children born in Catalonia) usually define themselves as Catalans, independently of their knowledge or use of the Catalan language (Solé 1981, 1982). For the nationalist leaders this integrative definition is certainly linked to political and not merely electoral goals of nation-building. However the 'residence' factor is often played down in everyday life until it becomes almost epiphenomenal. In the previous chapter we saw how language gradually emerged as the core value of the Catalan nation. In this chapter we have also seen that many immigrants themselves see in it a crucible of Catalanness. The fact that language tends to be accepted as such by many immigrants is a measure of its integrative strength.

Hence we are faced with a series of concentric circles and progressively integrating concepts, like the layers of an onion. First there stands a civic territorial definition of nationhood based on the *jus soli*, a definition which has currency at least in political rhetoric. Then there comes a deserved and acquirable membership in the nation through voluntary efforts, symbolised by mastering the language. The idea of 'nation of will' has to be actively demonstrated through a 'will of the nation', a longing to be part of the nation. Here, we can find some parallel in the French concept of citizenship: '*Etre Français, cela se mérite*', cried the French assimilationists. 'To be a Catalan cannot be bought or sold, it can only be earned. And [the immigrants] will not be Catalans until they speak like us, until they make our needs [and feelings] their own..., until they feel personally hurt in seeing all things Catalan despised' (Cruells 1965: 32). Finally, perhaps limited to rural strongholds, stands a declining stress on origin and descent, usually provable by a person's double Catalan surname. This definition is occasionally used among the assimilated Catalan diaspora as a tool to rediscover a Catalanity which has been

---

ascriptive definition of Catalan identity.

lost in its cultural aspects. However, its application has never implied an extreme stress on race, as with the Basques.

These three concepts of Catalan identity are often situational. The proposition that language is more important than residence at a more intimate and popular level is well addressed by Woolard (1986: 58), who mentions that 'many leaders object vigorously to any reference to "two communities" within Catalonia, but their broad-based definition of Catalans is rarely if ever employed by individuals to talk about themselves. Even those who are in sympathy with the Catalan leaders' political goals find it difficult to avoid the basic Catalan–immigrant dichotomy that the political definition attempts to abolish. In any extended or serious discussion, the dichotomy inevitably surfaces' (Woolard 1986: 58).

Language is thus the hallmark of integration, but not its only avenue. Immigrants often find an easier way into Catalan identity by participating in folksy events of popular culture, such as popular dances, *colles de castellers* (human towers), choral singing, trekking etc. In the crucial years of resistance and transition these activities provided a relatively painless means of integration, where not much personal reputation or sacrifice was at stake. 'They were readily available and, unlike language, risked little loss of face' (Johnston 1991: 120). A particular symbolic element of integration has been provided by the Catalan national dance, the *sardana*, created during the *Renaixença* by the Andalusian immigrant Pep Ventura (1817-75) on the basis of a folk tradition dating back at least to the sixteenth century. It was 'launched' in 1859 at the Liceu theatre and thereafter acquired increasing popularity (Rebull 1976, Barrera 1985: 300-8, Brandes 1990). A typically invented tradition, the *sardana* can be seen as a symbol of the inclusive nature of Catalan culture: 'By stressing the inclusion of everyone who learns the rules, the dance is a microcosmic reflection of the general Catalan belief in ethnicity as an achieved status. However, the *sardana* also excludes those who neither know nor follow the detailed rules of the dance' (Brandes 1990).

Children's entertainments and shows were aimed at the immigrants' offspring. As an example, in several Barcelona suburbs the *Roda d'Espectacles Infantils* (Children Shows Group) organised shows based on the study of Catalan traditions and the revival of lost celebrations. The *Roda* was founded in 1977 by the initiative of neighbourhood associations and recreation groups, at a time when it was still imperative to revive customs and traditions which had been suffocated by years of clandestine existence.[45]

Comparative trends. Several factors can be singled out as determining the more or less successful extent of the immigrants' cultural integration in Catalonia and Euskadi:

(1) The region of origin. According to a survey conducted in the Catalan town of Mataró, the most adaptable of the immigrants came from regions near to Catalonia but also from Andalusia; the more refractory came from the Castilian centre (Duocastella, cited by Maluquer 1963: 59).[46] In Euskadi, Castilian immigrants outnumber those from other regions and are known to be more resistant to assimilation (Blanco 1990).

(2) The structural difference between the two languages. The ease of learning Catalan cannot be matched by the difficulty of learning Basque, which is completely unrelated to Castilian.

(3) The prestige associated with each language. Catalan enjoys a higher prestige, not only culturally but also because it is associated with a dynamic entrepreneurial part of Spanish society. No such prestige has hitherto been accorded to Basque.

(4) Its value in the labour market. This may make the language a valuable means of economic integration. 'Instrumental' motivations for language learning are pervasive in an environment where Catalan is used in almost every sector of the economy. By contrast, notable attempts to introduce Euskara in the public administration have not been matched by equally successful efforts to introduce it into the private sector. As a consequence, economic integration is more important in the Basque country than cultural integration.

(5) The local population's reception of the immigrants' efforts to assimilate. In contrast with Catalonia, the Basques' initial isolationist attitudes implied that the locals were not particularly interested in promoting the knowledge of their language. This may have influenced the respective success of the two countries' integrative efforts.

(6) The nationalist leaders' different interpretations of national identity. Their formulations may finally have influenced both the

---

[45] Lluísa Celades, 'La integració dels fills dels immigrats mitjançant la cultural', *Avui*, 4 June 1986.

[46] The survey simply asked the interviewees if they understood Catalan.

attitudes of the natives towards the immigrants and the immigrants' confidence of being accepted in the host society, so that their efforts of assimilation will be rewarded. In the Basque country and Catalonia, we are faced with two different concepts of nationhood and potential citizenship. Perhaps this distinction runs parallel to the one between the German and French concepts of citizenship, the former based on the *jus sanguinis* the latter on the *jus soli* (Brubaker 1992).

Other related factors can be added to the above. For instance, before venturing into learning a new language, an immigrant may ponder what its intrinsic worth is, what has this language to offer *per se*. Again Catalan was greatly advantaged by its rich and ancient literature.

In this chapter we have seen that immigration not only plays a central role in the formation and evolution of nationalism, but also that immigrants can be active participants in the nationalist movement. This is most likely if the latter promote a new inclusive vision of national identity, which is non-ascriptive and not based on putative descent. But in order to do so, the nationalist movement has to concentrate on inclusive myths, symbols and core values which are not always available. Yet the construction of an oppositional ideology can achieve the same effects, bypassing the cultural dimension. The Basque case shows that some immigrants are likely to participate in nationalist politics where there is extreme polarisation between the nationalist movement and the state, while the state lacks widely accepted legitimacy. As we have stressed throughout, Catalan identity was originally conceived as integrative, while Basque identity had an exclusivist bent. In Catalonia, only marginal intellectuals (never the intelligentsia) adopted racist or segregationist approaches. Such trends, whenever they emerged, were quickly superseded by the nationalist leaders' integrative goals. Barcelona has been a destination for immigrants since the late nineteenth century (Jofre 1978). However, the steadiest migratory wave in modern Catalan history was in the 1960s and early 1970s, coinciding with the final phase of Franco's dictatorship. In a few years, nearly 1 million immigrants, mostly from Andalusia, settled in the insalubrious peripheries of Barcelona's 'industrial belt' and in other cities such as Tarragona.[47]

Unlike Catalonia, the Basque provinces had never experienced a massive population influx before the industrial revolution. Hence the Basques had correspondingly little preparation for integration and faith in it. We have mentioned the special *fueros* which did not allow non-Basques to reside in the country. According to Arana, the immigrants were *maketos* from despised *Maketania* (Spain or the rest of Iberia), fifth columns of the hated Spanish foe. For many Catalanists the immigrants were instead uneducated people who needed human care and full integration into the more European and modern Catalan 'civilisation'. Catalonia turned this sense of confidence into foundation on which its successful drive to turn the immigrants into 'new Catalans' rested. Arana himself recognised this when he opposed his solipsist philosophy to the Catalan aims (see Chapter 7).

From Arana's virulent statements one might infer that ethnic conflict between immigrants and natives would be much more acute in the Basque case, but it is not exactly so. On the contrary, Catalonia has a tormented history of strife between natives and immigrants, which reached its peak in 1909 with the anti-Catalan populist revolt of Alejandro Lerroux. It is important to consider that such anti-Catalan feelings barely depended on the language gap. Periods of great expansion of the Catalan language at the official level were not characterised by particular inter-ethnic strife. The main cause of tension was the identification of Catalanism as a pure bourgeois product. Indeed, an often inflexible Catalan bourgeoisie was notoriously unable to meet the workers' demands. In contrast, Arana's anti-capitalism and emphasis on social Christianity made him less a target of class hatred than people like Cambó or even Prat. In a period of rabid social conflict all over Europe, the fact that Arana appeared as a racist mattered less than his visceral anti-capitalist sermons. Moreover, Lerroux's mobs saw the Catalanists as representatives of a surreptitious hidden power, the power of finance and industry. In Basque nationalism the bourgeois sector of Sota was

---

[47] *Desarrollismo* (fast and savage industrial and urban development) is the nick-name for the last economic phase of Francoism, when the regime devoted itself to unbridled technocratic development as a panacea for the centuries-old economic gap between the peninsula's North and the South. The government tried to find a 'remedy' for this economic imbalance by encouraging 'internal' migration.

always contrasted by more radical elements, who were liable to make common cause with the working class.[48]

Only after the Second World War was race banished altogether from the nationalist vocabulary. In the aftermath of the Nazi Holocaust, appeals to race became universally discredited and Basque nationalists had to face a serious challenge in their search for new core values to adopt in its place. Immigrants in both Catalonia and the Basque Country experienced suburban segregation. And both nationalist movements, as they developed in the 1960s, increasingly resisted these trends. However, although the aim became the same (incorporation of the immigrants), the tactics were different. Catalan nationalism tried to *attract* the newcomers through the mobilisation of cultural symbols, presenting linguistic identity and participation in cultural networks as the final prize of successful incorporation, whereas postwar Basque nationalism tried instead to *penetrate* immigrant milieux by voicing their class concern through workers' mobilisation and the creation of a new solidarity. Direct participation in nationalist networks through active politics, rather than culture, was presented as the ultimate prize of successful incorporation.

In Catalonia, attempts at stigmatising and segregating the immigrants have been defeated by several factors. First, the natives' traditional predisposition to redefine their 'ethnic borders' in flexible terms helped to limit segregationism. This implies a remarkable capacity to absorb external cultural elements. Secondly, as working-class leaders and nationalists formed a common front of resistance against Francoism, Catalanism was assumed by relevant fringes of the immigrant proletariat. Thirdly, Catalonia's economic vitality made its original inhabitants into a reference group for the newcomers. Fourthly, the Generalitat more recently took over the main instruments of secondary socialisation, particularly education.[49] Since Catalonia was granted autonomy, Catalan has knocked down most

[48] See, for instance, Gallastegi's (1993) identification with the exploited workers in Chapter 3 (Espinosa 1993).

[49] The role of television has been of even greater importance in fostering the spread of Catalan as a language of 'high' culture. Since football is the most popular sport among immigrants and natives alike, the broadcast in Catalan of national and international matches and other sport events has been central for its diffusion.

of the remaining resistance to be accepted as a vehicle of high culture.[50]

Apart from some general similarities, the two regions face different immigration patterns resulting from different timing, local conditions and forms of adaptation for the immigrants. As a result their nationalist movements have tackled the issue of immigration in opposite ways.

---

[50] Should this integrative trend still persist, Catalonia could constitute a model for those who fear immigratory waves from the Third World as a threat to European cultural 'integrity'. A slow process of natural integration has occurred in Catalonia in the time-span of a few generations, without any of the official means which a bureaucratic state apparatus normally has at its disposal: without schools, without mass-media, and even without the official presence of the language in any public domain.

9

THE ROOTS OF VIOLENCE

The previous two chapters have shown how two national patterns of nationalist mobilisation developed through the focus on different core symbols and values and how far the latter achieved an integrating effect. Our main hypothesis was that the stress on different values influences the formation of different patterns of mobilisation, integration and identity, and that nationalist élites are limited in their choice by existing cultural conditions. We noted the contrast, from the 1960s to the 1980s, between Basque nationalism's preference for violence and Catalanism's traditional pacifism, although Catalan society was itself riven by violent conflict in the past. In this final chapter we advance a further set of hypotheses: that cultural assimilation and fragmentation created the condition for the emergence of a violent form of nationalism. However, in order to materialise, this violent potential needed a further condition, namely state repression. Our focus will essentially be the Basque country. We argue that the two most relevant factors for explaining Basque violence are respectively anthropological and political: a lack of shared core values and the repressive action by the part of the state's military forces. These two factors are connected with all the other sub-factors.

But before considering our main argument we have to dispel some myths about the violent character of Basque society. First, was violence something peculiar to Basque nationalism, as compared to Catalanism?

Violence not endemic to Basque society

It is sometimes claimed that Basque society is inherently violent, but this can be shown to be false. In this the comparison with Catalonia does not hold. There have been times when Catalonia was one of the most violent societies on the continent. In the fifteenth century Catalan society was permanently wracked by civil war. In 1511 the Italian political writer Francesco Guicciardini (1482-1540) described Catalonia as a land infested with bandits and ruled by the anarchy of violence (1993: 19-22). In 1603 a viceroy's report claimed that 'the majority of the population live in a state of fretfulness, belonging to bands and factions, which give rise to infinite excesses' (quoted by Reglá 1956: 124). In the 1830s, 'Barcelona led all other European cities in urban rioting and intermittent wholesale insurrections against central authority' (Payne 1975: 50). Engels described it as 'the city whose history records more struggles on the barricades than that of any other city in the world' (cited by Payne 1975: 50). Anarchist murders, urban rioting and burning of monasteries became commonplace in the 1910s. Barcelona was 'the most violent city of Europe during the early part of this century' (Hooper 1986: 234). Again, during the 1920s, it 'ranked first among Spanish cities in terms of absolute numbers of labour-related shootings, and second after Bilbao in terms of labour-related shootings as percentage of the total population' (Meaker 1974: 429-30). Finally, in the 1930s extremist factions began an escalation which led to the Civil War.[1] Pre-Civil War Euskadi, in contrast, was characterised by other kinds of phenomena, not specifically political.[2] This is in sharp contrast with the present, when the observer is struck by Catalonia's relative civil peace as much as by Basque radicalism.

Although before the Civil War Catalan urban society was more violent and fragmented than Basque society, this was basically true of Left-wing organisations, rather than the nationalists, who stuck to a clear definition of Catalan identity since at least Prat's compilation (1906).[3] Certainly, the PNV long remained the only significant force in Basque nationalism, in contrast with Catalonia's plural

---

[1] This heritage of violence has inspired some Catalan authors to identify an underlying vein of Catalan character: the term *rauxa*, or passionate extremism, has been used, among others, by Vicens Vives (1984: 190 ff.) to describe this intermittent feature of Catalan personality. Vives opposed the *rauxa*, to the *seny* (common sense, wisdom, consideration).

[2] For instance, Christian (1987, 1996) describes the amazing upsurge of millenarian visions, religious trances and other mystic happenings in the early 1930s. During the first half of the twentieth century, this phenomenon covered a much broader area, stretching from southern France (Lourdes) to Portugal (Fatima).

[3] The Catalanist ERC was a coalition of several groups which nevertheless shared a common vision of Catalan identity.

scenario. But Catalanism carried more weight in Republican Madrid, and was more coordinated in terms of its goals, identity and organisations. Rather, the fact that the cluster of Left-wing political ideologies stemming from Anarchism to Socialism and Republicanism were themselves divided may be a good indication of how ideological (and cultural) fragmentation is conducive to violence in non-nationalist conflicts as well.

Also important is which memories of the Civil War were selected and in what way, rather than the immediate impact of the Civil War in itself. But why did the memory of the Civil War have such an unparalleled impact on Basque nationalists? Was not the Civil War equally associated with national oppression in Catalonia? Unlike in Catalonia, the Civil War in the Basque country was experienced as a nationalist war. The nationalists had their own army, the *gudariak* (Basque soldiers), who fought for the Republic and whose memories created a nationalist myth of armed resistance. In Catalonia, the war was experienced as a fissiparous and self-destructive conflict between opposite extremisms. Today the Civil War is not celebrated by Catalan nationalists as part of their heritage.[4]

The first ETA activists considered themselves *gudariak*. For the Basque youth, the myth of the *gudari* remained alive, spread by a popular literature on events in the war. This is not the case for Catalonia, where only a few nationalists fought on the Republican side. One reason for this lack of prominence of Catalan nationalism during the Civil War was that, in contrast with the PNV, the main Catalan nationalist party, ERC (*Esquerra Republicana de Catalunya*), was a recently established coalition without a tested structure, historical experience or definite cadres. Born as a federation of about 100 nationalist centres, ERC represented an electoral venture more than a fully-fledged party such as the PNV, which was born more than fifty years earlier. Moreover, a vast sector of the moderate right was marginalised by the war and unable to take sides with either the Francoists or the Republicans.

Religious persecution was a key factor in this complex development. We have mentioned the 'tradition' of church-burning and priest-beating which developed in Catalonia. This did not happen in Euskadi, where religious persecution was limited to a few episodes

---

[4] I am grateful to Josep Benet for pointing out the very different impact that the Civil War had on Catalan and Basque nationalisms.

at the beginning of the war. Once the PNV imposed itself as the key resistance force, such cases ceased to embitter the faithful, at least in Vizcaya and Guipúzcoa. In contrast, anti-clerical persecution in Catalonia was so severe that many Catalanists had to move to the Francoist field for want of any alternative.

But was repression in the Basque country different from that in Catalonia or any more ferocious? There is no clear-cut answer. First, while in Catalonia cultural repression helped to accentuate awareness of the importance of language, in the Basque case the attacks were not so clearly targeted. Secondly, after 1959 Francoist repression became more widespread in Euskadi, so that at times the target seemed to be the entire Basque population. This stemmed from the two regions' different degrees of cultural fragmentation and assimilation into the Spanish state: language became the main target of repression in Catalonia precisely because it was the symbol of Catalan unity. Since no such clear element was identifiable in the Basque resistance, repression was blind and unable to distinguish nuances. According to Sullivan (1988: 34), 'there was never any serious attempt to prohibit the use of spoken Basque',[5] and instead all aspects of Basque identity were suppressed. Certainly Euskera was particularly under attack, at least up to 1968.[6] It is also debatable whether there was greater political persecution in Euskadi than in Catalonia. However, repression in Euskadi had a physical side that Catalonia only experienced in the early Falangist phase, with arbitrary imprisonment, police attacks on unarmed citizens, torture and suchlike.[7] From the late 1950s, repression in the Basque country achieved a much higher intensity then in the rest of the state: out of a total of eleven states of emergency decreed by Franco between 1956 and 1975, ten affected Vizcaya, Gipuzkoa or both of them at the same time (Jáuregui 1981: 208). It may still be argued that most of these states of emergency concerned strikes and other forms of workers' mobilisation, yet this polarised environment was ideal for ETA to prosper. 'The most distinctive feature [in Euskadi] . . . was

[5] However, Sullivan's interpretation is rejected by many Basques who blame on the Francoist regime a big share of responsibility for the decline of Euskara.

[6] For instance, the use of Basque names at baptisms or on gravestones remained forbidden till 1976 (Sullivan 1988: 34) together with a persisting general ban on all forms of written Euskara.

[7] On this see the various reports published by Amnesty International, especially from 1968 to 1975.

the intense physical repression of all resistance . . ., particularly since 1960' (Jáuregui 1981: 205).

This role played by the state had an immediate impact on the means of political mobilisation. The states of emergency reinforced the feeling of besieged identity that hovered over Basque society and were reflected in ETA's priorities. One of its leaders admitted: 'ETA has never been defined by an ideology (in the strict sense), but by its spirit of struggle'.[8] As continuous schisms created more fragmentation, there were new upsurges of activity directed at shifting the conflict away from within the organisation and against the common enemy. From a certain point onwards, action totally replaced ideology. The ideological and cultural vacuum was filled by direct action as the only means of giving the movement a sense of change and purpose. Only in this way could ETA demonstrate that it was still alive and reacting to its predicament. The choice of action was in-built into the very foundation of ETA. Their leaders declared in the 1950s: 'When a situation appears desperate, with no exit, action always precedes hope' (*Documentos Y*, vol. 1, p. 10).

In Catalonia cultural activities offered a way out. They presented an escape valve, as well as more opportunities for action. Cultural activism gave young people wishing to act something worth struggling for. 'In Catalonia, the defence of language could be carried out by everybody, independently of their political orientation. There was unanimity around the need to defend Catalan' (Benet, personal interview). For instance, the official magazine of the Communist Party, *Treball* (f. 1936, n.s. 1942), was published in Catalan, although most working-class immigrants spoke Castilian only. Nothing on a similar scale could be achieved in Euskadi.

The separatist dimension

It is often observed that the violent character assumed in the 1960s by Basque nationalism was related to its original separatist aim. However, separatism was also a compensatory device for the lack of shared cultural values and, in particular, for the Basques' severely restricted relationship with Madrid. In other words, it served to stress Basque determination *vis-à-vis* a state dominated by liberal centralism and unable to take into account peripheral

[8] Juan José Echave, in *Garaia*, no. 28, 1979, p. 29.

aspirations. It also enhanced the 'us-them' divide as a counter-strategy for the absence of clearly defined cultural borders. With his moralistic, purist and anti-immigrant crusade, Arana aimed at rejecting Spain and all Spanish elements before establishing a serious programme of nation-building. His invention of nationalist symbols was aimed at cementing a new oppositional loyalty, but his own definition of Basqueness was contradictory. Arana's deep-seated hatred of Spain often featured more prominently than his love for the Basques. Hence his confusion over a definition of Basqueness: he was good at rejecting, less so at constructing. Although he created the key symbols of Basque mobilisation (flag, name, hymn etc.), he was much more ambivalent over Basque identity. Arana's oppositional dichotomies served to push Spain farther apart from Euskadi. That was part of a border-making enterprise in which minor differences were exacerbated, as ethnic identities seemed to melt and overlap in his native Bilbao. Therefore, all contact with Spain was to be abolished, and anybody indulging in it would be branded as *españolista*. Arana's main qualm was that Bizkaia (and Euskadi) could be downgraded to the lower status of a Spanish region or province. He stressed continually that Euskadi was a nation, not a region. Hence, his vitriolic attacks against Catalanism: Euskadi would not follow the Catalan path to an integrationist regionalism at any price. The idea that Basque autonomy could be better protected by controlling the reins of Madrid's government was a Carlist one, and the Carlist wars had resulted in a devastating defeat for the Basques. The wars 'decimated the countryside, encumbered the population with huge debts in the form of war retributions, and left a standing army of occupation' (Douglass and da Silva 1971: 155-6). Defeat led to a climate of intimidation against the native culture, best expressed in the attacks by Unamuno and other pro-centralist intellectuals.

Stress on separation from Spain was also reinforced by powerful myths of origin lingering on despite assimilation. The postwar apathy of Basque society from 1939 to 1959 contrasts with the nationalist upheaval of the 1960s. This contrast testifies to the continuing resilience of memories and shared identities, when the nationalist movement appeared dormant. Since no political options could be freely expressed, memories of past suffering remained deeply entrenched, perhaps even being reinforced. When no uncensored history book is allowed to circulate, history is more likely to become myth or counter-myth. Hence nationalism assumes an even stronger potential for opposition.

State repression: the legacy of the past

In this section we consider two sub-factors of state repression, which were conducive to the violent turn of Basque nationalism: lack of pre-existing autonomous institutions – a direct consequence of state centralisation – and memories of the Civil War. Local autonomies were 'given up' only after prolonged military struggle and defeat (the Carlist wars). The absence of pre-existing autonomous institutions is often taken by analysts as encouraging violence rather than more accommodating attitudes. According to Kellas (1991: 112), 'violence erupts in areas where participative institutions are weakest; more sophisticated areas with an history of self-rule as the Baltic republics tend towards constitutional action . . .'. This observation seems correct in the short term, yet we also need to account for long-lasting periods of interrupted self-rule. In other words, cases of late centralisation and consequent disruption of local self-rule, as with the Basque *fueros*, do not correspond to cases in which a new form of self-rule was established, as in twentieth-century Catalonia. For instance, immediately before Francoism, the Catalans enjoyed a great degree of autonomy under the Second Republic. In contrast, the Basques were initiated to the experience of regional self-rule only under the dramatic circumstances of the Civil War; their autonomy statute was recognised by the Spanish Republicans too late to be put into practice. The Catalans also ran a semi-autonomous Mancomunitat in 1914-25, when Basque nationalism was still unable to build up alternative institutions.

However, if we go further back, we have to consider the persistence of Basque *fueros* right up into the early 1870s, while Catalan privileges were eroded more than hundred years before, in 1716. Hence, in 1914 (Mancomunitat) and again in 1931 (Generalitat), the Catalans started to rebuild their regional institutions virtually from nothing after two centuries of oblivion. In the same period, the more recently abolished traditional autonomies of the Basques could not be revived. Such precedents exerted their impact in the aftermath of Francoism: once a new decentralised constitution was approved in 1978, the Catalans were better equipped for self-government and ready to rebuild their institutions. Hence, the absence of pre-existing autonomous institutions can arguably be related to the need to resort to violence, insofar as the latter worked as a supplement to the former, and insofar as fragmented élites, unable to reach agreement over self-rule, could not control radical elements. But this absence was due to the state's opposition to nationalist demands, even during the short period of democracy under the Republic.[9] It was part of the more general factor of state repression. If they had not been hampered by centralist repression, local institutions might well have flourished. Indeed, we can identify centralisation and the abolition of the *fueros*, not merely as a process of state intervention but as overt acts of state repression: local rights were abolished without the consent of the people. The only sector of the population openly welcoming the elimination of the *fueros* was a small bourgeois oligarchy of mine-owners and iron industrialists.

Basque postwar resistance was characterised by a special discourse on the glorious memories of the Civil War and the horrors which accompanied it. We mentioned at the outset that the Civil War provided a moral and emotional watershed in Basque political culture. With the complete triumph of the winners, the humiliation of the losers became immeasurable. Under a ruthless militarisation of society, the war initiated a process of oppositional culture which had to last till the present day. In the wake of the Civil War, the Basques experienced destruction of their cities, enforced cultural assimilation and physical obliteration. A law-decree of 23 June 1937 declared Bizkaia and Gipuzkoa as 'traitor provinces'. 'Since 1936, all mention of the Basques was completely omitted from the administrative record of the Spanish state' (Jáuregui 1981: 206).[10] Remembrance of the Civil War, with its heroes and villains, was transmitted to the young generation in mythical terms. Hence, the legacy of totalitarian violence was felt all through the following decades. Much of these feelings are symbolised in Picasso's *Guernica*. What did the bombing of Guernica represent? In the words of Robert Clark, it 'is without doubt the most powerful and driving

[9] This point is in contradiction to Spain's relatively late efforts at state-building (Linz 1973, 1975).

[10] This official denial touched all aspects of the state's administration, so that Euskadi could not have a district either in the military sphere (*Capitanía General*), the judicial (*Audiencia Territorial*), the religious (archdiocese) or the educational (university district etc.) (Jáuregui 1981: 206)'.

symbol in the entire Basque political culture. For an American, it
would be Pearl Harbor, the Alamo and Bunker Hill all combined
in a single, searing metaphor' (in Aguirre 1991: 70-1).[11] The legacy
of the Civil War remained vivid in the new generation of Basque
nationalists. Most of the references in the bibliography of Zalbide's
Insurección en Euskadi are war studies or memoirs of the Resistance
against the Nazis, especially in France. Similarly, in the short
bibliography supplied by ETA's *Libro Blanco*, references include
works by the French partisans fighting the Nazi occupation.[12] The
comparison between the Basques under Franco and other European
peoples under Nazi occupation was frequent, because of the level
of violence experienced both during and after the Civil War. It is
important to remember that it was German planes of the Condor
Legion which bombed Guernica on a market day.[13] These were
constant topics among Basque radicals and emerged with new
virulence after the Americans opened up to Franco. The response
of the young nationalists to this disenchantment with the West was
a slow drift towards the adoption of Third World anticolonialist and

11 On the destruction of Guernica, see Southworth (1977).

12 Charles Tillon, *Les FTP. Témoignage pour servir à l'histoire de la Résistance*, Paris:
Julliard, 1962; M. Granet and H. Michel, *Combat. Histoire d'un movement de résistance
de julliet 1940 à julliet 1943*, Paris: Presses Universitaires de France, 1957; Jean-
Marie Domenach, *La Propagande Politique*, Paris: Presses Universitaires de France,
1955; Maurice Mégret, *L'Action Psychologique*, Paris: Fayard, 1959. Also considered
valuable was General T. Bor-Komorowski, *Histoire d'une armée secrète* (Paris: Les
Iles d'Or/Plon, 1952), on the Polish resistance movement against Nazi occupation
(1939-44). Three 'reactionary' manuals were included, in order to study the strategy
and tactics of the enemy: Dominique Ponchardier (*Les Pavés de l'Enfer*), Colonel
Roger Trinquier (*La Guerre Moderne*) and Curzio Malaparte (*Technique du coup
d'Etat*). The latter was read in its French edition (*Technique du Coup d'Etat*, Paris:
Grasset, 1948). Trinquier was translated into English as *Modern Warfare: A French
View of Counterinsurgency*, London: Pall Mall, 1964. Central to ETA was Trinquier's
view that the allegiance of the civilian population is one of the most vital objectives
for both insurgents and counter-insurgents, and his description of how to ensure
such allegiance. Finally, Claude Delmas, *La guerre révolutionnaire*, Paris: Presses
Universitaires de France, 1959, is a guerrilla classic, which was to be of the utmost
relevance for ETA activists who quoted it repeatedly. Focusing on Algeria, Tunisia
and Vietnam, as well as Communist insurgency in Greece and Iran, Delmas
theorised a tactical distinction between civilian terrorism and rural terrorism and
formulated the metamorphosis of the 'citizen-soldier' into a 'militant-soldier'.

13 Although the bombing of Guernica was the first and most famous one,
Catalonia was subjected to more aerial bombardments than the rest of Spain.

anti-imperialist models (Conversi 1993). But this drift can hardly be explained without the intervention of the crucial variable, state repression.

State repression: the impact on the present

After the devastation of the war, the Basques were ready for a true 'ethnogenesis', for a re-definition of their identity in relation to the state.[14] Many authors agree that under Franco Basque nationalism was reborn in a thoroughly new shape (Gurrutxaga 1990). Going further, it is legitimate to claim that not only a new Basque nationalism but a new Basque identity was forged in the process. This identity was based on the self-perception of the Basques as a heroic people fighting bravely for their survival against a powerful tyranny supported by the West. In turn, ETA's violence has been identified by several scholars as an offspring of the Franco era (Jáuregui 1981: 208, 1986, Clark 1979, 1984, Douglass 1988, Douglass and Zulaika 1990, Gurrutxaga 1985, 1990, Silver 1988) – a description which we basically subscribe to. We shall also consider ETA as the tip of the iceberg of a much wider popular resentment against Francoism. This cause-effect interpretation is central to nearly all studies on political violence in Euskadi. Accordingly, 'terrorism' is a result of the ruthless use of the Guardia Civil, police and other repressive forces to deal with nationalist dissent.

ETA's spiral 'theory of action/repression/action' tallied with reality: 'In the measure in which the nationalist forces in general, and ETA in particular, advanced in their struggle, the para-military occupation of Euskadi returned with extraordinary intensity' (Jáuregui 1981: 205). Yet each dismantling of an ETA cell through the use of torture was a pyrrhic victory for the regime: it brought about a massive amount of confessions, but it inspired an indelible hatred for the 'occupation forces'. This condition was clear in ETA from the beginning: 'Repression and torture, when they uncover the horrors of individual sadism and collective cynicism, become the best recipe for the youth's rebellion. Then no reasons or arguments are left. If morality only condemns the violence exercised

[14] As the anthropologist Richard Wilson puts the case, 'ethnocidal state policies imply ethnogenesis, and the two must be studied together if we are to grasp the full meaning of war' (Wilson 1991: 57).

by one side and justifies the other side's actions on the basis of order and authority, it loses its character of moderating social value and shows the reality of its ideological content at the service of specific interests'.[15]

There was another proof of the conscious and direct bond existing between state repression and nationalist violence. ETA's maximalist programme aimed at the liberation of all seven Basque provinces, including the three on the French side. Nevertheless, 'in all ETA's writings there is not a single reference to the need to use violent methods against France' (Jáuregui 1981: 213). This is surprising, particularly since ETA's main model of urban guerrilla came from Algeria's relentless struggle against the French. The obvious reason for this omission is that France provided a shelter for Basque refugees and a base where they could reassemble in the hope of launching new attacks.[16] There was also an understanding and mutual respect between Basque leaders and many Left-wing French intellectuals (in particular, Jean-Paul Sartre and other existentialists). However, another reason was more important: France was not an authoritarian state like Spain, at least not in its 'metropolitan territory'. Hence it was an unsuitable target for ETA's theory of action/repression/action. Only the Spanish state could be the chosen enemy, because of its predictable response with mindless repression. As Jáuregui puts it, 'it was precisely Francoism, with its repressive violence, which provoked ETA into the choice of violent methods of struggle; the lack of freedom, the impossibility to put into practice a legal political activity, . . . [all this] prompted ETA to adopt, nearly instinctively, a method of action with no relationship with traditional Basque nationalism, and which, furthermore, did not find precursors in any other European patriotic movement in those years' (Jáuregui 1981: 213).

One of the characteristics of nationalism can be described as 'blame-shifting'. Each side of the conflict attributes to the other exclusive responsibility for all current and past misdeeds. Francoist propaganda consistently described Basque nationalism as an evil force. In all ETA publications the blame for violence was diametrically reversed: state violence was continually described as the 'original', 'real' violence, which justified all ETA's actions. The

---

15 Reprinted in *Documentos Y*: vol. 1: p. 371.

16 On Basque nationalism in France, see Jacob (1994).

Francoist regime was not just bad, but it was evil incarnate. In this context any accusation of violence against Basque patriots was self-defeating. This view is clearly formulated in the first issue of *Zutik*:

> Several young Basques just happen to be condemned to large periods of detention. They are accused of having used violence to express their opposition to the regime. The accusers are Francoists, i.e. the same people who 25 years ago rose in arms against a constitutionally legitimate Republic, . . . the ones who launched against Euskadi an army of *Requetés* [Carlist militia], Falangists, Moors, Italians and Germans . . ., the people who set Guernica and Durango ablaze with barbarous bombardments, who murdered thousands of Basques.[...] These friends of violence unleashed a war which caused more than a million dead and stay in power only through force.[...] The violent are condemning violence.[...] They destroyed, trampled on and burned the flags of Euskadi. They persecuted our language and culture.[...] But violence generates violence. The Basque youth refuse to live as slaves. They are the *gudaris* of the new resistance. They have the right of the oppressed on their side.[17]

By the late 1960s this vision had spread to all corners of Basque society. A local magazine in the town of Itziar, Gipuzkoa, claimed in 1968 that 'there is already an ever-present institutional violence; any response to it, even pacifism, is violence. Violence therefore is the basic agent of social change; and whoever refuses to participate in it lacks personal commitment' (cited in Zulaika 1988: 55). Endless examples like this can be found in the Basque underground literature and media. Hence, state violence worked directly to legitimise nationalist counter-violence.

A consequence of state repression was the clandestine character of political opposition. This can account for both the choice and persistence of violence. On the one hand, illegality was attractive and prohibition exciting, especially for the young: ETA's challenge to authority was an irresistible invitation for some individuals, whatever the consequences. On the other hand, the regime was itself a victim of the illusion that the use of force could restore order. Francoist prohibitions created a secretive climate conducive to

[17] *Zutik*, no. 0, 1961, reprinted in *Documentos Y*, vol. 1, p. 371.

violence, which became a way of expressing one identity and asserting the popular will to survive repression (Pérez-Agote, 1984, 1987, 1993). In the fullest sense, violence replaced language and became itself a language.

The popular resonance of violent actions was crucial during the stalemate of Francoism. Violence became a most powerful political statement and a metaphor of the state's illegitimacy. The regime claimed that Basque nationalism had ceased to exist, and that 'separatism' had been overcome for ever. For the radical opposition the only means of demonstrating to world opinion that Basque nationalism was still alive was through continuous armed attacks. ETA broke the 'curtain of silence' imposed by the regime's censorship. In turn, ETA's actions were translated into an immediate loss of legitimacy for the dictatorship, which had always justified its existence as the supreme guardian of Spanish unity. Hence, Basque violence must also be understood as a method of communicating a people's existence, where no other means were available. ETA's violence in the 1960s became a supreme means of self-expression.

The ideological consequences of fragmentation: ETA's internecine conflict

We have already seen that ETA has undergone intense internal debate and splintering throughout its history, especially in the mid-1960s. But every time an ideological impasse emerged, the most violent factions took the lead and showed the way with their actions. 'The victory of the partisans of armed struggle was a constant feature during each crisis of the movement' (Jáuregui 1981: 310). What are the roots of this fragmentation?

The confusion in the nationalist goals and formulations dates back to Arana. In turn, these were related to Euskadi's pre-existing cultural peculiarities analysed in earlier chapters. Cultural fragmentation and assimilation were exasperated by mass immigration. When ETA attempted to involve the immigrant labourers in the nationalist struggle, it had to acknowledge this fragmentation in order to overcome it. ETA started to expand through participation in working-class disputes. But this was no easy choice. The debate over immigration and hence the continuous tension between class struggle and nationalism were at the heart of ETA's evolution. The only way for this impasse not to degenerate into a virtual break-up of the organisation was to 'externalise' the tension by fighting back against the regime. Once started, violence assumed a ritualised pace, a self-fulfilling dynamic of its own. Violence becomes a form of action 'not governed entirely (or even predominantly) by instrumental means–ends considerations. ETA's *ekintzak* . . . are condensed events, as well as public performances, in which chance plays a key role. Action for action's sake becomes quintessential to small militant groups and acquires a momentous efficacy that far surpasses its own instrumentality. As if by magic, each action, in its renewed challenge to authority, signals a new beginning which promises to trigger a revolutionary process aimed at transforming everything' (Douglass and Zulaika 1990: 255). This interpretation could explain why violence becomes an end in itself.[18] In turn, many Basques deemed ETA necessary to protect them from state encroachment.

As we have seen, most of the relevant ideological production of ETA dates back to its earliest years. The reader will recall that at least since 1970 ETA has abandoned any intellectual pretensions, giving absolute priority to practical politics over theoretical debate.[19] So it not surprising that since then the ideological output has been virtually nil. 'To all intents and purposes since 1970 ETA has been ideologically dead.[...] All theoretical and doctrinal activity was paralysed. All discussions after 1970 have centred only around problems of strategy and political tactics; even so they have been of greater intensity than previous debates' (Jáuregui 1986: 398).[20]

Indeed, in the 1970s violence began to plague the organisation from within. State repression increased not only ETA's violence but also its fragmentation in a spiral process: as a consequence of police

---

[18] However, lacking a historical approach, this interpretation may not adequately explain the origin of ETA's violence, i.e. why its leaders chose at a certain stage to adopt armed struggle.

[19] 'ETA never paused to analyse its previous evolution. It always moved forward, even during the most tormented ideological crises', guided by a 'sufficiently blind confidence in the nationalist principles' (Jáuregui 1981: 310).

[20] As ETA was more interested in practical action than in abstract theories or doctrine, its 'ideologues' did not attempt to justify their project of achieving Basque independence. Despite some intermittent debate over what are the central values of the Basque nation, there have been few attempts to theorise its aspiration to statehood in more precise terms than Arana's already vague ones. ETA was 'not preoccupied with the legitimacy or illegitimacy of the right to self-determination but with the need to set in motion the appropriate machinery in order to give credibility to this demand at the earlier opportunity' (Jáuregui 1986: 399).

swoops and the arrest of leaders, ETA's leadership was continuously changing. However, it was precisely from 1970 onward that, in the wake of the Burgos trial, massive demonstrations started to erupt in the streets, breaking forever the dictatorship's curtain silence. In this process the national symbols came into the open: 'nationalism became public, together with the symbols of difference;[...] a consciousness previously confined to intimacy was more and more openly expressed' (Pérez-Agote 1984: 116). ETA was the leitmotif behind all these changes.

The initial anti-bourgeois character of Basque nationalism has already been commented upon, both in the previous section and in the historical chapter about the birth of Basque nationalism. This factor is of little value in explaining the choice of violence, although it is useful in explaining both the stress on separation (lack of interest in maintaining economic ties with the centre) and on left-wing politics. Payne (1973: 80-3) labels Basque nationalism as an 'anti-bourgeois' movement supported by pre-capitalist classes, including peasants and small town businessmen with their rural values (Payne, cited by Zirakzadeh 1985). Linz (1975, 1980) identifies its main trend as 'an opposition to cosmopolitan corrupting influences'. However, Zirakzadeh (1985, 1991) challenges this viewpoint by showing how, at least in some phases the business classes were also interested in the nationalist movement. In chapter 3 we saw how anti-bourgeois ideologies latent in Basque nationalism periodically emerged when the movement radicalised its separatist demands, as in the case of Gallastegi. Hence separatist overtones increased every time anti-oligarchic radicals and pro-bourgeoisie moderates were at loggerheads within the PNV.

Fear of cultural annihilation.

Fear of cultural annihilation represents a crucial link between our two main variables. It was brought about by the eclipse of the traditional symbols of ethnic distinctiveness and reinforced by the state's repression of these very symbols and elements. After a centuries-long decline Euskara seemed on the verge of receiving its final *coup de grâce* with industrialisation. The lack of alternative core values made this sentiment particularly acute among nationalist intellectuals, who perceived the whole nation as being on the brink of extinction. This predicament was felt at the end of the nineteenth century as much as in the 1950s, yet Arana's followers never turned to violence. In the 1960s the full impact of state repression politicised the pre-existing divisions.

The fear of assimilation was exacerbated by the snobbish attitude of Basque mainstream intellectuals. Ramiro de Maeztu (1875-1936), the right-wing Catholic antagonist of Arana, cynically derided the attempts by the 'regionalists' to revive Euskara: 'The intellectual efforts of the Basque race have been squandered in this enterprise for half a century. And what has been achieved? A handful of philologists have learned Euskara, while many thousands of Basques have forgotten it. Just ten years ago it was still spoken by the children of San Sebastián, Guernica, Deusto . . .'[21] Unamuno reinforced this with an inflammatory speech against the use of Euskara which provoked utter radicalisation in the debate. He urged the Basques to drop their language, defining it as a grave obstacle to the spread of European culture (Ugalde 1979: 11). Arana's cohort had to drain the cup of misery to the dregs.[22] Their language loyalties under attack, Basque nationalists emerged from Unamuno's harangue more determined than ever to pursue their separatist programmes. Since Unamuno was a respected intellectual in Spanish mainstream circles (and eventually abroad), his words had a particularly exacerbating effect on nationalist feelings (Urla 1993: 106)

However, such wounded sensitivities initially affected a mere minority. Only with the Francoist onslaught did this perception spread to the masses. As we said, Ekin's founders were six or seven student-intellectuals. Witnessing the alarming decline of Euskara, with an overwhelming sense of cultural loss and under the threat of police persecution, the young students of Deusto University instinctively opted for an intransigent form of nationalism. Every member and supporter of ETA, especially its founders, had the sensation of living under a vital threat. For those who doubted, the menace materialised in increasing acts of police repression, which went hand in hand with the decline of traditional elements of Basque distinctiveness. State repression only enhanced this all-pervasive apprehen-

[21] In *El Imparcial*, 14 Sept. 1901. Reprinted in Maeztu (1981).

[22] In his journal *Euzkadi*, Arana, who claimed to be well acquainted with Unamuno, assured that the latter did not feel the way he spoke: Unamuno's attempt to hurt the Basques over such a sensitive matter was a purely personal yearning for attention. Arana also suspected that Unamuno wanted to wheedle Madrid's politicians in order to prop up his own career (cited by Villasante 1979: 292).

sion of being a people on the brink of extinction, adding to it an immediate fear of physical annihilation. 'Guerrilla mysticism found its justification in the sense of desperation latent in ETA since its origins. On several occasions ETA alluded to the idea that Euskadi was on the verge of disappearing, of being erased from the map of peoples, because its language and culture were slowly dying out and its customs were being replaced by alien ones. Hence, the peremptory and urgent need to put an end to this progressive disappearance' (Jáuregui 1981: 233).

As for the life of individual *etarras*, it simply reflected the broader one of the nation. Thus *ekintza* actions were not politics but acts of survival: 'ETA guys are like . . . cornered animals holding to their instinct of survival.'[23] The driving force behind the disinterested risking of one's own life was something that transcended personal circumstances. It related to a deadly challenge to one own's kin, extended family or nation. The latter challenge manifested itself as a blow to one's very existence and sense of being.

Proof of the personal commitment required of any sympathisers wishing to join ETA was given by the severity of its rules. Glancing through the 'security norms' which made up the *Libro Blanco* and other official ETA publications, we can see that the organisation was extremely demanding. It required that each member 'radically alter his/her own habits, lifestyles, friends, environment' etc. up to the point that this new way of life 'became natural'.[24] The tragedy was that all the 'security norms' were made useless by the use of torture: ETA itself recognised that 'during the interrogations, torture destroys all the patterns of behaviour and self-defence which the security norms pretended to create in the activist'.[25] Yet the fight went on, and there were always plenty of enthusiastic young people ready to immolate themselves for the cause.

Needing to attract more members, Ekin's founders had to expand in areas which were partly alien to their enterprise: cultural fragmentation and the urban/rural divide impinged on their original eclecticism. They were soon presented with a dilemma and had only two possible alternatives: either minimise (even drop) the ethnic

23 A woman 'closely involved with ETA' and 'extremely knowledgeable about most of its leaders', quoted in Zulaika (1988: 313).

24 See *Libro Blanco*, p. 3, reprinted in *Documentos Y*, vol. 1, p. 151.

25 *Documentos Y*, vol. 2, p. 369.

content of their struggle, in order to recruit assimilated Basques and even non–Basques, or limit their recruitment strictly to those areas which maintained a strong Basque identity (and where Euskara was still spoken). The first option would have meant a betrayal of ETA's original principles; the second would have confined their action to a select few, with little chance of expansion. The stress on ethnicity would have hampered ETA in an increasingly urbanised society undergoing cultural assimilation at breakneck speed.

The conflict between these options stands at the core of most of ETA's internal diatribes and schisms, whatever ideological disguise they have assumed. However, the choice between these two strategies was rarely spelt out. It was rather silently subsumed under the priority of fighting back against the pervasive external threat. Hence political fragmentation was determined by culture fragmentation and the loss of Basque culture. The two concepts of national liberation were related to two concepts of Basque identity. Indeed, these identities changed whether the emphasis was put on language or on other elements, but within ETA many activists never abandoned the cultural definition of Basqueness. As demonstrated in the study of other nationalist movements, a cultural definition of the nation serves as a reservoir of political legitimacy (Hutchinson 1987).

That political fragmentation was determined by cultural fragmentation is not easy to demonstrate, since both the nationalist struggle and the ideology supporting it served the purpose of binding internal fissions and, hence, of hiding any potential internal cleavages and lack of cohesion. The very emphasis on names indicating unity, as with the coalition Herri Batasuna (Popular Unity), was meant to deny this creeping fragmentation. The unity of the Basques was stressed in all major street demonstrations and other political manifestations, yet it could only be brought about by popular indignation against the state.[26] By definition, nationalism purports to be the ideology of a compact, unitary and clearly defined body. The nation is conceived in quasi-organic terms and no major internal divisions are acknowledged. Hence the strictly cultural-linguistic definition of the nation may clash with other definitions: civic, based on territory; ethnic, based on putative origin; racial,

---

[26] Without ETA's actions and the state's predictable reactions, Herri Batasuna would probably cease to be, since what binds together this plethora of small Left-wing groups is the climate of radicalisation induced by ETA.

based on biological determinants, and so on. Since all these elements were eroded, confused or not fully representative, the nationalist community felt threatened whichever of them was chosen. Certainly the lack of a shared culture was constantly felt as a grave handicap by most nationalists leaders.

However, preoccupation over the Basques' survival overwhelmed preoccupation over details. 'What mattered to ETA was that the nation found itself in a lethal situation and that, in order to save her, it was urgent to adopt a series of drastic measures. As a consequence, . . . it considered the *will* of the Basque people to recover their national identity as the only valid element to save the nation' (Jáuregui 1981: 151). Hence the adoption after 1963 of Ernest Renan's concept of the *nation de volonté*. But in the Basque case, the idea of the nation as a 'daily plebiscite' was to be implemented through the call to arms.[27]

Nationalism: cultural, political and military

Our analysis has followed the distinction between cultural and political nationalism highlighted by some recent works (Hutchinson 1987, 1992), but there is a further form of nationalism, the military, which we consider should be kept distinct from the two previous ones. Military nationalism became crucial when the radicals' armed branch started to act independently from political nationalists and finally became a self-propelling force. At the same time, cultural nationalism loomed in the background, exerting a wider legitimising influence over the general process of mass mobilisation.

One of the reasons for the resignation of Txillardegi and others from ETA in 1967 was that the organisation was no longer interested in promoting Euskara, and that all the articles in *Zutik* were now in

27 This also disproves a common assumption in the literature of nationalism, namely that Herderian principles are more rigid and less adaptable than the Renanian vision of the nation as a social contract. Voluntarist and contractualist visions of the nation can easily be used by radical separatists stressing opposition, rather than compatibility. Catalan nationalism was at the same time organicist and integrationist, while Basque nationalism was voluntarist and separatist. The influence of Herder and other German philosophers mingled in Catalonia to produce a moderate and integrationist scenario. The influence of Renan and other French thinkers mingled in Euskadi to produce a much more radical separatism. Again, these two different patterns can be traced back to pre-existing cultural factors, especially the diffusion of regional languages.

Spanish. The split, which resulted in the foundation of the group
Branka, came at a time of intense internal crisis. In their communiqué
the culturalists declared: 'ETA is no longer the adequate means to
achieve certain aims and has been converted exclusively into a
Marxist-Leninist party'.[28] ETA's new attitude was in sharp contrast
with the principles adopted by its First Assembly in 1962, which
stated that the movement's first task was to strengthen Euskara. Little
now remained of that aim. 'The defence of Euskara became a matter
of fighting for equality of treatment with Spanish. . . . As ETA
seriously tried to recruit immigrants, it was faced with its own
[Aranist] heritage' (Sullivan 1988: 48).[29] The subordination of
cultural to political goals is reflected in an eschatological vision of
independence as a panacea for all problems of cultural identity, in
particular the recovery of the language: 'There is only one path to
save Euskara: political independence for Euzkadi.'

What united opposite trends within ETA were occasional alliances of one or more trends against the other(s). For instance, culturalists and Third Worldists were united not by a common
understanding on Basque identity, or on how to liberate Euskadi,
but by a joint effort to defeat the *obreristas*, ('workerists'), who were
perceived as traitors of the Basque cause (Jáuregui 1981: 307).
However, after the expulsion of the *obreristas* (see Chapter 4), the
Third Worldists dominated the organisation, pushing Txillardegi
and his followers to resign. In turn, the Third Worldists' emphasis
on either urban or rural guerrilla warfare is also related to ideological
and cultural fragmentation.[30] The Third Worldist field was itself
divided between the proposers of urban and rural guerrilla warfare.
Frantz Fanon (1925-61), possibly the most influential foreign
theorist among the radicals, theorised about urban guerrilla warfare
and the mobilisation of the *lumpenproletariat*. Fanon's Algerian model
was in contrast to the Maoist, Vietnamese and, to a certain extent,
Cuban models of peasant war led by (urban) intellectuals.[31] These

[28] J.L. Alvarez Emparanza (Txillardegi), J.M. Benito del Valle and Xabier Imaz,
Por que dejamos E.T.A., 1-page 'communique', 14 April 1967 (reprinted in Caracas:
E.G.).

[29] *Zutik*, 3rd series, 15: 3, cited by Gurruchaga 1985: 245.

[30] This was recognised by Txillardegi, who later declared 'We were in favour of
a much more political, and much less military, form of struggle. . . . Urban guerrilla,
and guerrilla in general, . . . is not apt to a heavily industrialised country. . . It is
feasible in Vietnam, not here' (Kaufmann, cited in Jáuregui 1981: 308).

two concepts reflected two opposite visions of nationalist mobilisation, which in turn were related to two opposite visions of Basque identity. The supporters of urban guerrilla warfare tended to focus on assimilated Basques and immigrant workers. The supporters of rural guerrilla warfare tended instead to focus on the *Euskaldun* heartland. Again the conflict was resolved through action or, better, competition to act in the most prompt and effective way.[32] The fracture between the two trends was never truly formalised within ETA, although it was at the root of several splits.[33] The two currents were later included in the vague definition of *pueblo trabajador vasco* ('Basque working people'). The division remained latent, but on several occasions the unity of the organisation was saved at the price of increasing its external aggression.[34] Cultural nationalists in Euskadi were constantly under pressure from more radical elements, impatient to act. They had to adopt radical attitudes to maintain their credibility. The radicals kept on pressing them with this basic question: 'Certainly Euskara is a valuable tool, it is the proof of our unique ancestry, but how can we build a cohesive Basque nation if the language is spoken only by a minority?'[35]

✳ Nationalists also felt that their identity was being splintered. Thus

31 My thanks to Sebastian Balfour for pointing out this contrast.

32 Obviously this did not result in anarchy and chaos, since authority and respect were earned by those who were prepared to risk their lives.

33 Indeed, a clue to ETA's internal fragmentation is given by the fact that 'each single ideological line . . . [within] ETA assumed those aspects of [*Vasconia*] which most suited its political and ideological positions' (Jáuregui 1981: 225). This explains why Krutwig's book scored such a success and, despite its ambiguities, worked as a unitary framework for the radical movement.

34 To establish their hegemony, the Third Worldists were required to appropriate some of the tenets of both political and cultural nationalists. This resulted in a 'superficial' adoption, respectively, of Marxism–Leninism and the cultural struggle. However, both programmes were *de facto* rendered void: Marxism was subordinated to anti-colonial and anti-imperialist struggle, while Euskara was no longer used in official publications.

35 Zulaika explores the unsuccessful attempts by a local leader near to ETA-VI and the *obreristas* to convince his younger disciples of the primacy of class struggle over national liberation. He could not convince them, as 'they were definitely not interested in political groupings and polemics . . . [which] seemed to them just boring rhetorical subtleties' (1988: 61). Local groups still led by Marxist ex-seminarians 'offered a platform to raise political consciousness. The beneficiary was ETA', which overflowed with new members (Zulaika 1988: 61).

whether language, race or religion were taken as central elements of Basqueness, their upholders always felt that the Basque nation with which they identified was under threat. At the same time, these opposing trends created confusion over the core values to be adopted, and engendered the conditions for ideological fragmentation. In the Basque case the failure to define one core value steadily and consistently resulted in the impossibility of developing a popular form of cultural nationalism. The weakness of cultural nationalism led to the prevalence of other kinds of political activism in which an ambivalent attitude over the definition of cultural values concealed a deep conflict over forms of political mobilisation. We will now explore three other reinforcing factors: 'betrayal' by the West, religion and the economy.

Other reinforcing factors

Another situational factor influenced the radical choice of both violence and Marxism. This was the American about-face (see Chapter 5), which had long-lasting consequences for the Basques' morale. Hopes for Allied (especially American) military intervention to topple Franco were dashed in 1945. Since the PNV's reliance on an American 'salvation' plan justified much of the party's passive stalemate, the new generation was particularly anxious to get rid of the American model.[36] They were politically awakened during the period of decolonisation and thus unavoidably inspired by the newly-independent Third World 'nations'. It is possible to trace ETA's principal ideological influences from the short bibliography supplied in its *Libro Blanco* (White Book): only one Basque source is mentioned,[37] the other references being works from the protagonists of successful liberation movements or analysis of their struggle, normally in their Spanish or French editions.[38]

---

[36] The rejection of the American model and the subsequent drift towards Marxism did not imply an immediate renunciation of the principle of democracy. ETA's leaders vowed to fight all forms of dictatorship and never formally rejected democracy. Yet they believed its achievement impossible without the use of violence.

[37] It is *Ereintza: Siembra de Nacionalismo Vasco. 1894-1912*, an essentialist manual of separatism by Engracio de Arranzadi (San Sebastián: Editorial Auñamendi, 1980, 1st edn 1935).

[38] French was the foreign language most currently spoken by the Basques in Spain,

The most celebrated external inspiration came from the Algerian revolution (Conversi 1993). The main theorist of the Algerian model of decolonisation – also an advocate of revolutionary violence – was Frantz Fanon. The experience of Algeria seemed to hold out the promise that violence would pay off and lead the insurgents to victory. This theory of violence as the only solution was obviously also determined by the prevailing internal condition of ruthless dictatorship in Spain. As predicated by Fanon, state violence was an indispensable ingredient in spreading a general 'national awareness' among the wider population, instigating them to fight back. In synthesis, the adoption of Third Worldist models could not be realised without state repression. State repression was the central part of the 'theory of action/repression/action' as 'imported' by ETA.

The underlying religious character of Basque nationalism has been indicated as a possible inspiration for Basque violence, as manifested through abnegation and self-sacrifice. The media coverage of ethnic conflicts leads us to think that religious animosities are often exacerbated when they go hand in hand with nationalist claims.[39] However, four observations need to be made in order to place the link between nationalism and religion in the right perspective. First, although till recently the Basques considered themselves more religious than other Spaniards, they nevertheless share the same religion. Secondly, the strong Catholic attachment of the Basques long antedated the rise of nationalism. Thirdly, violence began to spread at the same time as religion was becoming irrelevant, as part and parcel of a process of secularisation common throughout the West: many recent surveys indicate that the process of secularisation in Euskadi is comparable to that of most Western industrialised societies.[40] Fourthly and finally, the religious emphasis of early Basque national ideology and the link between religion and nationalism were a consequence of the previous point, namely the lack of alternative cultural elements shared by the majority of the

---

for obvious reasons, given the continuous cross-borders contacts with their northern brethren and the presence in France of a large part of the Basque diaspora.

[39] The description of political violence as emanating from the religious background of their protagonists has been applied to other terrorist groups, such as the Italian Red Brigades (Acquaviva 1979).

[40] See for instance, FOESSA (1975) and Pérez-Agote (1990).

population. The dismissal of religion was also a tool for ETA to be further distanced from the PNV and its Christian-Democrat ideology. In May 1962 the participants to the First Assembly published the organisation's first formal statements of principles which called for the creation of a federated Europe based on ethnonationalities *not* guided by religion. They also rejected the idea of racial superiority and opposed all forms of dictatorships.

Is there a continuity between the original religious foundations of Basque nationalism and the new Basque political culture? We have noted the initial religious emphasis prompted by Arana, but Basque nationalism did not assume a violent face till the 1960s. Some authors have indeed demonstrated the deep religious vocation which animated many activists in the 1960s. In his study on the 'sacramental character' of Basque political violence, Zulaika (1988) observes the important influence exerted on ETA's militants by Catholic social doctrines, especially the ones emanating in those years from Acción Católica. Many *etarras* have lived through a phase of religious vocation followed by disillusionment with religion and the idea that their vocation cannot be carried out within the tracks of traditional Christianity. Basque nationalism has also been defined as a millennialist movement (Aranzadi 1981). Many nationalists passed from religion to secularism, this passage being rather a leap forward when they tried to adapt Marxism to such a purpose. Most of them came from Acción Catolica and its working-class branches, JOC (*Juventudes Obreras Católicas*) and HOAC (*Hermandad Obrera de Acción Católica*), and their 'apostolic' origin remained 'passionately [entrenched] with their personal frustrations'.[41] Students from different seminaries and novitiates (Franciscans, Benedectines, Jesuits, Carmelites etc.) participated jointly in the framework of local publishing in Euskara (Pérez-Agote 1986: 431). In most cases, protection by the Church was what made such enterprises viable. In the crucial phase of the early 1970s, when Marxist ideology permeated most nationalist discourse, the Church eventually withdrew its support, causing many local groups to collapse. Their disaffected members were faced with two options: either join one of a host of nationalist left-wing organisations or join ETA.[42] How

---

[41] *Documentos Y:* vol. 1: 371. See also Ortzi (1975: 276-7).

[42] See Zulaika (1988) for the example of the main radical group in the village of Itziar.

could this Catholic heritage have influenced the new generation of activist? Was there a link between their self-abnegation and the principles of Christianity? We have already analysed the importance of religion in both early and late Basque nationalism. However, it is difficult to infer a direct causal link. Zulaika (1988: 55) contends that radical nationalism was linked to Christian models of sacrifice and martyrdom. We have discussed above how violence itself can be seen as a ritual act, albeit a secular one, the finality of which goes beyond the mere physical damage caused (Douglass and Zulaika 1990).

A third factor which should be considered is the impact of economic transformation, notably the post-1973 recession. In popular wisdom, economic factors are often indicated as causes of nationalist mobilisation and even of nationalist violence. From the mid-1970s, the Basque country underwent a process of major recession and rises in the level of unemployment. This factor can be considered as collateral explanation and precipitant of nationalist violence rather than its cause. But the economic crisis was a general world trend commonly experienced in most of the industrialised capitalist world. Yet only in some areas was it accompanied by nationalist mobilisations, and even in fewer by nationalist violence. However, in some sectors this crisis differed from that experienced in other countries, and its effect in Euskadi took a particularly heavy toll: large industries were the main pillar of the Basque economy. As branches of multinational corporations dominated, Euskadi was severely hit by the international crisis and many factories had to close down (Zirakzadeh 1989: 321). When the international economy slumped in the 1970s, Euskadi suffered further because' of the relevance of its export sector and the specialisation in metallurgy and capital goods. Small and big industries alike found themselves without customers. Hence 'oscillation with international demand . . . led to a wave of popular support for nationalist parties aiming to protect the semi-peripheral areas from external economic pressures' (Zirakzadeh 1989: 323).

Yet wide-ranging economic change had already come about in the 1880s, but it did not prompt a violent reaction. In 1877 Vizcaya and Gipuzkoa were the poorest Spanish provinces, but within a few years they had become the richest, creating both social discontent and demographic displacement. The virulent anti-Spanish tones of Arana concealed the rage of many Basques, yet such rage was for the moment simply channelled through a non-violent nationalist movement. Still in 1973, Vizcaya and Gipuzkoa held the first and third place respectively among all Spanish provinces in terms of *per capita* income.[43] Moreover, the economic crisis came approximately ten years after ETA had adopted armed struggle. Undoubtedly, violence rose to a new peak because of the economic doldrums, when unemployment, recession and all their results reinforced social tensions. For instance, between 1975 and 1981 the adult labour force shrank by 11% and Euskadi's gross product had a negative growth-rate for three successive years (Zirakzadeh 1989: 327). ETA took advantage of these circumstances, but it would hardly be convincing to attribute the increase of violence to the economic situation alone. The electoral programme of Herri Batasuna (the political wing of ETA) included powerful appeals to the economically dispossessed 'through the use of pictorial representations of shovels, anvils and pitchforks', constantly alluding 'to its candidates' firsthand experiences of layoffs and job insecurity' (Zirakzadeh 1989: 328). Theories of 'relative deprivation' partly explain this outcome. But, again, it seems better to consider the economic situation as a powerful reinforcing factor rather than as a determinant of the choice of violence.

Declining legitimacy of the state and the persisting legitimacy of ETA during the Transition

State measures to defeat 'terrorism' have often prompted the fear of a much more indiscriminate kind of violence falling upon the Basques.[44] This perception of the state as a terrorist machine persisted after the demise of the dictatorship, defying the dialogue with the nationalists initiated by the King, the UCD, and other reformers. *Abertzale* parties alleged that repression continued unabated after Franco's death. For instance, several 'anti-terrorist laws', some of which were later condemned as unconstitutional, resulted in arbitrary arrests and detentions (Clark 1991).[45] Widespread opposition

[43] See García Crespo *et al.* (1981) and Payne (1975: 229-33).

[44] If one were to apply Weber's definition of the state as that agency within society which possesses the monopoly of legitimate violence, we would be inclined to conclude not only that Spain is not a nation, but that to many Basques it has not been even a state – at least in the 1970s.

[45] 'Part de la llei antiterrorista, considerada inconstitucional', *Avui*, 18 December 1987.

to the law has been expressed by popular demonstrations in several Spanish regions.[46] Furthermore, the murder of Basque political exiles in France by the GAL (*Grupos Antiterrroristas de Liberación*), a self-styled 'anti-terrorist' commando,[47] provoked angry popular demonstrations,[48] revealed a political scandal,[49] and prompted accusations of central government complicity.[50]

How was this situation of violent conflict reflected in the social texture? Since the 1970s, political violence seems to have become an intrinsic feature of Basque society,[51] and this has divided society into at least two opposite fields. With some exaggeration, Heiberg highlights the polarised atmosphere which pervaded most areas of public life: 'Political parties, artistic production, amnesty organizations, historical research, economic enterprises, schools, newspapers, public projects, popular festivals, publishing houses, etc. were forced into the mutually exclusive categories of *abertzale/españolista*, nationalist/non-nationalist, Basque/anti-Basque' (1989: 110). However, Heiberg's dichotomy cannot be extended to more recent developments: following the approval of the autonomy statute, internal tensions started to plague the nationalist camp along the radical–moderate line.[52] Non-political gatherings too have often degenerated into collective eruptions of youth violence.[53] The climate of antagonism has caused a lack of communication between

[46] 'Cinco mil personas pidieron en Barcelona la dimisión del ministro del Interior', *Egin*, 16 July 1983.

[47] This paramilitary organisation murdered several ETA militants living in exile in France, and was said to consist of security personnel (Korn 1989, Miralles and Arques 1990).

[48] 'Violentas manifestaciones en el país Vasco tras el doble asesinato de militantes de ETA por los GAL', *La Vanguardia*, 10 February 1984.

[49] 'On the bloody trail of ETA Agate', *Guardian*, 27 November 1989. A particularly detailed investigation is Miralles and Arques (1991).

[50] Chaffee (1988: 565) mentions graffiti which appeared in Basque cities and read 'GAL=PSOE', accusing the government that without the PSOE's approval the GAL commando could not operate.

[51] 'Erradicar la violencia en Euskadi', *El País*, 15 November 1987.

[52] 'Violents incidents entre des séparatistes et le président du gouvernement basque', *Le Monde*, 16 August 1983; Jesús Ceberio, 'Cisma en la tribu de Aitor', *El País-Domingo*, 23 November 1986, pp. 1-3.

[53] '45 heridos en choques entre jóvenes violentos y policías en Vitoria', *El País*, 9 August 1987, pp. 1 and 11.

different segments of society.[54] Although the Autonomy Statute helped to restrain support for ETA, its provisions fell short of the requirements of most Basque nationalists. In particular, the statute could hardly remedy the political hiatus which, at that time, separated the Basques from Madrid.

The environment was so polarised that Civil Guards and policemen lived isolated from the rest of society.[55] Nobody dared to speak to them, and anybody seen doing so was immediately suspected of being a police informer. One of the first duties for all committed *abertzale* was to shun any *chivatos* (suspected police informers, or at times people who had any sort of contact with the 'occupation forces'). The *chivatos* were rejected and ostracised by the community as moral outcasts. After decades of behaving as ruthless bosses of the region, the'occupation forces' experienced a dramatic anti-climax from the 1970s onwards: the Civil Guards' and policemen's extremely hard situation was reflected in a sharp rise in suicides among them.[56] This backlash was an unavoidable side-effect of the Spanish state's profound transformation.

Such boundless resentment against the forces of 'public order' testifies to the direct link between state repression and counter-repression. The security apparatus was considered a legitimate target for political violence because its members were popularly seen as the origin and prime actors of political violence. Hence policemen became symbolic targets. ETA's activists could hardly increase their campaign of terror against more important targets, such as industrialists and MPs, because this would have risked their actions becoming less popular. There were no other social figures in Euskadi who could command similar negative feelings.

The dynamics of political violence

In order to explore the double causes of the choice of violence and of its permanence, we need different interpretations. As has been pointed out, 'various theories may have differential utility

---

54 Patxo Unzueta, 'Euskadi invertebrada' *El País*, 25 November 1986, p. 16.

55 On the Guardia Civil as a powerful instrument of centralisation, see López Garrido (1982).

56 'El SUP previene sobre nuevos suicidios de policías en el País Vasco', *El País*, 19 July 1987.

at different phases of terrorist movement. In the early stages, theories that explore the political roots of collective violence may have relatively greater utility. Later, theories that emphasize the tendency for violence to become an end in itself may be more useful' (Thompson 1989: 694-5). In the 1970s a familiar pattern in ETA's evolution began to acquire a quicker tempo: as the more experienced and mature leaders of ETA were killed or forced into exile, younger and more radical ones quickly replaced them in a process that continues up to the time of going to press (1996). The Military Front, composed predominantly of very young people, became more and more uncontrollable, while its autonomous initiatives provoked further conflict. It clearly appears, especially during the 'Transition' phase, that violence has became a self-generating mechanism, a vicious circle very difficult to stop.[57]

Every exile, imprisonment or killing of ETA leaders created a vacuum which was soon filled by younger and more radical elements. For instance, in 1986, 'Txomin', at the time ETA's number one, was forced into exile. This action reached a new climax in the process of distancing the older leadership (the so-called *históricos*) from the emerging militant base.[58] New radical elements were swiftly incorporated into ETA's Executive Committee to replace the *históricos*. The new, more ruthless and determined guerrilla could move much more freely and safely across the border to France, while the known *históricos* could hardly deceive the French information services. In this way, the latter become increasingly displaced by the former inside ETA. In ETA 'it was not possible to be a militant while abroad'.[59] By being abroad, the older leaders lost many of their contacts with the closely- knit social networks of Basque resistance and the information and protection they provided. New ambitious young militants were eager to replace them in a process regulated by unrelenting internal competition.

Paradoxically, while the police exulted over the elimination of ETA's leaders, moderate nationalists expressed serious concern at

---

[57] Parallels with other guerrilla movements easily spring to mind: the IRA in Northern Ireland and the Khalistan movement in India's Punjab were – and are – plagued by a similar internal logic. In both, violence served to complement internal fragmentation.

[58] 'Los "históricos" de ETA dan paso a los jóvenes', *El País-Domingo*, 13 July 1986.

[59] Txillardegi, in *Garaia*, op. cit.

further uncontrollable violence.[60] Indeed, ETA's history has shown that the young entrants are unmistakably more radical, more un-compromising and less interested in negotiating. Thus Txomin's expulsion hampered the progress of peace talks, since he was one of the leaders most favourable to negotiation.[61] The elimination of the old guard in 1986 and 1987 can also explain why some of the most bloody terrorist acts occurred in the latter year.[62]

In the last phase of the Francoist dictatorship, popular mobilisa-tion was dependent on ETA's actions. As we have seen, each *ekintza* (ETA action) had a deep impact among the youth, especially in the slumbering villages of the countryside. ETA has also been a means through which the Basque-Madrid conflict, and the oppositional identity related to it, have been kept alive. And as the new Basque identity was (since the 1960s) founded on conflict and opposition, the prospects of any peaceful de-assimilation from Spain was closely linked to the possibility of creating a positive self-identity no longer based on negation of the enemy.

The trend towards 'de-ethnicisation' prevailed at the time of the Marxist 'conversion' in the early 1960s with its class politics and its lack of interest in Basque culture. Although the Military Front operated within the superficial legitimacy of Basque culture, it also used violence as an avenue for mobilisation by continuously redefin-ing the Basque-Spanish conflict in irreconcilable terms. Thus these military activists have tacitly pursued the option of reinforcing *ethnic borders* without reinforcing *ethnic content* (Barth 1969). The task of reinforcing ethnic content was left to the cultural nationalist who, though eclipsed by the military branch in the media, grew along with them. With its Maoist-derived emphasis on the countryside as the spearhead of revolutionary change, Krutwig's Third Worldist option was an attempt to reconcile cultural, political and military nationalism, to merge ethnic borders and ethnic contents. Yet although this direction apparently gave place of pride to culture, in ETA's practice culture was unavoidably subordinated to armed action, so that military nationalism became a separate force. In the

---

[60] 'Medios nacionalistas consideran "un serio error" el alejamiento de "Txomin"', *El País*, 12 July 1986.

[61] 'Los "históricos"...', *El País-Domingo*, 13 July 1986.

[62] 'ETA cometió en 1987, en Barcelona y Zaragoza, los atentados más sangrientos', *El País*, 29 January 1988, p.15. 'Algo cambiará tras Hipercor', *El País*, 28 June 1987.

aims of the nationalists, violence proved an effective substitute for culture insofar as it contributed to delineate the 'boundaries' of the Basque community by sharply demarcating outsiders from insiders.

We are now left to ponder whether this is the most useful way to understand what happened. Couldn't violence be an outcome of uncertainty over cultural values, rather than lack of cultural content? The answer is that the two are deeply interrelated, as we have repeatedly seen: first, Arana the philologist gave way to Arana the racialist; secondly, the urban/rural and Castilian/Euskaldun divide was at the core of ETA's lacerating dilemmas. These dilemmas were normally resolved by privileging action over introspection. Since at least the Fifth Assembly, 'action' became the core value promoted by ETA. The concept of *ekintza*, generally used to indicate an armed ETA attack, also conveyed a whole model of participating in the national struggle. Likewise the concept of *abertzale* became an inclusive one by virtue of ETA's expanding struggle: 'Abertzale is a status not defined by birth but by performance: an abertzale is one who participates in the political struggle.[...]You are not born abertzale. You make yourself one' (MacClancy 1988). Modern *batua* condenses these trends in the verb *abertzaletu* (to become a patriot) and the substantive *aberriordeko* (adopted homeland). Basques, in ETA's eyes, were distinguished from non-Basques mainly on the basis of their involvement in the struggle for Basque liberation. Lacking a discrete and visible element such as language, the requirements of Basque identity have shifted to a simpler voluntarist dimension. The more a person is involved in the struggle the greater that person's acceptance as a member of the national community. Hence the most radical option was likely to be considered also the most 'Basque' and thus the most morally acceptable. As a consequence, the social environment was far more polarised in Euskadi than in Catalonia, with each nationalist stressing his/her nationalist credentials in order to be accepted by the 'moral community'.[63] But does this mean that activists will not accept a Basque who is passive as a member of the Basque nation? No, the one does not imply the other; there is always a hope that those who are passive whether Basque or non-Basque will awaken from their lethargy and rejoin the nation by means of struggle. Hence, such a Renanian idea of

---

[63] The concept of the nation as a 'moral community' is due to Symmons-Symonolewicz (1970: 50 ff.).

the 'nation of will' is an open concept, which stands at the opposite extreme from Arana's closed vision. In Chapter 8, we saw that the crucible for second-generation immigrants' integration was their political involvement, which they can prove by participating in more and more demanding tasks, in a concentric circle of loyalties and identities, layer upon layer into the heart of the 'moral' community. Only then might they feel the urge to learn Euskara.

The border-making functions of violence have not always been self-conscious among activists. Obviously militants could see that violence exerted a powerful emotional impact and attracted more people into political action. But they seldom, if ever, conceived violence as a mere replacement for something else which was missing. Hence no ETA political writing theorises about violence as a substitute for culture. Because of the nationalist tendency to see the nation as an organic whole and to deny all internal cleavages, we have to infer these internal gaps.[64]

In this chapter, we have postulated several points. The first is that Basque violence is the product of the interaction between state repression and the nationalists' own internal tensions. These internal tensions were reflected in opposite ideologies and political trends co-existing inside ETA. Secondly, we have observed that such ideological and political fragmentation was related to cultural fragmentation. The different factions pursued different visions of Basque identity, aimed at different strata of the population (immigrant/native, rural/urban etc.), stressed different aspects of Basqueness, and adopted different strategies and tactics to achieve their goals. Thirdly, we have seen that cultural fragmentation was in part the result of cultural assimilation. The latter originated from several factors which have been discussed throughout the book: urbanisation, élites' Castilianisation, centralisation and, finally, mass immigration. At this point we must reiterate our picture of Euskadi's cultural space as plural and fragmented. In contrast with

---

[64] In a rare display of the border-making mechanisms of violence, the playwright Alfonso Sastre, a former Communist and sympathiser of radical nationalism, declared: 'Violence is one way of building a nation'. He meant that oppositional violence is a mobilising force which can create a sense of solidarity and a boundary where previously few or none were evident. This does not mean that the 'nation' is defined by violence; the latter is solely a means to its creation.'La violència és una forma de construir una nació', *El Món*, 204, 21 March 1986, pp. 20-1.

Catalonia, there is a lack of clear-cut and undisputed shared values. In Chapter 7 we related the latter particularly to the degree of language maintenance, the centrality of language in most European nationalist movements being an established fact. At no time have we argued that fragmentation has made Basque identity weaker. Quite the contrary, its strongly oppositional and antagonistic character guarantees a continuous rehearsal of the nation as a 'daily plebiscite'.

Finally, this chapter has emphasised how central was the role of state repression in cementing a common identity out of previous anthropological chaos. If we are to apply a purely functionalist approach, political violence responded both to an internal logic (the need to foster unity in the organisation) and an external logic (the need to respond to the challenge of the state). At any moment of stormy ideological debate within ETA, the initiative was seized by some violent factions. In this way, direct action, rather than ideology and culture, showed the way to be followed in order to achieve mass mobilisation with its concomitant effect of galvanising public support. While the theorists debated over the importance of this or that element of Basque culture, or about this or that ideological line or strategy to be adopted, the hard-liners overcame all of them. With their attacks, they demonstrated the simple reality that only direct action could achieve popular support and even extend mobilisation to non-ethnic Basques. The 'ideologues' thus had to face the music and bow to the argument that only a violent uprising could revitalise Basque nationhood, while disquisitions about the details of Basque identity retained a divisive effect. At least from 1973 (the year when Carrero Blanco was killed), ETA operated under the slogan 'Actions Unite, Words Divide'. ETA's activity has thus taken an anti-intellectual turn, the antithesis of Ekin's original philosophy.

A common feature of insurgent nationalist guerrillas in many countries is their relation with, and even dependence on, state repression.[65] All over the world, a plethora of nationalities and former tribes are drawn into violent confrontation with the state as

---

65 Wilson's study of the impact of state repression on Guatemala's Indian communities is illuminating: 'Acting on Mao Tse-tung's famous dictum that guerrillas depended on the population like fish on the sea, the army set about draining the sea. In the end, Q'eqchi villagers suffered far higher loss of life than the armed combatants. Repression itself was the most significant factor of all that led to Q'eqchi's joining the guerrilla' (1991: 40).

a result of decades of coercion by central authorities which are felt to be largely illegitimate.[66] The more recent the memories of suffering and horrors, the more acute the conflict seems to be. Of all Krutwig's ideas, his principle of 'retaliation', as expressed in the theory of action/repression/action, was the only one which in practice remained constant in ETA throughout its long history of mutations and splits (Jáuregui 1981: 220). Lacking the cultural link or other clearly defined rallying points, the guerrilla could only rely on action. We have also indicated who were the foreign ideologues exerting the most profound influence on both ETA's strategies and new ways of conceiving the nation: Renan and Fanon. The fact that both were French-speaking and French-educated was no coincidence.[67] As many Basque nationalists were well versed in French, most foreign ideologies were imported into Euskadi via France. French intellectuals, especially in the 1960s, exerted an unparalleled impact on the Basque radical intelligentsia.[68]

Recent studies have stressed the cultural components and ethnic origins of ethnonationalist movements (Hroch 1985, Smith 1986, 1991). However, movements which were initially forms of cultural activism altered their strategies and objectives in the course of their struggle. Thus at different stages ETA relegated the cultural struggle to second rank, in order to deploy its full resources for a frontal clash with the state. How was this possible? This chapter has postulated two modes (normally opposed) of political mobilisation: culture or violence. Where differential cultural elements were available as *ethnic boundaries*, the ethnonationalist movement tended naturally to use them. In this way the movement could also present itself as their saviour, while promoting a new militant vision of national culture. Operating through semi-legal institutions, Catalan leaders could more easily advance their claims under a unified platform and find internal cohesion around the centrality of one (or more) values. In contrast, nationalist leaders are compelled to choose other types of mobilisation when they cannot take advantage of pre-existing ethnic

---

[66] In many Third World countries this had been one of the legacies of decolonisation, whereas local élites have proved unable to impose their rule and values except by force.

[67] We cannot define Fanon as a Frenchman at heart, but his French education had a great influence.

[68] We mentioned the impact of the existentialists, especially Sartre.

borders. Cultural assimilation also highlights and uncovers a vital threat against a group's basic identity. Through the conceptualisation of this existential crisis, nationalist leaders can formulate a strategy of direct defence against central power. In one breath the state is blamed for military repression and for destroying the national culture. Hence, in conditions of cultural assimilation, cultural, political and military nationalists all have a grudge and a reason to welcome violence.

The transition to democracy reinforced the pre-existing trend at a time when the old order was collapsing and the new one was still undefined. However, as both radical and moderate nationalists attempted to build up consensus on the idea of the nation, a cultural revival became possible. Autonomy concessions seriously under-mined ETA, offering a chance to try out the new constitutional arrangements. Through the reinstatement of fundamental freedoms (and that does not necessarily mean independence), the Basque community had its first chance to experience a positive sense of self-realisation. But the process was continuously hampered by persisting state repression and indecision over Basque identity. Since Basque identity was not so strongly defined by discrete cultural elements (such as language), the nationalists needed a constant process of mobilisation in order to raise collective awareness.

10

CONCLUSION

This book has continually stressed the importance of culture, particularly language, in the project of identity construction of ethnonationalist élites, and sought to show that, to a different degree, modernity has eroded the traditional markers of ethnicity through the subsequent processes of state centralisation, assimilation of local élites and finally mass immigration. All these processes have deeply altered the anthropological structure of Catalonia and the Basque country, but have not impaired their basic identity and sense of separateness. On the contrary, they have reinforced the determination of the local leaders and their followers to pursue an autonomous status for their nation and even political independence. This epilogue formulates some conclusions on the oppositional character of nationalism through a comparison of the two movements.

Let us first recapitulate the main similarities between the two movements. They both (1) operated within the same *state* structure, Spain; (2) arose broadly at the same *time*, the end of the nineteenth century; (3) are among the most *popular* nationalist movements in Western Europe; (4) belong to regions that have been at the vanguard of the Spanish *economy*; and (5) have received a vast number of *immigrants* and thus had to face the challenge of integrating them.

However, the dissimilarities – economic and historical – were greater:

(1) The Basque bourgeoisie was pro-centralist. The Catalan bourgeoisie wanted to control the central state but, failing in this, turned to regionalism.[1]

---

[1] Economic élites diverged in their attitude towards the state: the Basque semi-oligarchy was staunchly liberal, free-marketeer and centralist, while Catalan industrialists were protectionists and lobbied for increasing tariffs to shelter their production.

257

(2) The Basque bourgeoisie was small in numbers (the six to ten families who controlled the local economy can be defined as a *semi-oligarchy*), but big in capital concentration. The Catalan bourgeoisie was more diversified, with several family-run enterprises scattered across a wider area, but none so rich and financially powerful as the big Basque firms.

(3) The timing of industrialisation was also different, or at least its impact radically differed: After the abolition of the *fueros* in 1876, Basque industrialisation was massive and abrupt.[2] Catalan industrialisation took longer.[3] Hence, Basque society had less time to cope with such radical changes.

(4) Some of the economic factors are obviously related to cultural ones. Basque industries were concentrated in a particular area of Bilbao, the left bank of the river Nervion. But Bilbao was never the 'moral' capital of Euskadi, a place for which it had to compete at least with San Sebastián and Pamplona. Indeed, the choice of Vitoria/Gasteiz as the capital of today's Autonomous Community responds to the need to choose a neutral centre, alien to the traditional cultural, geographic and economic divergence. In contrast, Barcelona was the centre for both the regional culture and the industrial revolution – which, however, was not really concentrated in a single area, several towns in Barcelona's province being seats of the most important textile factories.[4]

(5) Politically Catalan autonomies were crushed in 1716, whereas centralism reached Euskadi more than a century and a half later, in 1876.

(6) According to local historians, the Basques had an 'egalitarian ethos', whereas the Catalans had a 'bourgeois ethos' tied to small family enterprises.

(7) Religiously, we have seen that Basque society was more

---

[2] The only exceptions were the coastal areas of Guipúzcoa and Vizcaya, which became 'centers of commerce, trade and manufacturing as early as the sixteenth century' (Huxley, cited by Clark 1979: 8). The shipbuilding industry also developed on a quasi-industrial basis, but no large-scale industrialisation began before 1876. Economic fragmentation was also typical of the Basque provinces. See González Portilla (1989).

[3] Catalan industrialisation was also more autochthonous, i.e. less influenced by foreign capital.

[4] In particular, Mataró, Sabadell and Terrassa.

traditional, Catholic and conservative than its Catalan counter-part. It was also less modernised when nationalism emerged, and more alienated from the central government.

The dissimilarities in national identity patterns, illustrated par-ticularly in Chapters 6-8, have several *explanations*:

(1) A 'popular' explanation focuses on their different *'national characters'*. Obviously, such a concept is more apt to reinforce stereotypes than to analyse.

(2) The economic explanation privileges *uneven development* be-tween core and periphery as a catch-all factor. This is difficult to relate to the two regions, since they were both advanced sectors of the Spanish economy.[5] Furthermore, their economies were not, and still are not, internally homogeneous.

(3) The class explanation focuses on the different role assumed by the *local hegemonic classes*.

(4) The historical explanation considers that the Basques never achieved *statehood*, if we except the *fueros* granted by the monar-chy until 1876.[6]

(5) The political explanation focuses on the role of *state repression*. It is useful in accounting for the intensity of Basque radicalism, but only after the emergence of ETA.

(6) The anthropological/cultural explanation focuses on the role of the *local culture*. The latter supplied the raw material to the first nationalist formulations.

Our account has tended to privilege the last two factors. Let us now reiterate the main contrast between the two movements, taking into consideration the different kinds of relationship with the Spanish state that they championed. First, Basque nationalism was intransigent and *separatist* from its very inception. In contrast, the initial Catalan appeal was mildly *regionalist* and pro-Spanish, rather than fully nationalist. Secondly Basque separatism has developed from the 1960s a notoriously *violent* component. Catalan nationalism is more accommodative and broadly *non-violent*. For many onlookers

[5] However, the impressive decline of mining, siderurgy and other big industries in the 1970s affected the Basque economy to a much greater extent then Catalonia (Zirakzadeh 1989, 1991).

[6] This point is disputed by Agirreazkuenaga (1987) who describes Vizcaya before 1876 as a quasi-independent state.

the former personifies blind irrationality, as the latter exemplifies bourgeois rationalist calculations. However, Catalan nationalism was a form of Spanish regenerationism which aimed at regenerating the entire Spanish state. By contrast, Arana's drive to independence implied a break of major proportions with the Spanish state, aimed at withdrawing from the state and drastically re-drawing its borders. This emphasis was rarely found in Catalonia, a country which could always boast obvious linguistic markers in order to advance its national 'credentials', both *inwardly* (dissemination among the people of the idea of belonging to the same Catalan nation) and *outwardly* (cultural legitimation of Catalan ethnic claims *vis-à-vis* Castile).

Intransigence and maximalism remained a central tenet of Basque nationalism throughout the years, but the Basque separatist option did not translate itself into an immediate recourse to violence. In fact, Arana and his followers were convinced apostles of *non-violence*. Until the Civil War no violent form of nationalism had gained any popularity. Other crucial conditions had to intervene in order to foster violence.

Fragmented constituencies and authoritarian leadership

We have seen that the Basque Nationalist Party remained the sole representative of Basque nationalism, dominating nationalist politics for most of this century up till the 1970s. In contrast, early Catalanism was not represented by a single party (all the main historical Catalanist parties emerged from coalitions of pre-viously established groups), but its lack of political unanimity was compensated for by its common aim and breadth of appeal.[7] We have also seen how the situation was partly reversed in the 1980s, when nationalism was represented by a single main party in Catalonia (CiU) but by several parties in Euskadi (PNV, EE, EA, HB).

In the early historical chapters, we analysed how Basque nationalism was centred around a single leader, Sabino Arana, while Catalan nationalism had been articulated through the voice of several intellectuals and political figures. But appearances are deceptive

---

[7] Catalanist parties won elections and swept the polls much earlier than their Basque counterparts.

Paradoxically, Basque nationalism emerged from a fragmented political environment, while Catalonia was moving around a platform of consensus, which was basically provided by the undisputed need to regenerate Catalan culture as a minimum demand. Preceded by the *Renaixença*, Catalan nationalism could always refer back to the revival of powerful cultural symbols, epitomised by a literary renaissance. Basque nationalism was much more subject to bitter internal rifts, rivalries and ideological confrontation than Catalan nationalism was at any time. Only the charismatic-authoritarian personality of Sabino Arana could hold together under a single banner an archipelago of often solipsist and quaint local figures. Indeed, without Arana and his intransigent programme Basque nationalism might never have arisen in its present form. Probably, no PNV could have emerged and no unitarian nationalist programme would have been able to gain popularity. When Arana died, he left a legacy of firm principles, a line of assertiveness, a radical credo, a political bible made up of a few simple slogans, which were to be followed by several generations without significant ideological alterations till the 1950s. Attempts by bourgeois elements to infiltrate the party and mollify its line had only temporary success. A hardcore of unswerving *sabinianos* always emerged to claim for themselves the reins of the party.

Yet Arana's legacy was in itself confused and its commitment to language maintenance should not be taken at face value. An interesting episode shows clearly the incapacity of Arana to conceive a language with any integrating power, even among the Basques. At the beginning of the century, a significant effort was made to reunite in Fuenterrabia the most relevant Basque linguists and philologists from both sides of the Pyrenees for a congress on orthographic unification. Most illustrious scholars 'trembled at the news that Arana was going to participate with 320 of his followers, most of them incompetent, blind and unconditional henchmen of their master. The congress . . . was a complete fiasco because of the intransigence of the Aranists.[...] The colleagues from the French Basque country withdrew in disgust, and the orthographic disagreement between them and us persists until the present day'(Villasante 1979: 294-5).[8] For Arana language had to remain exclusively an

---

[8] Ever since Arana, the struggle to revive Euskara remained a subject of passionate debate among nationalists. In their heart and mind, Euskara remained the vessel of

ethnic barrier, and all efforts to dampen its purism met with his total opposition. Hence his credo was coherent only in its *opposition* to Spain, but not as Basque identity was concerned.

This oppositional character is present in all nationalisms and indeed in all forms of group identity. However, opposition can be articulated either through the appraisal of one own's identity or through a negative and constant comparison with an external enemy. We have seen clearly the contrast between these two models. Catalan mobilisation has been centered on the positive assertion of the group's culture. Conversely, since Arana, Basque politics has been based on negation and confrontation. This is related to the two original patterns, Basque *exclusivism* and Catalan *integrationism*. The latter proposition does not imply that oppositional movements are always exclusivist. Authoritarian leadership persisted after Arana's death and was revived during Francoism. As no personality like Arana could emerge in a captive society deprived of any freedom of expression, a strong authoritarian leadership could only arise in the underground, through a faceless organisation. That was one of the main roles filled by ETA. It lacked a charismatic central figure, but even as an organisation it possessed charisma.

In such a society, where no other communication was possible, the 'logic of action/repression/action' was indeed a form of communication. In Catalonia an underground but rich cultural life could convey veiled messages of self-determination and hopes for future resurgence. In Euskadi no high culture meant no hope, while the nationalist intelligentsia had to invent new ways of mobilisation. The de-Basquisation of Basque élites was one of the prime causes for this confusion.

In short, we have seen that Basque nationalism progressed from political unity to fragmentation, while Catalan nationalism moved in the opposite direction, from political fragmentation to unity. The influence of core values was crucial to this evolution. To clarify this point, we should stress again the role of *cultural nationalism* in its dialectics with *political nationalism*. There was a difference in the way cultural nationalists interacted with the state. In Catalonia they used cultural arguments as a disguise for political mobilisation, not only as an end in itself. Thus Catalanists carved up a non-political space

---

Basque uniqueness, yet, although hailed as a symbol of nationhood, its promotion was rarely put into practice.

for themselves and for a while, from the 1950s, were able to elude total censorship. As cultural arguments were weaker in Euskadi, culture could not unite the democratic opposition, but Basque nationalists were more intransigent in their demands. Since the state was also more intransigent in dealing with Basque opposition, the latter had to act in complete secrecy. Following Frantz Fanon and other radical political theorists, Basque nationalists set out to regenerate their nation morally through violence. 'Moral regeneration' is a task normally accomplished by cultural nationalists (Hutchinson 1987). However, the lack of a robust cultural nationalism and shared cultural elements implied that regeneration had to be carried out by other means. The opposite process occurred in Catalonia, where the slow lifting of censorship allowed a timid but steady revival of the national culture, which served as a focus for the opposition.

Immigration

The relationship between cultural nationalism and political nationalism had also to withstand the test of mass immigration. In Chapter 8 we saw how immigration influenced the evolution of Catalan and Basque nationalism. Contrary to Heiberg's (1989: 196) thesis that 'nationalism has created two antagonistic political communities', postwar Basque nationalism had helped instead to compound and smooth pre-existing ethnic divisions, but at the cost of magnifying the overall opposition between Basques – both immigrants and natives – and Madrid.[9]

The perception of immigrants as bearers of the oppressor's culture characterised late nineteenth century Basque nationalism (Arana 1982: 197-9). Sabino de Arana was particularly concerned with the fate of the language but, unlike what happened in Catalonia, he felt it impossible to assimilate the immigrants. To many Basques the language appeared irreparably lost, so the emphasis was increasingly put on more ambiguous concepts as defining traits of the Basque nation. Arana's ideology focussed on a nostalgic mythification of the past and on Basque racial purity. The goal was therefore not the assimilation of newcomers but the opposite: a nostalgic striving for

---

[9] I do not pretend to deny that fracture still exists between natives and immigrants, but does not depend on nationalism.

an uncontaminated sense of Basqueness. This self-enclosure was bound to fail because the increasing wealth of the region continued to attract immigrants. These could not be culturally integrated for several reasons: because of the central regime's oppression of Basque culture, because of the hostile attitudes of some of the natives and because a difficult language like Euskara could not be properly learned without its own school system.[10] The failure to transform Basque culture into a high culture must again account for its failure to attract immigrants.

In contrast, rejection of immigrants has not traditionally featured as a prominent Catalanist concern. The firm grip of the Left and Social-Catholic leadership on the nationalist movement prevented an anti-immigrant backlash. Knowledge of Catalan became an important feature of civil participation, and a powerful stimulus to adaptation for many immigrants (the more so. from the second generation onwards). Given the similarity between Catalan and Castilian, Catalan identity was based on highly permeable borders and non-Catalans could easily 'become' Catalans by adopting bilingualism. And because the stress on language was evident, such borders were also more clearly identifiable and thus easier to cross. Immigrants were encouraged in their identification with Catalonia by the obvious stress on language as a carrier of national identity. With the twilight of Francoism and during the democratic transition, Catalan assumed a key role on the political scene. Most political, intellectual, artistic and religious forces fully committed themselves to the recovery of the language. Their purpose was to elevate it into a communicative instrument fully appropriate to the needs of a rapidly changing society.[11]

The belief in the capacity of Catalan culture to absorb newcomers was one of the main reasons why no anti-immigrant reaction surfaced in spite of the immigrants' numbers. Cultural vitality is the basis of what can be broadly defined as Catalan optimism, as opposed to Basque pessimist attitudes. As many immigrants coming from the underdeveloped Andalusian countryside perceived Catalan culture as 'superior' to their own, they were both encouraged and willing

[10] In Eusdaki the language gap between immigrants and natives is even wider than in most industrialised countries.

[11] The centrality of language also explains the existence of a prolific school of sociolinguistic studies. See Vallverdú (1980) for an exhaustive overview of Catalan sociolinguistics up to the year 1979.

to learn it despite the fact that another high culture, Castilian, had the one and only support from the state.

Language maintenance

Since the late nineteenth century, the Basque language has been stressed over and over again as the most important distinctive element of Basqueness by politicians and scholars, both foreign and local. The founders of Basque nationalism were also cultural nationalists and saw Euskara as the quintessence of Basque identity. However, their dream of reviving it clashed with the reality of a declining tongue. This sociolinguistic situation influenced Basques politics in at least five ways:

(1) It radicalised potential cultural nationalists as they faced the possible disappearance of Euskara. Their compensatory reaction was to forge an uncompromising movement stressing separation from Spain. After understanding that a language revival on the Catalan pattern was not viable, Sabino de Arana focused on race and religion, beating a retreat into separatism away from his original Carlist inspiration.

(2) Cultural assimilation prompted a contrast among nationalist over which element(s) of Basqueness should be fostered. These tensions were recurrent in ETA's internal quarrels. Although strictly political discussions were to the fore, cultural debates often loomed in the background.

(3) This lack of definition of the central elements of Basqueness created a vacuum in political programmes. Once political violence was triggered under Francoism, this vacuum was easily filled by military actions.

(4) It added a powerful element of accusation against the centralist regime which was identified as bearing the main responsibility for cultural assimilation and loss. Accusations of cultural genocide served internally to justify armed struggle as a defence from, and response against, the state.

(5) It fomented a sense of despair since many Basques perceived themselves as a people on the verge of extinction. Only drastic counter-measures such as a mass insurrection could save them from their doom and moving into a state of abeyance.[12]

---

12 Jáuregui (1981) uses the powerful expression *sentimento agonico* (that is, a feeling

All these conditions remained confined to a coterie of committed militants until a decisive external factor contributed to spread it to the masses. State repression at a time when the regime was changing and declining was the main trigger of popular support for armed reaction against the dictatorship. Although cultural nationalists such as Txillardegi did not overtly embrace violent strategies, they were nevertheless radical die-hards not prone to compromise. In the 1960s Txillardegi's attempt to build a unitary front in which cultural nationalism was supported to provide the bond for a plethora of mutually arguing factions. Nevertheless, cultural nationalists could not put a halt to the increasing spiral of political violence – and perhaps they also did not want to.

As for the case of Catalan, the dictatorship prolonged a highly abnormal situation: the language was alive and widely spoken in many walks of life, but its public use was strictly forbidden, forcibly confined to domestic life, far from police inspection. Subsequently the vitality of civil society has turned it into one of the most creative non-official languages in Europe. Today it is used in all domains, it is a scientific language with a continuously expanding output of neologisms, it has a rich literature, it is the main language of theatre, arts, universities and television, and it is making great inroads in the movies, as well as in the daily and weekly press. All this progress was unthinkable not many years ago when the country came out of an uncertain transition from autocratic rule to Western-style democracy (1975-82).

How can we explain the different impact of cultural nationalism? An answer lies in the different role played by the two nationalist intelligentsias. Nationalist leaders normally pursue three tasks:
(1) mobilising their constituencies through common symbols and values;
(2) allocating a 'division of labour' within the movement, controlling radical deviations and inter-generational tensions; and
(3) conveying the message that, if the nation is fatally threatened, they are able defend it through their programme of moral regeneration.

These three points have had opposite effects on the Catalan and the Basque programmes:

---

of anguish and despair, of impending collective threat, of living on the threshold of oblivion).

(1) The Catalan intelligentsia could mobilise vast numbers through the use of specific symbols and values (namely, language) and in their defence. The Basque intelligentsia could not achieve the same result.

(2) At a time when political nationalism was still quiescent, the Catalan youth were drawn into the struggle for cultural regeneration. Lacking a similar tradition of cultural nationalism and without a corresponding 'division of labour', the alienated Basque youth was more prone to engage in other forms of struggle.

(3) The Catalanist leaders could reassure their constituencies that the nation could be saved through their own programme of cultural regeneration. In contrast, the Basque youth were disenchanted with the incapacity of the old leadership to put forward a programme of national regeneration and decided to act on their own.

These three factors prompted Basque radicals to drift towards political violence, a drift continuously reinforced by state repression. Cultural nationalism functions not only as a binding force but particularly as a way to channel the energies of enthusiastic young nationalists who are eager to act with all available means. It follows that without a thriving cultural nationalism the chances are greater for such nationalist youth to engage in political violence.

Nationalism as border-making

The state is the most powerful institution in the modern world. Given that nationalism is also an ideology aimed at the control of the state by the 'nation', it is not surprising that nationalism is also the most powerful contemporary ideology. Nevertheless, the study of nationalism has only belatedly emerged as an academic discipline in its own right. Hence theories of nationalism are deficient in various ways and omit essential aspects of the phenomenon. For instance, few of the mainstream theories start from the crucial consideration that nationalism is a form of border creation and/or maintenance.[13] Borders are activated to ensure a distinction between two or more differentiable groups, or the spaces they inhabit, which could otherwise be confused and intermingle with each other. Borders are a mechanism of both individual and group

13 For a theoretical overview of these approaches, see Conversi (1995).

defence and are a universal phenomenon occurring among all living beings.

However, the process is enormously facilitated when such borders include some clear differential markers or signposts.[14] In the process of universal homogenisation which has characterised modernity, many ethnies have lost their distinctive customs, laws, mores, traditions etc. In many cases this process of erosion of traditional societies has left almost unscathed historical memories and even myths of original independence which are at the heart of national identities (Smith 1986, 1991). Hence the potential for nationalist mobilisation and conflict has remained intact despite cultural assimilation. The nationalist leaders' job is to reawaken such 'slumbering' human material, giving voice and order to a set of often confused popular perceptions and myths. This job will be facilitated enormously if the leaders can focus the loyalty of their people around some shared symbols of identity or core values, and express it in a distinct language.

We have looked at how this process of national reawakening has worked in two opposed cases: cultural persistence (Catalonia) and cultural assimilation (Euskadi). First, we have seen that cultural conditions and the anthropological landscape have had a decisive impact on the evolution of the two nationalist movements. Secondly, it appeared that cultural fragmentation brings with it fragmented conceptions of national identity; hence cultural fragmentation paves the way to political fragmentation. We have analysed, thirdly, the role of state repression in reinforcing previously weak or confused ethnic boundaries and, fourthly, the influence of cultural vitality on the non-violent character of nationalist mobilisations.

An underlying rationale has been to uncover the fallacy that the advent of a global culture could inspire peace, prosperity and a general lessening of conflict. This is far from the truth and a rapid glance at the map of world conflicts (Gurr 1993, Gurr and Scarritt 1989, Harff and Gurr 1989) enables us to see that all of them have emerged in situations of close cultural contact, and for most of them such contact has resulted in assimilation of the weaker culture by the dominant one. Thus in countless cases violent conflicts have been revived by weak identities, and weak identities have been rejuvenated through violent conflict. However, nationalist violence

14 The concept of 'cultural markers' has also been used by Gellner (1973).

results in a further contradiction: it brings about more homogenisation, disruption of the local culture, and massive human losses. Yet it also reinforces boundary perceptions, disrupting multicultural coexistence and reviving centuries-old antagonisms, which, once triggered, have a power of their own. These numerous cases, among which the Yugoslav conflict stands out, show that once a conflict is initiated, people are helplessly drawn into it on each side. The more violent the conflict, the more likely that 'un-hyphenated' individuals with no predetermined allegiances are compelled to take sides.

We have reappraised the role played by cultural factors and related them to the process of boundary-making and boundary maintenance. The vitality of these cultural factors is thus related to the vitality of cultural nationalism, which in turn is linked to the élites' different formulations of national identity. A final finding has been that violence is used to reinforce ethnic boundaries when the latter are particularly weak or under threat.

BIBLIOGRAPHY

Acquaviva, Sabino 1979. *Il seme religioso della rivolta*, Milano: Rusconi.

Agirreazkuenaga, Joseba 1987. *Vizcaya en el siglo XIX (1814-1876): Las finanzas públicas de un Estado emergente*, Bilbao: Universidad del País Vasco.

Aguirre, José Antonio de 1991. *Escape via Berlin: Eluding Franco in Hitler's Europe*, Reno, Nevada: University of Nevada Press (1st edn 1994). The present edition includes annotations with an introduction by Robert P. Clark.

Alba, Victor 1975. *Catalonia: A Profile*, New York: Praeger/London: C. Hurst.

— 1983 *El Partido Comunista en España*, Barcelona: Planeta (1st edn 1979).

Alegret, Joan 1977. Entry 'Ateneu' in the *Gran Enciclopèdia Catalana*, vol. 3 (Ar-Bah), p. 318. Barcelona: Enciclopèdia Catalana.

Allières, Jacques 1977. *Les Basques*, Paris: Presses Universitaires de France.

Almirall, Valentí 1979. *Lo catalanisme*, Barcelona: Edicions 62/La Caixa (1st edn Barcelona: Llibreria Verdaguer/Llibreria López, 1886).

Altabizkar 1974. *Euskadi nucléaire*, Baiona: Elkar.

Alter, Peter 1989. *Nationalism*, London: Edward Arnold.

Alvarez Junco, José 1990. *Lerroux. El emperador del Parallelo*, Madrid: Alianza.

Amiel, Charles 1983. 'La "pureté de sang" en Espagne', *Etudes Inter-Ethniques*, vol. 6 (annual), pp. 27-45.

Amnesty International 1985. *Spain: A Question of Torture*, London: Amnesty International.

Anderson, Benedict 1983. *Imagined Communities: Reflections on the Origin and Spread of Nationalism*, London: Verso.

Andrés, Juanjo de, and José Antonio Maisuetxe 1980. *El movimento ciudadano en Euskadi*, San Sebastián: Sendoa.

Aracil, Lluís V. 1982. *Papers de sociolingüística*, Barcelona: Edicions La Magrana.

Arana y Goiri, Sabino de 1910. *Deun-ixendegi euzkotara: edo deunen ixenak euzkeratuta ta ixentzat ezarten diran jayetako ixenan euzkerazko ikurpenak/Santoral vasco: o sea lista de nombres euzkerizados de los santos y traducción de los nombres de festividad aplicables como nombres propios adaptados*, Bilbao: Comisión Bizkaina de Euzkera del Partido Nacionalista Vasco/Bilbao Maritimo y Comercial.

— (n.d. but ca. 1982). *Obras completas*, 3 vols. 2nd edn, San Sebastián: Sendoa (1st edn Buenos Aires: Sabindiar Batza, 1965).

— 1980 *Bizkaya por su independencia*, Bilbao: Geu Argitaldaria (1st edn. 1892).

Aranzadi, Engracio de ('Kizkitza') 1931. *La nación vasca*, Bilbao: Verdes.

— 1980. *Ereintza: Siembra del nacionalismo vasco, 1894-1912*, San Sebastián: Auñamendi (1st edn 1935, Zarauz: Ed. Vasca).

Aranzadi, Juan 1981 *Milenarismo vasco. Edad de oro, etnia y nativismo*, Madrid: Taurus.

Arbos, Xavier, and Antoni Puigsec 1980. *Franco i l'Espanyolisme*, Barcelona: Curial.

Arenas, Joaquim 1986, 'De la llei general d'educació a la llei de normalizació lingüística', paper presented at 2nd International Congress of the Catalan Language, Tarragona, May.

Aretxaga, Begoña 1988. *Los funerales en el nacionalismo vasco*, San Sebastián: Baroja.

Argente, Joan *et al.* 1979. 'Una nació sense estat, un poble sense llengua?', *Els Marges*, 15, pp. 3-15.

Arnau, J., and Humbert Boada 1986. 'Languages and school in Catalonia', *Journal of Multilingual and Multicultural Development*, 7, 2-3, pp. 107-21.

Arpal, Jesús, and Augustín Minondo 1978. 'El Bilbao de la industrialización. Una ciudad para un élite', *Saioak*, II, no. 2, pp. 31-68.

Arpal, Jesús, B. Asúa and P. Davila 1982 *Educación y sociedad en el País Vasco*, San Sebastián: Txertoa.

Artís i Benach, Pere 1980. *El cant coral a Catalunya (1891-1979)*, Barcelona: Barcino.

Asamblea Conjunta de Obispos y Sacerdotes 1971. *Historia de la Asamblea. Discursos*, Madrid: La Editorial Católica.

Atxaga, Bernardo 1992. *Obabakoak: A Novel*, London: Hutchinson/New York: Pantheon.

Aulestia, Gorka 1994. *Improvisational Poetry from the Basque Country*, Reno: University of Nevada Press.

Avni, Haim 1982. *Spain, the Jews, and Franco*, Philadelphia: Jewish Publication Society of America.

Azcona, Jesús, 1984. *Etnia y nacionalismo vasco: una aproximación desde la antropología*, Barcelona: Anthropos.

Badia i Margarit, Antoni M. 1964. *Llengua i cultura als Països Catalans*, Barcelona: Edicions 62.

— 1966. 'La integració idiomàtica i cultural dels immigrats. Reflexions, fets, plans', *Qüestions de Vida Cristiana*, 31, pp. 9-103.

— 1969. *La llengua dels barcelonins. Resultats d'una enquesta sociolingüística*, vol 1. Barcelona: Edicions 62.

Balcells, Albert 1983. *Historia contemporánea de Cataluña*, Barcelona: Edhasa.

— 1992 *Història del nacionalisme català, dels orígens al nostre temps*, Barcelona: Generalitat de Catalunya.

— and Josep Maria Solé i Sabaté 1990. 'Aproximación a la historia de la oposición al régimen franquista en Cataluña' in Tusell, Javier, Alicia Alted and Abdón Mateos (eds), *La oposición al régimen de Franco. Estado de la cuestión y metodología de la investigación*, Madrid: UNED/Departamento de Historia Contemporanea.

— and Genís Samper 1993. *L'escoltisme català (1911-1978)*, Barcelona: Barcanova.

Balfour, Sebastian 1989. *Dictatorship, Workers and the City: Labour in Greater Barcelona since 1939*, Oxford: Clarendon Press.

Barbancho, Alfonso G. 1967. *Las migraciones interiores españolas. Estudio cuantitativo desde 1900*, Madrid: Instituto de Estudios Económicos.

— 1974 *Las migraciones interiores españolas en 1961-70*, Madrid: Instituto de Estudios Económicos.

Barnard, F.M. 1995. *Herder's Social and Political Thought: From Enlightenment to Nationalism*, Oxford: Clarendon Press.

Barrera, Andrés 1985. *La dialéctica de la identidad a Cataluña. Un estudio de antropología social*, Madrid: CIS, Centro de Investigaciones Sociales.

Barth, Frederick (ed.) 1969. *Ethnic Groups and Boundaries: The Social Organization of Cultural Difference*, London: Geo. Allen & Unwin.

Basaldúa, Pedro 1977. *El libertador vasco. Sabino de Arana y Goiri*, Bilbao: Geu–Argitaldaria (1st edn Buenos Aires: Ekin, 1953).

Basurto Larrañaga, Roman 1983. *Comercio y burguesía mercantil de Bilbao en la segunda mitad del siglo XVIII*, Bilbao: Servicio Editorial, Universidad del País Vasco.

Batista i Roca, Josep Maria 1959. 'Martí d'Eixalà i la introducció de la filosofia escosesa a Catalunya' in F. Pierce (ed.), *Hispanic Studies in Honour of I. Gonzalez Llubera*, Oxford: Dolphin.

Batista, Antoni and J. Playà Maset 1991. *La Gran Conspiració. Crónica de l'Assemblea de Catalunya*, Barcelona: Empúries.

Beltza (pseudonym of Emilio López) 1977. *El nacionalismo vasco en el exilio, 1937-1960*, San Sebastián: Txertoa.

Benet, Josep 1968. *El Dr. Torras i Bages en el marc del seu temps*, Barcelona: Estela.

— 1973. *Catalunya sota el règim franquista*, vol 1. Paris: Edicions Catalanes de París (2nd edn 1978, Barcelona: Editorial Blaume).

— 1992. *Maragall i la setmana tràgica*, Barcelona: Edicions 62 (1st edn 1963, Barcelona: Institut d'Estudis Catalans).

Beramendi, Xusto 1984. 'Bibliografía (1939-1983) sobre nacionalismos y cuestión nacional en la España contemporánea', *Estudios de Historia Social*, 28-29, pp. 491-515.

Bereciartúa, José María 1977. *Ikurriña. Historia y simbolismo*, Estella: Editorial Verbo Divino.

Bilbeny, Norbert 1983. 'Nacionalisme i cosmopolitisme en la teoria noucentista', *Recerques*, 14, pp. 131-8.
— 1984. *Entre Renaixença i Noucentisme. Estudis de Filosofia*, Barcelona: La Magrana.
— 1988. *La ideología nacionalista a Catalunya*, Barcelona: Laia.
Birnbaum, Pierre 1988. *States and Collective Action: The European Experience*, Cambridge University Press.
Blanco, María Cristina 1990. *La integración de los inmigrantes en Bilbao.* Bilbao: Bilboko Udala.
Blasco, Rogelio 1987. 'Nuevo rock vasco. Un fenómeno sociológico', *Cuadernos de Alzate*, 6, pp. 12-30.
Blinkhorn, Martin 1974. '"The Basque Ulster": Navarre and the Basque autonomy question under the Spanish Second Republic', *Historical Journal*, XVII, 3, pp. 595-613.
Boix, Emili 1993. *Triar no és trair. Identitat i llengua en els joves de Barcelona*, Barcelona: Edicions 62.
Brand, Jack 1985. 'Nationalism and the Noncolonial Periphery: A Discussion of Scotland and Catalonia' in Edward A. Tiryakian and Ronald Rogowski (eds), *New Nationalisms of the Developed West*, Boston, MA: Allen & Unwin, pp. 277-93.
— 1988. 'Andalusia: Nationalism as a strategy for autonomy', *Canadian Review of Studies in Nationalism*, XV, 1-2, pp. 1-10.
Brandes, Stanley H. 1990. 'The *Sardana*: Catalan dance and Catalan national identity', *Journal of American Folklore*, 103, 407, pp. 24-41.
Brezzi, Camillo 1979. *I partiti democratici cristiani d'Europa*, Milano: Teti.
Brubaker, Roger 1992. *Citizenship and Nationhood in France and Germany*, Cambridge, MA: Harvard University Press.
Bruni, Luigi 1980. *E.T.A. Storia dell'esercito di liberazione dei paesi baschi*, Milano: Filorosso (Spanish transl. *ETA: Historia política de una lucha armada*, Navarra: Txalaparta, 7th edn 1993).
Brunn, Gerhard 1992. 'The Catalans within the Spanish monarchy from the middle of the Nineteenth to the beginning of the Twentieth century' in Andreas Kappeler (ed.), *The Formation of National Elites*, Aldershot: Dartmouth.
Cacho Viu, Vicente (ed.) 1984. *Els modernistes i el nacionalisme cultural (1881-1906)*, Barcelona: La Magrana/Diputació de Barcelona.
Cambó, Francesc 1930. *Per la concòrdia*, Barcelona: Llibreria Catalònia.
Cameron, Euan 1992. 'Myths of a Basque bestseller', *The European*, 10 Sept.
Camps i Arboix, Joaquim de 1963. *La Mancomunitat de Catalunya*, Barcelona: Bruguera.
— 1970 *Història de la Solidaritat Catalana*, Barcelona: Destino.
Candel, Francesc 1964. *Els altres Catalans*, Barcelona: Edicions 62.
— 1985 *Els altres Catalans vint anys despres*, Barcelona: Edicions 62.

Cardús i Ros, Salvador 1987, 'Bases socials d'un projecte nacional' in S. Cardús *et al.*, *El nacionalisme català a la fi del segle XX*, Vic: Eumo, 1987.

Caro Baroja, Julio 1971-2. *Etnografía histórica de Navarra*, 3 vols. Pamplona: Aranzadi.

Carr, Raymond 1966. *Spain, 1808-1939*, Oxford: Clarendon Press.

— 1980. *Modern Spain 1875-1980*, Oxford University Press.

— 1983. *Spain 1812-1975*, Oxford University Press.

— and Juan Pablo Fusi 1981. *Spain: Dictatorship to Democracy*, London: Collins (1st edn 1979).

Carreras de Nadal, R. and Albert Manent. *Le Vatican et la Catalogne*, Paris: Edicions Catalanes de París (2nd extended edition; 1st edn Geneva, 1967).

Casassas i Ymbert, Jordi 1986. *L'Ateneu Barcelones: dels seus origens als nostres dies*, Barcelona: La Magrana/Institut Municipal d'Història, Ajuntament de Barcelona.

— 1989. *Intellectuals, professionals i polítics a la Catalunya contemporània (1850-1920)*, San Cugat: Els llibres de la frontera.

Castellanos, Jordi 1986. 'Modernisme i nacionalisme' in Termes *et al.*, *Catalanisme: Història, Política i Cultura*, Barcelona: L'Avenç/Xarxa Cultural, pp. 21-38.

Castells, José Manuel 1976. *El estatuto vasco. El estado regional y el proceso estatutario*, San Sebastián: Haranburu.

Castells, Luís 1987. *Modernización y dinámica política en la sociedad Guipuzcoana de la Restauración, 1876-1915*, Bilbao: Universidad del País Vasco.

— 1990. 'Los trabajadores en el País Vasco (1880-1914)', *Historia Contemporanea*, 3, pp. 59-74.

Cavalli Sforza, L.L., *The Great Human Diasporas: A History of Diversity and Evolution*, Reading, MA: Addison–Wesley, 1995.

Chaffee, Lyman 1988. 'Social conflict and alternative mass communications: public art and politics in the service of Spanish-Basque nationalism', *European Journal of Political Research*, 16, pp. 545-72.

— 1993. *Political Protest and Street Art: Popular Tools for Democratization in Hispanic Countries*, Westport, Conn.: Greenwood Press.

Christian, William A., Jr. 1987. 'Tapping and defining new power: the first month of visions at Ezquioga, July 1931', *American Ethnologist*, 14, 1, pp. 140-66.

—1996. *Visionaries: The Spanish Republic and the Reign of Christ*, Berkeley: University of California Press.

CIDC 1987. *Padrons municipals d'habitants de Catalunya. Coneixement del català. Dades provisionals*, Barcelona: Consorci de Informació i Documentació de Catalunya.

Clark, Robert P. 1979. *The Basques: The Franco Years and Beyond*, Reno, Nevada: University of Nevada Press.

— 1980. 'Euzkadi: Basque nationalism in Spain since the Civil War' in Charles R. Foster (ed.), *Nations without a State. Ethnic Minorities in Western Europe*, New York: Praeger, pp. 75-100.
— 1981. 'Language and politics in Spain's Basque provinces', *West European Politics*, 4, 1, pp. 85-103.
—1984. *The Basque Insurgents. ETA, 1952-1980*, Madison: University of Wisconsin Press.
— 1985a. 'Dimensions of Basque political culture in post-Franco Spain' in William A. Douglass (ed.), *Basque Politics: A Case Study in Ethnic Nationalism*. Nevada: Associated Faculty Press and Basque Studies Program.
— 1985b. 'Spain's Autonomous Communities: A case study in ethnic power sharing', *European Studies Journal*, 2, pp. 1-16.
— 1986a. 'Patterns of ETA violence, 1968-1980' in Peter H. Merkl (ed.), *Political Violence and Terror. Motifs and Motivations*. Berkeley: University of California Press.
— 1986b. 'Patterns in the lives of ETA members' in Merkl (ed.), *ibid.*
— 1987. '"Rejectionist" voting as an indicator of ethnic nationalism: The case of Spain's Basque Provinces, 1976-1986,' *Ethnic and Racial Studies*, 10, 4, pp. 427-47.
— 1990. *Negotiating with ETA. Obstacles to Peace in the Basque Country, 1975-1988*, Reno, Nevada: Nevada University Press.
— 1991. Introduction to Aguirre (1991).
Climent, Teresa 1986. *Realitat lingüística a la Val d'Aran*, Barcelona: Departament de Cultura/Institut de Sociolingüística Catalana.
Coco, Emilio 1992. 'Poeti baschi contemporanei', *Poesia*, V, 53, pp. 34-43.
Cohen, Anthony P. 1985. *The Symbolic Construction of Community*, London: Routledge.
Colomer, Josep Maria 1976. *L'Assemblea de Catalunya*, Barcelona: L'Avenç.
— 1978. *Els estudiants de Barcelona sota el franquisme*, 2 vols. Barcelona: Curial.
— 1984. *Espanyolisme i catalanisme. La idea de nació en el pensament polític català (1939-79)*, Barcelona: L'Avenç.
Colomer, Leandre and Mascarell, Feran 1977. 'Catalunya , Democràcia Cristiana i alta cultura', *L'Avenç*, 5, pp. 45-51.
Collins, Roger 1986. *The Basques*, Oxford: Basil Blackwell.
Connor, Walker 1972. 'Nation-building or nation-destroying?', *World Politics*, XXIV, pp. 319-55.
— 1973. 'The Politics of Ethnonationalism', *Journal of International Affairs*, 1, 1-21.
—1994. *Ethnonationalism: The Quest for Understanding*, Princeton University Press.

Conversi, Daniele 1985. 'Diglossia e conflitto nella sociolinguistica catalana', *La Critica Sociologica*, 74, pp. 91-6.

— 1986. 'Valori centrali e immigrazione in Catalogna' in *La formazione dell' insegnante di lingue in contesto bilingue*, proceedings of a congress in Perugia, March 1985, Roma: Edizioni LIS, pp. 289-304.

— 1987. 'Teorie dell' etno-nazionalismo,' *La Critica Sociologica*, 81, pp. 71-88.

— 1987. 'L'insegnamento in Catalogna: verso una società bilingue?', *La Riforma della Scuola*, 1, pp. 28-36.

— 1988. 'L'integrazione degli immigrati a Barcellona', *Études Migrations/Studi Emigrazione*, 89, pp. 67-82.

— 1989. Considerazioni sul caso catalano in una prospettiva comparata', *La Crítica Sociológica*, 88, winter, pp. 42-60.

— 1993. 'Domino effect or internal developments? The influence of international events and political ideologies on Catalan and Basque nationalism', *West European Politics*, 16, 3, pp. 245-70.

— 1994. 'Violence as an ethnic border: The consequence of a lack of distinctive elements in Croatian, Kurdish and Basque nationalism' in Justo Beramendi, Ramon Maiz and Xosé M. Nuñez (eds), *Nationalism in Europe: Past and Present*, Santiago de Compostela University Press.

— 1995 'Reassessing theories of nationalism. Nationalism as boundary maintenance and creation', *Nationalism and Ethnic Politics*, 1, pp. 73-85; reprinted in John Agnew (ed.) *Political Geography: A Reader*, London: Edward Arnold, 1997.

Corcuera Atienza, Javier 1979. *Orígenes, ideología y organización del nacionalismo vasco, 1876-1904*, Madrid: Siglo XXI.

— 1984. 'Nacionalismos y clase en la España de la Restauración', *Estudios de Historia Social*, 28-29, pp. 249-82.

Cortada, James W. (ed.) 1982. *Historical Dictionary of the Spanish Civil War, 1936-1939*, Westport, Conn: Greenwood Press.

Crexell, Joan 1977. *Premsa clandestina 1970-1977*, Barcelona: Crit.

— 1982. *Els fets del Palau i el consell de guerra a Jordi Pujol*, Barcelona: La Magrana.

— 1987. *La caputxinada*, Barcelona. Edicions 62.

— 1992 *La 'manifestació' de Capellans de 1966*. Barcelona: Publicacions de l'Abadia de Montserrat.

Cruells, Manuel 1965. *Els no Catalans i nosaltres*, Barcelona: Edicions d'Aportació Catalana.

Cucurull, Felix (ed.) 1975. *Panoràmica del nacionalisme català*, Paris: Edicions Catalanes de París.

Cullà i Clarà, Joan B. 1977. *El catalanisme d'esquerra (1928-1936)*, Barcelona: Curial.

— 1986 *El republicanisme lerrouxista a Catalunya, 1901-1923*, Barcelona: Curial.

— 1989. 'Del pla d'estabilització a la fi del franquisme (1959-1975)' in Pierre Vilar (ed.), *Història de Catalunya*, vol. VII: *El franquisme i la transició democràtica, 1939-1988*, Barcelona: Edicions 62.

Del Campo, Salustiano, Manuel Navarro and J. Felix Tezanos 1977. *La cuestión regional española*, Madrid: Cuadernos para el Dialogo.

Della Porta, Donatella and Liborio Mattina 1985. 'I movimenti politici a base etnica: il caso basco', *Rivista Italiana di Scienza Politica*, XV, 1, pp. 35-67.

Dickson, Paul 1968. 'The separate land', *Saturday Review*, 7 Sept., pp. 50-1.

Díez-Medrano, Juan 1989. 'Nationalism and Independence in Spain: Basques and Catalans', unpubl. Ph.D. thesis, University of Michigan.

— 1995. *Divided Nations: Class, Politics, and Nationalism in the Basque Country and Catalonia*, Ithaca, NY: Cornell University Press.

Di Giacomo, Susan 1984. 'The Politics of Identity: Nationalism in Catalonia'. Unpubl. Ph.D. thesis, University of Massachussets.

— 1986. 'Images of Class and Ethnicity in Catalan Politics. The Elections of 1977 and 1980' in Gary W. McDonogh (ed.), *Conflict in Catalonia: Images of an Urban Society*, Gainesville: University of Florida Press, pp. 79-82.

Dobson, Andrew 1989. *An Introduction to the Politics and Philosophy of José Ortega y Gasset*, Cambridge University Press.

Domènech i Montaner, Lluís 1995. *Ensenyes nacionals de Catalunya*, Barcelona: Editorial 92.

Domínguez Ortiz, A. 1976. *Sociedad y Estado en el Siglo XVIII español*, Barcelona: Ariel.

Douglass, William A. (ed.) 1985. *Basque Politics: A Case Study in Ethnic Nationalism*, Reno, Nevada: Associated Faculty Press and Basque Studies Program.

— 1988. 'A critique to recent trends in the analysis of ethnonationalism', *Ethnic and Racial Studies*, 11, 2, pp. 191-206.

— and Milton da Silva 1971. 'Basque nationalism' in Oriol Pi-Sunyer (ed.), *The Limits of Integration: Ethnicity and Nationalism in Modern Europe*, Amherst, MA: Dept. of Anthropology Research Reports, 9.

— and Joseba Zulaika 1990. 'On the interpretation of terrorist violence: ETA and the Basque political process', *Comparative Studies in Society and History*, 32, 2, pp. 238-57.

Duocastella, Pere Rogelio 1965. 'Géographie de la pratique religieuse en Espagne', *Social Compass*, XII, 4-5, pp. 253-302.

Ehrlich, Charles 1993. 'Federalism, regionalism, nationalism: A century of Catalan political thought and its implications for Scotland in Europe'. Paper presented at ESRC Research Seminar 1992-4 on 'British

Regionalism and Devolution in a Single Europe', Glasgow, May 1993.

Elliot, John Huxtable 1963. *The Revolt of the Catalans: A Study in the Decline of Spain*, Cambridge University Press.

Elorza, Antonio 1977. 'En el tercer aniversario de "Gudari"', *Berriak*, 23, pp. 32-3 and 25, pp. 30-1.

— 1978a. *Ideologías del nacionalismo vasco, 1876-1937*, San Sebastián: L. Haranburu.

— 1978b. 'Sobre los origenes literarios del nacionalismo', *Saioak*, II, 2, pp. 69-98.

— 1984. 'Los nacionalismos en el Estado español contemporanéo. Las ideologías', *Estudios de Historia Social*, 28-29, pp. 149-68.

— 1989. 'El temido "Arbol de la Libertad"' in Jean-René Aymes (ed.), *España y la Revolución francesa*, Barcelona: Crítica, pp. 69-117.

— 1990. 'Las ideologías de resistencia a la modernización y el nacionalismo', *Historia Contemporánea*, 4, pp. 341-54.

Enders, Victoria Loree 1984. 'Jaime Vicens Vives, the *Annales* and Catalonia', unpubl. Ph.D. thesis, University of California, San Diego.

Ereño, Manuel 1979. 'El solipsismo lingüístico en el ensayo "Hizkuntza eta pentsakera" de Txillardegi', *Saioak*, III, 3, pp. 279-309.

Escudero, Manu 1978. *Euskadi: dos comunidades*, San Sebastián: L. Haranburu.

Espinosa, José Mari Lorenzo 1989. *Dictadura y Dividendo. El discreto negocio de la burguesía vasca (1937-1950)*, Bilbao: Universidad de Deusto.

— 1993. *Gudari. Una pasión útil. Eli Gallastegi (1892-1974)*, Tafalla: Txalaparta.

Esteva i Fabregat, Claudi 1978. 'Inmigració i confirmació ètnica a Barcelona', *Quaderns d'Allibrament*, 2/3.

Estivill, Jordi and Salvador Giner 1985. 'La identitat social de Catalunya' in *Actes de les Primeres Jornades Catalanes de Sociologia*, 1981. Barcelona: Institut d'Estudis Catalans.

Estivill, Jordi and Gustau Barbat 1980. 'Anticlericalisme populaire en Catalogne au début du siècle', *Social Compass*, 27, 2-3, pp. 215-30.

Estornés Lasa, Bernardo 1980. *Orígenes de los vascos*, 3 vols, San Sebastián: Auñamendi (3rd edn, enlarged and updated; 1st edn, 4 vols, Zarauz: Editorial Icharopena, 1959-66).

Estornés Zubizarreta, Idoia 1983. *La Sociedad de Estudios Vascos: Aportación de Eusko-Ikaskuntza a la cultura vasca (1918-1936)*, Bilbao: Asmoz ta Jakitez.

— 1990. *La construcción de una nacionalidad vasca. El autonomismo de Eusko Ikaskuntza (1918-1931)*, San Sebastián: Cuaderno de la Sección de Historia y Geografía no. 14/Eusko Ikaskuntza.

Euskaltzaindia 1976. *Sobre la Real Academia de la Lengua Vasca*, Bilbao: Euskaltzaindia.

— 1977. *El libro blanco del euskera*, Bilbao: Euskaltzaindia/Academia de la Lengua Vasca.

— 1979. *Conflicto lingüístico en Euskadi*, San Sebastián: Euskaltzaindia/Eds. Vascas.

Eusko-Ikaskuntza 1925. *Guillermo de Humboldt y el País Vasco*, San Sebastián: Imprenta de la Diputación de Guipúzcoa.

Fabre, Jaume and Josep M. Huertas 1981. 'CC, el moviment que va "morir" dos cops (1954-1962)', *L'Avenç*, 42, pp. 54-61.

— Huertas, Josep M., and Antoni Ribas 1978. *Vint anys de resistència catalana (1939-1959)*, Barcelona: La Magrana.

Farras i Farras, Jaume 1986. *La Patum de Berga*, Barcelona: Edicions de Nou Art/Thor.

Fernández de Pinedo, Emiliano 1974. *Crecimiento económico y transformaciones sociales en el País Vasco, 1100-1850*, Madrid: Siglo XXI.

Ferrater Mora, Josep 1980. *Les formes de vida catalana i altres assaigs*, Barcelona: Edicions 62/La Caixa (1st edn Santiago de Chile: Ediciones de la Agrupació Patriotica Catalana, 1944/2nd edn Barcelona: Selecta, 1955). This edition also includes other essays and speeches from 1955, 1960, and 1979.

Ferrer i Girones, Francesc 1985. *La persecució politica de la llengua catalana*, Barcelona: Edicions 62.

Figueres, Josep M. 1985. *El Primer Congrés Catalanista i Valentí Almirall*, Barcelona: Generalitat de Catalunya/Departament de la Presidència.

Fishman, Joshua A. 1966. *Language Loyalty in the United States*, The Hague: Mouton.

— 1972. *Language and Nationalism*, Rowley, MA: Newbury House.

— 1980. 'Social theory and ethnography: Language and ethnicity in Eastern Europe' in Peter Sugar (ed.), *Ethnic Conflict and Diversity in Eastern Europe*, Santa Barbara, CA: ABC-Clio.

— 1982. 'Whorfianism of the third kind: Ethnolinguistic diversity as a worldwide societal asset', *Language in Society*, 11, pp. 1-14.

— 1985. (ed.) *The Rise and Fall of the Ethnic Revival*, Berlin: Mouton.

FOESSA 1979. *Enquesta sobre la cuestión regional en España*, Madrid: FOESSA.

Fontana, Josep 1988. 'La nazione catalana in etá moderna e contemporanea' in *Le Autonomie Etniche e Speciali in Italia e nell' Europa Mediterranea. Processi Storici e Istituzioni*, Atti del Convegno Internazionale nel Quarantennale dello Statuto, Cagliari, 29 Settembre-1 Ottobre 1988. Cagliari: Pubblicazione del Consiglio Regionale della Sardegna, pp. 47-54.

Forest, Eva 1974. *Operación Ogro*, Hendaye: Mugalde/Ruedo Iberico (published under the pseudonym of Julen Aguirre). Engl. trans. 1975: *Operation Ogro: The Execution of Admiral Luís Carrero Blanco*, New

York: Quadrangle/Ballantine Books. French original, 1974, Paris: Seuil.

Fradera, Josep Maria 1990. 'Rural traditionalism and conservative nationalism in Catalonia 1865–1900' in Josep R. Llobera (ed.), *Family, Class and Nation in Catalonia*, London: Mare Nostrum Editions/Amsterdam: *Critique of Anthropology*, X, 2 & 3, winter 1990.

— 1992. *Cultura nacional en una societat dividida. Patriotisme i cultura a Catalunya (1838–1868)*, Barcelona: Curial.

Fusi Aizpurúa, Juan Pablo 1984. *Pluralismo y nacionalidad*, Madrid: Alianza.

Fuster, Joan 1977. *Nosaltres els valencians*, Barcelona: Edicions 62 (1st edn Barcelona: Edicions 62, 1962).

— 1988 *Raimon*, Barcelona: La Magrana.

Galien, Enric 1987. 'La literatura sota el franquisme: de l'ostracisme a la represa publica' in Riquer, Comas and Molas (eds), *Història de la literatura catalana*, Barcelona: Ariel, vol. 10, pp. 213–42.

Gallofré i Virgili, María Josepa 1991. *L'edició catalana i la censura franquista (1939–1951)*, Barcelona: Publications de l'Abadia de Montserrat.

Gallop, Rodney 1970. *A Book of the Basques*, Reno: University of Nevada Press (1st edn 1930).

García, Soledad 1990. 'Collective consumption and urban protest in Barcelona during the Franco era' in Josep R. Llobera (ed.), *Family, Class and Nation in Catalonia*, London: Mare Nostrum Editions/Amsterdam: *Critique of Anthropology*, X, 2 & 3, winter 1990.

García de Cortázar, Fernando and Manuel Montero 1983. *Diccionario de Historia del País Vasco*, 2 vols. San Sebastián: Txertoa.

García Crespo, Milagros, Roberto Velasco Barroetabeña and Arantza Mendizábal Gorostiaga 1981. *La economía vasca durante el franquismo (Crecimiento y crisis de la economía vasca: 1936–1980)*, Bilbao: Editorial de la Gran Enciclopedia Vasca.

García Soler, Jordi 1976. *La nova cançó* (with foreword by Salvador Espriu), Barcelona: Edicions 62.

García Venero, Máximiano 1967. *Historia del nacionalismo catalán*, 2 vols, Madrid: Editora Nacional (1st edn 1942).

— 1968. *Historia del nacionalismo vasco*, Madrid: Editora Nacional.

Garmendia, José Mari 1979 and 1980. *Historia de ETA*, 2 vols, San Sebastián: L. Haranburu.

— 1984. *Crisis de la violencia nacionalista en Euskadi*, in Reinares, Fernando (ed.) *Violencia política en Euskadi*, Bilbao: Desclée de Brouwer.

— and Alberto Elordi 1982. *La resistencia vasca*, San Sebastián: L. Haranburu.

Generalitat de Catalunya 1979. *Estatut d'Autonomia de Catalunya*, leaflet.

— 1983a. *La campanya de normalització lingüística*, Barcelona: Generalitat de Catalunya.

— 1983b. *La llei de normalització lingüística a Catalunya*, Leaflet.

Ghanime, Albert 1995. *Joan Cortada: Catalunya i els catalans al segle XIX,* Barcelona: Publicacions de l'Abadia de Montserrat.

Gil-Delgado, Francisco 1975. *Conflicto Iglesia-Estado,* Madrid: Sedmany.

Gilmour, David 1985. *The Transformation of Spain,* London: Quartet.

Giner, Salvador 1980. *The Social Structure of Catalonia,* London: Anglo-Catalan Society.

— 1984. 'Ethnic Nationalism: Centre and Periphery in Spain' in Christopher Abel and Nissa Torrents (eds), *Spain. Conditional Democracy,* London: Croom Helm, pp. 78-99.

— 1986. 'Nacionalismo étnico: centro y periferia en España' in Francesc Hernàndez and Francesc Mercadé (eds), *Estructuras sociales y cuestión nacional en España,* Barcelona: Ariel, pp. 436-60.

Gispert, Carlos and Josep M. Prats 1978. *España. Un estado plurinacional,* Barcelona: Blume.

Goldberg, David Theo 1992. 'The semantics of race', *Ethnic and Racial Studies,* 15, 4, pp. 543-69.

González Casanova, José Antonio 1974. *Federalisme i autonomia a Catalunya, 1868-1938,* Barcelona: Curial.

González Echegaray, Carlos 1989. *Catálogo de los manuscritos reunidos por el Príncipe Luís-Luciano Bonaparte que se hallan en el País Vasco: con un índice de nombres de personas, lugares, lenguas y dialéctos, y un catálogo,* Bilbao: Euskaltzaindia/Azkue Biblioteka.

González Portilla, Manuel 1989. 'Algunos aspectos de la transición en el País Vasco. De la protoindustrialización a la industrialización', *Historia Contemporánea,* 2, pp. 13-16.

Goti Iturriago, G.L. 1962. 'Los grupos sanguíneos de los vascos', *La Gran Enciclopedia Vasca,* vol. 1, pp. 39-65.

Granja Sainz, José Luis de la 1986. *Nacionalismo y II República en el País Vasco,* Madrid: CIS/Siglo XXI.

— 1994. 'La invención de la historia. Nación, mitos e historia en el pensamiento del fundador del nacionalismo vasco'. Unpubl. MS.

Greenwood, Davydd J. 1977. 'Continuity in Change: Spanish Basque Ethnicity as an Historical Process' in Milton Esman (ed.), *Ethnic Conflict in the Western World,* Ithaca NY: Cornell University Press, pp. 81-102.

Grilli, Giuseppe 1984. *Il mito laico di Joan Maragall. 'El Comte Arnau' nella cultura urbana del primo Novecento,* Napoli: Edizioni Sapere.

Gubern, Roma 1981. *La censura. Función política y ordenamiento jurídico bajo el franquismo (1936-75),* Barcelona: Península.

Guicciardini, Francesco 1993. *Diario del Viaggio in Spagna,* Pordenone: Edizioni Studio Tesi (1st edn 1514).

Gunther, Richard, Giacomo Sani and Goldie Shabad 1986. *Spain after Franco: The making of a competitive party system,* Berkeley, CA: University of California Press.

Gurr, Ted Robert 1993. *Minorities at Risk: A Global View of Ethnopolitical Conflicts*, Washington, DC: United States Institute of Peace Press.

— and James R. Scarritt 1989. 'Minorities at risk: A global survey', *Human Rights Quarterly*, 11, 4, pp. 375-405.

Gurrutxaga, Ander 1985. *El código nacionalista vasco durante el franquismo*, Barcelona; Anthropos.

— 1990. *La refundación del nacionalismo vasco*, Bilbao: Servicio Editorial Universidad del País Vasco.

Halimi, Gisele 1971. *Le procès de Burgos*, Paris: Gallimard (Span. transl. *El Proceso de Burgos*, Caracas: Monte Avila, 1976).

Hall, Jacqueline 1979. 'Immigration et nationalisme en Catalogne', *Perspectiva Social*, 14, pp. 93-136.

Hannum, Hurst 1990. *Autonomy, Sovereignty, and Self-Determination: The Accommodation of Conflicting Rights*, Philadelphia: University of Pennsylvania Press.

Hansen, Edward C. 1977. *Rural Catalonia Under the Franco Regime: The Fate of Regional Culture since the Spanish Civil War*, Cambridge University Press.

Harff, Barbara, and Ted Gurr 1989. 'Victims of the state: Genocide, politicide and group repression since 1945', *International Review of Victimology*, 1, 1, pp. 23-41.

Harrison R.J. 1977. *The Origins of Modern Industrialism in the Basque Country*, Dept of Economic and Social History, University of Sheffield.

Haugen, Einar 1966. 'Dialect, Language, Nation,' *American Anthropologist*, 68, pp. 922-35.

Heiberg, Marianne 1979. 'External and internal nationalism: The case of the Spanish Basques' in Raymond L. Hall (ed.) *Ethnic Autonomy. Comparative Dynamics*, New York: Pergamon, pp. 180-200.

— 1989. *The Making of the Basque Nation*, Cambridge University Press.

Hennessy, Charles Alistair Michael 1962. *The Federal Republic in Spain*, Oxford: Clarendon Press.

Hermet, Guy 1986. *Los católicos en la España franquista. Vol. II. Crónica de una dictadura*, Madrid: CIS.

Hernàndez, Francesc 1983. *La identitad nacional en Cataluña*, Barcelona: Vincens Vives.

Hills, George 1970. *Spain*, New York: Praeger.

— 1980. 'Basque autonomy: will it be enough?', *The World Today*, 36, 9, pp. 356-60.

Hobsbawn, Eric J. 1994. 'Nation, state, ethnicity, religion: Transformations of identity' in Proceedings of the International Conference on Nationalism in Europe: Past and Present. Santiago de Compostela University Press.

— and Terence Ranger (eds) 1983. *The Invention of Tradition*, Cambridge University Press.

Hollyman, John L. 1976. 'Basque revolutionary separatism: ETA' in Paul Preston (ed.), *Spain in Crisis: the Evolution and Decline of the Franco Regime*, Hassocks, Sussex: Harvester Press, pp. 212-33.

Hooper, John 1986. *The Spaniards*, Harmondsworth: Penguin.

— 1985. *Ethnic Groups in Conflict*, Berkeley, CA: University of California Press.

Hroch, Miroslav 1985. *Social preconditions of national revival in Europe: a comparative analysis of the social composition of patriotic groups among smaller European nations*, Cambridge University Press.

Humboldt, Wilhelm Freiherr von 1935. *Examen de las investigaciones sobre los aborígenes de España mediante la lengua vasca*, San Sebastián: Impr. de la Diputación de Guipúzcoa (2nd edn).

Hutchinson, John 1987. *The Dynamics of Cultural Nationalism: The Gaelic Revival and the Creation of the Irish Nation State*, London: Geo. Allen & Unwin.

— 1992. 'Moral innovators and the politics of regeneration: the distinctive role of cultural nationalists in nation-building', *International Journal of Comparative Sociology*, vol. 32, 1-2, pp. 101-117.

Ibarra Güell, Pedro 1987. *La evolución estratégica de ETA. De la 'guerra revolucionaria' (1963) a la negociación (1987)*, Donostia: Kriselu.

— 1994 'La evolución, a traves de su discurso, del nacionalismo vasco radical' in Proceedings of the International Conference on Nationalism in Europe: Past and Present. Santiago de Compostela University Press.

Ibarruri, Dolores 1976. *They Shall Not Pass: The Autobiography of La Pasionaria*, New York: International Publishers.

Ibarz, Merce 1981. *Breu història d'ETA, 1959-1979*, Barcelona: La Magrana.

Ibarzábal, Eugenio 1978. *50 años de nacionalismo vasco, 1928-1978*. San Sebastián: Ediciones Vascas/Argitaletxea.

— 1980. 'Sabino Arana y su herencia', *Muga*, I, 4, pp. 2-29.

Ibero, Evangelista de 1957. *Ami Vasco*, 3rd edn. Buenos Aires: Ekin (1st edn 1906).

Ille, Karl 1991. 'Discorso politico e glottopolitica all'epoca fascista: fascismo-nazismo-franchismo-Vichy', *Lingua e Stile*, XXVI, 1, pp. 17-34.

Izard, Miquel 1986. 'Cultura popular enfront de cultura oficial' in Termes et al., *Catalanisme. Història, Política i Cultura*, Barcelona: L'Avenç/Xarxa Cultural, pp. 39-46.

— and Borja de Riquer 1983. *Conèixer la història de Catalunya*, vol. 4: *Del segle XIX fins a 1931*, Barcelona: Vicens Vives.

Iztueta, Paulo 1981. *Sociología del fenómeno contestatario del clero vasco (1940-1975)*, Zarauz: Elkar.

Jacob, James E. 1994. *Hills of Conflict: Basque Nationalism in France*, Reno: University of Nevada Press.

Jardí, Enric 1977. *Francesc Macià, el camí de la llibertat*, Barcelona: Aymá.

Jáuregui Bereciartu, Gurutz 1981. *Ideología y estrategia política de ETA. Análisis de su evolución entre 1958 y 1968*, Madrid: Siglo XXI.

— 1986. 'National identity and political violence in the Basque Country', *European Journal of Political Research*, 14, pp. 587-605.

— 1993. *The Decline of the Nation State*, Reno: University of Nevada Press.

Jofre, P. 1978. 'Precedents de la immigració als Països Catalans', *Quaderns d'Allibrament*, 2/3, pp. 9-16.

Johnson, Chalmers A. 1982. *Revolutionary Change*, Stanford University Press (1st edn Boston: Little, Brown, 1966).

Johnston, Hank 1991. *Tales of Nationalism. Catalonia 1939-1979*, New Brunswick, NJ: Rutgers University Press.

— 1992 'The comparative study of nationalism: Six pivotal themes from the Baltic states', *Journal of Baltic Studies*, XXIII, 2, pp. 95-104.

Jones, Norman L. 1976. 'The Catalan question since the Civil War' in Paul Preston (ed.), *Spain in Crisis: the Evolution and Decline of the Franco Regime*, Hassocks, Sussex: Harvester Press, pp. 234-67.

Jorba, Manuel *et al.* 1992. 'Actes del Col.loqui Internacional sobre la Renaixença (10-22 de desembre de 1984)', *Estudis Universitaris Catalans*, XXVII. Barcelona: Curial/Edicions Catalanes.

Juaristi, Jon 1987. *El linaje de Aitor*. Madrid: Taurus.

Kaplan, Temma 1992. *Red City, Blue Period: Social Movements in Picasso's Barcelona*, Berkeley, CA: University of California Press.

Kaskla, Edgar 1992 'Five nationalisms: Estonian nationalism in comparative perspective', *Journal of Baltic Studies*, XXIII, 2, pp. 167-78.

Keating, Michael 1988 *State and Regional Nationalism. Territorial Politics and the European State*, New York: Harvester-Wheatsheaf.

Kedourie, Elie 1993. *Nationalism*, London: Hutchinson (1st edn 1966).

Kellas, James G. 1991. *The Politics of Nationalism and Ethnicity*, Basingstoke: Macmillan.

Khleif, Bud B. 1979. 'Language as an ethnic boundary in Welsh-English relations', *International Journal of the Sociology of Language*, 20, pp. 59-73.

Kimmel, Michael S. 1989. 'Defensive revolutionaries: The moral and political economy of Basque, Breton and Québécois nationalism', *Research in Social Movements, Conflict and Change*, 11, pp. 109-28.

King, Alan R. 1994. *The Basque Language: A Practical Introduction*, Reno: University of Nevada Press.

Kloss, Heinz 1967 'Bilingualism and nationalism', *Journal of Social Issues*, XXIII, 2, pp. 39-47.

Kaudsen, Jonathan B. 1986. *Justus Moser and the German Enlightenment*, Cambridge University Press.

Kohn, Hans 1968. 'Nationalism' in David L. Sills (ed.), *International*

Encyclopedia of the Social Sciences, New York: Macmillan and Free Press, pp. 63-70.

Korn, David A. 1989. 'State terrorism: a Spanish Watergate?', *Freedom at Issue*, 105, pp. 15-20.

Kreminitz, Georg 1993. *Multilingüisme social*, Barcelona: Edicions 62.

Krutwig, Federico 1963. *Vasconia. Estudio dialéctico de una nacionalidad*, Buenos Aires: Narbait (first published in 1963 under pseudonym of Sarrailh de Ihartza).

Lafont, Robert 1977. 'Sobre el procés de patoisització', *Treballs de Sociolingüística Catalana*, no. 1, pp. 131-36.

Lagasse, Marc 1951. 'Le "Séparatisme Basque" est-il un existentialisme?', *Cahiers Internationaux d'Etudes Humanistes* (Biarritz, unspecified issue).

Lahusen, Christian 1993.'The aesthetic of radicalism: the relationship between punk and the patriotic nationalist movement of the Basque country', *Popular music*, 12, 3, pp. 263ff.

Laitin, David 1989. 'Linguistic revival: Politics and culture in Catalonia', *Comparative Studies in Society and History*, 31, 2, pp. 297-317.

—1992. 'Language normalization in Estonia and Catalonia', *Journal of Baltic Studies*, XXIII, 2, pp. 149-66.

Lamarca, Henri 1976. *La danza folkórica vasca como vehículo de la ideología nacionalista*, Baiona: Elkar (Collection Oldar).

Lannon, Frances 1987. *Privilege, Persecution and Prophecy: The Catholic Church in Spain, 1875-1975*, Oxford: Clarendon Press.

Lancaster, Thomas D. 1985. 'Comparative Nationalism: the Basques in Spain and France', paper presented at the European Consortium for Political Research, 'Centre-Periphery Structure and the Revival of Peripheral Nationalism in Western Democracies' Barcelona, 25-30 March 1985.

Larronde, Jean-Claude 1977. *El nacionalismo vasco: Su orígen y su ideología en la obra de Sabino Arana-Goiri*, San Sebastián: Txertoa.

Lasa, J. Ignacio 1968. *Sobre la enseñanza primaria en el País Vasco*, San Sebastián: Auñamendi.

Lasagabaster, Jesús María (ed.) 1990. *Contemporary Basque Fiction*, Reno: University of Nevada Press.

Legarreta, Dorothy 1985. 'Basque refugee children as expatriates: Political catalysts in Europe and America' in William A. Douglass (ed.), *Basque Politics: A Case Study in Ethnic Nationalism*, Reno, Nevada: Associated Faculty Press and Basque Studies Program.

Lenski, Gerhard E. 1966, 1984. *Power and Privilege: A Theory of Social Stratification*, Chapel Hill, NC: University of North Carolina Press.

Letamendia, Pierre 1987. *Nationalismes au Pays Basque*, Presses Universitaires de Bordeaux.

Linz, Juan J. 1973. 'Early state-building and late peripheral nationalism against the state: the case of Spain' in S.N. Eisenstadt and Stein

Rokkan (eds), *Building States and Nations*, Beverly Hills: Sage, vol. 2, pp. 32-116.

— 1975. 'Politics in a Multilingual Society with a Dominant World Language: The Case of Spain' in Jean-Guy Savard and Richard Vigneault (eds), *Les états multilingues. Problèmes et solutions/Multilingual Political Systems: Problems and Solutions*, Quebec: Presses de I'Université Laval, pp. 367-444.

— 1979. 'Europe's southern frontier: Evolving trends towards what?', *Daedalus*, vol. 108, no. 1, pp. 175-209.

— 1985. 'From primordialism to nationalism' in Edward A. Tiryakian and Ronald Rogowski (eds), *New Nationalisms of the Developed West*, Boston: Allen & Unwin, pp. 203-53.

— 1986. *Conflicto en Euskadi*, Madrid: Espasa Calpe.

Llera ramo, Francisco José 1985. *Postfranquismo y fuerzas políticas en Euskadi. Sociología electoral del País Vasco*, Bilbao: Servicio Editorial Universidad del País Vasco.

Llobera, Josep R. 1983. 'The idea of *Volksgeist* in the formation of Catalan nationalist ideology', *Ethnic and Racial Studies*, vol. 6, no, 3, pp. 332-50.

— 1989 'Catalan national identity: the dialectics of the past and present' in Elizabeth Tonkin, Maryon McDonald and Malcolm Chapman (eds), *History and Ethnicity*, London: Routledge.

Llorens i Vila, Jordi 1992. ' L'associacionisme en els orígens del catalanisme polític', *Revista de Catalunya*, no. 60, pp. 39-49.

— 1993. *El federalisme català*, Barcelona: Barcanova.

López Antón, José Javier 1990. 'Juan de Iturralde y Suit (1840-1909)', *Muga*, vol. XI, no. 75, pp, 26-37.

López Garrido, Diego 1982. *La Guardia Civil y los orígenes del Estado centralista*, Barcelona: Crítica.

Lorés, Jaume 1980. 'Aproximació al pujolisme', *Taula de Canvi*, nos 23-24, pp. 5-37.

— 1985. *La transició a Catalunya (1977-1984), El pujolisme i els altres*, Barcelona: Empúries.

Loyer, Barbara 1990. 'Les nationalismes basque et catalan. Des représentations géopolitiques différents', *Hérodote*, no. 57, pp. 27-50.

McCarthy, M.J. 1975. ' Catalan *Modernisme*, Messianism and Nationalist Myths', *Bulletin of Hispanic Studies*, vol. 52, 379-95.

MacClancy, Jeremy 1988. 'The culture of radical Basque nationalism', *Anthropology Today*, vol. 4, no. 5, pp. 17-9.

McDonogh, Gary W. 1986. *Good Families in Barcelona*, Princeton University Press.

Mackay, David 1985 *Modern Architecture in Barcelona*, London: Anglo-Catalan Society.

Maeztu, Ramiro de 1981. *Artículos desconocidos 1897-1904*, Madrid: Editorial Castalia.

Magas, Branka 1993. *The Destruction of Yugoslavia. Tracking the Break-Up 1980-92*, London: Verso:

Maluquer i Sostre, Joaquim 1963. *L'assimilation des immigrés en Catalogne*, Geneva: Droz.

— 1965. *Població i societat a l'area catalana*, Barcelona: Editorial A-C.

Manent, Albert 1976. *La literatura catalana a l'exili*, Barcelona: Curial.

Mansvelt Beck, Jan 1991. 'Basque and Catalan nationalisms in comparative perspective' in Hans Van Amersfoort and Hans Knippenberg (eds), *States and Nations: The Rebirth of the 'Nationalities Question' in Europe*, Amsterdam: Instituut voor Sociale Geografie.

— 1992. 'Ethnic minorities and post-Franco territorial administration in Spain: Changes in the linguistic landscape', paper presented at the Third ISSEI Conference on 'European Integration and the European Mind', 24-29 Aug. 1992, Aalborg University, Denmark.

Mañé i Flaquer, Joan 1900. *El regionalismo*, Barcelona: Imprenta Barcelonesa (1st edn 1887).

Maragall, Joan 1929-55. *Obres completes de Joan Maragall*, 25 vols, Barcelona: Sala Pares.

Marcet, Joan 1987. *Convergencia Democratica de Catalunya. El partido y el movimiento político*, Madrid: CIS/Siglo XXI.

Marfany, Joan Ll, 1987. '"Al damunt dels nostres cants. . ." Nacionalisme, modernisme i cant coral a la Barcelona del final de segle', *Recerques*, 19, pp. 85-113.

Marí, Isidor 1987. 'Comunitat lingüística i comunitat nacional', in *El nacionalisme català a la fi del segle XX*, Vic: Fundació Universitaria de Vic/Eumo Editional, pp. 27-36.

Mar-Molinero, Clare 1989. 'The teaching of Catalan in Catalonia', *Journal of Multilingual and Multicultural Development*, vol. 10, no. 4, pp. 307-26.

Martin, David 1978. *A General Theory of Secularization*, Oxford: Basil Blackwell.

Martínez-Peñuela, Araceli 1989. *Antecedentes y primeros pasos del Nacionalismo Vasco en Navarra: 1878-1981*, Pamplona: Gobierno de Navarra-Departamento de Educación y Cultura.

Massot i Muntaner, Josep 1978. *L'Església catalana entre la guerra i la postguerra*, Barcelona: Rafael Dalmau.

— 1986. 'Cristianisme i catalanisme' in Termes *et al.*, *Catalanisme: Història. Política i Cultura*, Barcelona: L'Avenç/Xarxa Cultural, pp. 179-192.

— (ed.) 1987. *La persecució religiosa de 1936 a Catalunya. Testimoniatges*, Barcelona: Publicacions de l'Abadia de Montserrat.

Mayo, Patricia Elton 1974. *The Roots of Identity: Three National Movements* in *Contemporary European Politics, Wales, Euzkadi and Brittany*, London: Allen Lane.

Meaker, Gerald H. 1974. *The Revolutionary Left in Spain. 1914-1923*, Stanford University Press.

Medhurst, Kenneth 1987. *The Basques and the Catalans*, London: Minority Rights Groups (1st edn 1977).

— 1982. 'The Basques and Basque Nationalism' in Colin Williams (ed.), *National separatism*, Cardiff: University of Wales Press, pp. 235-61.

Melià, Josep 1967. *Els Mallorquins*, Palma de Mallorca: Daedalus.

— 1968. *La Renaixença a Mallorca*, Palma de Mallorca: Daedalus.

Mees, Ludger 1991. *Entre nación y clase. El nacionalismo vasco y su base social en perspectiva comparativa*, Bilbao: Fundación Sabino Arana.

— 1992. *Nacionalismo vasco, movimento obrero y cuestión social (1903-1923)*, Bilbao: Fundación Sabino Arana.

Mercadé, Francesc 1982. *Cataluña: Intelectuales, políticos y cuestión nacional*, Barcelona: Península.

—, Francesc Hernàndez and Benjamin Oltra 1983. *Once tesis sobre la cuestión nacional en España*, Barcelona: Anthropos.

Michelena (Mitxelena), Luis 1960. *Historia de la literatura vasca*, Madrid: Minotauro.

Miguel, Armando de 1974. 'Estructura social e inmigración en el País Vasconavarro', *Papers*, 3, 249-73.

Miguélez, Faustino 1984. 'Les Jornades d'Estudi Catalunya-Euskadi/Katalunia-Euskadi ikasketarako ihardunaldiak', *Papers*, nos 22-23, pp. 11-26.

— 1987, 'Immigració i mobilitat social' in *Visió de Catalunya. El canvi i la reconstrucció nacional des de la perspectiva sociològica*, Barcelona: Diputació de Barcelona, 1987, pp. 303-20.

— and Carlota Solé 1987. *Classes socials i poder polític a Catalunya*, Barcelona: Promociones Publicaciones Universitarias.

Minobis, Monstserrat 1988. *Aureli Ma. Escarré, Abad de Montserrat*, Barcelona: Edicions 62.

Miquel i Vergés, Josep M. 1944. *Els primers romàntics dels països de llengua catalana*, Mexico: Biblioteca Catalana (repr. Barcelona: Leteradura, 1979).

Miralles, Melchor, and Ricardo Arques 1990. *Amedeo. El estado contra ETA*, Barcelona: Plaza & Janés/Cambio 16.

Molas, Isidre 1972. *Lliga catalana: un estudi de estasiología*, 2 vols, Barcelona: Edicions 62.

Molas, Joaquim, Manuel Jorba and Antonia Tayadella (eds) 1984. *La Renaixença: Fonts per al seu estudi, 1815-1877*, Departament de Literatura Catalana de la Universitat de Barcelona/Departament de Filologia Hispanica de la Universitat Autonoma de Barcelona.

Molinero, Carme, and Pere Ysàs 1981. *L'oposició antifeixista a Catalunya 1939-1950*, Barcelona: La Magrana.

Monné, Enric, and Lluïsa Selga 1991. *Història de la Crida a la Solidaritat*, Barcelona: Edicions La Campana.

Morán, Gregorio 1982. *Los españoles que dejaron de serlo. Euskadi 1937-1981*, Barcelona: Planeta.

Morento, Luis 1988. 'Identificación dual y autonomía política: Los casos de Escocia y Cataluña', *Reis*, 42, pp. 155-74.

Muñoz, Xavier 1979. 'Història d'un moviment polític', *Serra d'Or*, 327, pp. 23-6.

— 1990. *De dreta a esquerra. Memòries polítiques*, Barcelona: Edicions 62.

Murgades, Josep 1986. 'El Noucentsime' in Termes el al., *Catalanisme. Història, Política i Cultura*, Barcelona: L'Avenç/Xarxa Cultural, pp. 99-114.

Nadal, Joaquim et al. 1986. *El Memorial de Greuges i el catalanisme polític*, Barcelona: La Magrana/Institut Municipal d'Història.

Nadal, Josep Ma. 1987. 'El català en els segles XVI i XVII', *L'Avenç*, 40. pp. 24-31.

Nadal, Jordi, and Emili Giralt 1960. *La population catalane de 1553 à 1717: L'immigration française et les autres facteurs de son développement*, Paris: SEVPEN.

Nagel, Klaus Jürgen 1987. 'Vasquismo y catalanismo hasta 1923. El catalanismo de izquierda y Euskadi' in Manuel Tuñon de Lara (ed.) *Gernika: 50 Años Despues (1937-1987). Nacionalismo. República, Guerra Civil*, San Sebastián: Servicio Editorial Universidad del País Vasco.

— 1991. *Arbeiterschaft und nationale Frage in Katalonien zwischen 1998 und 1923*, Saarbrücken: Breitenbach.

Ninyoles, Rafael Lluís 1969. *Conflicte linguistic valencià*, Valencia: Tres i Quatre.

— 1977. *Cuatro idiomas para un Estado*, Madrid: Cambio 16.

Nogué i Font, Joan 1991. *Els nacionalismes i el territori*, Barcelona: El Llamp.

Noyes, Dorothy 1992. 'Contesting the body politic: Spectacle and participation in the Patum of Berga' in Kataryne Young (ed.), *Bodylore*, Memphis: University of Tennessee Press.

Nuñez, Luiz C. 1977. *Opresión y defensa del euskera*, San Sebastián: Txertoa.

Nuñez Seixas, Xosé Ma. 1992. 'Historical Research on Regionalism and peripheral nationalism in Spain: A reappraisal, *EUI Working Papers in European Cultural Studies*, 92/6, Florence: European University Institute.

— 1993. *Historiographical Approaches to Nationalism in Spain*. Saarbrücken: Breitenbach.

Olabarri Cortázar, Ignacio 1981. 'La cuestión regional en España 1808-

1939' in Various Authors, *La españa de las Autonomías*, vol. 1, Madrid: Espasa-Calpe, pp. 111-99.

Ortzi (pseudonym of Francisco Letamendia) 1975. *Historia de Euskadi. El nacionalsmo vasco y ETA*, Paris: Ruedo Ibérico.

Otazu, Alfonso 1973 *El igualitarismo vasco: mito o realidad*, San Sebastián: Txertoa.

Ott, Sandra 1981. *The Circle of Mountains: A Basque Shepherding Community*, Oxford: Clarendon Press.

Pabón, Jesús 1952. *Cambó. 1876-1918*, vol. 1 (of 3) Barcelona: Alpha.

Parsons, Talcott 1975. 'Some theoretical considerations on the nature and trends of change of ethnicity' in N. Glazer and D. Moynihan (eds), *Ethnicity. Theory and experience*. Cambridge, MA: Harvard University Press, pp. 53-83.

— 1991. *The Social System*, London: Routledge (1st edn 1952).

Pascual, 'Angels and Jordi Cardelús 1987. 'El marc social dels desplaçaments de població a Catalunya' in *Visió de Catalunya. El canvi i la reconstrucció nacional des de la perspectiva sociològica*, Barcelona: Diputació de Barcelona, pp. 331-7.

— 1990. *Migració i història personal. Investigació sobre la mobilitat social des de la perspectiva del retorn*, Barcelona: Ed. 1990.

Payne, Stanley G. 1971. 'Catalan and Basque Nationalism', *Journal of Contemporary History*, vol. VI, no. 1, pp. 15-51.

— 1973. '*History of Spain and Portugal*, 2 vols, Madison: University of Wisconsin Press.

— 1975. *Basque Nationalism*, Reno: University of Nevada Press.

— 1976. 'Regional nationalism: The Basques and Catalans' in William T. Salisbury and James D. Theberge (eds), *Spain in the 1970s: Economics. Social Structure. Foreign Policy*, New York: Praeger.

Peers, Edgar Allison 1937. *Catalonia Infelix*, London: Methuen

Pérez-Agote, Alfonso 1982. 'Problemas de legitimación del Estado franquista en el País Vasco' in de Aberasturi and J.C. Jiménez (eds), *Estudios de Historia Contemporánea del País Vasco*, San Sebastián: Haranburu, pp. 279 ff.

— 1984. *La reproducción del nacionalismo. El caso vasco*, Madrid: CIS.

— 1986. 'The role of religion in the definition of a symbolic conflict. Religion and the Basque problem', *Social Compass*, vol. 33, no. 4, pp. 419-35.

— 1987. *El nacionalismo vasco a la salida del franquismo*, Madrid: CIS.

— 1990. *Los lugares sociales de la religión: La secularización en el País Vasco*, Madrid: CIS.

— 1993. 'Silence collectif et violence politique. La radicalisation sociale du nationalisme basque, *Espaces et Sociétés*, 70-71, pp. 57-72.

—, J.A. Garmendia and R. Parra 1982. *Abertzales y vascos*, Madrid: Akal.

Petherbridge-Hernández, Patricia 1990. 'The recatalanisation of Catalonia's schools', *Language, Culture & Curriculum*, vol. 3, no. 2, pp. 97-107.

Pi i Margall, Francesc 1972. *Las nacionalidades*, Madrid: Edicusa (1st edn 1876).

Pinilla de las Heras, Esteban 1973. *Immigracó i mobilitat social a Catalunya*, fasc. 1, Barcelona: ICESB.

— 1979. *Estudios sobre cambio social y estructuras sociales en Cataluña*, Madrid: CIS.

Pi i Sunyer, Carles 1929. *L'aptitud econòmica de Catalunya*, 2 vols, Barcelona: Barcino.

— 1975. *La República y la guerra. Memorias de un político catalán*, Mexico City: Oasis.

Pi-Sunyer, Oriol 1971. 'The Maintenance of Ethnic Identity in Catalonia' in Pi-Sunyer (ed.), *The Limits of Integration: Ethnicity and Nationalism in Modern Europe*, Amherst, MA: Dep of Anthropology Research Reports, no. 9.

— 1980. 'Dimensions of Catalan nationalism' in Charles R. Foster (ed.), *Nations without a State*, New York: Praeger

— 1983. *Nationalism and Societal Integration: A Focus on Catalonia*, Amherst, MA: Program in Latin American Studies, Occasional Papers, no. 15.

— 1985. 'Catalan Nationalism: Some Theoretical and Historical Considerations' in Edward A Tiryakian and Ronald Rogowski (eds), *New Nationalisms of the Developed West*, Boston, MA: Allen & Unwin, pp. 254-76.

Poblet, Josep Maria 1973. *Anselm Clavé i la seva època, 1824-1879*, Barcelona: Dopesa.

Pons Prades, Eduardo 1977. *Guerrillas españolas. 1936-1960*, Barcelona: Planeta.

Prat de la Riba, Enric 1978. *La nacionalitat catalana*, Barcelona: Edicions 62/Caixa de Pensions (1st edn Barcelona, 1906).

— and Pere Muntanyola 1894. *Compendi de la Doctrina Catalanista*, Sabadell.

Preston, Paul (ed.) 1976. *Spain in crisis: The evolution and decline of the Franco regime*, Hassocks, Sussex: Harvester Press.

— 1986. *The Triumph of Democracy in Spain*, London: Methuen.

— 1993. *Franco*, London: HarperCollins.

Pujadas, Joan J. 1983. 'Antropologia catalana o antropologia a Catalunya. Tradicions i nous enfocaments', *Arxiu d'Etnografia de Catalunya*, no. 3, pp. 71-98.

— *et al.* 1988. 'Una bibliografia comentada sobre etnicidad y nacionalismo', *Actas del III Congreso de Antropología*, Donostia/San Sebastián.

Pujol, Jordi 1966. *La immigració, problema i esperança de Catalunya*, Barcelona: Nova Terra.

— 1988. (ed. Josep Faulí) *El pensament polític de Jordi Pujol (1980-1987)*, Barcelona: Planeta.

Racionero, Lluís 1985. *Raimon, o, El seny fantastic*, Barcelona: Laia.

Ramírez Goicoechea, Eugenia 1991. *De jóvenes y sus identidades. Socioantropología de la etnicidad en Euskadi*, Madrid: CIS.

Read, Jan 1978. *The Catalans*, London: Faber and Faber.

Rebagliato, Joan 1978., 'L'evolució demogràfica entre el 1940 i el 1975', in Josep Ma. Salrach (ed.), *Història de Catalunya*, vol. 6, Barcelona: Salvat.

Rebull, Nolasc 1976. *Als orígens de la sardana*, Barcelona: Rafael Dalmau.

Recolons, Lluís 1987. 'Les migracions a Catalunya en un nou periode demogràfic' in *Visió de Catalunya. El canvi i la reconstrucció nacional des de la perspectiva sociològica*, Barcelona: Diputació de Barcelona, 1987, pp. 257-302.

Regalado García, Antonio 1990. *El laberinto de la razón: Ortega y Heidegger*, Madrid: Alianza

Reglá, Joan 1956. *Els Virreis de Catalunya. Els segles XVI i XVII*, Barcelona: Teide.

Reixach, Modest 1975. *La llengua del poble*, Barcelona: Nova Terra.

— 1986. *Coneixement i ús de la llengua catalana a la provincia de Barcelona*, Barcelona: Departament de Cultura/Generalitat de Catalunya.

Renart, Joaquim 1992. *L'Orfeo Català que he viscut*, Sabadell: AUSA.

Ribó, Rafael 1977. *Sobre el fet nacional. Catalunya, Països Catalans, Estat Espanyol*, Barcelona: L'Avenç.

Riggs, Fred W. 1986. 'What is ethnic? What is national? Let's turn the tables', *Canadian Review of Studies in Nationalism*, vol. 13, no. 1, pp. 111-23.

— 1991(a). 'Ethnicity, nationalism, race, minority: A semantic/onomantic exercise', part 1; *International Sociology*, vol. 6, no. 3, pp. 281-305; part 2, ibid., vol. 6, no. 4, pp. 443-63.

Riquer, Borja de 1977. *Lliga Regionalista: la burguesia catalana i el nacionalisme (1898-1904)*, Barcelona: Edicions 62.

— 1979. *Regionalistes i nacionalistes (1898-1931)*, Barcelona: Dopesa.

— 1989. 'Un país després d'una guerra (1939-1959)', in Pierre Vilar (ed.), *Història de Catalunya*, vol. VII: *El franquisme i la transició democràtica. 1939-1988*, Barcelona: Edicions 62, pp. 425-73.

— 1990. 'Rebuig, passivitat i suport. Actituds politiques catalanes devant el primer franquisme (1939-1950)' in Javier Tusell, Alicia Alted and Abdón Mateos (eds), *La oposición al régimen de Franco. Estado de la cuestión y metodología de la investigación*, Madrid: UNED/Departamento de Historia Contemporánea.

— *et al.* (eds) 1985. *Industrialización y nacionalismo: Análisis comparativos*, Barcelona: Servei de Publicacions de la UAB (Coloquio Vasco-Catalán de Historia, 1: Sitges, Spain, 1982).

— and Joan B. Culla 1989. 'Epíleg: De la transició democràtica a l'autonomia política (1976-1988)', in Pierre Vilar (ed.), *Història de Catalunya*, vol. VII: *El franquisme i la transició democràtica, 1939-1988*, Barcelona: Edicions 62.

Rohrer, Judith Campbell 1984. *'Artistic Regionalism and Architecural Politics in Barcelona, c. 1880-1906'*, unpubl. Ph.D thesis, Columbia University.

Roig, Montserrat 1992. *Els catalans als camps nazis*, Barcelona: Edicions 62 (1st ed 1977).

Roig Rosich, Josep Ma. 1992. *La dictadura de Primo de Rivera a Catalunya. Un assaig de repressió cultural*, Monstserrat: Publicacions de l'Abadia de Montserrat.

Roiz Célix, Miguel 1984. 'Los limites de la modernización en la estructura social de Catalunya y Euzkadi', *Revista Española de Investigación Sociologica*, no. 25, pp. 199-212.

Rosenthal, David H. 1991. *Postwar Catalan Poetry*, Lewisburg: Bucknell University Press.

Ross, Christopher John 1993. 'Euskadiko Ezkerra (Basque Left). The Development of a Left-Wing Nationalist Party in a Context of System Change' unpubl. Ph.D. thesis, Dept of Politics, University of Leeds.

Rossinyol, Jaume 1974. *Le problème national catlane*, Barcelona: Minerva.

— 1982. *Nacionalisme i Federalisme*, Barcelona: Edicions 62/La Caixa (1st edn Barcelona, 1917).

Rovira i Virgili, Antoni 1930. *El nacionalismo Catalán*, Barcelona: Minerva.

— 1982. *Nacionalisme i Federalisme*, Barcelona: Edicions 62/La Caixa (1st edn Barcelona: Societat Catalana d'Edicions, 1917).

Rüdig, Wolfgang 1990. *Anti-Nuclear Movements: A World Survey of Opposition to Nuclear Energy*, Harlow: Longman.

Sabater, Ernest 1984. 'An approach to the situation of the Catalan language: social and educational use', *Internal Journal of the Sociology of Language*, no. 47, pp. 29-41.

Sàez, Armand 1980. 'Catalunya, gresol o explotadora? Notes sobre exploitació i creixement' in *Immigració i reconstrucció nacional a Catalunya*, Barcelona: Editorial Blaume/Fundació Jaume Bofill.

Sahlins, Peter 1989. *Boundaries: The Making of France and Spain in the Pyrenees*, Berkeley: University of California Press.

Sallés, Anna 1987. *Quan Catalunya era d'esquerra*, Barcelona: Edicions 62.

Salvi, Sergio 1978. *Matria e patria*, Firenze: Vallecchi.

Samsó, Joan 1990. 'El mecenatge cultural de postguerra. Benèfica Minerva', *Revista de Catalunya*, no. 37, pp. 41-52.

— 1991. 'Josep Benet i la recuperació nacional: l'esbart Verdaguer, la Comissió Abat Oliva i Miramar' in *Miscel.lània d'homenatge a Josep Benet*, Barcelona: Publicacions de l'Abadia de Montserrat.

— 1992. 'La cultura catalana. Entre la clandestinitat i la represa pública, Barcelona, 1939-1951', unpubl. doctoral thesis, Universitat de Barcelona.

Sanchis Guarner, Manuel 1972. *La llengua dels valencians*, València: Eliseu Climent.

San Sebastián, Koldo 1984. *Historia del Partido Nacionalista Vasco*, San Sebastián: Txertoa.

Sarasola, Ibon 1976. *Historia social de la literatura vasca*, Madrid: Akal.

Sauret, Joan 1979. *L'exili polític català*. Barcelona: Pora.

Scott, Jr, George M. 1990. 'A resynthesis of the primordial and circumstantial approaches to ethnic group solidarity: Towards an explanatory mode', *Ethnic and Racial Studies*, vol. 13, no. 2, pp. 148-71.

Serra i Garcia Antoni 1968. *Història de l'escoltisme català*, Barcelona: Editorial Bruguera.

Shafir, Gershon 1992. 'Relative overdevelopment and alternative paths to nationalism: a comparative study of Catalonia and the Baltic republics', *Journal of Baltic Studies*, vol. XXIII, no.2, pp. 105-20.

Sierra Bustamante, Ramón 1941. *Euzkadi. De Sabino Arana a José Antonio de Aguirre*. Madrid: Editora Nacional.

Silva, Milton M. da 1975. 'Modernization and ethnic conflict: The case of the Basques', *Comparative Politics*, vol. 7, no.2, pp. 227-51.

Silver, Philip W. 1988. *Nacionalismos y transición. Euskadi. Catalunya. España*, San Sebastián: Txertoa.

Simon, Antoni 1993. 'Patriotisme i nacionalisme a la Catalunya moderna. Mites, tradicions i consciències collectives', *L'Avenç*, no. 167, pp. 8-16.

Smith, Anthony D. 1971. *Theories of Nationalism*, London: Duckworth.

— 1981a. *The Ethnic Revival*, Cambridge University Press.

— 1981b. 'War and ethnicity: the role of warfare in the formation, self-image and cohesion of ethnic communities', *Ethnic and Racial Studies*, vol. 4, no. 4, pp. 375-97.

— 1986. *The Ethnic Origins of Nations*, London: Basil Blackwell.

— 1991. *National Identity*, Harmondsworth: Penguin.

— 1992. 'Chosen peoples: why ethnic groups survive', *Ethnic and Racial Studies*, vol. 15, no. 3, pp. 436-59.

— 1993a. 'A Europe of nations – or the nation of Europe?', *Journal of Peace Research*, vol. 30, no. 2, pp. 129-35.

— 1993b. 'Ethnic election and cultural identity', *Ethnic Groups*, vol. 10, no. 1/3, pp. 3 ff.

Smolicz, Jerzy J. 1981. 'Core values and cultural identity', *Ethnic and Racial Studies*, vol. 4, no. 1, pp. 75-90.

— 1988. 'Tradition, core values and intercultural development in plural societies', *Ethnic and Racial Studies*, vol. 11, no. 4, pp. 387-410.

Solà, Pere 1978. *Els ateneus obrers i la cultura popular a Catalunya (1900-1939)*, Barcelona: La Magrana.

Solé, Carlota 1981. *La integración sociocultural de los inmigrantes en Cataluña*, Madrid: Centro de Investigaciones Sociologicas.

— 1982. *Los inmigrantes en la sociedad y en la cultura catalana*, Barcelona: Península.

— 1986. 'Immigració a Catalunya', *Perspectiva social*, no. 23.

Solé i Sabaté, Josep Ma. 1986. *La repressió franquista a Catalunya. 1938-1953*, Barcelona: Edicions 62.

— (ed.) 1984. *Cataluña durante el Franquismo*, Biblioteca La Vanguardia.

Solozábal, Juan José 1975. *El primer nacionalismo vasco*, Madrid: Túcar.

Southworth, Herbert Rutledge 1977. *Guernica! A Study of Journalism, Diplomacy, Propaganda, and History*, Berkeley: University of California Press (translation of *La destrucción de Guernica, 26 Avril 1937*, Paris: Ruedo Iberico, 1974).

Strubell i Trueta, Miquel 1981. *Llengua i població a Catalunya*, Barcelona: La Magrana.

— and Josep Maria Romani 1986. *Perspectives de la llengua catalana a l'àrea barcelonina. Comentaris a una enquesta.* Barcelona: Departament de Cultura de la Generalitat de Catalunya/Institut de Sociolingüística Catalana.

Sullivan, John 1988. *ETA and Basque Nationalism: The Fight for Euskadi. 1890-1986*, London: Routledge.

Symmons-Symonolewicz, Konstantin 1970. *Nationalist Movements: A Comparative View*, Meadville, PA: Maplewood Press.

Tamayo, Virginia 1988. *Genesis del Estatuto de Gernika*, Gasteiz: Herri-Arduralaritzaren Euskal Erakundea.

Tejerina, Benjamin 1992. *Nacionalismo y lengua*, Madrid: CIS/Siglo XXI.

Termes, Josep 1976. *Federalismo, anarcofederalismo y catalanismo*, Barcelona: Anagrama.

— 1984. *La immigració a Catalunya*, Barcelona: Empúries.

— 1986. ' Les arrels populars del catalanisme' in Termes *et al.*, *Catalanisme. Història, Política i Cultura*, Barcelona: L'Avenç/Xarxa Cultural, pp. 11-20.

Termes, Josep and Augusti Colomines 1992. *Las Bases de Manresa de 1892 i els orígines del catalanisme*, Barcelona: Departament de Presidència/Generalitat de Catalunya.

Terry, Arthur 1972. *Catalan Literature*, London: Ernest Benn.

Thompson, J.L.P. 1989. 'Deprivation and political violence in Northern Ireland, 1922-1985: A Time-Series Analysis', *Journal of Conflict Resolution*, vol. 33, no. 4, pp. 676 ff.

Thomson, J.K.S. 1992 *A Distinctive Industrialization: Cotton in Barcelona. 1728-1832*, Cambridge University Press.

Torras i Bages, Josep 1981. *La Tradició Catalana*, Barcelona: Edicions 62/La Caixa (1st edn, Barcelona: Impremta F. Giró, 1892).

Torrents, Ricard 1995. *Verdaguer, un poeta per a un poble*, Vic: Eumo.

Torres, Joaquim 1977. 'Les enquestes sociolingüístiques catalanes', *Treballs de Sociolingüística Catalana*, 1, 137–146.

— 1988. 'Les enquestes sociolingüístiques catalanes de 1974 a 1984', *Treballs de Sociolingüística Catalana*, 7, 55–77.

Tovar, Antonio 1957 *The Basque Language*, Philadelphia: University of Pennsylvania Press.

— 1980. *Mitología sobre la lengua vasca*, Madrid: Alianza.

Trias Fargas, Ramon 1972. *Introducció a l'economia de Catalunya*, Barcelona: Edicions 62.

— 1974. *Introducción a la economía de Cataluña*, Madrid: Alianza.

Tremoleda, Josep 1967. *Cavall fort. Una experiencia concreta*, Barcelona: Editorial Nova Terra.

Ucelay da Cal, Enric 1986. 'L' Esquerra Nacionalista catalana, 1900–1931: unes reflexions' in Termes *et al.*, *Catalanisme: Història, Política i Cultura*, Barcelona: L'Avenç/Xarxa Cultural, pp. 129–146.

— and Borja de Riquer 1992. *Nacionalisme català i feixisme*, Vic: Eumo.

Ugalde, Martin de 1979. *Unamuno y el vascuence*, San Sebastián: Ediciones Vascas (1st edn, 1966?).

Unamuno, Miguel de 1968. *La raza vasca y el vascuence/En torno a la lengua española*, Madrid: Espasa Calpe.

Unzueta, José Luis 1980. 'La Vª Asamblea de ETA', *Saioak*, IV, no. 4, pp. 3–52.

Uranga, M.G. and J.L. Herrero 1983 (ca.). *Dinamica del capitalismo, crisis y economía vasca*, San Sebastián: Hordago.

Urla, Jacqueline 1987. 'Being Basque, Speaking Basque: The Politics of Language and Identity in the Basque Country', unpubl. Ph.D. dissertation, Department of Anthropology, University of California, Berkeley.

— 1988. 'Ethnic protest and social planning: a look at the Basque language revival', *Cultural Anthropology*, vol. 3, no. 4, pp. 379–94.

— 1993. 'Contesting modernities: Language standardization and the production of an ancient/modern Basque culture', *Critique of Anthropology*, vol. 13, no. 2, pp. 101–18.

Urrutia, José 1972. 'Pasado y presente del Euskera en la legislación española', *Estudios de Deusto*, vol. 20, fasc. 45, pp. 159–72.

Valle, Teresa del 1989. 'Basque ethnic identity at a time of rapid change' in Richard Herr and John H.R. Polt (eds), *Iberian Identity: Essays on the Nature of Identity in Portugal and Spain*, Berkeley: Institute of International Studies, University of California, pp. 123–40.

— 1993. *Korrika: Basque Ritual for Ethnic Identity*, Reno: University of Nevada Press.

Vallverdú, Francesc 1970. *Dues llengues. Dues funcions?*, Barcelona: Edicions 62.
— 1980a. *Aproximació crítica a la sociolingüística catalana*, Barcelona: Edicions 62.
— 1980b. 'Aspectes sociolingüístics de la immigració a Catalunya', *Taula de Canvi*, no. 20, pp. 6-12.
Vandellós, Josep Antoni 1935a. *Catalunya, poble decadent*, Barcelona: Edicions 62, 1985 (1st edn Barcelona, 1935).
— 1935b. *La immigració a Catalunya*, Barcelona: Fundació Patxot i Ferrer/Imp. Altes.
Van Der Berghe, Pierre 1981. *The Ethnic Phenomenon*, New York: Elsevier.
Vázquez de Prada, Valentín (ed.) 1978. *Historia económica y social de España*, vol. III, Madrid: Confederación Española de Cajas de Ahorro.
Vicens Vives, Jaume 1958. *Industrials i politics del segle XIX*, Barcelona: Vicens Vives.
— 1984. *Notícia de Catalunya*, Barcelona: Destino/Edicions 62 (1st edn 1954, 2nd edn 1969).
Vilar, Pierre 1967. *Spain: A Brief History*, Oxford: Pergamon Press (transl. of *Histoire de l'Espagne*, Paris: Presses Universitaires de France, 1947).
— 1977. *Catalunya dins l'Espanya moderna*, Barcelona: Edicions 62, 3 vols (French original *La Catalogne dans l'Espagne moderne*, 4 vols, Paris: Flammarion, 1962).
— 1980. 'Spain and Catalonia', *Review*, vol. III, no. 4, pp. 527-77.
Villa, Ignasi 1986. 'Bilingual education in the Basque Country', *Journal of Multilingual and Multicultural Development*, vol. 7, nos 2-3, pp. 123-45.
Villasante, Fr. Luís 1979. *Historia de la literatura vasca*, Burgos: Aranzazu (1st edn Bilbao, 1961).
Vinyes, Ricard 1990. 'Música, ball i cant en els moviments socials. El cas Clavé', *Revista de Catalunya*, no. 37, pp. 81-94.
Waldmann, Peter 1989. *Ethnischer Radikalismus. Ursachen und Folgen gewaltsamer Minderheitenkonflikte am Beispiel des Baskenlandes, Nordirlands und Quebecs*, Opladen: Westdeutscher Verlag.
Watson, Cameron 1992. 'Culture, identity and ethno-nationalism: The case of the Scottish Highlands and rural Basque Country', unpubl. MS.
Weber, Max 1991. 'Class, Status and Party' in H.H. Gerth and C. Wright Mills (eds), *From Max Weber: Essays in Sociology*, London: Routledge (1st edn 1958).
— 1979. *Economy and Society: An Outline of Interpretive Sociology*, Berkeley: University of California Press (1st edn 1968).
Weinreich, Uriel 1968 *Languages in Contact. Findings and Problems*, The Hague/Paris: Mouton.
Wilson, Richard 1991. 'Machine Guns and Mountain Spirits: The cultural

effects of state repression among the Q'eqchi' of Guatemala', *Critique of Anthropology*, vol. 11, no. 1, pp. 33-61.

Woolard, Kathryn A. 1982. 'The problem of linguistic prestige: evidence from Catalonia', *Penn Review of Linguistics*, no. 6, pp. 82-9.

— 1986. 'The crisis in the concept of identity in contemporary Catalonia, 1976-82' in Gary W. McDonogh (ed.), *Conflict in Catalonia: Images of an Urban Society*, Gainesville: University of Florida Press, pp. 54-71.

— 1989. *Double Talk: Bilingualism and the Politics of Ethnicity in Catalonia*, Stanford University Press.

Wright, Alison 1977. *The Spanish Economy, 1959-1976*, London: Macmillan.

Zabala, Federico 1980. 'Fidel de Sagarmínaga', *Muga*, 5, 1980, pp. 36-49.

Zirakzadeh, Cyrus Ernesto 1985. 'The political though of Basque businessmen, 1976-1980' in William A. Douglass (ed.), *Basque Politics: A Case Study in Ethnic Nationalism*, Nevada: Associated Faculty Press and Basque Studies Program.

— 1989. 'Economic Changes and Surges in Micro-Nationalist Voting in Scotland and the Basque Region of Spain', *Comparative Studies in Society and History*, vol. 31, no. 2, pp. 318-39.

— 1991. *A Rebellious People. Basques, Protests, and Politics*, Reno: Nevada University Press.

Yan, Ma Shu 1990. 'Ethnonationalism, ethnic nationalism, and mininationalism: a comparison of Connor, Smith and Snyder', *Ethnic and Racial Studies*, 13, 4, pp. 527-41.

Zulaika, Joseba 1988. *Basque Violence: Metaphor and Sacrament*, Reno: Nevada University Press.

DAILY NEWSPAPERS

Avui (Barcelona), 1976-80.

Diari de Barcelona (Barcelona), 1986-8.

Egin (San Sebastián), 1976-80.

El País (Madrid), 1976-80.

El País (Barcelona edition), 1976-80.

La Vanguardia (Barcelona), 1976-80.

The Guardian (London), 1988-93.

The Independent (London), 1988-93.

WEEKLY MAGAZINES

El Món (Barcelona), 1986-8.

Muga (Bilbao), 1986-92.

Punto y Hora (Bilbao), 1986-8.

The Economist (London), March 1979, pp. 89-90; 10 April, pp. 72-3.

The European (London), 1990-2.

OFFICIAL PUBLICATIONS

Constitución Española/Regulamento del Senado (1982), Madrid: Publicaciones del Senado. (See also *La Constitución Española de 1978*. Albacete: Ediciones de la Diputación de Albacete, 1990; *Constitución española*, Almería, 1990; *La Constitución Española, 1978*, San Sebastián: Ediciones Vascas, 1978; *Constitución Española, 1978*, Madrid: Editora Nacional, 1978.)

Cortes Españolas, *Diario de Sesiones del Congreso de los diputados*, Ex: n. 66, 12 May 1978: 2332.

DGPL/Departament de Cultura (Generalitat de Catalunya). Law 7/1983 of 18th April on Linguistic Normalisation in Catalonia. Leaflet, Barcelona.

Euskal Hitz. (1987), *Euskararen I. Erakusketa Orokorra*, Vitoria: Eusko Jaurlaritza.

I.N.E., Instituto Nacional de Estadística (1988), *Anuario Estadístico de España*, Madrid.

Información Commercial Española, combined nos. 467 and 468 (1972) and no. 598 (1993). Special issues on the Basque economy.

PARTY PUBLICATIONS

Euskadi, official magazine of the PNV.

El Partido Nacionalista Vasco hoy. Declaración de principios del PNV. Bilbao: PNV, 1972.

ANNUAL REPORTS

AEH (Anuario de Euskal-Herria), Bilbao: Editorial de Amigos del Libro Vasco, 1987-9.

Amnesty International 1968, 1969, 1970, 1971, 1972, 1973, 1974, 1975.

Anuario El País, Madrid, 1988, 1989, 1990, 1991.

Cuadernos Vanguardia, Equipo de Sociología Electoral (1982). Barcelona: Universidad Autónoma de Barcelona.

Euskadi 1987, Euskadi 1988, Euskadi 1989. Yearly reports by the daily newspaper *Egin* San Sebastián).

OTHER SOURCES

Documentos Y, 18 vols (includes most of ETA's publications). San Sebastián: Hordago.

Lettre aux fédéralistes basques, unpublished pamphlet.

DICTIONARIES/ENCYCLOPEDIAS

Aulestia, Gorka 1992. *Basque-English, English-Basque Dictionary*, 2 vols, Reno: University of Nevada Press.

EGIPV (*Enciclopedia General Ilustrada del País Vasco*), 21 vols (last volumes still in print), San Sebastián: Editorial Auñamendi, 1970.

GEC (*Gran Enciclopedia Catalana*), 18 vols, Barcelona: Edicions 62, 1969–93.

INDEX

aberri, 64 n. 45
Aberri Eguna (Basque national holiday), 53, 54
abertzale(s), 64 n. 45, 85 n. 14, 103, 141, 150, 151, 153, 183
Acadèmia de la Llengua, 120 n. 34
Acció Catalana, 32, 38, 75 n. 71
Acció Catalana Republicana, 38
Acción Catolica, 204 n. 23, 245
Acción Nacionalista Vasca (ANV), 75
action/repression/action, theory of, 231, 232, 244, 255
Aguirre, José Antonio, 74 n. 69, 81, 83 n. 6, 94 n. 43, 145
Aguirre, José Manuel, 89
Aguirre, Julen (psued. of Eva Forest), 106 n. 65
Alava, 46, 70 n. 59, 76, 152, 200 n. 20, 201
Alba, Duke of, 44
Albanians, 192
Alfonso XII, 12, 18
Alfonso XIII, 12
Algeria, 232, 244
Algerian model, 241, 244
Almirall, Valentí: 17-19; *passim*, 20, 21, 22, 27, 42, 78, 169-70, 214 n. 44; compared with Prat de la Riba, 30; father of political Catalanism, 17
Alsasua, 150
America, 114; *see also* United States
American(s): 84, 86, 230; 'betrayal' of Basques, 89
amnesty, 153-4
Anarchism, Anarchists: 29, 40, 41, 224
Anarcho-syndicalists, 39
andereños, 201
Annales school, 116 n. 27
antagonistic identity, 5
anteiglesias, 55, 196
anti-catalanism, 113

anti-clerical: atrocities, 94; forces, 63; stand, 75
anti-militarism, 29 n. 36
anti-semitism, 113
Aragón, Crown of, 11
Arana, Luis, 54 n. 21, 56, 57, 72
Arana, Santiago, 55, 56
Arana y Goiri, Sabino de: 53-68; *passim* 72, 73, 74, 77, 78, 80, 84 n. 9, 90-1, 93, 107, 108, 122 n. 40, 125, 168 n. 11, 173-8, 182, 185, 188, 197-9, 200, 204, 219, 227, 234, 235 n. 20, 237, 245, 246, 253, 260, 262; and Basque language, 57-8, 64, 65, 175-6, 261; and Catalanism, 57, 62, 77, 175-6; and immigrants, 60, 175-6, 261; and Krutwig, 107-8; coins name *Euzkadi*, 53, 66, 200; 'conversion' to moderation, 68; 'conversion' to nationalism, 56-7; death, 69; designs *Ikurriña*, 54; early Carlism, 55-6, 265; early writings, 53; founds EB, 59; founds PNV, 54; legacy of contradictions, 73; neo-traditionalist route to nationalism, 59; on race, 60-1, 65, 179, 198; religious influences, 56, 62, 63; role in foundation of Basque nationalism, 53, 261; sentenced to jail, 59, 68; Vizcayan nationalism, 58-9
Aranism, 91, 93
Aranist: concept, 186; idea, 152; ideology, 182; principles, 75; spirit, 202
Aranists, 71, 93, 203
Aranzadi, Engracio de, 84 n. 9, 199 n. 19
'Argala', 105
Aribau, Bonaventura Carles, 13
armed struggle, 108, 203, 247
Asociación Euskara, 50, 51, 167; *see also Euskaros*

32, 35, 42, 78, 170-1, 214 n. 44, 219, 223; cf. Arana, 54; President of Diputación, 32

Premi de les Lletres Catalanes, 121

press law (*ley de prensa*), 122

Primo de Rivera, General Miguel: 73, 123, 134, 140, 167, 191; abolishes Mancomunitat, 37; declares dictatorship, 36; dictatorship boosts nationalism, 74

'primordial' traits, 207

Provençal, 188 n. 1

provincialisme, 13 n. 5

PSC-PSOE, 143

PSOE: 143, 147-8, 151, 205 n. 25, 206; and GAL, 248 n. 50

PSUC (*Partit Socialista Unificat de Catalunya*), 130, 131, 132, 143; *see also* Communist Party

Pueblo Trabajador Vasco (Basque Working People), 97, 242

Puig i Cadalfach, Josep, 32

Pujol, Jordi, 120, 129, 130, 136, 172, 214 n. 44; on integration of immigrants, 195-6

Punjab, 250 n. 57

Quart, Pere, 115

Quebec, 156 n. 47, 192 n, 6

Quebecois nationalism, 192

statute of autonomy (Basque Country), 76; *see also* Autonomy Statute (Basque country)

rabassaires, 40

race, 9, 6 n. 10, 67, 72, 74, 77, 91 n, 32, 93, 108, 162, 166, 176, 177, 178-82, 186, 193-4, 197-9, 201, 202, 203, 207, 220; and Basque nationalism, 60-1

racism, 193-6, 198

Raimon, 121

rauxa, 223 n. 1

Radical Republicans, 28 n. 34

Reconquest, 181

Red Brigades, 244 n. 40

Red Cells (*Céllulas Rojas*), 99-100

Regeneracionismo, regenerationism, regenerationist: 26, 198, 260

regionalism: 227, 257, 259; Catalan, 20; and *Euskaros*, 53

relative deprivation, 247

relationship between Basque and Catalan nationalism, 3

religion, 77, 155, 170, 177, 201, 244, 245, 259; and Basque nationalism, 74, 108; and Catalan nationalism, 26-8

Renaixença: 13-17 *passim*, 34, 42, 50, 140, 167-8, 194, 216; as response to modernisation, 16; precedes nationalism, 261

Renan, Ernest, Renanian: 95, 240, 252, 255

Rentería: 70; vote in, 204, 205-6

repression: 225, 226, 256; state, 10, 222, 228, 229, 233, 236, 238, 244, 253, 259, 266, 268

Republic: 145, 213, 224, 229; First, 12; Second, 38, 87 n. 17, 103, 201, 203

Requetés, 233

Resistance Committee, 82

Restoration governments, 40

Riba, Carles, 115

Right, 103, 143, 213

rojoseparatistas, 41, 110, 214

Roca i Farreras, Josep Narcís, 42, n. 52

Roosevelt, President Theodore, 68

Rossell i Vilar, Manuel, 194

Rovira i Virgili, Antoni, 13 n. 5, 32 n. 43, 75 n. 71, 214 n. 44

Rubió i Ors, Joaquim, 13-14

Sagarmínaga y Epalza, Fidel de, 46, 52

San Sebastián, 38, 74, 237, 258

sardana, sardanistes: 111, 133, 216

Sartre, Jean-Paul, 89, 100 n. 55, 232

Scout movement, 133-4

Second World War, 80, 167, 220

secularisation, 61, 244

secularism, 75, 245

seigniory, 45 n. 5

seminaries, 245

312   *Index*